Bataan Diary

An American Family in World War II, 1941-1945

Bataan Diary

An American Family in World War II, 1941-1945

by Chris Schaefer

Riverview Publishing

Publisher's Cataloging in Publication

Schaefer, Chris.
Bataan Diary: An American family in World War II, 1941–1945 / by Chris Schaefer

Includes bibliographical references and index
1. World War, 1939-1945—Campaigns—Pacific Area. 2. World War, 1939-1945—Philippines. 3. World War, 1939-1945—Underground movements—Philippines—Luzon. 4. Philippines—History. 5. Pacific Area—History. 6. Guerrillas–Philippines–Luzon I. Title

Library of Congress Control Number: 2004097157

ISBN 0-9761084-0-2

Published by
Riverview Publishing
Houston, Texas
First Printing, October 2004

Manufactured in the United States of America

Dedicated to
Primitivo Leonzon,
Placido Filomeno,
and all of the Filipinos
who helped save the lives
of American soldiers during
World War II

Contents

Maps

Southeast Asia

U.S.S.R.
ALASKA
Aleutian Islands
HAWAII
Pearl Harbor
Eniwetok
Kwajalein
Marshall Islands
MICRONESIA
Solomon Islands
Guadalcanal

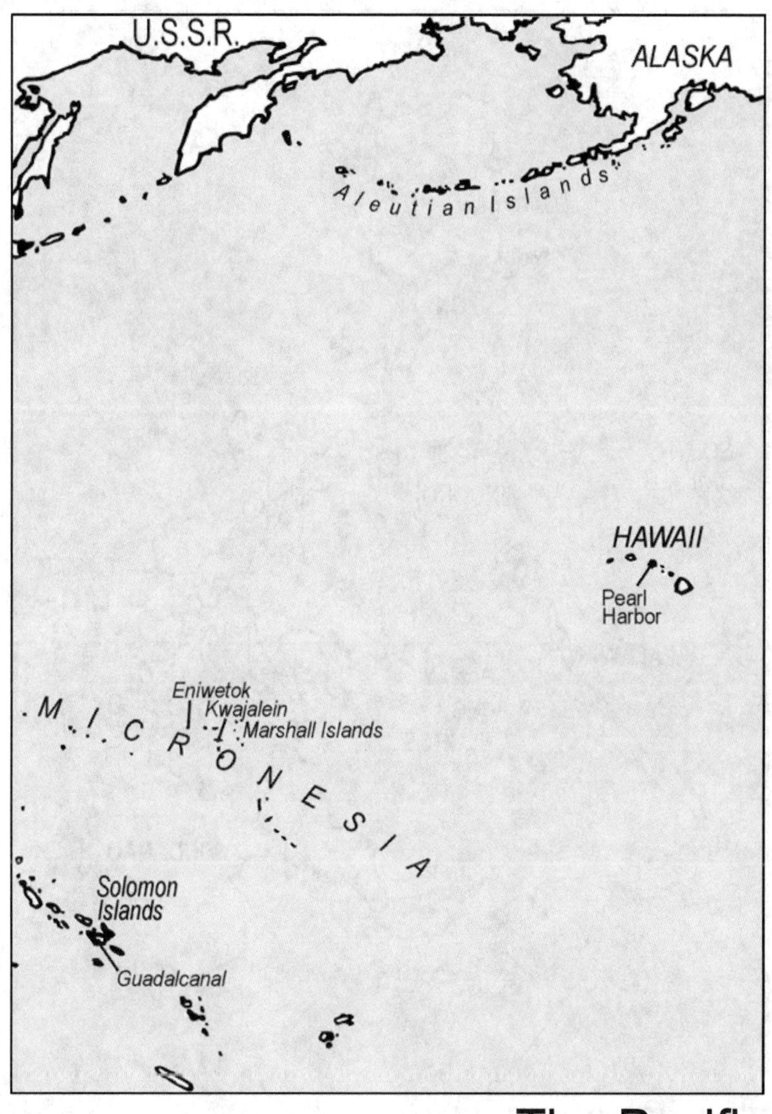

The Pacific

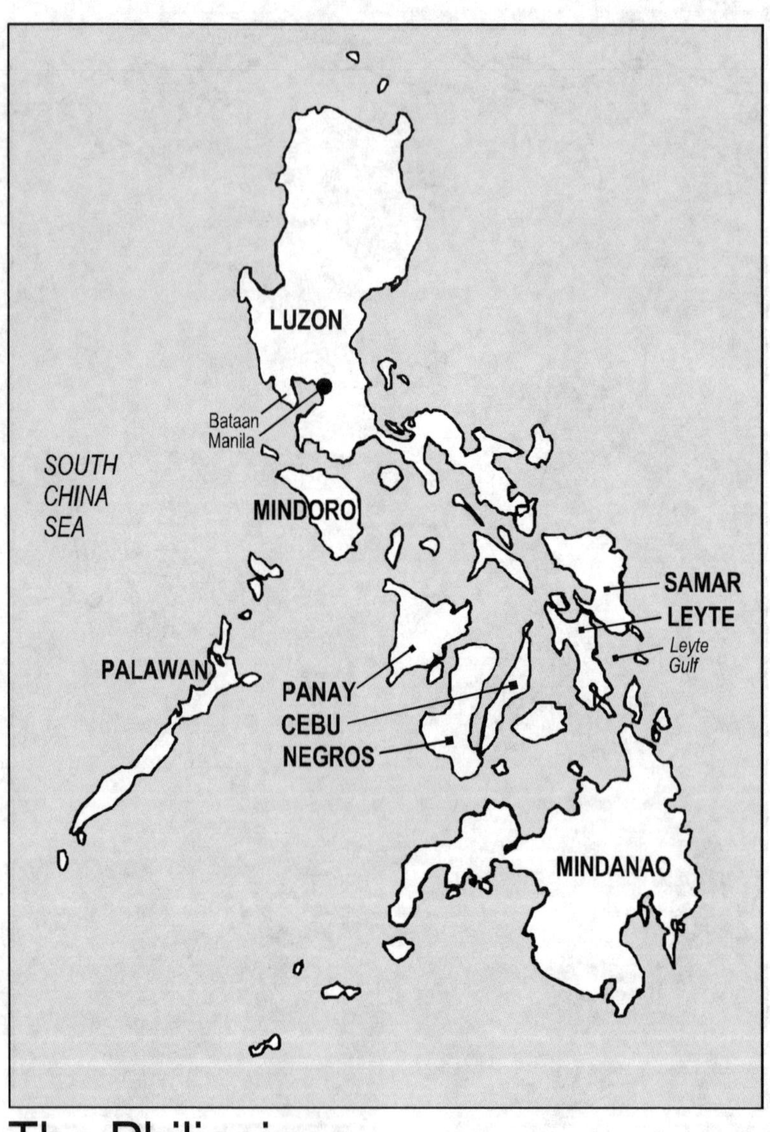

The Philippines

Kabugao
Apayao
Forest
KALINGA
Tuguegarao
Pinukpuk
ISABELA
Balbalan
Lubuagan
Baguio
Itogon
BENGUET
IFUGAO
Sierra Madres
Lingayen
Cabanatuan
Camp O'Donnell
Clark Field
Banaba
TARLAC
Mt. Pinatubo
ZAMBALES
Dibut Bay
Angeles
San Fernando
PAMPANGA
BULACAN
RIZAL
TAYABAS
BATAAN
Corregidor
Manila
Ft. McKinley
CAVITE
BATANGAS
Legaspi
MINDORO

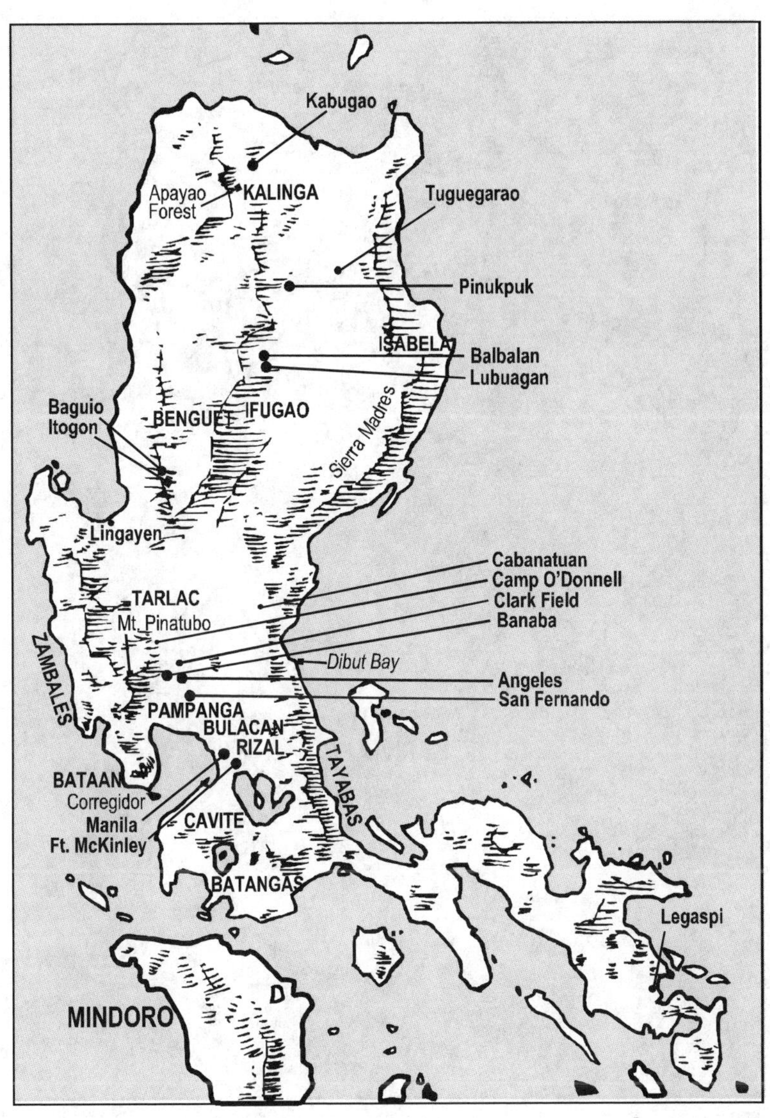

Luzon

San Marcelino
Aglao
Natividad
Floridablanca
Guagua
Castillejos
Dempe
PAMPANGA
Gutad
Fassoth
Camps
Mount Malasimbo
ZAMBALES
Dinalupihan
Fishponds
Zig-Zag
Kulo
Layac
Olongapo
Bamban
Hermosa
SUBIC
BAY
Meyete R.
Mount
Santa
Rosa
Orani River
Tala
Orani
Samal
MOUNT
NATIB
Mabatang
Abucay
MANILA
BAY
Balanga
Morong
Pilar
Bayside Hwy
Mount
Samat
SOUTH
CHINA
SEA
Bagac
Orion
MOUNT
MARIVELES
Mamala R.
Limay
Alangan R.
Lamao
Mt. Limay
Silaiim Bay
Little Baguio
Quinauan Point
Cabcaben
Mariveles
Longoskawayan Point
CORREGIDOR

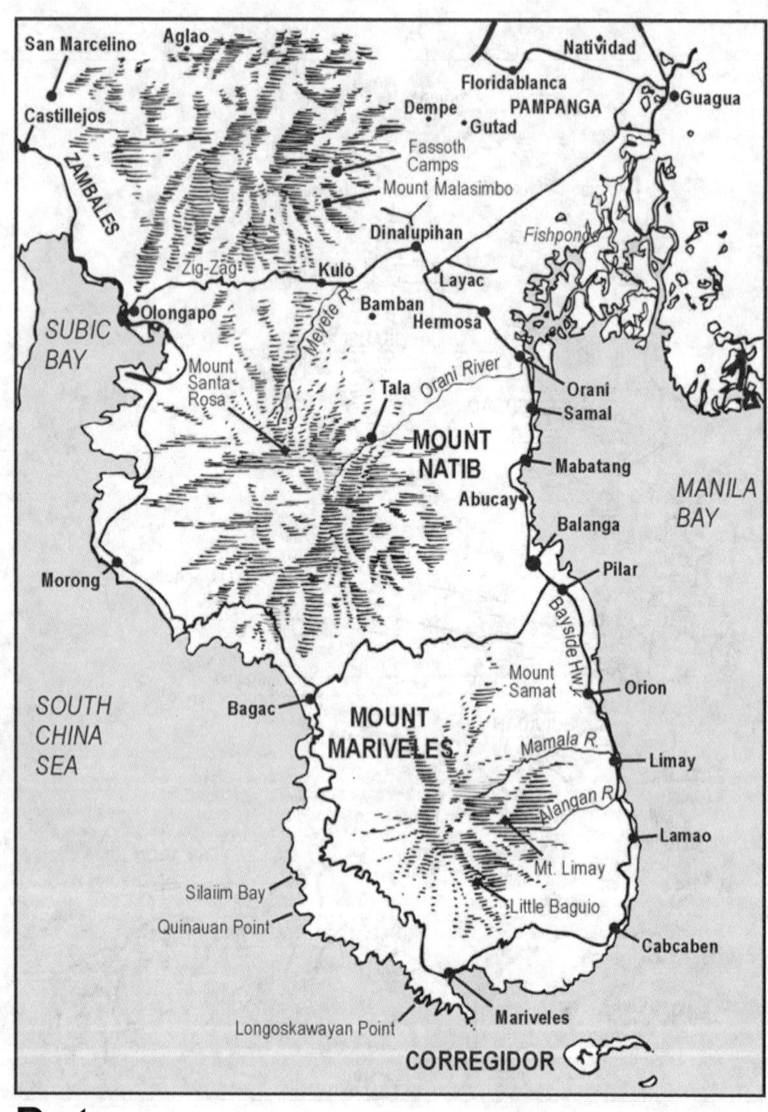

Bataan

Prologue

1941 dawned on a world as surreal as a George Orwell novel. Fascist governments controlled more than a third of the earth. Another group of uniformed dictators, the communists, controlled the vast landmass of northern Eurasia. The only major democracies left in the world were the United States and the surviving members of the British Commonwealth.

By May 1941, Nazi Germany had conquered most of Europe and was moving east. The Battle of Britain was at its height. Italy invaded North Africa, and Japan was fighting a bloody war of attrition in China.

You are about to read the story of a couple whose lives were torn apart that year, and who followed separate paths through the dark times that followed. He was missing in action and presumed dead. She served the war effort at home and struggled to keep her faith and family together.

Frank and Evelyn Loyd attempted to contact each other, dreamed about each other—and kept diaries. For three years he wrote on scraps of paper, hid them in the jungle in coffee cans and jars, and gave them to friendly natives to preserve and send to Evelyn if he did not survive. Hers was kept on her desk at home, among letters, old photographs and newspaper clippings that helped her keep up hope that he was still alive.

This is a true story.

I. Separation

Evelyn Loyd looked to her left, over the white iron railings of the *USAT Washington*, out over the glassy surface of Manila Bay.

Manila Bay is deep. Its waters take on a dark blue cast only a few yards from the beach, and the bay is big enough that Evelyn could not quite see the far shoreline from the deck of the *Washington*. Where a horizon should have been, her vision was filled by a panorama of smoky green mountains dominated by two extinct volcanoes—Bataan Peninsula.

The peninsula looked so big, and distant. She had visited Bataan in January with her husband and two children, and enjoyed horseback rides through the shady, hot jungle. Cool nights under mosquito-netted beds, noisy monkeys in the treetops, and colorful birds dotted her memory. The children had even caught a glimpse of a few

Negritos, the reclusive, pygmy-size forest people that inhabit the mountains of Bataan.[1] She had no idea, of course, that the name of that pristine place would soon become synonymous with incredible cruelty, and death.

***

Major Frank Riley Loyd was pleased to bring his family to the Philippines in June, 1940. For years Evelyn and their two children, Bonnie, age nine, and Frank Jr., age eleven, had followed him through a series of small, cold infantry posts in Alaska, Washington State and Oklahoma. For Evelyn and the children, their trip to the tropics was a welcome adventure.

Just before the Loyds boarded their ship in New York, Nazi Germany had invaded France and attacked England by air. The Germans had already overrun most of northern and eastern Europe. The United States was a "neutral" country, and President Franklin Delano Roosevelt, bowing to public opinion, had vowed to keep the United States out of the European war.

North of the Philippines, Japan and China were also at war. The Japanese attacked China in 1937 and easily captured the eastern portion of the country. Since then, the two countries had been locked in a drawn out war of attrition with little progress on either side.[2] South of China, the nations of Southeast Asia and the Pacific were quiet and peaceful.

Frank was appointed Provost Marshall of Fort McKinley, a large Army post seven miles south of Manila. Evelyn enjoyed the post's relaxed work schedule. Frank and the other officers worked mornings, six days a week, and had the afternoons off. Evelyn taught fourth grade at the post elementary school. The Army quartered the Loyd family in a roomy, government-supplied home across from the parade ground, and she got home in plenty of time to supervise the household. On Manila's low wages the officers could afford to staff their homes with cooks and housekeepers, and there were cocktail and dinner parties at one home or another almost every night.

At five o'clock every afternoon a cannon fired and a bugler stood next to Fort McKinley's flagpole to play "Taps" while the American flag was lowered. All traffic on the post stopped. Men stepped out of their vehicles or stopped on the sidewalks and saluted the flag. This daily ceremony not only re-affirmed the loyalty of the men at Fort McKinley, it also signaled the start of the cocktail hour, which was immediately followed by the dinner hour. Evening attire at the Officer's Club consisted of formal, white "mess jacket" uniforms, with evening dresses for the ladies.

In April 1941, ten months after they arrived in the Philippines, Evelyn and Frank Loyd dressed for dinner. He wore his tropical white uniform, and told her that she looked "sexy" in her black, straight evening dress. She looked at herself in the mirror and liked what she saw. Most of all, she liked it when he noticed.

The children, Bonnie and "Junior," were sitting down to a nice dinner prepared by Gonzales, their cook. As Evelyn kissed them goodbye Junior winced at hearing his nickname. He had made it clear that he wanted to be called "Frank," or at least "Frank Jr." All of his friends at school called him "Frank." Frank Sr. ignored the grimace, as usual.

They strolled a block and a half down the street to the home of Evelyn and Arthur "Maxie" Noble, a couple they had met since arriving in the Philippines. Dinner at the Noble house was always a treat because Maxie, a small, wiry West Pointer, could be counted on to entertain his guests with ragtime music on his piano.

As they entered the house, the other guests were talking excitedly. The War Department had ordered all Army and Navy wives and children to return to the United States. All military dependents were to be out of the Philippines by May 13, just thirty days away.

They had their drinks and sat down to dinner. Conversation quickly focused on the war. President

Roosevelt had just signed the "Lend-Lease Act," authorizing shipments of war materials to all of the countries fighting Germany, Italy and Japan. The U.S. was sending more aid to China and to the British, and Roosevelt had demanded that the Japanese get out of China.

"What kind of neutrality is that?" one woman wanted to know.

As drinks were consumed, the dinner conversation became more animated.

"What could Roosevelt be thinking?"

"What will Japan do now? Attack us?"

"It must mean war. Why else would they evacuate us from the Philippines?"

"Not much chance of that," a woman said. "The Japs may be little, but they're not stupid. At least I don't think they are!"

Everyone laughed. After four years of bloody warfare, the Japanese had still not beaten the Chinese. They certainly posed no threat to the United States.

Evelyn helped herself to a few drinks from the bar and thought about the coming trip home—without Frank. After a couple of hours, and many more drinks, Frank was ready to leave. To Evelyn, the evening had become a blur. She took "one for the road" and staggered off behind Frank. A few houses down, she stopped in front of Evadne and Montgomery McKee's house. The Loyds and McKees were old friends. Frank and Montgomery had been stationed together in Alaska.

"You go on," she told Frank. "I don't want the children to see me like this."

She stumbled into the McKees' front door, found Evadne, and talked, drank and cried with her all night. As dawn broke the next morning she took her shoes in one hand, held her head with the other, and walked home.

***

The Philippine Islands extend like stepping-stones down the east side of the South China Sea, from mainland China to Indonesia. The 7,000 islands are the world's second largest island archipelago, extending north and south for more than 1,100 miles, roughly the length of the U.S. West Coast.

Indonesia, stretched along the equator to the south, is the world's largest island archipelago and the world's fourth largest country in population. In 1941, Indonesia was called the Dutch East Indies and was owned and controlled by the Netherlands. Borneo, the largest island in the Indies, sits atop massive oil fields. Her major customer for that oil was Japan. In fact, in 1941 the Dutch East Indies and the United States supplied ninety percent of Japan's oil.[3]

Due west of the Philippines, the Malay Peninsula creates the western boundary of the South China Sea, extending from mainland Indo-China in the north to the island city of Singapore at its southern tip, almost touching western Indonesia. The Malay Peninsula is rich in mineral deposits such as tin, tungsten, and titanium, and in rubber trees. The lowlands of Indo-China are covered with rice fields and rubber plantations. In 1941, Malaya was a British colony, Indo-China was a French colony, and they both supplied food, raw materials and rubber to Japan.

The Philippine Islands sit in the middle of all this, between Japan and its Southeast Asian suppliers. The largest island in the Philippines is Luzon, similar in size and shape to England. At its center is Manila Bay, a protected and nearly perfect natural harbor. Because of its central location, a naval base in Manila Bay, or an air force bomber base anywhere on Luzon, could theoretically control all shipping between Japan and her Southeast Asian suppliers.[4]

In 1941, as now, Japan was totally dependent upon foreign sources of food and raw materials to sustain its people and its industry, particularly its arms industry. To the fascist military leaders of Japan, the Philippines were, potentially, "a clot in the bloodstream of the Japanese Empire." [5]

***

The week before the May 13 sailing date, Frank Loyd took his family to the seacoast town of Legaspi on the tip of the long, hilly Bicol Peninsula to celebrate Evelyn's birthday. She was charmed by the quaint two-story hotel with its whitewashed walls, dark brown hardwood floors and hand-carved shutters. The hotel sat right on the beach and was mostly empty except for a few British and Dutch vacationers.

The days passed quickly. Frank experimented with his new 8mm movie camera and its telephoto lens. He made movies of Bonnie and Junior as they played on the beach and dug in the sand. While the children played outside, Evelyn and Frank found a little time to spend with each other.

On the way back to Fort McKinley they talked about how to manage their bank accounts and other details essential to a couple about to live apart. Frank promised that he would have the movies of their vacation in Legaspi developed and mail them to her. He would keep the movie camera and make films of whatever happened after she left. They promised to write each week. And they made plans for a reunion someday in San Francisco—just the two of them.

Frank instructed Evelyn to find good schools for the children, even if she had to put them in private school. He was a stickler for education, a man who strove to speak every sentence correctly, and who insisted that his children do so as well. His friends had long since nicknamed him "The Professor." A name and a concept that, when applied to Frank, made Evelyn smile.

On Tuesday, May 13, 1941, they drove up Dewey Boulevard to the Manila waterfront, noisy at mid-morning with cars, trucks, and horse-drawn *calesas*, the two-wheeled carriages used for picturesque taxi service in downtown Manila. Frank parked the car near the entrance to Pier 7, just behind the Manila Hotel. Pier 7, the world's longest pier, provided berthing places for ocean liners, cruise ships and the *USAT Washington*.

Odors of fish, exhaust fumes and horses greeted Evelyn as they stepped out of the car and followed other couples into the shade of the covered, wooden pier. They walked about halfway out, to the berth of the *Washington*, a sleek German ocean liner confiscated by the U.S. Army in 1917. The ship's white decks and superstructure gleamed in the hot, bright sunlight. A large crowd had gathered—young women, their khaki-uniformed husbands, and myriads of running, squealing children. Off to one side a small military band played bouncy tunes, trying to give the day a festive atmosphere.

Evelyn's eye was drawn across a small inlet next to Pier 7, to the whitewashed stucco walls of the elegant Manila Hotel. Sunlight glowed brightly off the sides of the five-story building. Its dark green tile roofs and awnings perfectly matched the surrounding lawns and shade trees. The hotel was the center of Manila's highest society. She peered at the row of penthouse windows along the top floor, overlooking Pier 7. That was the home of General Douglas MacArthur, reputed to be the most famous man in the United States Army and the smartest, most powerful man in the Orient—if you believed Douglas MacArthur, that is.

***

In the library of the elaborate wood-paneled suite on the top floor of the Manila Hotel, General Douglas MacArthur contemplated a tough problem. The tall, bony General had forged an impressive reputation, a place in history, over the years and now that reputation, and his beloved Philippines, appeared threatened. But a threat was a challenge, and Douglas MacArthur welcomed a challenge.

When he graduated from West Point in 1903, he had been First Captain, the top cadet in the corps, with the highest academic record posted at the academy in more than thirty years. MacArthur guided the U.S. Army's Rainbow

Division through Europe in 1917 and gained a worldwide reputation for bravery, leadership and flamboyance. When he retired from the U.S. Army in 1935 he was the youngest Chief of Staff of the Army, ever.

Instead of retiring to civilian life, MacArthur had accepted an invitation from President Manuel Quezon, the newly elected President of the Philippine Commonwealth, to undertake the task of founding and building the new Philippine Army. The Philippines were to be granted independence from the United States on July 4, 1946 and would then be responsible for their own defense. Creating an entire army from scratch was a huge undertaking—a project Douglas MacArthur considered worthy of his considerable talents.[6] Plus, it would give him an opportunity to return to the country that his father once governed, and where he had completed two tours of duty as a young engineering officer. In a ceremony at Malacañang, the presidential palace, in 1936, President Quezon had bestowed upon Douglas MacArthur the title "Field Marshall" of the as yet non-existent Philippine Army.[7]

Field Marshall MacArthur devised a training program whereby U.S. Army soldiers stationed in the Philippines would put Filipino recruits through five and a half months of basic infantry training. Every six months President Quezon was to draft 20,000 twenty-year-old Filipino men to go through the program. The young soldiers would then be assigned to one of ten reserve infantry divisions, similar to the U.S. National Guard.[8] Once the program got under way, MacArthur's Philippine Army took over responsibility for training its own personnel.

But things began to go awry. The Philippine Military Academy and college ROTC programs could not produce enough officers to staff the new divisions. Budget cuts created severe shortages of equipment. MacArthur's appeals to the Philippine legislature did no good. In fact, Quezon and the legislators, eager to provide roads and other amenities to their constituents and cronies, cut back the number of men who could be recruited and trained each year.

Field Marshall MacArthur, therefore, had a problem. He headed a Philippine Army that consisted of half a division of regular army "trainers" and ten under-strength divisions of poorly equipped, poorly trained reservists. Hardly worthy of himself, and hardly able to defend the islands in case of trouble.

To the north, Japan was pressing its war in China. President Roosevelt was badgering the Japanese to get out of China. The U.S. Army had only one division of soldiers in the Philippines, and suddenly President Roosevelt had ordered all U.S. military dependents to go home. It was supposed to be just a precaution. But there was trouble brewing in the Pacific, and General MacArthur's Philippine Army was far from ready.

***

As Evelyn's ship prepared to pull away from the dock, she recognized a tall, thin officer in a white dress uniform standing near Frank. He was Major General Jonathan Wainwright, commander of the U.S. Army's Philippine Division. Wainwright was an old cavalryman who liked to wash the dust out of his throat at the end of each day with a cold beer at the Officer's Club. He had come to the Philippines for his last tour of duty before retirement.[9]

Here and there along the rail of the ship were Evelyn's friends. Evadne McKee and Evelyn Noble were just down to her left with Evelyn's two daughters. Betty Wilson was further along the rail to her right with her three children. Her husband, O. O. "Zero" Wilson, was General Wainwright's aide.

Absent from the families on the ship were the wife and young son of General Douglas MacArthur. General MacArthur was keeping his family with him in Manila.

Evelyn watched Frank standing on the dock. She knew that he would rather be at his office this morning. As

Provost Marshall of Fort McKinley, Frank was responsible for the military police and for security. His men were constructing a series of new buildings and enclosures—to house Japanese prisoners of war. Air raid shelters were being dug also, one by the entrance to the Officer's Club and another one right behind their house. They were supposed to be "mere precautions." Frank had work to do, but there was no question that he would bring her and the children to the ship this morning and see them off. Evelyn knew that a tremendous weight was being lifted from his shoulders. No matter what happened next, at least Frank would know that his family was safe.

As the *Washington* backed into the bay, the band struck up a shaky rendition of *Auld Lang Syne.* Evelyn mustered another smile as she watched Frank. His small, dark eyes were fixed on hers. She waved. He grinned slightly and slowly returned the gesture. Over the roof of a warehouse, Evelyn could see the twin barrels of an anti-aircraft gun pointed skyward.

Evelyn and the children stayed on deck as the Manila skyline drifted into the distance. When they went below to their cabin, there was a bouquet of orchids. The note said, "I love you." It was signed simply, "Frank."

With Frank's note in hand, and thinking of those months of separation that could be facing her, Evelyn sat down on the bed and cried.

Within an hour, the *Washington* approached the mouth of Manila Bay. Frank Jr. and two of his friends, Gail Wilson and Ted Lilly, went up to the deserted deck to look over the channel islands on each side of the ship. On the left they could see the fortified islands of Fort Franco and Fort Drum. Fort Drum was, literally, a concrete battleship perched on a rock in the mouth of the bay, bristling with cannons. On the right was the larger Corregidor Island, with the mountains of Bataan Peninsula looming behind it. Corregidor was dotted with large caliber coastal artillery batteries that could hurl shells twenty to twenty-five miles out to sea with great accuracy. These fortified islands were manned by "Philippine Scouts," well-trained, professional Filipino soldiers serving in the United States Army.

Beyond the islands were the open waters of the South China Sea and, half a world away, the first stop on their voyage home...Pearl Harbor.

II. Bataan

Two months later, on July 23, 1941, the Japanese sent troops into French Indo-China. Japanese Ambassador Kichisaburo Nomura informed President Franklin Roosevelt that Japan found it necessary to secure the rather considerable supplies of rice, rubber and tin produced in Indo-China, because Roosevelt had recently ordered reductions in trade between the United States and Japan.[1] Intercepted Japanese messages, however, indicated that the new Japanese bases would be used to attack China, and perhaps the Dutch East Indies.[2]

President Roosevelt reacted immediately. The United States, Britain and the Dutch embargoed all trade with the Japanese Empire, cutting off her supplies of oil and raw materials.[3] Under these circumstances Japan's war machine in China would soon grind to a halt—literally out of gas.

The next day Roosevelt recalled General Douglas MacArthur into the United States Army. He placed MacArthur in charge of a new military organization, the United States Army Forces in the Far East (USAFFE). MacArthur's new command included the U.S. Army's Philippine Division and Far East Air Force, several National Guard units hastily sent in from the United States, and the nationalized Philippine Army—a total of more than 100,000 American and Filipino troops. President Roosevelt began to ship tons of supplies to General MacArthur, including squadrons of fighter airplanes and B-17 bombers. With an authorized strength of 272 B-17s, Clark Field, sixty miles north of Manila, was slated to become the Army Air Corps' biggest bomber base in the world.[4] Between the bombers at Clark Field and the twenty-nine Navy submarines stationed in Manila Bay, the United States should easily control the South China Sea.

In case the Japanese attacked the Philippines, sufficient ammunition and supplies were stored on Bataan Peninsula to sustain the USAFFE army for six months—plenty of time for the U.S. Navy to assemble a convoy to bring additional supplies and reinforcements from the States.[5]

In October, the first flight of thirty-five B-17s arrived at Clark Field. General MacArthur was confident that his Philippine Army and his Far East Air Force could repel any Japanese attack, so he moved tons of supplies from Bataan to warehouses in north and south Luzon. He wanted his supplies close to the front lines—the beaches where his Philippine Army would repel the Japanese.

On December 7, 1941, the Japanese Empire launched one of the biggest surprise attacks in military history.[6] They attacked Luzon Island in the Philippines, Pearl Harbor in Hawaii, British Malaya, and British Hong Kong, simultaneously. Just a few hours after sinking the U.S. Navy's Pacific Fleet at Pearl Harbor, Japanese bombers appeared over Clark Field and destroyed General MacArthur's Far East

Air Force sitting on the ground. The few bombers that escaped destruction flew south to Australia. The U.S. Navy's small Asiatic Fleet, based in Manila Bay, retreated south to join the Dutch Navy in the Indies.

The aggressive, well-trained Japanese Army landed on the beaches of Luzon, and MacArthur's front lines crumbled. General MacArthur ordered his army to retreat to Bataan Peninsula and nearby Corregidor Island. But the retreating Filipinos and Americans had neither the vehicles nor the time to haul their supplies back to Bataan. They abandoned huge quantities of food, medicine and fuel to the enemy.

MacArthur positioned his new front line across the north end of Bataan, broken in the middle by Mount Natib, the northernmost of the two extinct volcanoes that formed the peninsula. He placed General Jonathon Wainwright's I Corps on the west side of the mountain, and on the east side General George Parker's II Corps.

The Filipino and American soldiers were ordered to dig in, guard Manila Bay, and wait for the Navy convoy to bring reinforcements from the States.

***

On January 2, 1942, amidst the chaos of trucks, horses and troops maneuvering around General George Parker's headquarters, Lieutenant Colonel Frank Loyd got what he considered a most peculiar order: all units were to immediately turn in their food rations.[7] Frank had brought a small supply of food for Parker's staff as they retreated into Bataan.

As the rations were being loaded into a truck, Frank took one of the quartermaster officers aside.

"What's going on?"

"Keep this quiet, but we think that there is only enough food on Bataan to feed everybody for one or two months," the man confided in him. "Particularly with the refugees to feed."

There were almost 70,000 Filipino and American troops on Bataan now, and 20,000 Filipino refugees.[8]

After the quartermasters left that day, Frank got new orders: everyone would be cut back to two meals per day, served at dawn and at dusk, effective immediately. Daily food intake was set at twelve ounces of rice per day, per American, supplemented by a small portion of canned meat and beans or other condiments; less for the smaller Filipinos.[9] The meager, twice-daily meals were referred to as the "Bataan Ration." By restricting food in this manner, it was believed that the available rations could be stretched to last three months, through March 1942.

Only three months—a lot depended on that reinforcement convoy.

As General Parker's staff car drove Frank south down Bataan's bayside highway that afternoon, he looked forward to getting back to his troops. He had been called to serve briefly on Parker's staff during the retreat but now he was going back to the Philippine Constabulary, the Philippines' national police force. General MacArthur had inducted the 1st and 2nd Philippine Constabulary Regiments into USAFFE to guard against sabotage when the Japanese attacked. The General had assigned Frank Loyd to be Chief Instructor of the Philippine Constabulary—he and his four assistants were to drill the men in basic infantry tactics. As Frank worked with the constables he had become confident that these men, his men, given enough time and training, could be whipped into an effective fighting force. As effective, perhaps, as the U.S. Army's Philippine Scouts.[10]

Hot, gritty air blew into the open windows of the car as dust rose from the shoulders of the two-lane highway, the only paved road on Bataan. Trucks, buses and ox-carts filled with refugees competed for pavement. Looking to his left out the driver's window, Frank could see a black plume of smoke rising from the Manila waterfront where the retreating USAFFE forces had torched their fuel and oil supplies. Suddenly, a flight of Japanese Zeros flashed overhead firing streams of machine gun bullets down the center of the crowded highway. What little order there was dissolved into chaos as drivers wrenched their vehicles into ditches or ran up side roads, and civilian refugees fled in terror from the strafing airplanes.

Frank's driver pulled off the road at a spot just past Lamao, near the south end of the peninsula. He pulled Frank's duffel bag and cot out of the trunk and hoisted it onto his back. Frank slung his musette bag and pack over one shoulder and too much other gear over the other, and the two men hiked up the trail to the headquarters of the newly constituted 4th Philippine Constabulary Regiment. At the small, bamboo headquarters building Frank met Colonel Rafael Jalandoni, the regimental commander.

The no-nonsense Jalandoni was taller and heavier than most Filipinos, and he welcomed Frank to his new command. Jalandoni had been in charge of the Constabulary Department of Central Luzon when the Japanese attacked. He rounded up the provincial constabulary units on Luzon and the palace guards in Manila, and ordered them all to go to Bataan with the retreating army. Colonel Jalandoni was an intelligent man, and a man who showed initiative—two characteristics that Frank liked. General MacArthur designated Jalandoni's organization the "4th Philippine Constabulary Regiment," and he assigned Frank Loyd to train its 1,800 constables to be infantrymen.

Late that afternoon Frank pitched his tent in a bamboo thicket near a large Banyan tree, about one hundred yards uphill from the 4th PC Regiment's bivouac. Two constables dug a foxhole for him at the base of the tree. Montgomery McKee joined him the next day. At the height of the retreat to Bataan, Montgomery had rounded up groups of clerks and retired Philippine Scouts around Fort McKinley to help pack up the post headquarters, then commandeered a fleet of Manila taxicabs to bring them all to Bataan. They left in such a rush that Montgomery had no tent, bedding or extra clothes.[11] Frank moved Montgomery into his own tent and gave him his two blankets to sleep on.[12] Frank had brought his Artic Woods sleeping bag with him in General Parker's convoy.

***

On January 3, at USAFFE headquarters on Corregidor Island, General MacArthur received a disturbing radio message from Army Chief of Staff General George C. Marshall in Washington, D.C. General Marshall said that due to losses at Pearl Harbor, the U. S. Navy's ability to convoy reinforcements to the Philippines had been seriously impaired.

On the other hand, Marshall's message also said:

> A stream of four-engine bombers, previously delayed by foul weather, is en route with the head of the column having crossed Africa. Another stream of similar bombers started today from Hawaii staging at new island fields. Two groups of powerful medium bombers of long range and heavy bomb-load capacity leave next week. Pursuit planes are coming on every ship we can use.... Every day of time you gain is vital to the concentration of the overwhelming power necessary for our purpose.[13]

The air power was badly needed. MacArthur had no bombers left, and all but eighteen of his Far East Air Force's 107 P-40 fighters had been destroyed on the ground or shot down by Japanese Zeros. He knew that the new bombers would help, but they could not feed his troops. He radioed a plea to General Marshall to send fast ships that could run the naval blockade the Japanese had thrown up around the Philippines, to bring in needed supplies. Marshall replied that he would do what he could.

On January 10, MacArthur crossed the channel to confer with his commanders on Bataan Peninsula. The previous day he had gotten good reports—a Japanese attack down the bayside highway had been repelled by the Philippine Scouts' artillery.

On Bataan that day, General MacArthur visited the field hospital, met with General Parker at II Corps headquarters, and assured Parker's staff that reinforcements were on the way. He told Parker that intelligence expected the Japanese to attack again the next day, and that both I Corps and II Corps would be hit. Then he went forward to the front line, to survey Parker's defenses.

General Parker's line stretched across a large, cultivated area called Abucay Hacienda. In the center of the line he had placed General Vincente Lim's 41st Infantry Division. Brigadier General Vincente Lim, the oldest and one of the most respected Filipino generals, had been the first Filipino to graduate from the U.S. Military Academy at West Point back in 1917, and the 41st Division, under Lim's leadership, was one of the stronger Philippine Army units. To Lim's right, astride the critical bayside highway, General Parker placed the 1st Battalion of the Philippine Scouts' 57th Infantry Regiment, commanded by Major Royal Reynolds.

Major Reynolds, an intense, dark-haired West Pointer, had burned down Mabatang village in front of his positions that day, to provide clear fields of fire for his Filipino Scouts. He instructed machine gunners to remove all tracers from their ammunition belts so as not to reveal their positions once they commenced fire. His men were well dug in, with overhead cover to conceal their positions from enemy reconnaissance planes and bombers. Major Reynolds' Scouts were ready.

The previous day, though, specially trained and equipped Japanese snipers had infiltrated the Scouts' positions. These men, virtually on suicide missions, tied themselves into tall mango trees near and behind the Scouts' lines. They were excellent marksmen, and several Scouts had been killed just that morning. Machine-gun fire into the trees had been effective in some cases, and the bodies of several dead Japanese snipers hung grotesquely from the tree branches when General MacArthur arrived on the scene.

Major Reynolds briefed MacArthur on the previous day's action. Then, in spite of the snipers and the occasional artillery shells that crashed through the trees and exploded in the Scout's positions, the tall, confident general walked around the area talking to the men and inspecting their defenses. His eyes were covered by dark sunglasses. He wore a soft cap, no helmet, carried a riding crop under his arm and smoked his pipe. He looked as if no artillery shell, or sniper's bullet, would even dare approach him.

MacArthur's appearance was awe-inspiring and gave a big boost to the troops' morale.

After a while, satisfied with what he saw, General MacArthur assured Major Reynolds that "the sky will soon be black with planes," climbed back into his staff car and headed for General Wainwright's I Corps headquarters.[14] There, he delivered the same message, then returned to Corregidor.

That afternoon, formations of Japanese bombers appeared overhead, scattering a terse, 160-word leaflet from Lieutenant General Masaharu Homma, the Japanese commander. The leaflets "advised" General MacArthur's unconditional surrender "to avoid needless bloodshed." [15] On the heels of the bombers, a rolling barrage of artillery fire swept across Abucay Hacienda. Behind the exploding shells, Japanese troops attacked down the bayside highway.

Major Reynolds' Scouts were ready. Their machine guns, artillery, and M-1 Garand semi-automatic rifles devastated the attackers.[16] At times Japanese bodies were piled three deep in front of the Scouts' positions, but the Japanese kept coming, leaping and crawling over the bodies of their fallen comrades in a furious *banzai* attack. Eventually, after hours of bloodshed and hundreds of losses the surprised Japanese broke off contact and pulled back out of range.[17]

Over the next few days, the Japanese did everything they could to dislodge the Fil-American defenders. Special rifle rounds were used, that shot two firecrackers instead of a bullet. The firecrackers would explode in back of the Fil-American lines, sounding like two more rifle shots, intended to instill panic in the Filipino troops. Birdcalls echoed through the dark jungle at night to make the Filipinos and Americans think that the Japanese were sneaking up on them. Airplanes flew overhead, bombing constantly and dropping propaganda leaflets that promised safety to any Filipino who would desert his American commanders and surrender. Loudspeakers blared across the front lines, delivering the same message in pleading women's voices.

***

Farther south, along the east coast of Bataan Peninsula, Lieutenant Colonel Frank Loyd conducted last-ditch training sessions for the men of the 4th Philippine Constabulary Regiment while Japanese bombers and Zero fighters swooped down the coastline attacking anything man-made. Anti-aircraft batteries on Corregidor and at nearby Cabcaben airfield blazed away at the attacking planes, so Frank's constables had to dodge falling anti-aircraft shells as well as Japanese bombs and machine gun bullets.

Training progressed well considering the circumstances, and the constabulary regiments were assigned to defend sectors of the coastline around the south end of Bataan. The 4th PC's area was on the east side, the Manila Bay side, from Lamao to Cabcaben. Their mission was to fend off any attempt by the Japanese to make an amphibious assault from across Manila Bay.

Late one night, Frank got an urgent call from Colonel Jalandoni to come quickly to the beachfront—sentries had spotted lights out on the water. Frank and Jalandoni told the constables to hold their fire. Through his field glasses Frank could see several white lights moving around, but in the darkness it was impossible to tell how far away they were, or how high off the water. Colonel Jalandoni sent a message to the gunboat *Oahu* to go investigate. Later, a report came back from the *Oahu*—the lights were small, bamboo buoys, each with a flashlight battery and bulb tied to the top. Apparently, the Japanese had floated them down the bayside currents in an effort to draw fire from the beach defenses.[18]

The *Oahu* found no enemy boats, so Frank and Jalandoni left the sentries on alert and headed back to their tents. Whatever trick the Japanese were up to, it had not worked.

But over the next several nights the Japanese floated buoys and iridescent logs past the beach defenses in another attempt to draw fire. When that did not work they towed a barge with a cannon and machine guns mounted on it along the beaches, and fired into the constables' positions.[19] This time the constables did not hold back. They blasted the barge with a barrage of artillery and .50 caliber machine gun fire.

The next day, the constabulary gunners paid the price. The Japanese had emplaced long-range artillery pieces at Cavite on the south side of Manila Bay, and they opened up on the constables' positions. The men scrambled for their foxholes as deadly phosphorous and high-explosive shells rained in.[20]

***

At Abucay Hacienda the Japanese stampeded a herd of carabao [water buffalo] through the Fil-American mine fields then followed in the animals' tracks, and over their dead bodies, to attack once again.[21] They broke through General Lim's 41st Division in the center of the line, but then were driven back as the Philippine Scouts and the American 31st Infantry Regiment counter-attacked to regain lost ground.

Under the constant onslaught, the front lines began to falter. By mid-January the Japanese again penetrated the Abucay line, and General MacArthur ordered his troops to retreat farther south to the next defense line, a dirt road that snaked across the middle of the peninsula from Pilar on the east coast to Bagac on the west.

The tired troops crept out of their positions on the Abucay line late that night and walked wearily south along the roads and trails to re-assemble in the new, as yet not fully prepared, positions. Reports came into Frank's 4th PC headquarters of Japanese troops pursuing the withdrawing USAFFE troops down both coasts. As units rotated into reserve for a much-needed rest, gaps were left in the line that were quickly filled by the pursuing Japanese, leaving pockets of enemy units dangling within the Fil-American lines.

In the midst of the withdrawal, a Japanese amphibious force landed on the west coast of Bataan just opposite Frank's positions on the east coast. The landings were made at night, in spots on the rugged peninsula that most of the Americans had never heard of and could not pronounce: Quinauan Point, Longoskawayan Point, and Silaiim Bay. The jungle was dense to the point of impassable, and largely unmapped. To the American officers it was obvious that the Japanese planned to cut the dirt road up the west coast and thus isolate the I Corps troops at the Pilar-Bagac line.[22] Battalions from the 1st Philippine Constabulary Regiment moved out to meet the enemy.

At the height of it all, Frank and the troops were treated to an encouraging message from their commanding general:

> Help is on the way from the United States. Thousands of troops and hundreds of planes are being dispatched. The exact time of arrival of reinforcements is unknown as they will have to fight their way through Japanese attempts against them.

It is imperative that our troops hold until these reinforcements arrive.

No further retreat is possible. We have more troops in Bataan than the Japanese have thrown against us, our supplies are ample; a determined defense will defeat the enemy's attack.

It is a question now of courage and determination. Men who run will merely be destroyed, but men who fight will save themselves and their country.

I call on every soldier in Bataan to fight in his assigned position, resisting every attack. This is the only road to salvation. If we fight we will win; if we retreat we will be destroyed.

MACARTHUR [23]

Our supplies are ample? Frank could see that the two-meals-a-day Bataan Ration was beginning to take its toll. To supplement the canned rations, the quartermasters had set up a bakery near the southern tip of the peninsula, and a fishery and slaughterhouse at Lamao, just north of Frank's troops. The slaughterhouse took in carabao, horses, mules and anything else that walked, crawled or swam, but the fishery shut down shortly after it got started—Frank's constables could not protect the Filipino fishermen from Japanese patrol boats or the ubiquitous Zero fighters, and hungry soldiers stole most of the catch on the beach before it could be processed.

As Frank talked to the Filipino officers and men, he found them to be optimistic and confident in spite of their hunger. General MacArthur said that help was on the way, so help would surely be here soon. The Americans Frank talked to looked across the bay toward the safety of MacArthur's headquarters in the Malinta Tunnel on Corregidor, and began referring to the general as "Dugout Doug." He had not set foot on Bataan since his first and only visit to the front lines, at Abucay Hacienda.[24]

Rumors began to circulate wildly: The reinforcement convoy was over one hundred miles long, laden with men, equipment, ammunition, and food! At the field hospital on the side of Mount Mariveles men climbed tall hardwood trees to look out to sea and watch for the convoy. When they spotted two ships anchored off Corregidor, word spread that the 9th Cavalry had arrived and that black soldiers on white horses would shortly cross over to Bataan and attack the Japanese.[25]

But the ships turned out to be two blockade-runners that made it to Corregidor with a few days' rations and some ammunition, and the "Buffalo Soldiers" never came.

At night, Frank and the other men would gather around a radio to listen to the "Voice of Freedom" broadcast from a small transmitter on Corregidor. The announcer, a diminutive Filipino newspaperman named Carlos P. Romulo,[26] gave the news events of the day, played a little music, berated the Japanese and, the best part, predicted that American ships and planes were on their way to relieve the men on Bataan.[27]

On January 26, Frank and a few other officers were listening to radio station KGEI in San Francisco over the short-wave radio at 4th PC headquarters. There, they heard the first report of American troops finally arriving overseas. The broadcast reported that a convoy of ships carrying the first contingent of American Expeditionary Forces into World War II had just landed—in Northern Ireland.[28]

Ireland?

The men were stunned. American troops had landed in Ireland, but none had yet shown up in the Philippines. What could it mean?

The more optimistic soldiers interpreted the news to mean that the Philippine relief convoy was somewhere en route, but had just not made it yet. The less optimistic gave the news a darker interpretation. Frank tended to go with the optimists.

In spite of the lack of reinforcements, the Fil-American soldiers held their positions along the Pilar-Bagac road and counter-attacked the Japanese beachheads on the "Points" along the west coast of Bataan. The constables, air corps and naval personnel who had been assigned to guard the rocky coastline were joined by U.S. Marines from Corregidor, and eventually by Philippine Scouts from the 45th and 57th Regiments. The Fil-American forces pushed the Japanese back to the very cliffs they had scaled to make their landings. With their backs to the sea, hundreds of Japanese soldiers dove over the cliffs to their deaths rather than surrender or be captured.

In the "Pockets," farther north, the Filipinos counter-attacked the Japanese who had infiltrated behind their lines, driving them back in tough fighting. Frank was pleased with the reports he heard from the front. The combined Fil-American assaults, spear-headed by the Philippine Scouts, wiped out the Japanese pockets and the Pilar-Bagac Line held.

Frank's Constabulary troops had fought alongside the Scouts in the tough and bloody battles, attacking the Japanese with bayonets. Frank was proud of his men. The Filipino soldiers had held the Japanese at the Pilar-Bagac line, and they soundly defeated them at the Pockets and at the Points. The victories gave a big boost to everyone's morale, in spite of their meager diets. Frank felt a renewed sense of hope. Maybe they really would be able to hold out until that relief convoy arrived.

***

From the High Commissioner's apartment in the U.S. Embassy building a few blocks south of the Manila Hotel, Lieutenant General Masaharu Homma had a magnificent view of Manila Bay and of the hazy, twin peaks of Bataan Peninsula just beyond.

The Filipino and American soldiers, so easily overwhelmed on Luzon's beaches when Homma first landed in the Philippines, were holding their own on Bataan. Homma's soldiers were tired, riddled with disease and decimated—his 65th Brigade had taken almost twenty-five percent casualties in its attack on Bataan, and half of the remaining men had malaria.[29] The Brigade's 20th Regiment was literally wiped out in the ill-fated attacks on the Fil-American lines and the landings at the Points on the west coast of Bataan. Of the 2,881 troops in that regiment, only 377 were still alive.[30]

On February 8, the day by which he was supposed to have conquered the Philippines, General Homma called a meeting of his staff officers at his forward headquarters in San Fernando.[31] He told the commander of the 65th Brigade that the attack on Bataan would, for the time being, be abandoned.

Homma then posed a question to his generals: Could they, after some rest and recuperation, take Bataan? Alternatives were called for and considered.

A staff officer concluded that up to this point, Homma's army had been beaten. He suggested that there was no need to take Bataan. MacArthur and his army were bottled up there and could neither attack nor last long without re-supply and reinforcements. With Pearl Harbor in shambles and the Japanese Navy blockading the Philippines there was no possibility of that, so why risk the lives of thousands of soldiers to eliminate a threat that, in reality, posed no threat?

If Homma insisted on attacking Bataan, his staff concluded, he would have to go to Tokyo and ask for more troops and supplies.

Requesting help from Tokyo would be a bitter pill to swallow—a significant loss of face. Particularly since General Tomoyuki Yamashita and the other army commanders were meeting their objectives ahead of schedule. The British had been defeated in Malaya and Hong Kong, and Singapore was on the verge of collapse. Japanese armies were about to sweep over the Dutch East

Indies. Thailand and French Indo-China had capitulated without a fight. Even the Pearl Harbor attack had been a great success.

But not a single Japanese ship floated on Manila Bay, and none could possibly get past the guns of Corregidor. As long as MacArthur's troops occupied Bataan and Corregidor everyone could see that General Homma, alone, had failed to make his objective.[32]

Per Homma's orders, the Japanese pulled back to regroup.

***

Across Manila Bay, the Bataan Ration was cut again. Men who got their full daily allotment received a slice of bread, about ten ounces of rice, a small portion of canned fish, some canned milk, and a portion of canned vegetables—either string beans or tomatoes.[33] Many of the men, particularly those on the front lines, got less.

Scraps of news circulated around the relatively quiet Fil-American camps. The U.S. submarine *Trout* crept into Corregidor one night with a load of anti-aircraft ammunition and news about Pearl Harbor. Contrary to previous reports, destruction there was almost total. Admiral Husband E. Kimmel and General Walter C. Short had both been sacked for their failure to detect and counter the attack.[34] A Japanese carrier fleet had struck Darwin, Australia in much the same manner as the attack on Pearl Harbor, sinking or damaging virtually every ship in port.

The disturbing news quickly spread through the camps on Bataan. Frank calculated that to avoid the Japanese Navy the relief convoy would have to refuel in Hawaii, proceed to Australia, then sail south of the Dutch East Indies to Singapore before entering the South China Sea. How could they do that with Pearl Harbor in ruins and Australia under attack?

Then word came in that Malaya and "impregnable" Singapore had fallen to the Japanese. The radio station in

Manila and thousands of leaflets dropped by Japanese airplanes crowed about the victory, and referred to General Tomoyuki Yamashita as the "Tiger of Malaya." Before long, rumors were circulating that General Homma had been called back to Tokyo in disgrace for having failed to take the Philippines. Supposedly he had committed *hara-kiri* rather than face failure. That was great! General Yamashita, it was said, was taking over the Philippine campaign. That was not so good.[35]

By mid-February, flour supplies ran out and the bakery shut down. The rice supply was dwindling. The men were encouraged to scavenge for food, and the gaunt soldiers began to take chances crossing into the no-man's land in front of the Pilar-Bagac Road to look for rice in the fields, and animals they could eat. To their surprise, they often saw no trace of the Japanese, even when foraging hundreds of yards in front of their lines.

Prolonged hunger causes profound changes in one's priorities and thought processes. The hungry men no longer talked about sex, women, booze, or sports. Food occupied their minds. Reminiscing about restaurants and meals gone by became a favorite pastime.[36] The men sat in the dirt of their foxholes and talked about white tablecloths, silverware and steak dinners. Frank thought about his house at Fort McKinley and the delicious spreads prepared there by Gonzales, their cook. Where was Gonzales now? Some Japanese officer undoubtedly occupied the house. What did he eat? Frank remembered his tour of duty at a small infantry post in Alaska. In the middle of winter the post had been snowed in and the cook ran out of meat. Frank asked for volunteers for a deer hunt, but no one wanted to venture out into the cold and snow. Frank went himself and shot a bear. He skinned and dressed the bear, gave the meat to the cook and kept the hide for himself. After eating bear meat for a week, plenty of soldiers volunteered for the next deer hunt. Frank wished he had that bear on Bataan.

Morale began to suffer. Even the most loyal and optimistic Filipino soldiers had to question, or express their discontent with, the army that could not feed them. There were epidemics of dysentery and diarrhea. It was estimated that only fifty-five percent of the troops could be considered combat-effective, defined as a soldier who could walk 100 yards without staggering and still have enough strength left to shoot his weapon.[37]

Quinine supplies ran low and the dense mosquito population caused a sharp increase in malaria. By the first of March, 500 new malaria cases were reporting in to the two open-air field hospitals each day. Six hundred of Frank's 1,800 constables were absent from duty, committed to the hospital with malaria. Hunger and other diseases undermined the morale of the rest.

Rumors made life worse. It was said that Japanese reinforcements were arriving at Lingayen Gulf, and were being trucked down the Luzon central plain to Bataan. But these were not just rumors. Even the Manila newspapers reported it.

***

On Corregidor, General MacArthur received a radio message from President Roosevelt. The President ordered MacArthur to leave the Philippines and proceed to Australia, "where you will assume command of all United States troops." [38]

MacArthur was stunned. The President of the United States had ordered him to abandon his men. He considered his options, which were few. He could not refuse an order from his Commander in Chief and remain a general in the United States Army. He talked with General Richard K. Sutherland, his closest advisor, and considered the possibility of resigning his commission, enlisting as a common soldier, and joining the troops at the front.[39]

From a practical standpoint, the option was not a good one. He was sixty-two years old, his wife and small son were on Corregidor with him, and if he were captured as a private in the front lines it would not make any difference to the Japanese propagandists. To the rest of the world, he would still be General MacArthur.

Why would Roosevelt even suggest such a thing? MacArthur agonized over the order, and had his staff review all messages received from Washington since Christmas, searching for a reason. Taking command of the relief convoy was the only acceptable answer. Finally, after further consultation with Sutherland, he concluded that he had no choice but to comply with the orders of the President. He decided to evacuate himself, his family, and his key staff members to Australia.

On the evening of March 11, 1942, a party of twenty-two persons boarded four PT boats at the Army Dock on the north side of Corregidor. The fast boats sped out into the darkness, dodging underwater mine fields and Japanese destroyers as they headed for Mindanao, the southernmost island in the Philippines.

General MacArthur, like the Far East Air Force and the U.S. Navy's Asiatic Fleet before him, was gone.[40]

***

The next morning, General Wainwright announced MacArthur's departure to his officers. The Voice of Freedom broadcast the news to the troops, saying that MacArthur left, "to continue the fight from Australia." General Wainwright was promoted to Lieutenant General and placed in overall command of the Philippines. Major General Edward P. King took command of Bataan.

As Frank talked with the men around him he found that, as usual, the Filipinos maintained their faith in General MacArthur—they were certain that he had gone south to take command of the relief convoy, which would surely arrive soon. But many of the American soldiers believed that MacArthur had deserted them. Some of them began stashing supplies against the day they might find themselves on their own.[41]

The barrage of Japanese propaganda continued. Radio broadcasts increased, and paper leaflets from the ever-present Japanese bombers told the soldiers that MacArthur had deserted them to save his own skin, and no reinforcements were coming.[42] They promised the Filipino soldiers food, safe conduct to their homes, and the opportunity to reunite with their families. Some of the leaflets pictured drawings of young Filipino men engaging in sex with beautiful women. In another day and time, the idea would have been of great interest to any soldier. But to the starving men of Bataan, sex was no longer a motivator. What they craved most was food and medicine. They used the leaflets for toilet paper.[43]

On March 15, the last bony cavalry horse went into the slaughterhouse. Meat supplies, such as they were, ran out. The slaughterhouse closed.

The Bataan Ration was cut, yet again. Each soldier's total daily food allotment was dropped to fifteen ounces per day, about one-fourth of the U.S. Army's standard daily intake, half of which was rice. The sparse rations were divided in two—half served in the morning and half at night. The new measures were supposed to make the food last through April 10.[44]

Frank Loyd was dismayed. Up until this point, he believed that the men were doing pretty well and could continue to hold on. But Frank did not see how they could last more than a few more weeks on the meager diets they were now being given. Virtually all of the men had lost about twenty-five percent of their normal body weight. Fat was gone, muscle was deteriorating. Digging a foxhole, a task that normally took about an hour, now took all day. Gaunt artillerymen found that they could no longer lift the heavy shells up to the breech of their cannons.

The men needed food and medicine. There were persistent rumors that the relief convoy would arrive tomorrow. But each day was like the day before, and relief never came. Air corps crews worked to expand the two hidden airfields on Bataan, and pilots were periodically given extra rations so they would be in shape to fly the new airplanes that General Marshall had promised. But except for the two small blockade-runners, no ships or airplanes came.

Every day, the thin, lanky figure of General Wainwright could be seen around the front lines on Bataan, encouraging the troops and conferring with General King. Wainwright, a decisive officer who genuinely cared about his men, estimated that now only about twenty-five percent of the troops could be considered combat-effective. The two open-air hospitals were jammed with more than 10,000 wounded and seriously ill soldiers, down with malnutrition, malaria, dysentery and other diseases. New malaria cases were coming in at a rate of 700 per day, and the supply of quinine was dwindling.[45] When he visited Bataan, General Wainwright himself walked with a cane—his legs were painful and weak from beriberi.[46]

On Thursday afternoon, March 19, Japanese airplanes flew over Bataan and dropped thousands of empty beer cans, each containing a letter. The 4th PC constables recovered one of the cans and brought it to Colonel Jalandoni. Jalandoni called Frank into his headquarters, and together they read the message:

> March 19, 1942.
>
> To His Excellency Major-General Jonathon Wainwright, Commander-in-Chief of the United States in the Philippines.
>
> Your Excellency,
>
> We have the honor to address you in accordance with the humanitarian principles of 'Bushido', the code of the Japanese warrior.
>
> It will be recalled that, some time ago, a note advising honorable surrender was sent to the

> Commander-in-Chief of your fighting forces. To this, no reply, as yet, has been received…
>
> Your Excellency, you have fought to the best of your ability. What dishonour is there in avoiding needless bloodshed? What disgrace is there in following the defenders of Hongkong, Singapore, and the Netherlands East Indies in the acceptance of honorable defeat? Your Excellency, your duty has been performed. Accept our sincere advice and save the lives of those officers and men under your command. The International Law will be strictly adhered to by the Imperial Japanese Forces and Your Excellency and those under your command will be treated accordingly. The joy and happiness of those whose lives will be saved and the delight and relief of their dear ones and families would be beyond the expression of words. We call upon you to reconsider this proposition with due thought.
>
> If a reply to this advisory note is not received from Your Excellency through a special messenger by noon of March 22nd, 1942, we shall consider ourselves at liberty to take any action whatsoever.[47]

It was signed by General Homma, "Commander-in-Chief of the Imperial Japanese Army and Navy."

This, thought Frank, *from an army that would court-martial and probably execute any soldier that actually surrendered.*

After he received General Homma's message, Wainwright commented, "The bastards could at least have sent a few full cans of beer." [48]

Ominous signs began to appear. Artillery observers near the front could see a large, dark shape rise up over Abucay Hacienda—a Japanese observation balloon to be used in directing artillery fire, just out of reach of their own artillery.[49] Aerial bombing increased sharply. Men at the front could hear trucks dragging artillery pieces into position behind the hills on the north side of the Pilar-Bagac Road, and tanks moving in.

On March 22, having heard nothing from Wainwright, Homma ordered the “softening up” to begin. Sixty heavy bombers, recently flown in from Malaya, began a round-the-clock schedule of attacks on the USAFFE positions. Long-range, heavy artillery opened up from Cavite and joined Japanese Navy bombers plastering Corregidor and the southern coasts of Bataan.[50]

General Wainwright ordered normal radio communications from Corregidor temporarily curtailed so the soldiers of Bataan and Corregidor could transmit 30,000 applications for government life insurance policies to the United States.[51] He had 40,000 "C" rations transferred from Corregidor to Bataan, in hopes that a decent meal would help the men face what was coming.[52]

Frank Loyd gathered his few remaining possessions together: his war diary, his 8mm movie camera and telephoto lenses, and two rolls of color film he had taken of the first Japanese planes bombing Corregidor. He wrapped it all in a piece of canvas and tied the bundle with heavy twine. He wrapped the bundle in what had long been one of his prized possessions, his Arctic Woods sleeping bag, and placed it in an empty footlocker. He wrote a letter to Evelyn, folded it, wrote her address on the outside, and put the letter in the footlocker. With the help of a couple of constables, he lowered the footlocker into the bottom of his foxhole.[53] The constables filled in the foxhole and covered it carefully with brush and leaves. If Frank survived the war he intended to come back one day and retrieve his property. If not…Colonel Jalandoni, his friend Montgomery McKee, and several constables knew where the footlocker was buried. Perhaps one of them would forward it all to Evelyn after the war.

Frank was worried about Evelyn and their two children. How would they survive without him, particularly as the children grew up? They might never know what happened to their father. But Evelyn was a strong and resourceful woman. One way or another, he knew she would be all right.

Frank joined Colonel Jalandoni at the 4th PC command post. During the battle Frank's role would be to handle communications with General Parker's headquarters, and to coordinate the actions of the 4th PC Regiment with adjacent units on each side.

***

On Good Friday, April 3, at three o'clock in the afternoon, after more than a week of almost constant bombardment, the thundering of the Japanese artillery suddenly stopped.

Along the Pilar-Bagac Line, the emaciated, hungry soldiers of General Vincente Lim's 41st Infantry Division crouched in their foxholes and lifted their eyes up to the sky. Waves of Japanese bombers passed overhead, dropping sticks of incendiary bombs into the dry, hot jungle. As the flames welled up around them, many of the men jumped out of their foxholes and ran for the reserve line to their rear, only to be cut down by the Japanese artillery, which shifted its fire into the area behind the main line.

Through the ringing in their ears, through the hot, smelly clouds of acrid smoke that stung their nostrils in the bleak and splintered jungle, the gaunt soldiers who remained could hear the faint sounds of boots on the hard earth. As the noise intensified, they heard the snapping of brush being pushed aside, cries of "*Banzai*!" and the roar of tank engines, which grew increasingly louder.

Out of the hills and ravines in front of them burst waves of fresh Japanese infantrymen, running toward them with fixed bayonets.

III. The Fiddlers' Club

For weeks after the Japanese attacks on Pearl Harbor and the Philippines, Evelyn Loyd's morning newspaper featured stories of U.S. troops on Luzon beating back the Japanese almost every day. In one front-page article, Associated Press reporter Clark Lee said that the Japanese soldiers were just "an ill-uniformed, untrained mass of young boys…equipped with small-caliber guns."[1] There were stories about Igorot headhunters riding on top of U.S. tanks and hacking their way through the thick jungle with machetes to get at the Japanese.[2] According to the headlines, American and Filipino pilots were shooting down lots of Japanese airplanes and the Dutch Navy was sinking Japanese warships around the East Indies, nearby. Evelyn Loyd read every word of every article. She listened to every radio news broadcast hoping to hear some word about Frank or his unit, the Philippine Constabulary.

Several of the wives who had been evacuated from the Philippines the previous year had formed a loose-knit social group in San Antonio called the "Fiddlers' Club," that met occasionally for lunch. When the war started, their numbers grew to about forty-five and they began holding regular weekly meetings at the Fort Sam Houston Officers' Club.[3] Evelyn attended when she could, in hopes of hearing some news from Bataan. The women also met from time to time to roll bandages for the Red Cross. It wasn't much, but it was at least something they could do to help. For Christmas, Evelyn knitted green wool gloves for her three brothers-in-law in the Army.

Evelyn soon realized that except for the women in the Fiddlers' Club, most people she met had only a vague idea where the Philippines Islands were and many were not even aware that the islands were a U.S. possession. Evelyn and some of the other wives of servicemen became popular speakers at local events. Evelyn got a call from Frank Jr.'s teacher, who asked that she come to the school and give a talk about the Philippines. She did, and she took the movie films of their beach vacation at Legaspi and showed them to the class.

But as Evelyn Loyd searched through the papers each day she noticed the news reports becoming less optimistic. By February, the American army was clearly bottled up on Bataan and Corregidor, and the press reported that the Japanese were sending in reinforcements. Japan had attacked the Dutch East Indies, sunk a number of Dutch ships, and was capturing island after island with relative ease. Japanese submarines were patrolling up and down the U.S. West Coast, sinking American freighters and tankers within sight of the California beaches. It was getting hard for Evelyn to find news stories about the Philippines—the newspapers and radio had turned their attention to the war in Europe, and to the Japanese and German submarine attacks off the coasts of California and New Jersey. Evelyn had not gotten one word from or about Frank since

December, when she received some Christmas packages that he had mailed just before the attack, and a cable wishing her and the children "Merry Christmas."

Evelyn anxiously perused every newspaper looking for some indication that the Philippine relief convoy President Franklin Roosevelt had alluded to so often was finally on its way to Bataan.[4] On February 23, the day Roosevelt was to deliver his monthly "Fireside Chat" radio broadcast, his Executive Assistant, Eugene Casey, told a gathering of Fort Worth Democrats that "the time is not unreasonably distant when it will no longer be impossible to reinforce General MacArthur." [5]

As Evelyn listened to his speech that night, Roosevelt, hoarse from a severe cold, talked about increasing industrial production, supplying the British, and winning the war. His only mention of the Philippines was when he referred to the battle there as a "delaying action," and said that it would be "almost impossible" to rescue the men on Bataan. While he spoke, a Japanese submarine surfaced off the coast of California and shelled an oil refinery near Santa Barbara.[6]

Early in March, Evelyn read a newspaper article that said the government was suspending the pay of all soldiers who were killed or missing in action. A few days later she opened her mail and found an official notice stating that her monthly allotment from Frank's paycheck had been cut off. The notice was a standard form, and there was no explanation.

Truly frightened, Evelyn picked up the telephone to find out if other wives had received similar notices.

When she got her friend Evelyn Noble on the phone, the woman was clearly upset.

"What's the matter?" she asked, cautiously.

"Oh, Evelyn, haven't you heard?"

"No. What is it?"

"It's Maxie—he's dead!"

She could barely understand the shaky voice on the other end of the line. Evelyn Noble was a small, strong woman, raised on a south Texas farm. She was always in control, but today—only barely. Back in January there was a rumor that her husband had been wounded and put on the hospital ship *USS Mactan*, bound for Australia. Everyone thought he was safe.

But Marge Wright had just called from San Francisco. The paper there printed a long article about Maxie Noble, with his picture, saying that he had been killed in action on Bataan.[7]

Evelyn Loyd called another friend, Betty Wilson, and found her upset as well. She had received two sympathy letters from other friends. They said that her husband, Zero, was missing in action. None of the women had received any kind of notification from the War Department.

Alarmed, the three women telephoned friends they knew in Washington. Later that afternoon they all sent telegrams to the War Department asking for information about their husbands.

The next day they received telegrams back—the War Department knew nothing about any of their husbands, except that none of them appeared on official lists of soldiers killed, wounded, or missing in action.[8]

It was little comfort. Evelyn Loyd began a daily ritual of telephone conversations with Evelyn Noble and Betty Wilson to exchange whatever news each might have heard, and to do what she could to calm the other women's fears.

On March 18, the radio and newspapers reported that General Douglas MacArthur had been ordered out of the Philippines and sent to Australia to take command of all Allied forces in the Southwest Pacific. To Evelyn and the other wives in the Fiddlers' Club it seemed like a sudden ray of hope. They were certain that General MacArthur was going there to take command of the Philippine relief convoy. The men on Bataan had been holding on now for three months. Very soon, Evelyn expected, MacArthur and an army of reinforcements would sail for Bataan to drive the Japanese out.

***

What General Douglas MacArthur found in Darwin, Australia when he arrived on Tuesday, March 17, 1942, left him bitter and angry. He and his family flew in on an Army Air Corps B-17 that picked them up on Mindanao Island and spirited them out of the Philippines. But there was no brass band to greet him, and no divisions of soldiers formed up on the tarmac ready to follow him back to the Philippines. In fact, he and his entourage were forced to quickly scramble across the airfield, board a waiting DC-3 transport, and take off again to avoid being hit by Japanese bombers coming in to attack the airfield.[9]

As he traveled on to Melbourne, MacArthur learned the real truth—there was no Philippine relief convoy. The United States Navy had no ships standing by, on the way, or even planned, for a Philippine relief expedition. No U.S. Army troops were waiting in Australia.[10] Everything had been sent to Europe. And where were those "streams" of airplanes that General Marshall had promised? The fact is, they never existed.[11] The 86,000 men of the USAFFE army, clinging desperately to the rocky hillsides of Bataan and Corregidor, had been abandoned.[12]

Douglas MacArthur would never trust Franklin Delano Roosevelt again.[13]

***

Back in the States, the newspapers talked Douglas MacArthur up as a big hero, and possible future president. Roosevelt had felt compelled to extract MacArthur, a potential political rival, from the Philippines—it would be unthinkable for America's popular hero to be pictured in chains on the front page of a Japanese newspaper. On March 26, 1942, President Roosevelt awarded General Douglas MacArthur the Congressional Medal of Honor, for his "conspicuous gallantry and intrepidity in action against the invading Japanese forces in the Philippines." [14]

Two weeks later, Bataan would surrender.

IV. Days of Decision

How had it come to this? Frank Loyd wondered.

On, April 6, 1942, Frank's 4th Philippine Constabulary Regiment had been ordered to abandon its beach defenses and move north to Bataan's Mamala River.[1] General Edward P. King's front-line troops were falling back under the Japanese assault, and General King ordered every available unit into the battle. As new units moved forward, the broken remnants of the defeated divisions began to stream southward out of the combat zone.

At mid-afternoon, Frank and Colonel Rafael Jalandoni rousted their men out of their foxholes, and had them tear down their heavy equipment and assemble along the bayside highway. There, they boarded a convoy of buses and cars to drive north up the peninsula, along Manila Bay, to the front. As his driver wrestled his staff car up the shell-pocked highway, Frank watched wounded, defeated men walking south down both sides of the road heading the other way. Here and there were pairs, one holding the other up. Americans and Filipinos together. Bandaged and bloody, their clothes soaked with sweat. Some dragged improvised litters made by wrapping the edges of a blanket around two tree branches. Bumping along on the litters were their buddies who were too sick or too badly injured to walk.

Frank's convoy snaked northward along the shell-pocked road, past steep gullies and over shallow streams that flowed from the sides of Mount Mariveles, the extinct volcano that formed the south end of Bataan Peninsula. Above him, dense jungles covered the rugged sides of the mountain. Frank thought about the time he brought Evelyn and the children to Bataan for a camping trip. Since then Bataan had become a panorama of Hell itself.

At dusk the convoy turned off the highway onto Trail 2, a small road cut through the jungle. Speed dropped to a crawl as the staff cars and buses bounced over the uneven roadbed heading for the front line, thought to be somewhere north of the Mamala River.

Shortly after dark, the lead units of the 4th PC Regiment crossed the Mamala and ran headlong into the Japanese Army. As Philippine and American Army units retreated around them, the constables at the front of the convoy engaged the enemy and stood their ground, covering the retreating soldiers. Frank and the rest of the men jumped from their vehicles and scrambled into defensive positions along both sides of the trail.[2]

The battle went on sporadically. Then a messenger brought word that the front lines had been overrun and the defense along the Mamala River had failed. Frank ordered his men back into their vehicles to withdraw. As the buses and cars backed down the narrow trail, bullets and artillery shells crashed into the trees around them. The units at the front of the line were cut off by the enemy and lost.[3]

When they arrived back at the bayside highway, the 4th PC Regiment was ordered to retreat farther south to the

Alangan River. There, U.S. forces were regrouping, desperately preparing a new defense line to make another stand against the Japanese. In the dark, with headlights dimmed, Frank's driver picked his way back down the road, dodging bomb craters, retreating soldiers, and refugees. Frank could see that some of the stragglers were still carrying their weapons. Their units had been overrun and dispersed, leaving the men leaderless. They were fatigued, hungry, and barely strong enough to walk.

Frank studied the vehicle in front of his car. It was a commercial bus that had its top cut off, apparently by a blowtorch. A peculiar sight in any other circumstances, but not at all out of place here on Bataan. The ragged body of the bus was covered with dust and grime, and Frank could make out the name "Pambusco" painted beneath the molding that once held a rear window. Inside, the heads and shoulders of about forty of his constables bobbed about as the bus lurched from crater to pothole. The men were sitting bolt upright, staring around them at the fleeing soldiers.

At six o'clock in the morning, Wednesday, April 8, 1942, the 4th PC got to their new positions. Colonel Jalandoni received his orders: block the bayside highway just south of the Alangan River.[4] The 4th PC Regiment's mission was to stop the Japanese from advancing down the highway, the only road into American-held southern Bataan.

As the sun rose over Manila Bay, Frank and Jalandoni stood in a tree line on a small rise south of the river and studied their intended battlefield. The highway wandered down from northern Bataan alongside Manila Bay, which was off to their right, and crossed the Alangan River in front of them, just to their left. From the river, the road climbed a gentle slope then curved east, passing in front of them for about 300 yards before turning south again. Between the river and the road were open fields of tough, chest-high Cogon grass. On the south side of the curve, behind Frank, the ground sloped up for a few hundred yards, covered with tall, shady hardwood trees broken by clumps of brush and bamboo. At the top of the rise, the trees became more dense and merged into a thick jungle that extended south along the highway and west toward Mount Mariveles. It would have been a peaceful, tranquil morning, standing there on that hillside, except for the Japanese bombers roaring over the treetops, and the rumble of explosions off to their left, farther down the defense line.

Jalandoni gave orders for the disposition of his troops: he ordered the 1st PC Battalion and the 2nd Engineer Battalion to dig in under the tree line on the south side of the curve in the road. From the hillside they would have clear fields of fire north across the road and into the Cogon grass fields, as well as up the road itself. He ordered the 2nd PC Battalion to dig in closer to the river, in an area left of the road where they could bring grazing fire across the highway and the grass fields.[5] Frank and his assistant, Major McClellan, inspected each battalion and made sure that every machine gun and automatic weapon was positioned to bring maximum fire onto the road, and could then shift to defensive fire across the front of the constables' lines. The highway and the Cogon grass fields would be their battlefield. Here, they would wait for the Japanese.

The men began digging in. Dust from the hard, tan earth added a gritty smell and taste to the breeze blowing off Manila Bay. The men were weak and work progressed slowly. While they worked on their foxholes, cooks came around and distributed the morning meal. Frank got two tablespoonfuls of boiled rice and half of a tin of tuna fish. That would be it until the end of the day. Frank and everyone else wondered, *where is that reinforcement convoy?*

Back in the tree line, up the hill from the road, the constables dug a hole under a thatch of Nipa palm bushes to serve as the 4th PC Regiment's command post. From the dugout, Frank and Colonel Jalandoni would have a clear view of the battlefield through the widely spaced trees. They could see the 1st PC Battalion's foxholes in the tree line in front of them, the road curving past the foxholes, the grass fields on the other side of the road, and the river. Behind the command post, among scattered thickets of bamboo, Colonel Jalandoni hid his medical aid station, vehicles, and cooks. Frank felt confident that they had picked the best possible site from which to ambush the advancing Japanese. The highway was still alive with fleeing refugees and military stragglers, quietly trudging south. There was nothing they could do about that. So far, there was no sign of enemy soldiers.

As the morning sun climbed higher, two Japanese dive-bombers spotted the activity in the tree line and began swooping and diving on the 4th PC's positions. Japanese artillery joined in. The constables grabbed their rifles and scrambled into their unfinished foxholes.

Dodging the dive-bombers, Frank scouted the 4th PC's flanks. He found that the air corps and infantry units that were supposed to hold the line on his left had withdrawn under the artillery and bombing attack, leaving an unmanned area of jungle on his left.[6] Frustrated and angry, he returned to the command post and reported the problem to Colonel Jalandoni. Jalandoni sent a messenger to II Corps Headquarters to bring troops forward to fill the gap.

Although the men were jittery from the dive-bombers and sporadic artillery fire, they continued working through the morning, digging and preparing their positions in the smoky, dirty heat. The work was exhausting. Many of the men were weak from malaria. Nonetheless, they were digging, hauling ammunition up to their foxholes, and getting ready for the Japanese.

At noon, the bombing stopped and was followed immediately by a heavy artillery barrage. The exhausted constables dropped their shovels, dove once again into their foxholes, and readied their rifles and ammunition. Safeties were clicked off. Machine guns were sighted down lanes of fire.

The refugees had disappeared from the highway. Nervously, the constables peered out at the road and into the tall Cogon grass. Japanese soldiers might already be moving in on them, crawling through the high grass.

Gradually, they came into view. Brown uniformed men armed with rifles and automatic weapons walked along both sides of the highway, passing through the smoke, coming up the hill from the river toward the 4th PC. Behind them, a few light vehicles mounted with machine guns picked their way through the craters in the roadway.

The constables held their fire.

As the lead elements of the Japanese force drew directly in front of the line of concealed foxholes, the bulk of the Japanese troops were still about 400 yards away. Colonel Jalandoni shouted the command: "Fire!" The constables opened up with everything they had.[7]

Along both sides of the roadway startled Japanese soldiers dropped, mortally wounded. Those who were not hit in the first fusillade dove into the ditches and scrambled to see where the gunfire was coming from. The vehicles stopped and began backing away as their gunners sprayed the tree line with machine gun fire.

More Japanese soldiers appeared on the hillside, moving through the grass fields toward the constables. Somewhere an officer had taken stock of the situation, rallied his troops and sent them up the hillside into the battle. As Frank watched, his constables poured small arms fire into the fields and raked the roadsides with their machine guns. Frank watched his men. They were performing exactly as ordered. Exactly as they had been trained.

Frank left the command post, running and crawling along the line of foxholes toward Lieutenant Colonel Vincente Torres' 2nd Engineer Battalion. It was Frank's job to maintain communications between the front-line units during the battle.[8] He found Torres wounded in the neck but crawling forward to send an automatic rifleman after some Japanese approaching from the left.[9]

In front of the tree line, a squad of Japanese suddenly burst out of the Cogon grass and charged across the road. Before they could be stopped, they found a foxhole and fired their rifles point-blank into the hapless constables inside. As those Japanese were brought down by fire from nearby foxholes, another group burst out of the Cogan grass with fixed bayonets. Frank, trying to get Torres back out of the line of fire, looked up and saw the Japanese machine gun vehicles moving forward on the road. More troops were coming up behind them. Another squad of Japanese rose up out of the grass and charged across the highway into the constables' line.

Colonel Jalandoni, having survived an artillery round that hit the mango tree above his command post, leaped from his dugout. He ran to the rear, into the bamboo clumps. There, he rallied and organized his cooks, truck drivers, medics and anyone else he could find. Grabbing their rifles, Jalandoni and his rag-tag reserves counter-attacked the Japanese, killing those within his perimeter and driving the lead elements of the assault back across the road into the grass field.[10]

Seeing their leader and his rear-echelon men charge past them, the constables of the 4th PC rose out of their foxholes and attacked. Colonel Torres and Frank Loyd rallied the 2nd Engineers, ordered them out of their foxholes and joined the assault. As they moved forward, PC machine gunners poured fire down the road at the Japanese vehicles.

As Torres moved forward, a Japanese sniper off to the right hit him again.[11] Badly wounded, he fell to the ground while a squad of engineers moved out to drive the sniper off a nearby cliff.

The Japanese began to fall back, covered by their machine guns, and soon by artillery fire. The heavy shells crashed into the Cogon grass and the tree line, sending the constables scrambling for cover. They had been firing so intensely that many of them were out of ammunition.

As Frank, Torres and Jalandoni exhorted the men to get back into their foxholes, other PC officers scrounged the battlefield for ammunition.[12] They ran through bursting shells, pulled bandoleers off of dead soldiers, and redistributed the ammunition to the line of foxholes.

Gradually the Japanese withdrew. The firing died down. The firefight had lasted about an hour.

Frank moved from point to point across the defensive front, taking stock of the damage and yelling at commanders to get their men back on line. There were thirty casualties among the enlisted men, plus Colonel Torres and several other officers.[13]

On checking the flanks, Frank found that no troops had been brought forward to plug the gap in the line on his left. He was furious. Then, on his right flank, he found that the provisional infantry unit that was supposed to hold the line between the 4th PC and the shores of Manila Bay had also disappeared during the attack.[14] The 4th PC Regiment was isolated and alone on the front line, with both flanks exposed. Ammunition was dangerously low.

After hearing Frank's report, Colonel Jalandoni dispatched his executive officer, Major Gaspar Baylon, to II Corps headquarters to bring back reinforcements and ammunition. The need was urgent. Baylon and his driver ran back to a staff car and took off south down the bayside highway.

Japanese artillery shells crashed sporadically into the constables' positions and Zero fighters swept down the defense line spraying the area with machine-gun fire. But there was work to be done. Wounded men were sent to the rear area aid station, and the dead were dragged back to the bamboo thickets to be buried. Constables were moved and reassigned to fill gaps in the line of foxholes. Despite the artillery fire, Colonel Jalandoni walked through his constables' positions, encouraging each man and telling him that help was on the way.

Major Baylon returned with bad news. The entire defense line was under attack. Every unit had already been committed. No reinforcements would be coming.[15] Frank and Baylon met with Colonel Jalandoni and told him the truth—if they stayed where they were, without reinforcements and ammunition, the constables could not hold up against another attack.[16] The units on each side of them had pulled out and left them alone, exposed on the front line. They had best withdraw south until they could find friendly lines.

Farther off to their left they could hear artillery and gunfire. Somewhere down the defense line, Fil-American forces were under attack but apparently still holding on. Jalandoni thought it over: the bayside highway was the critical route into southern Bataan—if the 4th PC left their positions it would open the highway to the Japanese with disastrous consequences. Colonel Jalandoni made a decision—the 4th PC would hold the line at all costs. If necessary, they would fight to the death. He sent Major Baylon back to II Corps again to beg for the desperately needed reinforcements.

Frank knew that unless the reinforcements arrived, they would not survive the next Japanese assault. But losing the bayside highway would probably mean losing Bataan. Holding the road at all costs was the right thing to do. Frank admired the Colonel's guts. As bad as it was, it was the decision Frank knew Jalandoni had to make.

By three-thirty in the afternoon, the 4th PC's officers finally got all the remaining men back in their positions and re-supplied with the available ammunition. The Japanese artillery had fallen off to sporadic interdiction fire. The dive-bombers were gone but before they left they dropped incendiaries into the grass fields in front of the constables' positions, and the fields were on fire.

The constables sensed the danger they were in. Everyone was on edge. They had had little to eat for two days, and no sleep. Dead Japanese littered the road and the grass fields in front of them. Smoke burned the constable's eyes and lungs.

The relative quiet was unnerving. They knew the Japanese were preparing another assault, but nothing seemed to be happening. Here and there, dog-tired constables fell asleep in their foxholes. Major McClellan, Frank's assistant who was now commanding the 2nd PC Battalion, crouched down in his command post near the river. His head drooped over his rifle as he fought to stay awake in the stifling heat. Like many of the men around him, his eyes grew heavy and he dozed off. When he awoke an hour later, he was alone. McClellan crawled out of his dugout and looked around. He walked up and down his line. The foxholes were empty. The entire 2nd PC Battalion was gone. There was not a constable or a Japanese in sight. His men had deserted.[17]

Frank listened to McClellan's report in characteristic silence. A knot of disappointment, followed by a deep concern for the remaining troops, tightened his stomach. The 4th PC Regiment now consisted of only two battalions, the 1st PC and the 2nd Engineers. Both units were at half strength at best, hungry, weak with malaria and short on ammunition. There was no possibility of reinforcements. And it was their mission to prevent the Japanese Army from advancing down the critical highway.

Just short of five o'clock in the afternoon, Frank was in the command post and Colonel Jalandoni was out by the line of foxholes talking to the men. Frank heard the distinctive sound of a tank or half-track moving on the highway behind the 4th PC's positions. He turned to see what was going on. Perhaps reinforcements were coming after all.

As he turned to look, two tanks broke through the bamboo and trees behind the command post, and sprayed the area with machine gun fire. Japanese infantry burst out of the jungle behind them, and viciously attacked the constables from the rear. With cries of "*Banzai! Banzai!*"

they rushed out of the darkening jungle and attacked the line of foxholes.[18]

Surprised, stunned, and frightened, the constables turned and fired, but it was too late. A few stood fast and managed to shoot some of the on-rushing Japanese before they were shot or bayoneted in the foxholes that now became their own graves. Frank watched in horror as the rest of the men jumped from their positions and stampeded in every direction, many of them out into the burning Cogon grass, trying to escape. The Japanese charged after them. The whole attack had happened in an instant. The excited Japanese troops rushed past the command post without even seeing Frank.

Everything was chaos as the Japanese soldiers ran out into the grassy fields to hunt down survivors. All of the constables were gone, disappeared. It was incredible. Jalandoni's men had been in position and ready to fight one moment, and they were either gone or dead the next.[19]

Some of the Japanese soldiers returned and began poking around the abandoned foxholes, moving toward the command post.

Frank pushed through the brush at the back of the dugout and crawled out under the jungle bushes. He yearned to draw his pistol and kill the first Japanese he saw, but the effort would be useless—and suicidal. He crawled into the trees, away from the tanks and the Japanese soldiers, and away from the highway. In the distance behind him a few PC officers shouted at their fleeing troops. He could hear the distinctive "ping" of Japanese rifles, and the chatter and roar of the Japanese tanks.

Frank got up and ran to his right, hoping to rally some constables he had spotted and to set up at least a small defensive position. A few of the men joined him.

As one of the tanks turned toward Frank and the men around him, they ran toward the jungle, weaving and dodging, looking for a protected spot that they could defend.

The tank rumbled after them. Machine gun bullets zinged overhead and smashed into the tree trunks. Behind them, the voices of Japanese soldiers rose in excitement. The tank's cannon fired, striking a tree directly in front of them. Frank could hear shrapnel sprinkle the ground as he darted to his left, down a small trail. The men who had been with him ran to their right, headed west.

To Frank's horror, another tank was stopped on this trail—directly in front of him. He had been spotted again. As the tank prepared to fire, Frank saw Japanese soldiers pushing through the brush on each side of it, coming around it, coming after him. He quickly lunged to his right. Fire flashed at the muzzle of the tank's cannon. Frank's ears throbbed with the impact of the round as it exploded behind him.

His heart racing, Frank dashed through the darkening woods. He had a good head start on the Japanese soldiers. Around him were thick hardwood trees that he knew the tanks could not get through. He only had to elude the soldiers.

Frank ran like hell through the trees. He dodged clumps of brush and entangling vines, and kept running. Slowly the noises faded behind him. He slowed and began running more carefully, as quietly as possible, staying in the shadows. His heart pounding in his ears, his breath was hot and harsh in his chest. As he ran, the other noises faded. He paused to look around, to catch his breath, and to listen. The sun was setting over the mountain ridges to his right and the light was growing dim. He heard no one coming after him. No tanks behind him. He was exhausted.

The sounds of the battle had died down, but rifle shots still cracked sporadically in the distance. He could still hear the cries of wounded soldiers. Frank found himself standing on a small north-south trail.

He decided to move cautiously up the trail, back toward the 4th PC's positions. As he walked north in the darkening jungle, Frank glimpsed movement on the trail ahead of him just past a slight bend. He stepped aside, behind a large tree. He waited for the men to get closer, close enough for them to recognize that he was an American. As he fidgeted and waited, the dark shapes came around the bend into full view. It was a group of ten Japanese soldiers walking single file.

The lead man had not seen him. Frank inched slowly back, keeping the tree between himself and the approaching Japanese. He crouched down in the brush and held absolutely still and quiet. The Japanese soldiers trudged by, heading south with their rifles slung over their shoulders.

The dark shapes passed within a few feet of Frank. As they walked, their boots kicked up small clouds of dust. Nervous sweat trickled into Frank's eyes as he watched. His own breath seemed to ring in his ears, and his nostrils became clogged with the puffs of dust that drifted by.

As the patrol disappeared into the darkness, Frank remained motionless. He listened.

The jungle was almost pitch-black. He had no weapon except his pistol. He had had nothing to eat since that morning. He had not slept for two days. His eyes, his head and his stomach all ached, and his legs felt like lead. He took a few steps back from the trail and stumbled into some bushes.

***

When Frank Loyd awoke it was still dark. He lay still.

He heard engines, but in the dense jungle the vehicles sounded like they could be anywhere, or everywhere, around him. Farther distant were the muffled rumbles and booms of artillery. Somewhere, the battle was continuing but it did not sound close at hand. Cautiously, he stood up and looked around.

Frank was alone in the jungle and could see only a few yards through the brush and trees. His mouth was dry and parched, his eyes were blurry and the air smelled of burnt fuel and gunpowder. Frank's shoulders and legs ached. He stepped through the trees and found the north-south trail he had run down the night before, parallel to the highway.

After looking carefully up and down the dark trail, he began feeling his way north, back toward the bend in the highway, to the 4th PC Regiment's old position. His confidence rose somewhat as the first rays of dawn began to lighten the sky.

Suddenly, Frank noticed movement in the bushes to his right, and to his left. He stopped dead in his tracks. His eyes blinked to attention.

Dark shapes in the brushy jungle began to move, stand up, stretch, and yawn. He recognized the rattle of mess kits being opened and the rustle of bedding being rolled up in the jungle grass.[20] In a ritual as old as armies on the march, a sergeant was walking around in the pre-dawn shadows waking his men, turning them out for breakfast. The language he was muttering was Japanese.

The skin on Frank's back crawled. He had walked right into a Japanese camp. Somehow, the sentries had missed him. They must have pulled in from their guard posts just as he approached the camp, their duty done for the night. So far, he had not been noticed.

He put his head down slightly, hiding his Caucasian features with his hand, and looked out of the corners of his eyes. It was a small camp, platoon size, about thirty or forty men. To his left, about twenty feet away, a group of four or five had gathered—probably the platoon leader and his sergeants. Around the camp the soldiers were beginning to move about, paying attention to their bedding and equipment on the ground, and stumbling off into the trees to urinate. Incredibly, he still had not been noticed. Frank stretched a little and, keeping his hand in front of his face, stumbled off to his left into the jungle, trying to look like a sleepy soldier who needed to go.[21]

At the edge of the camp he slipped behind a large tree. He crept cautiously through the trees, away from the camp. Slowly at first, then faster. In a few moments he had done it. He, a senior American officer, had walked into an encampment of Japanese soldiers, walked right on through it and out the other side, undetected. Mentally he kicked himself for being so stupid. Gathering his wits, Frank decided he had better get away from the highway and head west, hopefully toward friendly troops farther down the defense line. He walked faster and faster, and then broke into a run.

Frank had a new mission now—escape and evade. It was Thursday morning, April 9, and it was his duty to get back to friendly lines and rejoin his unit. He had no idea how far south the Japanese had advanced down the bayside highway, but as far as he knew, I Corps was still in its original positions along the west coast of Bataan. He decided to cross over the foothills of Mount Mariveles and find his way to I Corps. Frank followed his compass west through the jungle.

About noon, he found himself at the foot of a rocky hill. He climbed up to an outcropping to look around. As he peered out from behind the rocks, he heard voices.

Cautiously, Frank crouched down, drew his pistol, clicked off the safety, and listened. Someone was coming up the trail exchanging brief, quiet comments—in English.

Frank looked down from his hiding place and saw two American soldiers walking toward him. Relieved, and barely able to conceal his smile, Frank stood up, returning his .45 to its holster. He stepped out from his hiding spot and in good military fashion called out, "Who's there?"

The men looked up startled, then grinned.

"Lieutenant Leonard Mills, US Navy!"

"Sergeant James Wools, US Army! Who the hell are you?" [22]

They seemed to be as pleased to see Frank as he was to see them.

Frank identified himself, but the three men's elation quickly turned to disappointment as they realized that they were all stragglers, cut off from their units during the previous day's battles.

Lieutenant Mills was a big man who, Frank thought, looked curiously clean and well fed for someone who had been on Bataan for three months. Sergeant Wools was smaller, thin, and his clothes were dirty and torn. He looked like he had been in the thick of it for much longer than three months.

Wools and Mills, it turned out, were headed for Mariveles, the southernmost town on Bataan Peninsula, to re-join the Fil-American forces. They said that there was a collection point there, where stragglers were being re-grouped into fighting units to go back to the front. If anyone was left from the 4th PC Regiment, Frank would most likely find them in Mariveles. As they talked, they shared a tin of tuna fish that Sergeant Wools had brought along, the only food they had among them. Frank decided to join the men and go to Mariveles.

When they started walking Frank had the other two separate, staying about fifteen yards apart. They took turns on the "point," leading the way. They headed southwest, looking for Trail 20, a north-south access road the Army Engineers had cut through the jungle.

The men moved cautiously through the jungle until well after dark, picking their way along, stopping frequently to listen.

Before dawn, they reached Trail 20, a rutted dirt path through the trees that served as a supply route from the rear areas to the front lines, wide enough for vehicles to pass in single file. They were on a crest of high ground that flowed down from a ridge on the east side of Mount Mariveles. They should be within friendly territory now. All they had to do was walk south down the trail until they encountered friendly forces.

As the men looked and listened, they heard trucks approaching from the north.

Frank and Lieutenant Mills crawled into a brushy ditch by the roadside, but Sergeant Wools stepped out onto the trail to flag down the trucks.

"Get back here and get down!" Frank ordered.

"Why? They'll pass us up. Let's stop 'em!"

"Get down. And be quiet!"

Wools looked confused. He looked at the road as if to bolt out in front of the approaching trucks on his own. Mills pulled him back.

The trucks grew closer as the three men hid in the ditch and watched. Frank thought it odd that their headlights were on—certain to draw artillery fire if an observer spotted them. Two trucks passed by, only a few feet away. As the trucks passed, Frank could see that they were filled with Japanese soldiers.[23]

"Jesus, those were Japs!" Wools sputtered.

The jungle was deathly quiet as Frank stepped out into the middle of the dark roadway. The only sound was the fading growl of the two truck engines as they continued south, down Trail 20. There had been almost no artillery fire or bombing since noon. Obviously, the Japanese had been more successful than Frank expected. He concluded that the U.S. Army must have fallen back farther south, probably to Cabcaben, to make a stand there. If the Japanese had gotten that far, their supply lines would be stretched. They must be re-grouping and planning their next attack, a process which would take at least two days. The men would have plenty of time to get to Mariveles.

Frank decided that they should continue moving west. They would climb up the side of Mount Mariveles to a saddle between the peak of the mountain and a smaller outcropping known as Mount Limay, then walk down the south face of Mount Mariveles to the town.

At mid-morning on Friday, April 10, they made it to the saddle and crossed onto the south slope of the mountain. Through the trees, Frank caught occasional glimpses of the seaport town of Mariveles and its small, blue harbor below them. Three miles off shore was the island fortress of Corregidor. From high on the mountainside, Mariveles looked beautiful. There they could get something to eat, they could find out what was going on, and they would be safely back with the U.S. Army.

The men headed west around the south slope, then turned onto a jungle trail and went down, walking single file, about ten yards apart. At three o'clock in the afternoon Mills, the point man, waved the other two off the trail and into the brush. Ahead he had spotted a small group of Filipinos. The Americans hid in the bushes until the five men were just in front of them on the trail. Mills could see that there was no one coming behind them.

Mills bellowed out, "Halt, who's there!"

The surprised Filipinos turned out to be Philippine Army soldiers wearing civilian shirts. They were tired, nervous, and anxious. They quickly told the three Americans why: "General King has surrendered. Bataan is lost!"

"What?" The Americans' words were filled with emotions that ranged from disbelief to dismay. If General King had surrendered Bataan, then all of Luzon Island was under Japanese control.

"Japanese all over Mariveles. General King says, 'All Americans and all Filipinos in Bataan lay down their guns, turn themselves in.' Everyone to go to Mariveles or Bagac, so Japanese can take them to prison camp."

The Filipinos explained that the Fil-American Army had finally collapsed under the Japanese onslaught. Whole divisions had been destroyed in the retreat. The two field hospitals were packed with thousands of sick and wounded soldiers. Food supplies had all but run out. The soldiers were out of ammunition and the tanks were running out of gas. Rather than see any more of his men die, General King had surrendered.[24]

The stunned Americans pressed for more information. "What about Corregidor?"

"Corregidor still holding. General Wainwright refuse to surrender."

"Can we get to Corregidor?"

"No."

The Filipinos said that after the surrender, thousands of soldiers in Mariveles had clambered into every boat they could find, to flee to Corregidor. There were no boats left. Some of them made it, but while the boats were crossing to the island Japanese planes strafed them with machine guns. Hundreds of men had been killed. Some men even attempted to swim to Corregidor. But before they could get away, the Japanese arrived. Japanese marksmen stood on the shoreline and shot at the bobbing heads in the water, killing many of the men. Sharks got more.

At that point, these Filipinos and several hundred others slipped away from Mariveles into the jungle, before the Japanese could surround the city. An American officer from the 26th Cavalry fled with them, but he was sick. He was so weak from malnutrition that he could not make the climb up the mountainside. When they stopped at a Negrito village halfway up the mountain trail, the natives said that they would feed and take care of him, so the Filipinos left him behind.

The five Filipinos wanted to move on quickly, before Japanese patrols came up the mountain after them. They were going to return to their homes and wait until General MacArthur returned with the reinforcements to liberate the Philippines, as he had promised. After brief good-byes they continued up the trail, into the jungle.

Frank was numbed. After two days of dodging the Japanese trying to get back to U.S. forces, there were no U.S. forces to join. He slumped to the ground and looked at the others.

"We've missed the last train." [25]

***

On the morning of April 9, 1942, the day General King surrendered, the tired and hungry troops of the Fil-American Army on Bataan destroyed their weapons as ordered. They blew up the firing mechanisms from their cannons, threw their pistols into the sea, and wedged the barrels of their rifles into the crotches of trees and bent the barrels. Many of the men sat down where they were, too tired to do anything but wait for the Japanese. Others walked and stumbled toward the bayside highway or the Pilar-Bagac Road, preferring to meet the Japanese and get it over with as quickly as possible. Those near food depots broke open the last remaining rations and enjoyed their first full meal in three months. In all, 11,000 American and 55,000 Filipino soldiers were about to become prisoners of war. Twenty-four thousand of them were wounded or seriously ill—more than 10,000 of those needing hospitalization.

A small detachment of U.S. Army Air Corps men manned General King's radio communications station on the southwest side of Mount Mariveles, a few hundred yards above General King's headquarters at Little Baguio. Lieutenant Henry Clay Conner and the rest of the men gathered around to talk about the surrender order, which they had received by radio. The detachment commander, Colonel Gregg, suggested that instead of surrendering they could take off into the jungle and head north to find Lieutenant Colonel Claude Thorp.[26] Back in January, Colonel Thorp had left on a secret mission into the Zambales Mountains north of Bataan, with a party of sixteen men and two women. Thorp and his crew had established a hideout in the mountains where they could monitor Japanese bombers taking off from Clark Field and report them to General King by radio.[27] The communications center had monitored Colonel Thorp's radio reports.

Colonel Gregg reasoned that Thorp would still be in radio contact with General Wainwright on Corregidor and with General MacArthur in Australia. If the men could get to

Thorp's hideout, Thorp might be able to arrange for a ship or a submarine to pick them up and take them to Australia where they could re-join the USAFFE forces. To Lieutenant Conner and several of the others it sounded like a better option than spending the rest of the war in a Japanese prison camp.

The men talked it over. Most of the younger ones agreed to go, but the older men, including Colonel Gregg, were simply too weak, too hungry or too sick to survive in the rough terrain of Bataan's mountains and jungles. They decided to surrender, as ordered.

That afternoon, while the older men hiked down the trail to surrender, Lieutenants Henry Clay Conner and Bert Pettit, Captain Bernard Anderson, Sergeant Samuel Dawson, and Privates Howard Mann and Ernest Kelly blew up their radios, left the communications center, and climbed up to the peak of Mount Mariveles.[28]

***

Near the west coast of Bataan, Lieutenant Colonel Arthur "Maxie" Noble called his troops together after the surrender and walked with them into a large clearing to hear the commander of the 11th Division, Brigadier General William E. Brougher, give a farewell speech.

As Maxie Noble entered the clearing with his men he ran into a friend, Lieutenant Colonel Martin Moses—they were both regimental commanders in the 11th Division. They gathered around with their troops to listen to General Brougher while they waited for the Japanese. They expected to be there for a while as Brougher had a reputation for giving rather extended talks. In that respect, they were not disappointed.

However, as General Brougher concluded his remarks, Japanese soldiers suddenly burst out of the nearby wood-line with rifles and machine guns blazing. Bullets slashed through the crowd of several thousand unarmed Filipinos and Americans. Panic ensued. As wounded and dying men fell to the ground around them, Maxie Noble, Martin Moses, and everyone else who was able to do so fled into the nearby jungle.[29]

Once they escaped from the carnage, the two colonels vowed that they would never surrender to the Japanese, whom they now hated with a passion. They decided instead to make their way north through the dense jungles of Bataan and to head for the mountains of northern Luzon. There, they believed, several battalions of the Fil-American army were still holding out against the enemy.[30]

***

Frank Loyd and his two companions sat for a while by the mountain trail after the five Filipinos departed, and stared at each other. Lieutenant Mills spoke first.

"I guess we have to go to Mariveles and turn ourselves in. General King's orders."

"That means prison camp," Frank snapped back.

"Maybe it won't be so bad. At least we're alive. We'll have a place to sleep and something to eat. At the end of the war we go back to our families."

Frank thought for a moment about Evelyn and his two children. How long would he be in prison? Would they even know where he was or if he was alive? Frank also thought about the carnage he had seen on the bayside highway, and the bodies of dead constables in their foxholes. He thought about the cries of wounded soldiers he had heard, followed by rifle shots. The war was not over and he had no desire to wait out the rest of it in a prison camp.

Frank turned to Mills. "Do you know what the Japs did to prisoners in Nanking? They won't treat us any better. Besides, we've got other options. We can go to Corregidor."

"Colonel, we don't have a boat. Even if we found one, you heard what those guys said about the Jap planes. Prison camp wouldn't be any worse than rotting out here in the jungle—like we have been for the last three months."

"You've never been in a Japanese prison camp."

"Well, neither have you."

Sergeant Wools finally spoke up. "Maybe it wouldn't be so bad."

Frank thought about it. To disobey General King's orders could result in a court-martial. But suppose he got to Corregidor and joined General Wainwright's forces? If he sat out the war in a prison camp he would be useless. But if he re-joined the American Army he could still do what he was trained to do, what he wanted to do, and what the Army paid him to do. Technically, he supposed, he would not have disobeyed General King's order. When the reinforcement convoy finally arrived, General Wainwright would be in charge of re-capturing the Philippines.

Frank made his decision. He hoped Mills and Wools would go along with it.

Frank explained to the other two that he was going to Corregidor, even though he had not yet figured out how to do it.

"But I am not going to turn myself in. Are you with me?"

Sergeant Wools looked up. He hesitated. Then, "Whatever you say, Colonel."

Lieutenant Mills looked surprised. He stared off into the distance. "We don't have anything to eat. How will we survive?"

Frank had two problems: how to get food, and how to get to Corregidor. Getting food was the most urgent problem, and solving it might make Mills feel more confident. He would have to think about the other one.

Frank gave the men assignments to go out and scavenge for edible plants and fruit, telling them, basically, what to look for. They would meet back at this same spot by the trail in the afternoon. Sergeant Wools headed off to see what he could find. Lieutenant Mills followed.

A little before dark, Lieutenant Mills brought in some leafy plants for Frank to inspect and cook. Sergeant Wools had a hat full of green and purple berries from a large tree he found on the mountainside. Frank had caught an iguana-size lizard he found sunning on a boulder. The men built a small fire while Frank skinned and cleaned the lizard. Wools filled their canteens from the nearby stream and set them in the fire to boil. They had to hurry. The fire had to be doused before nightfall.

While they prepared the food, Frank tried to interest Mills in the idea of sailing a boat across the channel to Corregidor at night, but without much success. Peculiar, he thought, since Mills was a Navy man. The leaves Mills had brought in looked a little like watercress, so Frank washed them with hot water and took a bite. The leaves were bitter to taste but seemed edible. The men tried the berries, which turned out to be sweet and juicy. Mixed together, the "salad" was at least palatable. Frank and Sergeant Wools ate as much as they could while Lieutenant Mills ate his share of the berries and picked at the bitter leaves.

When the lizard was cooked and ready, Frank distributed the meat. It was hardly enough for three men but better than nothing. As he and Sergeant Wools chewed and swallowed the stringy meat, Lieutenant Mills stared at the white strips in front of him. Frank watched him carefully.

After a while Mills declared, "I'm no animal, and I am not going to eat a lizard. Not under any circumstances!" [31] He got up, went over to a large rock, sat down, and stared at the sunset.

As darkness closed in they talked some more about the possibility of stealing a boat and crossing the channel to Corregidor. They agreed to rotate sentry duty during the night and Sergeant Wools volunteered for the first shift.

Frank pulled his army-green mosquito net out of his musette bag, strung it between two bushes and crawled under. As he settled in, he thought again about General King's orders, and then about Corregidor. To get there, they would have to get a boat. If there were none in Mariveles, perhaps one of the smaller fishing villages along Manila

Bay… Frank drifted off to sleep while Lieutenant Mills and Sergeant Wools talked quietly nearby.

The next morning, Lieutenant Mills seemed to have developed a new, more positive attitude. He approached Frank and proposed that he and Sergeant Wools go down to the Negrito village and ask the natives for food. While they were there, they would check on the American officer the Filipinos had left behind. If he was in a good situation, perhaps they could all join him. In the meantime Frank could scout the mountainside for sources of wild fruit or other food, and for a better campsite. They would meet again at the end of the day.

Frank opposed this plan, saying he saw no point in letting the Negritos or anyone else know they were there. But Mills persisted. Sergeant Wools said that he had to go along also, to help bring back the food. Hunger gnawed at Frank's stomach as they talked and he knew the Negritos would have food—but that did not mean they would share it. Reluctantly, Frank agreed. Mills and Wools headed off down the mountain.[32]

Once they were gone, Frank explored the mountainside for a better campsite. They were only about 1,000 feet above the town of Mariveles—dangerously close to the Japanese in Frank's opinion—so he hiked upstream to look for a better site.

At noon, he encountered three Filipino stragglers carrying a supply of army rations up the mountain trail. As the men all stopped and stared at each other, Frank rested his hand on his pistol. The Filipinos looked Frank over, wondering what he wanted. Drawing his pistol, Frank motioned for them to drop the rations and back away. Surprised, they set the food packages on the ground in front of them and stepped back. One of the men began to plead that it was all they had and that they had a long way to go to get back to their homes in Pampanga. As the men watched, Frank sorted through the cans and packages on the ground and took enough for a good meal for himself, Wools and

Mills. Hopefully, the two men would bring more food from the Negrito village and they would be set for a couple of days. Frank backed off from the small pile of items that were left. He waved his pistol at the Filipinos. They shot him a dirty look, gathered up their food and left.

From his vantage point on the mountainside, Frank Loyd could clearly see Corregidor Island and he longed to get there. The island, located three miles off the tip of Bataan, looked like a big tadpole swimming out to the South China Sea from Manila Bay. Its body was a mile-long rock hill about 500 feet high, with a flat tail stretching two miles back into the bay. On top of the hill were the wreckage of an old Spanish lighthouse and the bombed-out stone buildings of Fort Mills, the U.S. Army post on the island. Here and there, Frank could spot the concrete fortifications that housed the big guns of Corregidor.

As Frank watched, Japanese soldiers began to line up artillery batteries along the road and beaches east of Mariveles. Soon they were firing on Corregidor. Frank could see the shells explode on the island's rocky hilltop, ripping apart the few stands of trees still there. A breeze blowing in from the South China Sea brought the sulphureous odor of burnt gunpowder up the mountainside.

After a few minutes, a large group of men appeared on the road from Mariveles, walking toward the Japanese artillery emplacements. Once they arrived at the line of guns they began marching back and forth, from battery to battery. Other groups followed. After watching curiously for a few minutes Frank felt a bitter anger boil up inside him. The groups of men on the road were American and Filipino prisoners of war. The Japanese were using them as shields.[33] The guns on Corregidor could not fire back at the Japanese artillery without hitting the prisoners.

Frank went back to the rendezvous point that afternoon and waited for Mills and Wools. He was bitter about the way the Japanese were treating the prisoners, but he felt that his day had been pretty successful. In addition to hijacking a supply of rations from the Filipinos, he had found a more suitable campsite higher on the mountainside, a short distance from a stream. His plan to steal a *banka* [a wooden outrigger boat common in the Philippines] from a fishing village along the bay had begun to take shape, and he was anxious to discuss the plan with Mills and Wools. It would take the three of them to get such a boat, wrestle it out into the water in the dark, and sail it to Corregidor.

Frank watched the sun set over the South China Sea. He waited for Mills and Wools.

***

As Lieutenant Mills and Sergeant Wools approached Mariveles that morning, they were joined by several more tired, hungry men walking into town from various stations on the mountainside. At a checkpoint, Japanese guards took them into custody. They were searched and relieved of their watches, rings, and the few Philippine pesos they had in their pockets. Lieutenant Mills started to protest when a guard demanded his gold college ring, but he kept quiet. He was an officer and expected to be treated as such. But there might be bigger issues ahead to worry about.

The guards pushed the men toward the center of town, walking them through a scene of almost total destruction. Bombs and artillery fire had hit virtually every building in Mariveles. The superstructures of several ships stuck grotesquely out of the harbor waters, some still burning.

When they got to the highway at the edge of town, Mills and Wools joined thousands of American and Filipino prisoners standing and sitting by the roadside, waiting. After several hours of milling around, the prisoners were made to form up in two columns, four abreast. The American column was on the right side of the road, Filipinos on the left. The Japanese guards made the prisoners count off, separating each column into groups of 100 prisoners. Four Japanese guards were assigned to each group. After alternately sitting and standing in the hot sun for another hour, the groups of prisoners were herded up the road a little way and made to walk back and forth between the Japanese artillery batteries firing at Corregidor. A smiling Japanese guard told them that they were there to "practice marching." For hours they moved back and forth without being given water, and without being allowed a break to relieve themselves.

At dusk, the prisoners were ushered off the road into small pens surrounded by barbed wire fences. Close to 2,000 men were packed into one enclosure, many of whom had wounds and various diseases, including dysentery. Along one side, someone had dug a large, rectangular latrine. The men were dehydrated and hungry. A nauseating stench wafted through the enclosure, emanating from the latrine and from the filthy pants of sick soldiers.

The Japanese guards gathered into groups outside the fence and stood idly watching. Each group of guards was armed with a machine gun in addition to the soldiers' rifles.

As the exhausted prisoners searched for places to sit or lie down, one of the Americans went to the latrine, dropped his pants and squatted to relieve himself. From one side, a Japanese soldier stepped through the crowd of prisoners, unslinging his rifle as he approached. Without a word, he drew back, then lunged forward, driving his bayonet deep into the chest of the startled prisoner crouched over the latrine. Blood gurgled out of the man's throat as his eyes sought the face of his attacker.

The guard attempted to jerk the bayonet out of the American's bony chest but the blade would not come loose. The Japanese put his left boot against the man's chest, grasped the rifle with both hands, and pushed the man off the blade. The dying American soldier toppled backward and disappeared into the latrine.

The prisoners stood frozen in stunned silence as the last rattle of breath escaped from the body in the latrine. Glancing around, the men could see that the Japanese guards had their rifles at the ready. The machine guns were manned and pointed directly into the crowd of prisoners.[34]

The prisoner's troubles had barely begun.

***

That night on the mountainside above Mariveles Frank Loyd heard noises in the brush and a faint sound of voices somewhere down the mountain. A Japanese patrol, perhaps. The next morning he gathered a few more wild berries and moved his camp farther up the hillside.

Once again he turned his attention to Corregidor. His heart sank. More than one hundred Japanese artillery pieces were lined up along the Bataan beaches, shelling the island continuously. Planes flew overhead every hour unloading more explosives on the little island. With each explosion Frank knew that his chances of re-joining the U.S. Army on Corregidor grew slimmer.

As he watched, Frank saw explosions on the beaches below him. The lines of American prisoners were gone.[35] The big guns of Corregidor were firing back! But the fire was sporadic. Only the two mortar batteries could train their weapons on Bataan—all of the other guns were permanently fixed in place, pointing out to sea.

Frank stayed on the mountain for ten days, living off berries and leaves, hunting unsuccessfully for a wild pig or other edible animal, and evading Japanese patrols. Every day he scanned the horizon of the South China Sea looking for signs of the U.S. Navy's reinforcement convoy. All he could see were Japanese warships, sailing almost peacefully across the tranquil water.

From the beaches of Bataan, the bombardment of Corregidor continued. Lieutenant Mills and Sergeant Wools did not come back. It could be weeks, maybe months, Frank decided, before General MacArthur and the reinforcement convoy could fight their way back to the Philippines.

It was time to make a new plan.

V. Days of Hope

Evelyn Loyd found her daily telephone conversations with Evelyn Noble increasingly depressing. Evelyn Noble was certain that the newspaper article about Maxie's death must be true, even though the War Department said they had no word about it at all. Evelyn Noble, a slight woman before, had become physically ill from worry and she was rapidly losing weight. But Evelyn Loyd still held out hope for both of their husbands. Perhaps they had escaped to Corregidor.

Then, less than a week after the surrender of Bataan, the women in the Fiddlers' Club began to receive letters and telegrams from their husbands. The messages had been written in March, a month before the surrender, and loaded onto a submarine.[1] Once the sub reached Australia, the Army had flown the mailbags to the United States. Evelyn Loyd's telephone rang constantly as one wife after another called to relate whatever information they had about their husbands' status before the surrender. Betty Wilson got a telegram from Zero that said he was well, and to keep her chin up. Everyone seemed to have a letter, or at least a telegram. Everyone, that is, except Evelyn Loyd and Evelyn Noble.[2]

Evelyn Loyd was convinced that if the other wives had received letters, there must be one for her as well. At the first of March she had taken a job as an "English Interpreter" (censor) at the United States Post Office in downtown San Antonio, and she had met the postmaster, Dan Quill, several times. So she went to see him and she asked for his help, then followed up each day to see if he had traced down a letter from Frank. But he could find nothing for her. He tried to keep her hopes up by telling her that perhaps Frank had been wounded. Or he was sick with malaria and was just too ill to write.

Evelyn sat at home in the evening and thought about Frank. At this point she had heard nothing from or about him in more than four months. Then, one by one, day by day, every letter Evelyn Loyd had written to Frank since the previous November, since before the Japanese attack, came back unopened.[3]

However, mysteriously, her pay allotment started again. In response to her inquiry, the War Department said that Frank was not on their casualty lists and therefore he was considered missing in action (MIA). His pay would be continued for twelve months. After that time, if the Japanese did not list him as a prisoner of war (POW), the War Department would make "a final determination."[4]

***

Nine days after the fall of Bataan, Evelyn Loyd was startled to hear CBS News' John Purcell report from Washington:

"We have no official confirmation here of Axis reports that Tokyo has been bombed.

"The War Department says it has no confirmation of the reported attack, and the Navy Department says it has no official information on the bombing." [5]

Evelyn's newspaper that day described American bombers battering Tokyo, Yokohama and Kobe, Japan, in prolonged attacks. But the Japanese claimed that the damage was negligible, and even pooh-poohed the attack as nothing but a Roosevelt publicity stunt.[6]

The effect on American morale, however, was electrifying. America had struck back! Radio reports came in all day from places like London, Sydney and Chungking, conveying the enthusiasm of America's allies all over the world.

President Roosevelt refused to divulge any information about the raid or to acknowledge, officially, that it had even taken place, adding to the mystery and to the excitement. A reporter asked him where the bombers came from.

"Shangri-La," replied the smiling president, referring to the mythical land in the popular novel, *Lost Horizon*.

It was the stuff that news stories, legends, and wild rumors would be made of throughout the United States, the world, and especially the Philippines.[7]

However, the euphoria of that single, isolated air raid on Tokyo was lost on Evelyn Loyd and the other wives in the Fiddlers' Club. Bataan had surrendered on April 9, and all of the 66,000 American and Filipino soldiers there who were not confirmed dead were listed as "missing in action." [8] As yet, no one had been officially designated a prisoner of war. Then, the newspapers reported that the Tokyo air-raiders captured by the Japanese had all been executed.[9]

Up to this point, Evelyn had written and mailed a letter to Frank every week. Now, the post office would not accept her letters. At the suggestion of the Red Cross, she and the other wives prepared boxes of supplies to send to their husbands in case they turned up as prisoners of war. But so far, the Red Cross had no information about Frank

Loyd or any of the other men. Evelyn kept up hope that one day soon she would get some kind of confirmation that he was alive and well. But the fact is, she had heard nothing about him since December 1941, and she had no real idea whether he was dead or alive.

The next month, just off the coast of Australia, General MacArthur sent Australian troops into New Guinea and Admiral Chester W. Nimitz landed American Marines on nearby Guadalcanal to prevent the Japanese from launching an attack on Australia itself. To Evelyn Loyd, it seemed that no one was even trying to get back to the Philippines.

VI. Escape and Evade

On the hot, rocky, south slope of Mount Mariveles Frank Loyd decided to make his way north up the Bataan Peninsula, then across the upper end of Manila Bay and south down the other side to Manila.[1] He would sneak into the city at night, locate some Filipino friends and, hopefully, get them to smuggle him onto a ship bound for Australia. In Australia, he could rejoin General MacArthur's forces and again lead troops against the Japanese. This time he would have a chance to pay the little bastards back.

The north face of Mount Mariveles is a formidable precipice of steep cliffs, deep ravines and thick jungle. Two weeks had passed since the surrender of Bataan and there were Japanese on all the trails now, so Frank had to climb down a series of bare rock faces and ford a thankfully shallow river to get down.

Once he got to the lowlands he waited until night and walked east toward the bayside highway. In the dark it would be easier to walk across the flat, open farmlands by the bay than to contend with the jungle.

Traveling only at night, he went first to the 4th PC Regiment's old headquarters near Lamao and scavenged some cans of food from what was left of the mess area. That took two nights. Then he made his way north, parallel to the highway, until he came to the Mamala River where the 4th PC had first run into the Japanese. Early in the morning he lay down in the brush on the south side of the river to get a few hours sleep. Before long the heat of the rising sun woke him up. Fearing that the Japanese might patrol the river-banks, he crossed the river by crawling over a brush snag well out of sight of the highway.

As he climbed up a sandy gully on the opposite side, Frank's ears perked up—he heard a cough.

He spied a small brush pile in a crevice on the east side of the gully, so he crouched behind it and waited. A Japanese patrol came into view a few hundred feet down the riverbank, walking toward him.

Frank carefully lifted a limb that protruded from under the brush pile. The limb lay across a log under the brush, and Frank slipped quietly into the damp space by the log, moving his feet and hands slowly to keep from breaking twigs or making any noise. He inched up to the log, lay on his right side, and slowly lowered the limb and the brush down on top of himself.

The four Japanese soldiers meandered up the riverbank, drawing closer to the gully and Frank's brush pile. Eventually he could see one of them, and then another, as they poked around the entrance to the gully. One of the soldiers stopped where Frank had just crossed. He was looking down at the ground. He spoke and several others joined him, looking at Frank's footprints in the sand.

Frank's heart pounded as the soldiers raised their heads and looked around, looked up the gully, then looked down again, talking all the while.

As Frank watched the soldiers discuss his footprints, he felt a movement against his leg. It stopped. Then, movement again. Something heavy.

Frank bent his head slightly down and peered into the brush. He caught a glimpse of dark skin undulating under the sticks. Moving, actually, under the sticks and over his leg. He remembered stories about a large snake in the Philippines called the "nooner" snake—if it bites you at noon you're dead by dinner. Sweat broke out on Frank's forehead. He gritted his teeth and held still.

He could see the snake's back more clearly as it passed over his leg, cleared the edge of the brush pile and slithered under some leaves farther up the gully. It was huge. About four inches in diameter, he guessed. It seemed to take forever to slip completely over him and out of the brush pile.

Frank slowly raised his head again and peered out at the Japanese soldiers. They were still looking around and talking. But they were taking no interest in the brush pile and soon they wandered out of Frank's field of vision.

Frank remained motionless. He had been lying on his right side for about twenty minutes and his left arm ached where the limb was resting on it. He decided to remain where he was until dark.

As darkness settled in that evening, Frank cautiously lifted the limb and extracted himself from the brush pile. He had slept a little, but he felt exhausted and his body ached all over from the cramped position he had been in. He seemed to be alone. He stretched, and continued walking north up the gully and then out into the grasslands and trees on the north side of the river.

As he approached the Pilar-Bagac Road in the pre-dawn darkness a few days later, Frank began to notice a certain odor. It was faint at first, but grew to a heavy, obnoxious stench as he drew closer to the road and to the former battlefields. Soon, Frank stumbled over a dead human body, bloated and decomposing, in the dark. They seemed to be everywhere, lying in the deep grass all around the deserted fields, covered with swarms of large blue flies and infested with hordes of inch-long maggots and other vermin.

Gagging and covering his face, Frank approached the road just as a Japanese Army truck passed by. He could not stand to hide there among the filth of all those pitiful, dead men so, as dawn broke, he cautiously crept into the weeds at the edge of the roadside. The road was clear. He bolted across. Frank began picking his way up an old jungle trail, headed north.

Two nights after he crossed the Pilar-Bagac Road, Frank Loyd passed through the Abucay Hacienda. The area was still burned and wasted, dotted by dark mounds—the rotting bodies of dead cavalry horses. He managed to catch a chicken, and in the early morning he built a small fire to cook it before he moved on. The next night, as morning broke, he found a gully in a tree-line well away from any roads and lay down to rest, quickly drifting off to sleep.

Around noon the bright sunlight, mottled by the trees above him, seeped into Frank's consciousness and he became aware of a Filipino crouched down only a few feet away, watching him intently. The man was squatted down on his heels, knees almost touching his shoulders in that peculiar, awkward-looking position men throughout the Orient seem to find comfortable.

"What do you want?" Frank asked.

"You okay?"

Frank was pleased that the man could speak English. It had been almost three weeks since he had had a conversation with anyone, since Lieutenant Mills and Sergeant Wools left and did not come back. After a brief conversation the man, Rudolfo Repollo, offered to take Frank to his home in nearby Orani.[2] Frank was grateful. The temptation of spending even a few minutes in a real house again was strong. Frank was hungry and he knew that once he was inside Rudolfo's home he would be offered a meal, as is the Filipino custom. Perhaps Rudolfo could help him get to Manila.

Together, the two men set off down the tree-line toward Orani, a large town at the north end of the bay.

The evening meal turned out to be better than anything Frank could have imagined—rice and carabao meat served at a real table with chairs, utensils and even a finger bowl. And a real bed to sleep on, in a shack behind Rudolfo's house. It was the first bed he had seen since he left Fort McKinley in December, four months ago.

Frank dropped his musette bag on the floor by the bed, dropped his rifle and pistol belt next to the bag, and took out his wallet. The wallet contained his military identification card, pictures of his wife and family, and twenty pesos. Comforted by the pictures of his family, Frank relaxed on the bed and soon fell into a tranquil sleep—his first in many months. Reality came back with a jolt, though. During the night he was awakened by barking dogs, footsteps, and Japanese voices outside his window.

The next morning Rudolfo gave Frank disturbing news. After the surrender the Japanese had grouped all of General MacArthur's soldiers, American and Filipino alike, including the sick and the wounded, into bunches of 100 or so and made them walk sixty miles up the bayside highway in the blistering heat. The men were allowed little water or food as they plodded along for five days from the holding pens in Mariveles and Bagac, through Orani to San Fernando farther north. Occasionally a soldier would fall out of ranks, overcome by exhaustion, thirst or disease.

"The Japanese guards dealt quickly with such failures," Rudolfo said. "At first they shoot the downed prisoners. Later they just bayonet them where they lay in the road—to conserve bullets."

So many prisoners died or were killed as they marched up the highway that bodies were strewn up and down the road in both directions. The Japanese made no effort to remove or to bury them; in fact they would generally go through the pockets of the dead men and loot the body of anything of value. Some of the men had been hung on a barbed wire fence while they were still alive, then their bowels were ripped open with bayonets as an example to the others.[3] Another was tied to a tree, stripped to the waist, and bayoneted to death.[4]

Any Filipino civilian who tried to help the prisoners was immediately chased away—or shot. The Japanese warned the civilians not to ever talk about what they had seen, and no newspaper was allowed to mention what had happened to the USAFFE prisoners on what everyone now called the Death March. The secret was well kept. It would be more than a year before anyone outside of Bataan learned about the slaughter along the bayside highway.

"We bury as many as we can," Rudolfo went on, "as many as the Japanese let us. But the whole bayside highway is still covered with thousands of bodies. You can even smell it right here." [5]

Rudolfo told Frank that he could not stay at his house. There was a large Japanese garrison in Orani, and if they discovered Frank they would arrest Rudolfo and all of his family. Frank told Rudolfo that he was anxious to get on his way to Manila.

"No. Too many Japs on the roads. Checkpoints. Patrols looking for escaped soldiers. It is too risky."

"Also, you must be careful who you talk to." Many Filipinos welcomed the Japanese, and others felt that they had to cooperate with them since they were clearly in charge now. Several people accused of helping Americans had been arrested by the Japanese, tortured, and even killed. Recently, the Japanese offered rewards to anyone who brought in Americans—five pesos each, dead or alive.[6]

Rudolfo, however, knew someone who could help Frank.

***

To the groups of gaunt prisoners that had been prodded up the bayside highway by Japanese guards, the Death March was a brutal ordeal that was clearly a matter of life or death. The prisoners forced themselves to keep up the pace, and did their best to help their buddies keep moving lest they be executed on the spot.

Every now and then there would be a bit of confusion, as when a convoy of trucks went past, or there was a stream to ford next to a blown-out bridge, or the guards broke ranks to chase off townspeople who tried to hand the prisoners bits of food and cups of water. At these times a man who was alert and cautious could slip out of the column unnoticed. If he was spotted he would be shot. But if he was lucky he could hide until the rest of the group passed by. Such was the case with Colonel Gyles Merrill, a leathery cavalry officer who stepped out of line near dusk and crawled away from the roadside during the night.

Gyles Merrill was a tough, by-the-book cavalryman who had spent much of his career riding horseback through the deserts of Texas and New Mexico, and who bought his tequila by the case. He was in his early fifties but looked much older. After years of service in the deserts, Merrill's skin was said to be so tough that mosquitoes were afraid to bite him. Colonel Merrill was a strict disciplinarian, but he was known to take off his uniform at the end of a long day and spend the night drinking in the bars with his men. The next morning it would be business as usual.[7]

After his escape, sick, physically debilitated and weak from hunger, Merrill fell exhausted into a sugarcane field. The next morning he had the good fortune to be discovered by two Filipino farmers who knew someone who might help him. That night they took him to a sugarcane plantation on the east side of Mount Malasimbo, just northwest of the municipality of Dinalupihan, at the north end of Bataan. The plantation belonged to William and Martin Fassoth, American twin brothers in their early fifties who had immigrated from Hawaii years before to seek their fortunes as Philippine sugar growers.

The Fassoths' home had been destroyed by Japanese bombing and the family was living in a small camp near a waterfall in the jungle. By the time Merrill arrived, Bill Fassoth had accepted several other Americans and a Filipino soldier into his camp—all escapees from the Death March. Fassoth got together with his good friend and fellow sugar grower, Vincente Bernia, whose plantation was at Gutad in the lowlands northeast of Dinalupihan. They made an agreement: the Fassoth brothers would take in and care for any American soldiers who might escape from the Death March. Bernia would take care of Filipino escapees and help them return to their homes.[8]

Bernia put out the word to local villagers that anyone who brought an escaped soldier to him or to the Fassoths would be rewarded: fifteen pesos for each man—about a week's wages for most Filipinos.[9]

Within a few weeks more than fifty American escapees were collected and taken to Fassoth's camp. But the camp was getting crowded and Colonel Merrill soon became concerned that the Japanese would get wind of what was going on, even this far back in the jungle.

Merrill struck out on his own and moved into a little fishing shack in the midst of the huge complex of fishponds near Guagua, east of Dinalupihan, at the north end of Manila Bay.[10] An unlikely place, he reasoned, for the Japanese to look for an American Army officer. He decided he would hide there, alone, until General MacArthur came back.

***

Lieutenant Colonel Peter Duryea Calyer, a West Pointer from Orange, New York, had been Operations Officer of the 31st Infantry Regiment on Bataan. He was a handsome young man who, in a pistol accident at West Point, shot the index finger off of his left hand. The Filipinos called him "Putol" [cut-off], as a result.[11] Calyer was one of those men who was always calm and cheerful in the face of adversity.

After the surrender, as Japanese soldiers were systematically looting their American and Filipino captives of money, jewelry and souvenirs, Peter Calyer stepped over to the side of the road to relieve himself. With his back to the assemblage of men on the road, he unbuttoned his pants. He slipped his West Point ring off his finger, pulled a string from the frayed cuff of his shirt, and tied the ring to his testicles. Thus, when he buttoned his pants and re-joined his comrades, he was able to preserve that which, at the moment, was most precious to him while all the men around him were losing theirs.[12]

As Calyer stumbled north along the bayside highway on the Death March he was struck by a truck from a passing convoy and knocked into a ditch. There he lay unconscious while the Japanese guards looked him over and, fortunately, decided that he was already dead. Rather than shoot or bayonet his body for good measure, the guards hurried off after their group of prisoners.

Peter Calyer regained consciousness that night, and his moans attracted a group of Filipinos who took him to a safe house in the fishponds, near Guagua. In this small, dark house they were attempting to nurse four other Americans and a Filipino soldier back to health, all of whom they had rescued from the Death March.

After a few weeks, the Filipinos told Calyer about another officer, Colonel Merrill, hiding in a shack in the fishponds nearby. Once Calyer regained enough strength he went to call on Colonel Merrill and the two men pledged to stay in touch. They were certain that MacArthur would soon return with the relief convoy, and re-take the Philippines.

VII. The Sickness at Tala Ridge

Frank Loyd was close to exhaustion after two hours of climbing the steep trail up the side of Mount Natib, so he was relieved to follow Rudolfo down a small path into the gorge of the Orani River. There, partway down the river-bank, was a house built up on stilts, almost obscured by thick jungle foliage. The gorge was damp and cool, with the sound of river water tumbling down the rocks nearby, a welcome relief from the mid-day heat.

They went inside and Rudolfo introduced Frank to a Filipino named Margarito. Rudolfo told Margarito that he was looking for a place to hide Frank. Margarito assured Rudolfo that he could take care of him.

In addition to Margarito and his family, there were three American men in the small house: Lieutenant Henry Clay Conner, Sergeant Samuel Dawson and Private Howard Mann.[1] The men said that they had been part of an Air

Corps group that manned General King's communications center, and that they had climbed up Mount Mariveles with Captain Bernard Anderson after the surrender to evade the Japanese. As they talked, Frank noticed Lieutenant Conner and Sergeant Dawson shivering from malarial chills.

The three men told Frank that they planned to go to Australia. They intended to contact an American colonel named Thorp who was hiding somewhere in the Zambales Mountains to the north. Thorp, they said, was in radio contact with General MacArthur's forces in Australia and he could arrange for a boat or a submarine to pick them all up. As they talked, Margarito told them about another safe haven, at the Fassoth sugar plantation on the east side of Mount Malasimbo. Mr. Fassoth was an American and he had collected a large number of soldiers at his camp.

Convinced that his best chance for re-joining MacArthur's forces would be to go with these men and contact Thorp, Frank abandoned his plan to go to Manila. Margarito, though, insisted that they wait. The Japanese were actively looking for American stragglers, and Frank and the others should wait until it was safe to travel. Margarito knew of a small refugee settlement farther up the mountain where they could stay. His house was too small and he did not have enough food to take care of everyone himself.

That afternoon Frank followed Margarito about three more miles up the mountainside. The settlement, named Tala, turned out to be a collection of six thatch-roofed farmhouses arrayed alongside the trail. The first house was on the right of the trail, under the trees but facing out, clearly visible as they approached it. The trail wound around to the left and Frank could barely make out the roof of a second house situated behind some huge banana trees down in the Orani River gorge, like Margarito's place. The trail turned right again and as they walked a little farther up they came into a clearing where three more houses stood in a neat row along the left side of the trail. Off to the right across the clearing sat a smaller house, tucked by itself back in the trees.[2]

Margarito stopped at the first house in the clearing. An old man came out on the porch. After a brief discussion, Margarito called Frank over.

"This is Filomeno. He will take care of you."

The Filomeno family, like most of the other inhabitants of the Tala settlement, were refugees from Batangas, a province south of Manila. They had fled here in December with the retreating Fil-American army. The family included the old man, his wife, their son Placido, about twenty-five years old, and their daughter who looked to be about eleven, the same age as Frank's daughter, Bonnie. The old man was a character and he insisted that Frank sit down at his table to talk. He spoke a little English and, with Placido's help, he told Frank about fighting in the insurrection against the Americans in 1903. Eventually, the insurrection had died out and the American governor of the islands, General Arthur MacArthur, father of General Douglas MacArthur, had proven to be a good man. At the direction of Arthur MacArthur, the U.S. Army built schools all over the islands and the Philippines had thus became one of the most literate countries in the Orient. All of the children learned English in school, and the islands adopted English as a universal language—the Spanish, after all, had only taught their language to the elite.

Mr. Filomeno went on to talk about the roads the Americans built, the improvements in agricultural production, and the fact that the American government was about to grant the Philippines its independence when the Japanese started this war. Mr. Filomeno made it clear that he was a great admirer of the United States of America, of General Arthur MacArthur, and of his son, General Douglas MacArthur.

As they talked, Mr. Filomeno took Frank outside for a brief tour of the settlement. He said that an American sergeant and two privates, one of whom was a medic named

"Panama" Pierce Wade, were living in the home of Hippolito Sayas, the first house on the trail. Francisco Silva and his family occupied the house in the river gorge. The next house above the Filomeno house, the middle one of the three in the clearing, was the home of Jimmy Espino, who had two Americans living with him. One of them was a very tall, strong soldier named Frank Gyovai. The family in the third house up the ridgeline was caring for an American soldier who was very ill. The house in the woods on the other side of the clearing belonged to a mysterious Filipino known only as Troubadour, who was seldom seen by the other refugees. There was an American soldier with him who also was very ill and, it was said, who had a great deal of money with him.

Frank asked Mr. Filomeno if he knew someone who could be his guide and take him north to find Colonel Thorp in the Zambales Mountains, or at least take him as far as the Fassoth plantation. Mr. Filomeno said that he would be pleased to take Frank there himself, but unfortunately, being only a refugee from Batangas, he did not know the way. He was honored, however, to have one of General MacArthur's officers stay in his home. He promised to make inquiries the next day to see if he could find a suitable guide.

The next morning Frank was anxious to get started on his trip north. Mr. Filomeno's son, Placido, immediately volunteered to go with him to be his interpreter and to help get food and shelter.

"But unfortunately," Mr. Filomeno interrupted, "Placido does not know the way. There is no one to guide you there.

"Orani, Dinalupihan, and the highways are patrolled by the Japanese. They move the checkpoints every day. Even if you get to Zambales, you have no way to contact the Americans there. You will surely be captured or killed by the Japanese."

Reluctantly, Frank conceded that Mr. Filomeno was right. He decided to stay in Tala for a few weeks and see what developed with regard to the war. Mr. Filomeno made it clear that he wanted Frank to stay with them until General MacArthur and the American Army returned.

From the stories he had heard in Orani, Frank was concerned that if the Japanese found him in the Filomeno home they would arrest, and might even kill, the entire Filomeno family. So he went around and visited the other houses in Tala and encouraged each American living there to come with him and set up a separate camp farther back in the jungle, for the safety of their Filipino hosts. Many of the men, it turned out, were in pretty bad shape. Only Sergeant Samuel Dawson and Private Howard Mann agreed to go with him.

The next morning Frank, Placido and the two soldiers hiked up the river and found a spot in the trees where they could construct a shelter. Mr. Filomeno had loaned them bolo knives, and as they erected a bamboo lean-to and cut Nipa palms to make a thatch for the roof, Frank learned that all was not well with Dawson and Mann. Sergeant Dawson was weak from his illnesses and despondent over his situation. He was genuinely afraid that he would die if he did not get medical treatment soon. He was utterly convinced that there was no help coming, and that MacArthur was safe in Australia and was going to stay there. Howard Mann was in better shape physically and mentally, but ill-equipped to live in the jungle—his shoes were worn out, his clothes were in tatters and Frank found that he was almost helpless in the woods.

Mosquitoes swarmed around their new hideout that evening—strange for such a high altitude, almost two thousand feet up the mountainside. After two miserable nights the three men climbed higher up the trail and began work on a new, larger shelter under a thick canopy of trees. That night, they rested and talked. Dawson had grown even more depressed, and he announced that he had decided to start walking to Manila. If he made it and could find help there, that would be good. If the Japanese took him into custody along the way, so be it. At least as a prisoner of war he would get medical treatment. Howard Mann made a decision too. He agreed with Frank that it was dangerous to stay in Tala, but he just did not believe that hiding out in a shelter in the jungle was that much safer. Frank was disappointed. He had hoped that when the three of them moved out of Tala into the jungle it would inspire the other Americans to do the same.

In the morning they all shook hands, and Dawson and Mann left.

Alone in the shelter, Frank took stock of his situation. For tools, he had the bolo knife lent by Mr. Filomeno and an Army rifle he had picked up while crossing one of the battlefields. His other possessions were the uniform on his back, his Army-issue .45 caliber semi-automatic pistol with fifteen bullets, and his musette bag. The bag contained an extra shirt, his mess kit, toothbrush, a small bottle of iodine and his mosquito net. In his shirt pocket was a message pad on which he had jotted down a brief description of the events of April 6 through 12, when his Philippine Constabulary troops tried to hold back the Japanese on the bayside highway. He also had a pencil and a small notebook that served as his daily diary. He wrote a few notes about his physical condition and the options that were open to him. Frank decided that he would stay put for ten more days, and then he would head north.

Placido soon climbed up the trail for a visit, and Frank told him about his decision.

Placido squinted up at Frank in the bright sunlight. The young man was a short, dark Filipino whose high cheekbones seemed to draw the corners of his mouth up into a perpetual, chipmunk-like smile. He warned Frank again of the danger of being caught by the Japanese, and pleaded with him to stay. To Frank's surprise he offered to use his own savings, fifty pesos, and to sell his carabao to buy food for Frank. Placido reasoned that General MacArthur would surely be back soon, so why risk death to go to Colonel Thorp? Placido said that the next time he went to Manila to sell the *camotes* [Philippine sweet potatoes] they grew on his father's farm, he would contact Frank's friends and ask them to notify Evelyn in the States that Frank was safe.

The young man's reasoning made sense. Frank proposed a deal: he would stay for a few more weeks if Placido would go to Orani, purchase rice for Frank, and bring it to him each Saturday. Frank would pay him with IOUs and record their agreement in his diary. Then, if Frank did not survive the war, Evelyn would still know to compensate Placido for his help. Placido agreed to get the rice and to carry a message to Frank's friends in Manila.

On Monday, May 4, 1942, Placido went into Orani and brought back some good news. Corregidor was still holding out. Germany had surrendered. American bombers were already hitting Japan. Placido assured Frank that he had heard this news from reliable sources.[3]

The next Saturday, Placido brought bad news—Corregidor had surrendered.

Frank was concerned, but not terribly so. If Germany had already surrendered, then Japan could not hold out more than a few months. MacArthur's relief convoy must already be in motion. Given the prevailing winds and currents, and the necessity of taking some of the islands south of Luzon to establish bomber bases, Frank calculated that MacArthur and the U.S. Army should be landing on Luzon in about sixty days. The war, he felt confident, should be completely over by February 1943.

That being the case, he decided to just stick it out until the American forces returned. He told Placido about his decision. Together, they scouted out a better location for his hideout—higher up the mountain to avoid the mosquitoes, and deeper in the jungle to avoid the Japanese.

They picked a spot across the Orani River, about two hours walk from Tala. It was off the trails, behind the ridgeline, and about 300 yards from the nearest stream. Frank reasoned that if the Japanese chose to patrol this high on the mountain, fully a day's climb from Orani, they would come via the animal trails or streambeds and would not be likely to stray into the jungle.

In a clear area under the thick jungle canopy they constructed a small *bahay*, or Philippine house. It measured twelve feet by twelve feet with a dirt floor. The Nipa thatch roof was low at the sides, but tall enough in the center for Frank to stand erect in the room. Placido brought Frank some woven palm mats called *sawali*, and they lashed them to the bamboo framework to make the outside walls. There was a door at one end, but no windows. Frank made a table and Placido made a bed, both of bamboo poles. In the center of the room they dug a small pit and lined it with rocks so a fire could be built inside. It would be cold on the mountain at night during the coming rainy season. They made several containers for storing food by cutting a piece of large bamboo just below two successive joints, resulting in a round container with one end open and the other closed.

After Placido left, Frank made further improvements. He constructed a split-bamboo gutter along the sides of the roof to collect rainwater and save the 300-yard walk to the stream. He made a rattan pack frame with woven shoulder straps to carry an emergency supply of food and other gear in case he should have to run into the jungle to avoid a Japanese patrol. As time went by, he built an animal trap to catch meat to supplement the rice and fruit Placido brought each week.

The trap occasionally yielded a large lizard or a small monkey that Frank slaughtered, cooked and ate. The lizard meat was not bad, if you could put out of your mind where it came from, with a kind of sweet, light taste. The monkey meat was tough and stringy, but a monkey was usually good for two meals. Frank would cook and eat one leg and the liver the day it was killed, and smoke, dry and salt the other leg to be enjoyed later.

On one of his supply runs Placido brought two helpers: a small Negrito man named Damaso Caballero and his son, Angel. Damaso was the mayor of the Negrito barrio near Tala. The two little men, barely four feet tall and dressed only in cloth g-strings, spoke neither English nor Tagalog,[4] but seemed eager to help and glad to have the friendship of an American officer. They, too, began to bring food from time to time, primarily wild pig, which they skillfully brought down with their bows and arrows and butchered with their bolos.

Placido continued to bring sporadic war news. Apparently, Germany had not surrendered. There were rumors of a big naval battle near the Caroline Islands in which the British and Americans sunk twenty-seven Japanese ships.[5] There was also news of other Americans: the Japanese caught five American soldiers in a boat near Manila, and shot them all.

For Frank, life at the jungle *bahay* was sheer boredom. The hot, humid days stretched by, one just like the other, with little for Frank to do and no contact with any other beings except Placido and occasionally Damaso.

At the end of May, the rainy season started and Frank thought he could feel all of the Filipinos on Luzon heave a collective sigh of relief. Soon temperatures would drop, the mosquito population would be washed away, and the farmers would take to the fields to plant rice, slogging through the mud to banjo time.[6]

Frank rested, exercised, fought off boredom and thought about his family. On Wednesday, May 27, 1942, he wrote in his diary:

> Surprising Sweetheart Evelyn, how much time is required just for cooking, washing mess kit and doing my laundry... Menu today: rice, monkey meat, green mango and some citrus fruit like dwarf limes.[7]

A year ago Frank had watched Evelyn sail off aboard the *USAT Washington*. Only a year, but the horrors of war warp a soldier's perception of time to the point that one year becomes half of a lifetime. All the preceding years are just the other half.

***

With Corregidor out of the way, the Japanese Army began to get organized and take control of Bataan.

The commandant of the Orani garrison, Major Nakai, had some problems to attend to.[8] First, it was expected that food and basic supplies for each garrison would be obtained locally. Therefore, it was important that the local farmers get back to their fields and crops quickly so the Japanese soldiers could be properly fed. Also, malaria was a major problem throughout Bataan and many of Major Nakai's soldiers were already off duty and in the hospital because of it. Malaria was also rampant among the local Filipinos and getting worse.[9] To assure that there would be enough medicine to treat his soldiers, Major Nakai would have to collect all of the quinine and Atabrine he could find in the area before the Filipinos used it up. A Red Cross doctor named Romeo Atienza and his very vocal Lithuanian nurse, Rosena Utinsky, were requesting that the Japanese provide medicine for the Kalaguiman hospital in barrio Samal, near Orani.[10] Major Nakai reminded them that the Imperial Japanese Army had a war to fight, and the matter was thus closed.

Next, there were reports of American and Filipino soldiers still loose in Bataan, stragglers who did not turn themselves in properly after the surrender. These men had failed to obey the lawful orders of their superiors. They were to be considered deserters, subject to immediate execution. Major Nakai intended to find each of them. It was expected that each man captured could be forced to lead Major Nakai's soldiers to others.

***

At the end of June, Placido reported that a number of Filipinos in Bataan and Zambales provinces had taken to the hills to form guerrilla groups to continue to fight the

Japanese until MacArthur returned. "But they are not guerrillas at all," Placido said. "They are just bandits. Criminals. They claim to be guerrillas so they have excuse to rob from people." He also said that two of the families in Tala, including the Filomenos, were planting rice crops, just in case the war was not over by October as Frank was now predicting.

When Placido brought supplies up to the *bahay* the next week, he told Frank that the malaria epidemic in Bataan had spread to the Tala settlement. Three of the Americans in Tala had died of malaria and it looked like Lieutenant Conner, who was now being cared for by Francisco Silva's family, was going to be next. Some of the refugees had malaria, too, and there was no medicine available anywhere. The only two Americans who were not sick were the big man, Frank Gyovai, and Panama Wade, the medic.

"Last night," he said, "they go to Orani with Jimmy Espino. They go to the Japanese hospital to get medicine. They do it at gunpoint, if necessary."

Frank was shocked, but impressed.

"Jimmy Espino was a Red Cross medic," Placido continued, nervously. "They have not come back—and they may bring the whole Japanese Army."

Placido left Frank's supplies and went back to Tala.

For days, Frank was worried about the situation in Tala, and mad at Wade and Gyovai for taking such a foolish risk. On the other hand, without medicine there was a good chance that malaria would kill more of the men hiding there. There was nothing Frank could do but wait. And wish them luck.

When Placido brought Frank's supplies the following Saturday, he reported that Wade and Gyovai had broken into the Kalaguiman Hospital at night and had stolen all of the quinine and Atabrine they could find.[11]

"They got back to Tala safely but there is not enough medicine to go around. They saved Lieutenant Conner. But two of Francisco Silva's children are dead."

Frank's own health had held up well, so far, but at the end of June he developed a bellyache that would not go away. In a few days it turned from a nuisance into "much griping and colic" in his stomach. He stopped eating and tried a Filipino remedy recommended by Placido: boil rice in a pot until it burns, drink the liquid off the rice, and then eat the burned rice. It did no good.

Frank was not terribly concerned about dysentery. He had taken care to boil all water before he drank it. He cooked all of his food except fruit he could peel, and he peeled that carefully. He sterilized his mess kit and his spoon over the fire before each meal. He did remember, however, eating some uncooked sugar a few days before which had been stored in a bamboo joint with a piece of old canvas for a stopper. No flies should have been able to get into it but there might have been germs on the cloth, or in the bamboo container.

At noon on Thursday, July 7, Placido visited Frank before going to Orani. An hour after he left, Frank had an urgent feeling for a bowel movement, but produced only white mucous and blood—symptoms of amoebic dysentery. By the next evening, he felt like his liver and bowels were inflamed, and he was having periodic fevers. The symptoms persisted the next day. When Placido brought supplies on Saturday he suggested another Filipino remedy: rice wine mixed with burned dirt. Frank passed on that one.

Over the next few days the fever and white mucous discharge continued. Placido tried to buy quinine tablets in Orani but could not find any. He made Frank a brew of Dita bark tea, which some Filipinos, notably the Negritos, take for malaria.[12] The remedy seemed to help sooth Frank's stomach, but only for a few days.

Exactly a week after the symptoms began, Frank was seized with a violently upset stomach and constant urges to have a bowel movement. When he went to the latrine and strained to force it out, all he could produce was white, sticky mucous. He knew that dysentery, untreated, was often fatal. The amoebic form, characterized by blood in the stool as well as mucous, is usually fatal even with competent treatment. Dysentery gives a person a recurring, almost constant urge to go, as many as a hundred times per day. The frequent attempts to satisfy that urge dehydrate the body to the point of exhaustion and breakdown.

Frank knew he had to do something. He left his *bahay* and lay on the bank of the running stream where he could use the cool water to sooth his fever. He drank as much water as he could to maintain his fluids, but as a few days went by there seemed to be no improvement.

Frank devised a treatment. With his knife, he cut a large section of bamboo to make a tube that was closed at one end, about three inches in diameter. He smoothed out the interior. Over the next two days he fashioned a wooden plunger to fit into the open end of the tube and bored a small, round hole into the bottom of the tube. Then he cut a smaller bamboo tube leaving it open at both ends and inserted one end tightly into the hole in the large tube. He filled the device with boiled, soapy water, and mixed the only medicine he had, iodine, into it. He inserted the plunger into the open end of the large tube. Finally, he applied the treatment.

Within two days it seemed that the makeshift enema had worked. Frank's stomach was back to normal.

The very next day, however, he had a new problem. When Frank awoke that morning his left thumb, left shoulder and right knee were swollen and painful. That night he could not sleep. The next morning was worse—he could not move his left arm or right leg. He could barely maneuver to sit up and hobble around the small confines of his *bahay*. Using his rifle as a crutch he was able to get to the latrine outside. By the third day he was in extreme pain and could not get up from his bed at all.

Placido headed down to Orani to find a doctor. He left Frank propped up in bed, his rifle in his right hand, with a roll of sticks and rags under his right knee to relieve the pressure and make it more comfortable.

During the late afternoon, movement near the *bahay* door caught Frank's eye. A large lizard was dragging his right shoe across the floor and out the door. Frank raised the rifle, took aim, and squeezed the trigger. The animal jumped in pain, dropped the shoe, and lay twisting on the floor. Obviously it was still alive, but incapacitated. Frank, satisfied that at least his right hand and eye were still steady, decided to leave the lizard as it was for the time being. At least the meat would still be fresh when Placido got back.

That night was a bad night. The pain was intense. Frank sweated heavily, and dreamed about pulling his leg off and putting it on a shelf. When Placido returned at ten o'clock the next morning, Frank was mad at him for having taken so long and he let him know it. That afternoon, as a heavy rain washed through the jungle outside, they made splints for Frank's knee. Then more pain, fever from early evening until two o'clock in the morning, and heavy perspiration until dawn. Frank was not sure what he had contracted, but he was certain that at least part of it was either malaria or dengue fever.

As the rains continued, Placido stayed with Frank. Some use of his left arm returned, and Frank and Placido used the time to make some needed equipment. A bamboo container became a bedside urinal. They made a bedpan by splitting a large section of bamboo horizontally, leaving the joint in place at one end. Frank rigged a pole and pulley above his bed, so he could pull in another bamboo joint positioned at the end of the roof gutter, to get rainwater when Placido went to Tala or Orani for food. Placido stacked small sticks of firewood by the bed so Frank could build a fire for warmth or cooking. Finally, they made a brace for Frank's knee and suspended his leg from the roof of the *bahay*, to relieve the pain and limit the swelling. Frank Loyd's leg would remain tied to the ceiling of the *bahay* for the next five weeks. He would not stand or walk again for seventy-three days.

Frank lay on his cot with pains that were always present and often severe. Fever came and went, sometimes alternating with chills on a particularly bad night. He learned that heavy perspiration often followed the fever bouts, and that his body seemed to relax during these periods. So when the fevers were at their peak he drank hot water, forcing himself to perspire during the fever and thus reduce the overall pain, which had now spread to his back and both hips. Placido learned that if he found Frank soaking wet in the morning, it meant it had been a good night. Relatively speaking.

And still, there was no quinine. The doctor in Orani simply had none. So Frank continued to drink Placido's Dita bark tea, but found little relief in it.

Early in August, Frank's right knee began to yield a little. One morning he found that he could bend it thirty degrees. After a week or so of practice and attempted exercise, the knee could be bent as much as ninety degrees. Placido made a second bamboo cot and set it outside the *bahay*. Once a sunny day came along he carried Frank, who was now little more than skin and bones, outside to get fresh air. Slowly, the pains began to lessen, although Frank still could not stand or walk.

Placido told Frank that he was going to move him closer to Tala. It would be warmer and drier there, he would be able to get some sun, and Placido could more easily care for him. Frank agreed to go. Placido brought two soldiers from the settlement, Howard Mann and Eddie Keith. They wrapped Frank in a wool blanket and carried him down the narrow, slippery trail and across the river to his new home, a tool shack in a banana patch just outside of Tala.

And a shack it was. A one-room farm hut, barely six feet by ten feet, built on stilts with a wood floor a little more than three feet off the ground. The place was furnished with a cot and a small table. It looked pretty solid and Frank could see out the one window and even get some sunshine. No distinct trail led to it. Placido had brought a bag of foodstuffs with them, and after the other men left, he cleaned up and put everything in order. Placido stayed with Frank that night and the next, sleeping on the floor next to the cot. He worked on the thatched roof and got it into good enough shape to be able to fend off a rainstorm. On the third day he headed home, promising to come back quickly and bring medicine.

Lying on his cot in the shack the next morning, Frank heard flights of aircraft nearby. He listened carefully. There were deep rumbling engines that he had not heard before. Mixed with the deeper sounds were higher pitched engines, probably fighter escorts for the bombers. It was a moment that reinforced his hopes—either the Japanese were flying out to bomb attacking American ships, or American pilots had returned to bomb Japanese positions in the interior of Luzon. Either way, the war must surely be drawing to a close!

Then more good news. Placido returned with fifty quinine tablets, half the doctor's supply. Placido said that U.S. troops were reported to be in Burma and Thailand.

Frank began to feel better. After taking the quinine, the swelling in his left hand and right knee subsided perceptibly, although his shoulders ached to the point where he could not sleep. He tried to stand on one foot and dangle his bad leg but the strain was prohibitively painful. However, he found that he could scoot across the cabin floor on his rear end, using his one good arm and one good leg. Sleep was constantly denied. On Friday, August 21, Frank wrote in his diary:

> This ailment of mine could not be better designed to cause discomfort if the devil himself had devised it. Last night typical: Unable to rest on either side on account of disabled left shoulder and right knee and sore (neuritic) right hip. When on

> back while I have fever, tail bone becomes so hot I cannot sleep. Have to pull heavy pad under hips; then hips ache. After midnight go to sleep and awake an hour later because of aching shoulders. Alternate sitting up and lying down till morning, with perhaps one hour more sleep.[13]

A few days later he added:

> Another sweating spree, the worst yet. Started midnight last night and still going strong. Put on dry clothes at 8 am but in a short time was so wet as if I had fallen into the river.

So it went. On August 25, 1942, his daughter's birthday, Frank wrote:

> More fever and less sleep than usual last night. This is Bonnie Beth's 12th birthday, but will not be a very happy one for her. Bonnie, Placido is making a corn cake and some tea to celebrate your birthday this afternoon. While I am thinking of you, perhaps you will have a pleasant dream of your daddy to cheer you on your birthday. I am wishing you many, many happier ones. Before my birthday, September 17th, I hope to be able to radio my family.

Placido brought many rumors of American successes in the war against Japan. Frank was confident that things were going well. October was coming and with it, he hoped, the end of the war.

By early September, Frank ran out of quinine pills and Placido was unable to get any more. The rains continued. Frank's symptoms worsened and he went back to drinking Dita bark tea. His left thigh gradually atrophied to about half the size of his right one.

Frank Loyd continued to remain optimistic. His September 12 diary entry reads:

> Today completes two months and two days on my back. Many good things could happen in next 30 days. Might walk, recover from malaria. U.S. forces retake Luzon. Certainly the weather will improve.[14]

The next day it stopped raining.

***

Down in the lowlands, at the Japanese garrison headquarters in Orani, Major Nakai looked over a news report that said recent campaigns to eradicate guerrillas and renegade American soldiers had been quite successful. However, the *Kempei-tai* in Balanga reported that there was an American officer at large in the mountains above Orani, raising a guerrilla army. A U.S. Army colonel named Frank Loyd.[15]

VIII. The Unwelcome Visitors

In mid-September 1942, Lieutenant Henry Clay Conner and Private Frank Gyovai decided to become guerrillas. Jimmy Espino told them about a secret meeting to be held late at night in Samal, a town south of Orani. At the meeting, the men in the village were going to discuss ways they could oppose the Japanese. Jimmy agreed to take the two Americans to the meeting.

That night Clay Conner and Frank Gyovai were greeted warmly when they arrived at the meeting place, a large room in the home of Jimmy's uncle. Some of the men gathered there told them that more than 3,000 people had lived in Samal before the war, but only about 1,000 were left. Almost 2,000 people had died during the recent malaria epidemic, during which the Japanese authorities had provided no medical care, whatsoever.[1] As things got under way Conner got the feeling that there was little enthusiasm for taking action against the Japanese. One of the villagers explained how life was lived in Samal:

"Everyone is required to have a *cedula*, an identification card, which he must carry with him at all times. To get one, you have to take an oath of loyalty to Japan.

"On the front of each house the Japanese have posted a sign called a *monpai*, that lists the residents of the house. Each evening, the authorities come around and check the houses. Any extra male found in a house, and anyone who cannot produce a valid *cedula*, is arrested.

"The house patrols also note the absence of any resident. If a number of persons are absent at the time a guerrilla raid takes place, mere absence is taken as proof of guilt. The entire family will then pay the death penalty or, at the least, have their house burned to the ground.

"If we sow trouble for the Japs," he said, "we will harvest only our own dead." [2]

The discussions went on all night. Conner could see that the men at the meeting clearly hated the Japanese, especially those who had lost family members during the malaria epidemic—and that was virtually everyone. But the men concluded that there was nothing they could do to the Japanese without seriously endangering their families. This they were unwilling to do. Conner decided that if he was going to recruit men to become guerrillas, Samal was not the place.

As the meeting broke up early the next morning, the sound of marching boots could be heard outside. The men at the meeting peered out the window and watched the entire Japanese garrison from Samal march up the road toward Orani to attend an assembly.

With the Japanese gone, Conner and Gyovai stepped out of the house into the sunlight and strolled down the main street of Samal in broad daylight, being greeted and cheered all the way by the townspeople.[3]

As they hiked back up the trail to Tala that afternoon, Conner and Gyovai encountered a group of armed Filipinos.

They, it turned out, were communist Hukbalahap guerrillas from Pampanga, the province northeast of Bataan.[4] They were headed down the peninsula toward Mariveles to salvage guns and ammunition from the old battlefields.

Conner had heard of the Hukbalahap, "Huks" as they were commonly called, but knew little about them. They stopped on the trail and talked, and Conner told the Huk leader about his desire to get back into the war as a guerrilla fighter.

"If you want to be a guerrilla," the Huk leader said, "you come with us when we go back to Pampanga."

Conner and Gyovai agreed to go. A few days later, the Huk leader and a few of his men stopped in Tala on their way back from the battlefields. Conner and Gyovai left with them.[5]

After Conner and Gyovai left, a larger group of about sixty Huks appeared, surrounded the Tala settlement, and ransacked each house looking for weapons. They pushed the residents aside and took whatever they wanted.[6]

But the Filipino refugees at Tala would not be had so easily. Most of them had hidden their own guns in the jungle, away from their homes in case of a Japanese visit. As the Huks searched their houses, the refugees melted away into the jungle and retrieved their rifles and ammunition. The Huks departed in a hail of gunfire.

Shortly after the Huks left, another band of "guerrillas" showed up to raid Tala. They robbed and beat up the elderly Hippolito Sayas and his wife while trying to find firearms. Again, several of the refugees slipped off into the jungle to retrieve their rifles, and drove the bandits away.

***

Frank Loyd, meanwhile, lay sweating and in pain in the Tala banana patch. On September 20, Placido walked in the door. With him were Jimmy Espino and a doctor's assistant from Orani. They gave Frank an injection of quinine urea, some salicylate tablets and some cough medicine.[7]

The quinine did the trick. Frank's condition began to improve. Within a week he stood on his own feet for the first time in almost three months. When he tried to hobble about the shack on his crutches, though, his "good" leg was almost as useless as the bad one due to lack of exercise.

October 1, 1942, the date Frank had looked forward to as his best estimate of U.S. forces returning to the Philippines, came and went. But there was no American army anywhere in sight. There had been no U.S. invasion.

Frank decided to push himself to regain strength. He worked out some exercises that he could do while sitting on his cot. When he struggled to get up and walk, pains shot through his knee and arm with each attempt. But gradually, during October, his limbs and joints showed improvement as he exercised and hobbled around on his crutches. Progress was slow and frustrating. He could not stand up straight, even on his crutches, and the increased activity seemed to aggravate his malaria. Eventually though, the exercise began to work and he graduated to a cane.

The doctor's assistant returned and gave Frank another quinine shot and more salicylate tablets. His condition continued to improve. He stretched out his exercise walks to 100 yards, then almost 200 yards. He was pleased to find that he could walk with his cane all the way to the home of the banana farmers on the other side of the banana patch. There, he could visit for a few minutes with their young son.

He learned that there were only four Americans still hiding in Tala. Some of the men, like Samuel Dawson, had surrendered to the Japanese. Four had died of malaria and other causes. Conner and Gyovai had gone to Pampanga with the Huks. Others, including the medic, Panama Wade, left to find safer hideouts such as the Fassoth camp farther north.

The banana farmers told Frank that the Japanese were aggressively pursuing Americans, and they were mounting a strong offensive against any guerrillas they could find. They said that the Japanese had raided the Fassoth camp and captured sixteen of the Americans hiding there.[8] The Fassoth brothers escaped, but the Japanese led the captives away and Filipinos who lived nearby said that the Japanese were going to kill them all.

***

When Lieutenant Colonels Maxie Noble and Martin Moses arrived in mountainous Benguet Province in northern Luzon, they were exhausted from their two-month long trip through the mountains and jungles of Bataan and Pampanga provinces. One night along the way a large thorn had badly damaged one of Maxie's eyes as they struggled through the dense jungle. They found that Colonel John P. Horan, the American commander in northern Luzon, had surrendered himself to the Japanese as ordered. Many of Colonel Horan's troops refused to follow their leader's example, though, and Moses and Noble took command of what was left. As senior officer, Lieutenant Colonel Martin Moses declared himself commander of all USAFFE forces in northern Luzon.[9]

For the next several months the two colonels recruited volunteers from the local populace, primarily Igorot tribesmen who thoroughly disliked the Japanese. They built up a guerrilla army reputed to include as many as 6,000 men, many armed only with bolo knives.[10]

Coordinating with local commanders from Colonel Thorp's guerrilla organization, Colonel Moses planned a massive attack to occur on October 15, 1942, in the area around Baguio.[11] He chose as a specific objective the Japanese Army garrison at the Itogon Mining Company headquarters.[12] If the guerrilla army could take this objective, they could capture a large quantity of arms, medicine and supplies. They could also eliminate a particularly onerous problem: a Japanese civilian named Okoda, the boss of the Itogon mine. Okoda was turning in pro-American Filipinos to the *Kempeitai*, revealing the locations of guerrilla hideouts in the mountains, and recruiting Filipino collaborators.

By holding the high ground around Baguio and the mines, Moses and Noble reasoned that they could cut Japanese communication and supply lines in the area, and establish an operating base in the mountains of northern Luzon. Here, they would hold out until General MacArthur's return, which they calculated would occur some time in December.

On October 15, 1942, they launched their attack.[13] Unfortunately, some trigger-happy guerrillas gave away the element of surprise at the mine itself. As a result Mr. Okoda was killed rather than captured, depriving the guerrillas of the pleasure of interrogating him.

However, Japanese communication and supply lines were cut, weapons were captured, and a great deal of damage was done. Moses and Noble held the mine area for almost a week. Then the Japanese counter-attacked with tanks and infantry, and retook the mines. As the two colonels withdrew into the mountains with their men, the Japanese began to level whole villages in the area. They slaughtered everyone they suspected of harboring or aiding the enemy.[14]

Maxie Noble and Martin Moses headed north into headhunter country, determined to hold out until MacArthur returned.

***

On Monday morning, October 19, Placido left to go to Manila. The purpose of his trip, ostensibly, was to collect money owed to his family for *camotes* he had sold in the city. While there, he was going to try to contact some of Frank's friends, including Colonel Rafael Jalandoni, Frank's old commander at the 4th Philippine Constabulary Regiment. Frank hoped that Jalandoni would be able to notify Evelyn that he was all right, and possibly find a way to book passage for him on a ship to Australia.

As Frank sat eating his noon rice, Damaso Caballero, the mayor of the nearby Negrito village, suddenly burst into the banana patch and ran toward Frank's hut hollering "*Sigue! Sigue!*" ["Go! Go!"]. With much gesturing and pointing, he excitedly conveyed the idea that the Japanese were in Tala.

Frank grabbed his emergency pack and did his best to ask, "How many?"

"Hundreds!" the little man seemed to be saying.

The two men started for the Orani River gorge, Frank hobbling on his cane as best he could with the little Negrito excitedly urging him on. Frank could not understand what the man was saying, but it was evident that Damaso considered Frank to be in considerable danger.

Once they got to the gorge, Frank lowered himself down the steep bank. The thick jungle along the river proved to be something of a boon, providing handholds and tree trunks for Frank to rest against as he descended with his one good hand and one good leg.

Deep in the canyon, they found a niche in the vines and undergrowth where Frank would be practically invisible from any direction. The crashing river rapids obliterated other sounds. The air was heavy with moisture and it smelled like rain, so Damaso helped Frank unroll his canvas shelter-half from his emergency pack and string it up between two bushes.[15] The Negrito then scrambled back up the hillside.

As he huddled in his small shelter trying to catch a sweaty breath of air, Frank took stock of his situation. After five months, the Japanese had suddenly shown up at Tala without any warning, as Frank always assumed they would. Placido was in Manila, if the Japanese had not arrested him. If that had happened they would surely arrest his family as well. Frank Loyd felt utterly helpless. The Filomeno family was undoubtedly in danger but there was nothing he could do about it. For now he was alone, trapped on the side of a steep canyon wall with mosquitoes and a band of little stinging flies that constantly swarmed around his hideout.

On the positive side, Frank was surprised to find that he had been able to walk and crawl over 400 yards down the steep embankment to this hiding place, exceeding his own expectations. An incentive like fear of Japanese bayonets could apparently work wonders.

Darkness that evening was accompanied by a steady rain. The shelter-half had not been positioned well, so water from the trees poured down on part of Frank while rivulets of muddy rainwater ran down the steep hillside and under his bed of leaves, wetting everything else. He alternately chilled and perspired until about midnight, when he finally began a fitful sleep.

Early the next morning, Damaso returned with another Negrito who spoke a few words of English. They told Frank that the Japanese had found Frank's hut in the banana patch. They did not know anything about the banana farmer, or Placido's family. After chattering back and forth for a few minutes the two Negritos said they were going to go find out where the Japanese were and they would come back to get Frank when it was safe.

Frank stayed in the shelter, hidden amongst the vines, drizzle and flies.

About four o'clock in the afternoon thick rain clouds turned the sky dark gray. Frank wiggled out of his shelter. Using his cane for an end pole, he re-erected his shelter-half. With his good hand and a stick, he dug a ditch around the high side of the shelter to divert the rainwater that would come running down the hill. He finished just in time. As he crawled back under the shelter-half, the sky opened up with a downpour.

It was a heavy, cold storm that quickly proved to be too much for Frank's small shelter. As wind and lightening slashed through the treetops, rain poured in around the sides of the shelter-half. More water poured in from the hillside, bubbling over the side of, and washing away, his protective ditch.

With the torrent of rainwater flowing into the river canyon, a flash flood became a real possibility—a greater danger at this moment than the Japanese soldiers in Tala. In the midst of the downpour, using his cane like a mountain climber's pike and pulling himself upward with his good right arm, Frank began climbing, as best he could, out of the gorge.

Soaking wet, muddy, cold and exhausted, he crawled over the lip of the canyon and dragged himself through wind-swept trees and debris to the banana patch. It was late evening now, and dark. Guided by lightening flashes, Frank picked his way to his shack. He crawled inside the door and collapsed on the floor.

Within minutes, like some sort of Filipino angel, Placido's father appeared in the doorway, laden with cooking implements and food.

"No Japs!" he said, cheerfully.

Between Mr. Filomeno's broken English and Frank's few words of pidgin Tagalog, Frank learned that the Japanese soldiers had left during the morning, headed toward the Negrito village. The two Negritos disappeared behind them. There had been seven Japanese soldiers, and with them were three Filipinos from the Bureau of Constabulary.

Mr. Filomeno built a fire and cleaned up Frank and his clothes. Before leaving for Manila, Placido had given his father instructions to come feed Frank if he was not back the next day. Mr. Filomeno cooked a dinner of rice, green *munggó* beans, some other greens seasoned with ground up little fish, and a small quail. Somewhere in the distant past, Frank Loyd had enjoyed a fine dinner at the elegant Army & Navy Club in Washington, D.C.—but he had never enjoyed a meal as much as this one. That night he gratefully fell into a deep, hard sleep.

***

Placido finally returned from Manila, and his trip had been an unqualified success. Not only did he collect the money that was owed his family but he was also able to contact Sergeant Marcelo Peralta, Frank Loyd's top sergeant in the Military Police company at Fort McKinley when Frank was Provost Marshall. Placido had stayed several extra days at Peralta's house.

Sergeant Peralta told Placido an interesting story. On the night the 4th Philippine Constabulary Regiment was overrun by the Japanese on the bayside highway, Sergeant Peralta was stationed at a road intersection farther south, near Cabcaben. He and his men were directing traffic when some stragglers from the 4th PC began to arrive. A PC officer told Peralta to send the men over to an irrigation ditch near the side of the road where they would regroup and again wait for the Japanese. Before long, Colonel Jalandoni arrived and he told Sergeant Peralta to be on the lookout for an American officer named Frank Loyd. Peralta told Jalandoni about his previous association with Frank, and insisted on walking up the road in the dark to look for him. He and Jalandoni started up the road, but they had gone only a short distance when they rounded a curve and ran smack into the Japanese Army. Both men were taken prisoner.[16] They had been imprisoned together at Camp O'Donnell, until the Japanese released Colonel Jalandoni and made him a senior officer in their new Bureau of Constabulary.

Sergeant Peralta then took Placido to see Colonel Jalandoni.

"What did he have to say?"

"He was surprised to hear you're alive!"

Placido handed Frank a handful of money, and said that Colonel Jalandoni promised that on his next trip to Manila he would give Placido more money and some books and medicine for Frank.

But Colonel Jalandoni said that Frank must not come to Manila. The Japanese controlled everything very closely, and it would be extremely dangerous for Jalandoni to try to hide Frank in Manila for any length of time. Jalandoni said it would be impossible to smuggle him on board a ship bound for Australia or anywhere else.

Frank was disappointed with Jalandoni's assessment.

Frank knew that he had been a financial burden to the Filomeno family as well as a danger, so he used Jalandoni's money to redeem some of his IOUs from Placido. But if Manila and Australia were not feasible, Frank needed to come up with a new plan.

He decided that when Placido brought some more money he would hire a guide to take him to Colonel Claude Thorp's headquarters. By joining Colonel Thorp he would relieve the Filomeno family of having to care for him, and he could also be of some value to the war effort. General MacArthur, he was sure, would be returning soon.

***

Claude Armenius Thorp, "Bill" or "Willie" to his friends, was a stocky rough-looking guy, forty-five years old, with brown hair and eyes, and bushy eyebrows and moustache. Several of his rear teeth were missing and "CT" was tattooed on his left arm. He had chased Pancho Villa across northern Mexico while serving under General Pershing, and fought in France during World War I.

In 1940, Major Thorp was appointed Provost Marshall of Fort Stotsenburg, adjacent to Clark Field. There, the Army assigned a small, thin, hard-working and very self-assured ex-schoolteacher named Herminia Dizon to be his secretary. She came from a good family in Pampanga Province and was well connected with local Filipino politicians. Over time, Herminia began to win his heart. Eventually, she became his lover.

When the Fil-American Army retreated to Bataan in January 1942, Thorp went to General MacArthur with a plan. He asked MacArthur to let him take a group of volunteers and sneak through the Japanese lines to a hideout

Thorp knew about in the mountains above Fort Stotsenburg. There, he would recruit Filipinos to spy on Japanese activity and he would radio intelligence reports back to MacArthur. Recognizing Thorp's initiative, MacArthur gave his approval and promoted Major Thorp to Lieutenant Colonel.

Thorp, Herminia Dizon, and sixteen volunteers set out in mid-January 1942, with Thorp still recovering from a bullet wound in his leg.[17] It took them almost a month to infiltrate the front lines and make their way into the Zambales Mountains, raiding a Japanese convoy for supplies as they went.[18] Thorp's hideout proved to be an ideal spot from which to spy on Clark Field, which was now a major Japanese airbase. Thorp's men monitored Japanese bombers taking off from Clark Field and radioed warnings to General MacArthur and his men on Corregidor and Bataan.

After the surrender of Bataan in April, Thorp turned to organizing a Philippine resistance movement. He divided Luzon Island into four districts and appointed officers to recruit guerrillas in each district.[19] He issued an official order placing himself in charge of all guerrillas on Luzon, as authorized by General MacArthur.[20]

After the fall of Corregidor in May, the Japanese turned their attention to eliminating Thorp. As General MacArthur's authorized representative, recruiting guerrillas in the mountains above Clark Field, Thorp was an obvious menace to Japanese security. Perhaps more importantly, he was also an inspiration to many Filipinos. The Japanese Military Police, the *Kempei-tai*, issued a wanted list naming Thorp and each of his lieutenants. They offered large rewards for each man, dead or alive.

The Japanese campaign bore little fruit and Thorp continued to build his organization. He sent Lieutenant Frank Young to travel to Mindanao Island in the southern Philippines, and from there to find a way to travel to Australia and report to General MacArthur. Thorp's district commanders fanned out into Luzon and began recruiting Filipino guerrillas.

In August an American sergeant named McCann, who was hiding out with his Filipina wife in the fishponds near Guagua, died, leaving a will in which he named Colonel Thorp executor. Incredibly, Sergeant McCann's wife took his will to the local courthouse to be probated. The magistrate turned it over to the Japanese authorities.[21] They immediately sent a force into the Zambales Mountains where an informer said Thorp could be found. They raided Thorp's camp. But Herminia had been forewarned by friendly Filipinos, and Thorp and his men slipped away shortly before the Japanese arrived.

About this same time, two American officers brought Lieutenant Colonel Thorp a letter from a man he knew well—Colonel Gyles Merrill, who was living with the Jingco family at a sugar plantation near the town of Natividad, Pampanga, in the lowlands below Thorp's mountain headquarters. Colonel Merrill and Major Thorp had both served in the 26th Cavalry at Fort Stotsenburg. Colonel Merrill's letter implied that, as ranking officer, he would be taking command of guerrilla operations on Luzon.[22]

Thorp was enraged at Merrill's attempt to take over his organization.[23] He carefully crafted a persuasive, though unsubtle, reply which pointed out that General MacArthur personally appointed Thorp to raise guerrilla forces on Luzon. Thorp said he was having trouble bringing the communist Hukbalahap guerrillas, who were based near Merrill in Pampanga Province, into his organization. Thorp said he needed Merrill's help. The letter closed by offering Merrill command of Pampanga Province if he would recognize Thorp's authority.[24]

Merrill's hackles may have been raised a little, but he decided to accept that for the time being. During September 1942, he made brief contact with a Huk squadron, but he quickly learned that the Huks used their affiliation with Colonel Thorp to persuade ordinary Filipinos that the Hukbalahaps were sanctioned by General MacArthur.[25] Since they were sanctioned by MacArthur, the Huks said, they were authorized to confiscate weapons, food and supplies from the general population, which they did repeatedly, often at gunpoint. A citizen's failure to cooperate with the Huks could quickly result in death.[26]

As Thorp's organization grew, Japanese pressure to catch him increased. Raids on his camps occurred regularly. Sometimes friendly Filipinos would warn him and Herminia a day or two in advance. Sometimes they would slip into the jungle, guided by the Negritos, just minutes before the arrival of a Japanese patrol.

In October 1942, with the Japanese on their heels, Colonel Thorp accepted an invitation from Herminia's uncle, a part-Negrito Filipino named Marcos Laxamana, to move his headquarters to a remote site farther north in the mountains. The site was in a rugged valley near a little town named Maamot. Thorp, Herminia, and a few of his men left for their new hideout with Laxamana's guide, a man named Andres de la Cruz.

On October 28, Thorp received word at his new headquarters that the Japanese had captured Marcos Laxamana. Sensing danger, Thorp's men began packing their camp to move on.

While Thorp's men prepared to clear the camp, a large contingent of Japanese soldiers arrived in Maamot with Laxamana in tow. Interpreting for the Japanese, Laxamana told the villagers that anyone who left town that night to warn Thorp would be killed.

The next morning, the soldiers surrounded Thorp's camp. After fourteen previous unsuccessful attempts, the Japanese captured Lieutenant Colonel Claude A. Thorp, several members of his staff, and Herminia Dizon.

While the soldiers were tying up their prisoners, another man was brought into the clearing with his hands tied—Andres de la Cruz. A Japanese interpreter saw him and quickly strode over to the guard commander. A brief conversation ensued. As Thorp and Herminia watched, the Japanese untied Andres de la Cruz and handed him his gun.

The Japanese took Claude Thorp down the mountainside to Fort Stotsenburg. On the way down the mountain they stopped in Maamot where the guard commander paid Marcos Laxamana a large cash reward.[27] Then, Thorp, Herminia and the others were locked up in the cells of a prison that Thorp had built when he was Provost Marshall at Fort Stotsenburg—a prison he built to house Japanese prisoners of war.

Claude Thorp sat in his small cell and thought about Herminia. He was thin and emaciated from his months on the run. His brown hair had turned completely white since he and his volunteers set out from Bataan ten months ago, in January 1942. He had no idea what was going to happen to him. And worse, he could only imagine what might happen to her.

***

Frank got Placido to help him move from the banana patch back up to the *bahay*. It was an extra two-hour walk for Placido to bring supplies, but it was also that much farther away from the Japanese garrison. Japanese soldiers and Constabulary men had visited Tala twice recently. They even searched Placido's house. Frank's legs were still unsteady but he could get along on his own now, and if the Japanese found him near Tala they would undoubtedly arrest Placido and his family.

On his next trip to Orani, Placido learned that Colonel Thorp and his staff had been captured. The news was disturbing. With Rafael Jalandoni saying not to come to Manila and Claude Thorp in the hands of the Japanese, Frank's options had narrowed considerably.

But Placido had also learned of a group of American officers hidden in the foothills of the Zambales Mountains near the South China Sea coast. As Placido described it, a Colonel named Collier and his assistant, Colonel Merrill, commanded the Americans. It might be some sort of headquarters. They were very secretive. Their Filipino guards would not let anyone approach the camp.

Frank considered this news carefully. Colonel James Collier had been Frank's classmate at the Army Command and General Staff School before coming to the Philippines. They had worked together briefly on General MacArthur's staff in Manila. He was an important officer. Perhaps these two men were taking over from Colonel Thorp. Perhaps General MacArthur had sent them to Luzon on some specific mission.

Frank decided to contact Collier. He realized that he might not be allowed to join Collier's organization in his present, near crippled, condition, but perhaps he could be of help to him in some capacity. Placido agreed to try to make contact with Colonel Collier.

***

By late December 1942, Frank Loyd was able to walk around his jungle clearing reasonably well, although he still had to use his cane to support his weak right leg. The rainy season had ended and the Philippine Islands were basking in that relatively pleasant between-seasons period of comfortable days and cool nights.

On a sunny afternoon he decided to go to the creek for a bath. He put on his uniform shirt and pants, and his leather shoes that had become cracked and rotted from the constant humidity in the jungle during the rainy season. He strapped on his holster with his loaded .45 caliber semi-automatic pistol just for safety, and in case he should happen to run across a wild pig or some other edible creature along the way. He carried the new bar of soap that Placido had brought him several days ago.

Sunshine filtered through the jungle canopy as Frank stepped out of his *bahay*. Because of the soft jungle floor and occasionally thick underbrush, it took him some time to cover the 300 or so yards to the creek. Frank had adopted a habit of taking a slightly different route each time he went, to avoid creating any distinct trails.

As he approached the creek the brush gave way to large boulders of various shapes, with smaller rocks and gravel under foot. The rushing waters echoed under the thick canopy of trees, providing a kind of pleasant music that blotted out other sounds.

Rounding the large gray boulder that marked the spot of his favorite pool in the stream, Frank looked up and was startled to see two men in the water in front of him.

They, just as startled, stared back.

On the ground immediately in front of him were two piles of clothes—Japanese Army uniforms—and two Japanese Army-issue rifles.

Frank looked up at the men again. Their eyes were fixed on him.

They all paused—a moment of stunned silence.

As the cold chill in his back turned to ice, Frank shifted his cane from his right hand to his left. He steadied himself. He reached for his .45.

The Japanese were moving toward him, pushing against the current with their arms held out of the water, moving toward a gravel patch on the creek bank just a few yards away.

Frank got his pistol free of its holster. He gripped it firmly in his right hand. He clicked off the safety.

The two Japanese reached the gravel patch. One put his hands on the bank and in one movement hoisted himself out of the stream. The other was right behind.

The two naked men paused for an instant as one muttered something to the other. Then they rushed toward Frank, one going right, the other left. It was a short distance, only a few steps.

Frank's years of infantry training kicked in. Go for the most difficult shot first—the man on the right. His hand brought the pistol up into his lower peripheral vision and steadied the end of the barrel squarely in the man's chest—the largest part of the torso. He fired.

As the first body staggered to his right, Frank twisted instinctively to his left, set the end of the barrel in the second man's on-coming chest and squeezed the trigger.

The .45 caliber bullet stopped the Japanese in mid-stride. His body slumped toward the ground and the man's head thudded into a rock by Frank's left foot.

Frank's initial sense of elation over having dropped the two men suddenly turned into an overwhelming feeling of revulsion and doubt at what he had done. He felt a dark weight settle into his heart. He looked at the bloody bodies, a large hole torn through the middle of each.

What were they doing here, so far up in the mountains? If they were searching for guerrillas there might be more soldiers around, and if so, the gun shots would bring them running.

As quickly as he could manage, Frank moved back into the brush behind a large rock where he could observe the streambed but not be seen. His pistol cocked and ready, he remained perfectly still, watched and waited. No one showed up. No voices called out. No one came looking for the two men. There was nothing but the rushing of the stream and an occasional breath of air through the trees.

After a while, Frank moved out from his hiding place and back to the stream. With considerable effort, and considerable pain in his arm, leg and hips, he dragged the bodies behind some boulders. He threw their clothes, some dirt, and branches from the stream over them. He took their rifles and threw them into the jungle. At least if anyone came looking, the men would be hard to find.[28]

Frank hobbled back to his *bahay*. He found it difficult to sleep that night, thinking about the two soldiers. What would happen if the Japanese caught him now?

IX. The Home Front

At the U.S. government censorship room in the San Antonio post office, Evelyn Loyd was "promoted" (no pay raise) from carrying bags of mail to the censors' tables, to being a censor herself. Every piece of mail coming into or going out of the United States had to be examined for confidential information. As government censors, Evelyn and her friend Betty Wilson opened and read letters and documents, and looked for any reference that might be threatening to national defense.[1] Anything about military units, ship movements, prison camps, weapons, or quantities of industrial production was prohibited. Evelyn used a big tube of jet-black ink to blot out any offending reference, or cut it out of the pages with a sharp knife or a pair of scissors. A letter could wind up looking like a lace doily after censorship. If she discovered text that seemed to be truly threatening, she attached that portion of the letter to a "submission slip" and passed it to Major Snyder, supervisor of the censorship room. After reading and censoring a letter, Evelyn put it back in its envelope, sealed it, stamped it with a red-ink rubber stamp, and initialed the stamp mark. She tossed the censored letters onto a pile where a postman periodically sacked them up for delivery.

Evelyn felt like she worked in a cattle-pen. The huge censorship room on the third floor of the post office operated twenty-four hours per day and bustled with more than 250 employees, mostly women. Major Snyder, the overall supervisor of the operation, seemed to be a good man stuck in a boring job. Mostly he sat at his desk and watched the girls. Questions of propriety were about the only subject of lively discussion among the female employees, and Major Snyder was the assumed protagonist of most of the off-color rumors that flew around the room.

Any expectations Evelyn had of finding juicy tidbits about friends and neighbors quickly faded and she was soon convinced that mail censor was the most boring job anyone had ever thought up. It was endless hours of reading invoices and shipping documents, and piles of letters about other people's babies, vacations, and car troubles.

In October 1942, Evelyn picked up her own mail from the mailbox by her front door. There among the bills and advertisements, was a letter from her husband, Frank Loyd.[2]

Stunned after ten months of no word at all, she ripped it open. The letter had been written on March 6, 1942, on Bataan, before the surrender. Apparently it had been brought out on a submarine, then lost somewhere in the postal system for the next six months. In it, Frank asked about Bonnie's artwork, Frank Jr.'s model airplanes, and Evelyn's finances. He described a little bit of the battle, but assured her that he was quite safe and that everything was mostly just boring. He even described the food as being pretty good. But Evelyn noticed that the food he described was rice, carabao meat, and a package of raisins.

After reading the letter over and over, Evelyn at least knew that he had been safe in March. That was more than she had known before. And in her heart, she was confident that he was still alive—somewhere. She called her friends, Evelyn Noble and Betty Wilson, to give them her good news.

***

In December, the Japanese finally released lists of the men taken prisoner in the Philippines. The War Department sent cablegrams and letters to their families, and all of the men who were from San Antonio had their pictures in the local newspapers.[3]

Frank Loyd and Maxie Noble were not there. Evelyn Loyd and Evelyn Noble telephoned the War Department and went to the Red Cross seeking information, any information. But to no avail. There was no word about Frank, or about Maxie Noble.

Betty Wilson showed Evelyn Loyd her telegram and letter, and the instructions she received for writing to Zero.[4] The materials from the War Department also included information about pay allotments. The wives of the prisoners of war would continue to receive their checks.[5]

As Evelyn waited for some kind of word, January turned unusually cold and rainy and everyone came down with the flu. Between bouts of fever and coughing, Frank Jr. occupied his time with his small, intricate models. Some had moving control surfaces on the wings and tail that were connected to the stick in the cockpit. He seemed to have his heart set on becoming a pilot and an Army officer. He got mad at Evelyn and Bonnie for coming to breakfast in their bathrobes, and he scolded Evelyn for using his razor. Evelyn silently mused that it was remarkable how much Junior was like his father. Together, the three of them prayed each night for Frank's safety.[6]

In the year that had passed since the Japanese attacks on Pearl Harbor and the Philippines, things had changed radically in the United States.[7] In addition to government censorship, many goods were rationed, such as shoes, meat, canned goods and coffee. Gasoline was rationed and was selling for $3.00 a gallon. Food prices were very high. Evelyn, like most of her neighbors, maintained a vegetable garden in her back yard called a "Victory Garden," but it produced little during the winter months. It was almost impossible to buy things like automobile tires or batteries now. And there were no new cars—the Detroit automakers had stopped building them. They only made trucks, tanks and military vehicles.[8] Women were taking jobs in the factories as their men enlisted or were drafted. Ships were being built at every port in the United States, and President Franklin Roosevelt expected the aircraft companies to build 60,000 airplanes during 1943.[9]

News from the war was mostly bad, in spite of the optimistic headlines in the newspapers. General MacArthur was still fighting in New Guinea. General Dwight Eisenhower was chasing German General Erwin Rommel around the deserts of North Africa. President Roosevelt and British Prime Minister Winston Churchill met in Casablanca, and the newspapers proclaimed that only the "unconditional surrender" of the Axis powers would end the war.[10]

Japan now controlled more than 4 million square miles of land and more than 500 million people—more than twice as many as the Germans.[11] The Japanese held virtually all of Southeast Asia and the Pacific, and were pushing the British out of Burma. Japanese news broadcasts, the only communications that came out of the Pacific, said that the small bands of guerrillas still loose in the Philippines were being hunted down and captured, or killed.[12] To Evelyn and most of her friends, the "unconditional surrender" of Japan sounded like a pipe dream.

In the evenings after the children went to bed Evelyn stayed up late, made notes in her diary and daydreamed about what it would be like when Frank came home. She had lost weight, so she decided that once she knew for sure when he was coming she would fatten up a bit, buy some good-looking clothes and dye her graying hair. She wanted to look really great when he arrived.[13]

***

In Australia, General Douglas MacArthur prepared for his next move. On January 2, 1943, Australian and U.S. forces captured Buna, a major Japanese stronghold on the north shore of New Guinea.[14] American Marines and soldiers pushed back the remaining Japanese on Guadalcanal.[15] MacArthur ordered his staff to begin planning for a thrust northward through the islands of the Southwest Pacific. A route that would one day, he expected, take him back to the Philippines.

Since December, MacArthur had been receiving radio traffic from two guerrilla radios in the islands—one operated by a Philippine Army major named Marcario Peralta on Panay in the central Philippines, and the other belonging to a Major Wendell Fertig on Mindanao, the southernmost Philippine island.[16] Peralta had established a rudimentary spy network that extended to Manila and enabled persons there to relay information on Japanese ship movements back to MacArthur through Peralta's radio. But a portion of the radio traffic from Majors Peralta and Fertig was given over to bickering about which one of them should be appointed USAFFE guerrilla commander over all of the Philippines.[17]

On January 3, MacArthur's headquarters received a radio message from a new source—Captain Ralph Praeger on Luzon.[18] It was the first radio contact MacArthur had had with anyone on Luzon since a last, desperate message came in from Captain Guillermo Nakar in north Luzon, in August 1942. MacArthur quickly put through promotions for Praeger and several of his chief lieutenants.[19]

On February 7, 1943 Praeger relayed messages from two other Americans, Lieutenant Colonels Martin Moses and Arthur "Maxie" Noble, describing how they had raised a small army on Luzon and attacked the Japanese at the Itogon mines.[20]

X. Joining Collier

Frank Loyd screwed a rusty top securely down on the second of two mason jars arrayed on the dark brown dirt in front of him. Inside, curved and tightly packed, were his diary pages for November and December 1942. Previously, he had given Placido Filomeno a sealed tin filled with more of the small pages covered with tiny pencil writing, his diary from April 6, 1942 up to November. Placido had promised to hide the tin and to keep it safe until the war was over.

These mason jars were another matter. Frank never believed in putting all of his money in the same bank, and he wanted to be certain that at least some of his diary survived the war. That night he paced off a short distance from the shack in the banana patch, dug a hole about three feet deep and buried the two mason jars. He covered the site with loose dirt and a few banana leaves, then sprinkled a little debris from the nearby forest floor over it. Satisfied, he stepped back and surveyed his work in the dim moonlight. There was no reason any Japanese, or anyone else for that matter, should ever be curious about or dig in that spot. But it was a spot Frank could easily find if he ever got the chance to come back to Tala to retrieve his diary.[1]

Frank went back into the shack and lay down on his cot. The previous night, his last night in the *bahay*, he had dreamed about being captured by the Japanese.[2] It woke him up. He had never dreamed such a thing before, but he had been nervous and concerned since the day he discovered the two Japanese soldiers in the stream near his *bahay*, and he had not slept well since that day. This night, alone in the banana patch, he again had trouble sleeping. The Japanese were getting too close.[3] Tomorrow, he was leaving Tala. He was going to join Colonel Collier.

In a fortuitous coincidence, when Frank came down from his *bahay* to the banana patch he learned that an American lieutenant had visited Tala earlier in the day, and brought a message to Placido from Colonel Collier.[4] Collier invited Frank to join him and Colonel Gyles Merrill at their headquarters in the Zambales Mountains, north of Bataan. The lieutenant left without identifying himself, but the fact that the message was delivered by an American officer was sufficient credentials for Frank. He was ready to go.

On Tuesday morning, January 5, 1943, Frank awoke to the song of a Filipino somewhere across the valley. He lay for a few moments on his bed as sunlight streamed in through the door, listening to the lilting words he could hear clearly but could not understand. The foliage outside was warming up in the sunlight and there was a crisp, clean smell to the morning air.

Frank got up and set to work shaving off his dark foot-long beard, using his knife and a sharpening stone Placido's father had lent him. It was a tedious and painful process that revealed a family of tiny lice residing on his jaw and cheeks. The lice notwithstanding, the beard would be a dead giveaway if anyone saw him from a distance, since

Filipinos have little facial hair. Frank could not possibly pass for a Filipino but he would not be quite so obvious clean-shaven.

About nine o'clock, Placido came. With him was the Negrito mayor, Damaso Caballero. Damaso would be their guide.

Frank hoisted his emergency pack onto his back, checked to be certain his .45 pistol was loaded and securely stowed in its holster, grabbed his cane, and set off behind Damaso and Placido down the mountain trail. He was limping slightly from the pains that still plagued his right leg.

Collier's messenger had given specific instructions. They were to travel through the jungle, away from the rice fields, staying close to the base of the mountains. They would go to a designated house and meet a man there who would take them to a rendezvous point outside of Kulò, a village on the south side of the Dinalupihan-Olongapo highway that stretched across the north end of Bataan. The highway was heavily used and heavily patrolled by the Japanese Army, so they must not try to cross to the north side by themselves. The messenger told Placido that Colonel Collier's headquarters was north of the highway, deep in the mountain jungles of Zambales Province and, as far as he knew, the Japanese were unaware of his presence.[5] Collier did not want any Americans being discovered or captured in this area.

They covered about twelve kilometers that day and found the designated house near barrio Bamban, situated in a narrow valley on the mountainside above Kulò. It belonged to a Filipino who was part of the anti-Japanese underground. Damaso left them there and that night their host served eggs for supper—a rare treat in most Filipino homes and a true feast as far as Frank was concerned.[6]

The next morning their host prepared fresh eggs for breakfast as well. After the meal he led Frank and Placido down a path through the woods to a small Nipa-thatched shed in the center of a rice field, about 200 yards south of the Olongapo highway. The field was flat and slightly mushy, with green and brown stalks sticking out of the ground, the rice having recently been harvested. The place had a pungent smell of animal manure and cut grass.

Across the rice field a row of thatched-roof houses stretched along the south side of the highway, blocking the road from view. This was barrio Kulò. Their host told Frank to wait there for a man named Francisco, who would take him to meet Collier's guide on the north side of the highway. He then took Placido and walked away into the barrio.

Frank waited nervously by the shed. His right knee and ankle were stiff and sore from the long walk down the mountain from Tala. As the day went by and the sun passed overhead, he moved around the shed to keep in the shade and to be as inconspicuous as possible. He kept an eye constantly on the village in front of him. His ears strained for any sound of bootsteps or of metal clinking on metal in the jungle behind him, the sounds of approaching Japanese soldiers.

At sundown, a stooped figure emerged from the darkening barrio and began making its way across the rice field toward the shed. It was a poor old woman with the butt-end of a cigar in her mouth, who came to share her supper with Frank. It seems that several farmers had spotted him lurking in the mid-day shadows of the shed and immediately recognized that he was an American. That afternoon, the "American hiding by the shed" became a general topic of conversation in the barrio. Since no one seemed to know anything about him, the old woman assumed he was alone and hungry and she brought her dinner of beans and bananas to share.[7] It wasn't much, but Frank was humbled by the thought that someone who had so little would come and share it with a complete stranger.

Later that night, Francisco finally showed up. He told Frank that Placido had gone back to Tala, but had promised to come check on Frank, and that he may join him in about a month at Colonel Collier's. Francisco had been unable to contact Collier's guide on the north side of the highway but he promised to come back and get Frank the next day.

***

As Placido climbed the last section of the trail into Tala it was well after dark, almost midnight.

He passed by Hippolito Sayas' house and turned up the path toward the clearing. Everything was quiet in the settlement. Faint moonlight illuminated the grassy clearing and reflected off of the thatched rooftops of the three houses that sat alongside the trail. No cooking fires or candles glowed from inside, but one would not expect to see activity at this hour. Most Filipino farmers and their families turn in shortly after sundown.

Placido climbed the steps to the front porch of his own house. He thought it odd that no dogs barked. It was still and dark inside the front room.

He stepped through the doorway.

He heard a faint clink of metal on metal from the back of the room. As his eyes adjusted to the darkness, the skin on the back of his neck began to crawl.

Out of the shadowy corner to his right stepped a Japanese officer.[8]

***

The late morning sun was bright and hot, and Francisco had still not returned. At the edge of the woods there was a giant hardwood tree that had blown down during a storm, and Frank found a narrow passage between two huge roots that led to a damp, circular cave about six feet in diameter under the tree. The entrance to the passageway was masked from view by a tangle of roots and dirt.[9] Crouched among the twisted roots, Frank could watch the Nipa shed while being relatively hard to spot from the barrio.

About mid-day, as Frank peered out from the tangle of tree roots, he saw an older Filipino man come walking out of the barrio toward the shed, apparently looking for him.

Frank went out to meet him and the two men sat down in the shade by the Nipa shed to talk. The man's name was Delphin Pamintuan, and he brought Frank a huge baked *camote*. While Frank ate, Mr. Pamintuan explained that Francisco had come to see him earlier in the day, and asked him to look after a Colonel Loyd for a few days, until Francisco came back to get him.

Mr. Pamintuan went on to say that as a prominent citizen of the area, he had certain contacts with the Japanese authorities, and that the Japanese were about to launch an all-out campaign to destroy guerrilla organizations in Zambales and Pampanga provinces. He said that he used what influence he had to direct the attention of the Japanese toward the "bandit" guerrillas who were causing trouble for honest Filipinos, and away from the legitimate guerrillas such as his own son-in-law, Ruben Bondoc. Ruben's headquarters were on the north side of the Olongapo highway, near the base of Mount Malasimbo. Ruben, alias "Captain Magtanggol," [the "Defender"] was well known in the area and had some plans of his own for the Japs.[10] In fact, he had plans for some pro-Japanese Filipinos, too.

As Mr. Pamintuan talked, he asked Frank a few questions, clearly probing for information. Frank gave him very little. When the conversation was over, Mr. Pamintuan assured Frank that someone would be coming for him, although he did not say how he knew this. He then walked slowly back across the rice field toward the highway.

Delphin Pamintuan returned to his home in Bamban that night, and turned in a little later than usual.

Deep in his thoughts, Mr. Pamintuan failed to notice a few faint noises outside his bedroom window, then a stirring in the front room of his house.

A gruff voice awoke him.

Around him were several armed Filipinos. They were men he had never seen before, men who said they were guerrillas.

They accused him of being a Japanese spy. They took him away.[11]

***

Frank woke up to the sound of gunfire.

From his hideout in the roots of the tree, he had a clear view across the rice fields to the trees and houses that lined the south side of the Olongapo highway. The shots, and a good deal of yelling in Japanese, were coming from across the road.

As Frank watched, he could hear the distinctive "ping" of Japanese rifles, the deeper "crack" of American-made rifles, and a smattering of other weapons. Occasionally, the "boom" and "crash" of a small artillery piece punctuated the melee.

The distinct smell of burnt gunpowder drifted by. Frank could not see flashes or explosions in the village, so he reasoned that the fight was going on in the jungle north of the highway—precisely where he wanted to go.

The gunfight continued through most of the day, tapering off as darkness approached. During the night he could hear trucks moving up and down the highway. The next day, through the narrow spaces between the houses in Kulò, Frank caught glimpses of Japanese soldiers and military vehicles on the highway.

The following morning Frank saw a familiar face coming toward him across the rice field.

Jose Payumo, a Filipino forest ranger Frank had met at the U.S. Army training camp on Bataan before the war, was walking toward Frank's hideout accompanied by Delphin Pamintuan.[12]

At the sight of Frank, Payumo's eyes filled with tears and he threw his arms around Frank's neck. Payumo, who lived in Dinalupihan, had heard about an American named Loyd hiding nearby and he came to see if it could be the same man that he had met on Bataan almost two years before.

My presence here, thought Frank, *is certainly no secret*. Even the small cave under the tree, it had turned out, was a favorite playhouse for children in the barrio.

Frank explained that he was trying to join Colonel Collier in the mountains north of the highway, but that he had apparently been abandoned by his guide, Francisco. Payumo did not know where Francisco had gone, but he did know that two American colonels had a camp in the jungle north of the highway, closer to Olongapo.

While Frank and Payumo talked, Delphin Pamintuan became increasingly nervous about the sounds of sporadic gunfire coming from the north side of the highway. He interrupted to say that even though the Japanese had not shown any interest in the south side yet, there were strange people in the area. Pamintuan related a story about being taken prisoner at night and held under guard for two days by some bandit guerrillas who threatened his life. They had released him just last night.

The gunfire on the north side of the highway intensified. A major battle was shaping up between the Japanese and the guerrillas. Payumo told Frank that the Japanese had lost a number of men fighting the guerrillas the previous day, and that they were striking back heavily to wipe out the guerrilla forces.[13] It was Tuesday, January 12, 1943, and all contacts between the Filipino resistance people on the south side of the highway and the guerrillas on the north side had been broken.

It was obviously getting dangerous around Kulò.

Payumo said that it would not be possible for Frank to go to Colonel Collier's hideout until things cooled down, but he knew another place where Frank could hide temporarily.

Concerned about the deteriorating situation around him and disappointed that Francisco had not returned, Frank agreed to go.[14]

Frank followed Payumo through the woods on a trail that ran parallel to the highway, past the west end of Kulò.

After almost an hour, they turned south up a shallow valley in the mountainside and followed another path between a jungle stream on the left and a row of rice paddies on the right. Their destination turned out to be a *palay* [unhusked rice] storage shed tucked back into the woods behind the stream. Standing outside the *palay* shed were three American army officers.

Frank recognized two of the men. Lieutenant Colonel Edgar Wright Jr. and his wife Marge had been on the same ship with Frank and Evelyn Loyd when they all came to the Philippines in 1940. Eddie Wright was Maxie Noble's roommate at West Point, and the three couples had socialized occasionally at the Nobles' house at Fort McKinley. Eddie was about the same height and build as Frank although several years younger.[15] Eddie Wright was one of those people who never forgot a name or a face, and he immediately recognized Frank.

The second man, Major Royal Reynolds, was a handsome, athletic West Pointer from New York, with bright, blue eyes and dark hair. At Fort McKinley Reynolds and his beautiful, red-haired wife, Jeannie, were well known around the Officers' Club where they were usually the center of attention—they both had a certain movie-star quality about them that captured the attention of Fort McKinley's children and young people.[16] Frank had always thought of Roy Reynolds as a young man with something of an attitude, but an attitude was okay with Frank as long as the man could deliver. Frank's constables had fought alongside Roy Reynold's men at the Battle of the Points on Bataan, and Frank knew that Roy Reynolds could deliver.

Wright and Reynolds were both officers in the Philippine Scouts.

The third man, Major Allie H. Romaine, was a reservist from Louisiana. He was the tallest of the three at well over six feet but looked flabby, even though he, like the others, was undernourished and thin. He reminded Frank of an old Collie dog. Shortly before the war he had been called to active duty, sent to the Philippines, and assigned to command a Philippine Army infantry company.[17] Frank wondered how he fit in with the other two.

The men talked and it turned out that the three of them had been hiding at this *palay* shed practically since the surrender. They knew nothing about Colonels Collier and Merrill, but they agreed that Frank could stay with them until he could make contact with Colonel Collier. Frank asked how they had come to this place to begin with.

The men said that they had been separated from their respective units in the confusion of the last big battle leading up to the surrender. Eddie Wright was cut off from his 45th Infantry Regiment as he and a few Philippine Scout soldiers tried to take out a Japanese machine gun that pinned them down at a trail intersection.[18] After spending the night in a deep ravine, they learned that General Edward King was about to surrender. Later that afternoon they met Roy Reynolds, who was cut off from his 57th Infantry Regiment while scouting a route the regiment could take to counter-attack the Japs.[19]

Wright, Reynolds, and a sergeant from the 45th named Esposito decided to move north in hopes of getting behind the Japanese lines, then turn west toward the American positions along the west coast of Bataan. Along the way, they met Romaine and several more Filipino Scouts. They all spent that night hidden together in another ravine.

The next day as they moved cautiously westward, they stumbled into a jungle clearing. Looking around the trampled grass and bushes, they were sickened by the sight of hundreds of dead bodies—Philippine Army soldiers from the 91st Infantry Regiment who apparently had surrendered to the Japanese per General King's orders.[20] They had disabled their weapons in the prescribed manner, throwing away the firing mechanisms and wedging their rifle barrels into the crotches of trees, then bending the barrels. It was apparent that when the Japanese found them they were disarmed and waiting to be taken prisoner.

Instead, they were slaughtered.

Hundreds of bodies lay scattered about, hands bound behind their backs with wire. Some of the men were killed by bullets fired into the backs of their heads. Others were used for bayonet practice, stabbed repeatedly until dead. Still others, many others, were made to kneel before their captors and they were beheaded by sword-wielding Japanese officers. Bodies and bloody heads, eyes and mouths grotesquely askew, covered the floor of the clearing.[21]

The 91st had been one of the more successful Philippine Army regiments, and had distinguished themselves in the Battle of the Pockets by wiping out a Japanese regiment attempting to break through the USAFFE lines. The Japanese, when they recognized who was surrendering to them, had exacted a terrible retribution on these brave, unarmed men.

At that point, Wright, Reynolds, and Romaine decided that surrender was out of the question. The few Scouts who were still with them, except Sergeant Esposito, discarded their uniforms and went off into the jungle to find their way back to their homes. In their shorts and bare feet they were hardly distinguishable from ordinary Filipino farmers.

The four men headed north. They crossed the Pilar-Bagac road at night and worked their way up to a point just south of the Olongapo highway. There, as they rested by a creek early one morning, a Filipino farmer named Primitivo Leonzon approached them. Seeing the pitiful condition of Wright and his companions, Mr. Leonzon gave them food and offered shelter for the three Americans.[22] He moved them into the *palay* shed near his rice fields. Sergeant Esposito returned to his own home in Olongapo.

For the past year "Tivo" Leonzon had kept these three Americans out of sight and reasonably well fed. Eddie Wright wanted to pay him for their upkeep, but Tivo was reluctant to accept any money. They finally made an arrangement where Tivo agreed to bring them weekly rations of rice and *munggó* beans for fifty pesos per month, per man. None of the men had any money, though, so Tivo agreed to carry them all on credit—credit based on the assumption that they would make it through the war alive and pay him later.[23] Frank agreed to join in the arrangement.

"Tivo is a God-sent angel," remarked Al Romaine.[24]

The *palay* storage shed was cramped for three men, much less four. Its leaky roof was so low the men could not stand erect inside. Along both walls were bamboo and wicker bins used to store the *palay*. Two men slept on top of the bins and one slept on the floor. They assigned Frank the only space left—on the floor between the bins.

The shed sat in a narrow gulch about ten yards from a stream and the path Frank and Payumo had walked up from Kulò. Frank learned that the men had not dug a latrine. When they needed to go, they simply walked out into the woods and went—a clear violation of the most rudimentary principal of field sanitation. Frank wondered why they did not all have dysentery.

At night the men spread a large community-type mosquito net over themselves like a tent within the shed. But the floor of the shed had spaces between the slats "wide enough for mosquitoes to fly through in formation," and varmints could easily crawl up through the floorboards and join the men within their own net. Eddie Wright and Al Romaine had recently recovered from malaria attacks, and Roy Reynolds was showing symptoms. Here in the lowlands mosquitoes were a problem year-round, particularly during the dry season. Frank decided that if he was going to stay here, even for a short while, he was going to make some changes.[25]

First, he got the men to gather bamboo leaves and lay a thin mattress over the floor of the shed to keep the mosquitoes out. He had them dig a small latrine back in the jungle and he instructed them to cover their leavings, not only for sanitary purposes but to keep smells from alerting any passing Japanese. The men freshened and thickened the rudimentary camouflage they had placed around the sides of the shed. Frank established procedures for stepping on stones and taking different paths when going to and from the stream to avoid leaving a trail.

The three men did not exactly welcome Frank's reforms. However, as senior officer—he outranked Eddie Wright by about three weeks—he felt it was his duty to get the camp back onto a more military footing, and he felt responsible for everyone's health and safety.

When Tivo Leonzon brought in his first load of supplies after Frank's arrival, Frank greeted him and shook his hand. He found Tivo to be an affable man, a little over five feet tall, of medium build, and about fifty years old. Tivo had a wife, seven children, and parents who all lived with him in a large house in barrio Myete, a few miles south of Kulò. Tivo owned the rice paddies Frank had passed along the trail, and he was proud of his ability to speak English in spite of only completing the third grade in school.[26]

Frank told Tivo that he would pay for his keep, along with the other men. As he had done with Placido, Frank wrote a note for Tivo Leonzon guaranteeing that if he did not survive the war Evelyn would pay off his debt, and he noted their agreement in his diary. Privately, Frank wondered what motivated this man to take on the care of four American strangers in addition to his large family, putting himself at considerable risk by doing so. The money aside, Frank decided that Tivo was getting something of value out of the arrangement even if he never got paid. In these times of outright lawlessness throughout the Philippines, having four armed soldiers guarding his rice twenty-four hours a day had to be worth something.

But the rations Tivo provided were meager, and the men's diet was worse than bland. Delphin Pamintuan came to the camp to visit Frank and, after seeing how the men lived, he began bringing a few vegetables, fish, sausages and other treats, such as coffee and milk, with each visit.[27]

Frank quickly got the impression that Tivo resented the Americans having contact with Pamintuan or any other Filipinos.[28] On every visit Tivo would ask if anyone had been there, and he was disturbed to learn that Pamintuan and Payumo visited several times. Payumo even brought his new wife, a nurse, to give the men shots for malaria, which also seemed to bother Tivo. Eddie Wright placed a lot of confidence in Tivo, but Frank decided to keep an eye on him.

Frank asked Payumo to see if he could locate Colonel Collier, and he talked to the other men about coming with him to join Collier.[29] He told them that James Collier apparently was in the Philippines on a mission from General MacArthur, and if they joined him they could all participate in his mission or, at the least, maybe find some way back to MacArthur's forces. Roy Reynolds agreed to go with Frank if Collier could be found. Eddie and Al declined, electing to stay with Tivo. Eddie said that if Colonel Collier was really in the Zambales jungle somewhere, he was probably just a fugitive like the rest of them.

"Colonel Thorp," said Eddie, "was MacArthur's man. Look what happened to him—the Japs got him."

Before Frank joined them, Eddie had sent one of Tivo’s sons to find Colonel Claude Thorp and volunteer the services of the three officers. The boy found Thorp’s camp destroyed. Local natives told him that Thorp and his staff had been taken prisoner a few weeks before.[30]

More recently, Tivo reported, the Japanese had brought Herminia Dizon, Thorp’s secretary, to Pampanga Province as part of a propaganda team that was trying to entice guerrillas to surrender. Accompanied by an armed escort of Japanese soldiers, she was touring Pampanga and delivering speeches on behalf of the Japanese administration.

Speaking in Kapampangan, or any of several Filipino dialects she spoke fluently, Herminia told the people that

Colonel Thorp had been captured, and that the guerrilla resistance movement was broken.

"The Japanese are our friends," she said. "We must all cooperate with them."

But the Japanese interpreter and the guards who accompanied her often did not understand the local dialects. In the middle of her prepared speech, Herminia would let slip a word or two, or an occasional phrase, such as:[31]

"Colonel Thorp lives!" a statement which would draw smiles from the crowd.

"Keep up hope—MacArthur will return," in place of a phrase about MacArthur's defeat, eliciting cheers from the crowd.

Gesturing at her companions, "These Japs are stupid. They will lose." A daring comment, which would bring gasps and laughter.

The Japanese guards never understood why the Filipino audiences laughed and cheered at inappropriate places during Herminia's speech.

These Filipinos, they would think, *who can figure them out?*

***

Early in February 1943, Delphin Pamintuan showed up at the camp with a former Philippine Scout named Sam Zozabrado, from Olongapo. Zozabrado had escaped from the Death March, and Frank figured that he must now be associated in some way with the guerrillas given that he was in the company of Delphin Pamintuan.[32] He had to assume that Zozabrado was trustworthy, based on his Philippine Scout background and the fact that Pamintuan brought him to the camp. Zozabrado was going to go to Manila, and Pamintuan brought him to meet Frank in case Frank might want him to contact anyone there.

At this point Frank figured that every soul from Olongapo to Dinalupihan must know about the four Americans and where they were hiding. But he told

Zozabrado how to find Colonel Rafael Jalandoni in Manila, and he said to tell Jalandoni that Frank and the other three Americans needed help, especially malaria medicine. Frank gave Zozabrado his Iowa State college ring to use for identification. He told Zozabrado that once he made contact with Jalandoni he should pawn the ring and use the money to buy Atabrine. The gold in the ring should be worth at least twelve tablets.

Days went by. Payumo was unable to locate Colonel Collier or Colonel Merrill, and he stopped coming to visit. Zozabrado did not come back. Supplies from the now-sullen Tivo dwindled, and deliveries became increasingly irregular. Delphin Pamintuan and one of his sons, Victor, took up the slack and began bringing food for Frank Loyd and the others.

On one of his visits, Victor Pamintuan mentioned that Corporal John Boone would be in the area the next day, visiting a large guerrilla unit that numbered almost 300 men.

Frank was immediately interested. Eddie Wright had mentioned a U.S. Army corporal named John Boone, a local guerrilla leader. At the time, Frank had paid little attention, preferring to avoid any contact with guerrillas, all of whom he regarded as little more than bandits. However, Corporal Boone might be able to take him to Colonel Collier.[33] He arranged with Victor Pamintuan to meet Corporal Boone the following night. For security reasons, the meeting would be held at midnight and would be attended only by Frank and Victor—the other three Americans would stay at the *palay* shed.

The next day, Frank downed eight quinine tablets to fend off his pains and fevers. Victor showed up that evening a little later than expected, with two young Filipinos carrying American Army rifles and short bamboo poles with kerosene-soaked rags stuffed in one end. Frank had his loaded pistol on his hip and his cane in his hand. He was feeling a little nauseous from the quinine when the four men started down the trail toward Kulò.[34]

As they neared the rice paddies, a small path jutted off into the trees. Here, the bamboo torches were lit and the men proceeded single file, with one of the torchbearers in front and the other behind. Victor and Frank silently followed the lead man, stumbling over tree roots and the uneven ground.

The path grew narrower. The jungle canopy overhead blocked out all moonlight and any view of the stars. Instead, the flickering torchlights illuminated a small arc of overhead growth, tree trunks and brush around them, giving the impression of moving through a narrow, dark cave. The clean night air held a slight chill and whiffs of burnt kerosene. As the leader turned onto other, smaller trails, Frank knew he would be totally unable to find his way back to camp, or to Kulò for that matter, if these men abandoned him in the jungle.

At almost exactly midnight, the leader veered off to the right of the trail and stepped through a small opening in the bushes. There, the trees and underbrush gave way to a small clearing. In the middle of the clearing was a thatched roof, open-sided shelter, and in the middle of the shelter sat a small, wiry American, Corporal John Boone.

Frank sat down, and the two men got acquainted.

Boone, it turned out, was in the 31st Infantry Regiment as the Fil-American army retreated into Bataan. Boone said that at Layac Junction, a road intersection on the north edge of Bataan, he and two other men were cut off and left behind when the 31st pulled back in the face of the Japanese onslaught.

Frank Loyd wanted one thing from John Boone.

"Do you know where Colonel Collier is? Can you take me to him?"

Boone knew of Colonel Merrill, but all he knew about Collier was that there was someone by that name with Merrill. Boone said that he might be able to take Frank there, but first he would have to confirm that Frank had, in fact, been invited to their camp.

"But that will take time. The trails on the north side of the highway have been blocked off by the Japs—it's hard to get around. Besides, I'm told that Merrill and Collier moved way back into the jungle to get away from the Japs.

"I'll let you know if I make contact with them."

Boone went on to say that his own headquarters was in the jungle on the side of Mount Malasimbo, north of Dinalupihan. He had other units scattered around the area as well, each with its own separate base of operations.

"Victor's brother-in-law is one of my lieutenants," he said, nodding toward Victor Pamintuan. "One of my best men. Although, a little too aggressive."

Frank remembered Delphin Pamintuan mentioning his son-in-law, Ruben Bondoc, alias Captain Magtanggol.

"He has some good ideas, though. He recently turned in a couple of informers to the *Kempei-tai*, claiming they were guerrillas. The stupid Japs arrested their own informers."

Boone went on to describe his guerrilla operation.

Lieutenant Edwin Ramsey, who had been one of Colonel Thorp's lieutenants, was his superior officer. Ramsey's headquarters were in the mountains on the other side of the Luzon central plain, north of Manila. Ramsey visited Boone from time to time, and they occasionally communicated by courier. By virtue of being under Colonel Thorp's authority, Ramsey's men were "official" USAFFE guerrillas, not bandits like the other guerrillas roaming around Luzon. Lieutenant Ramsey and Colonel Thorp had officially promoted Corporal Boone to Captain.[35]

Frank doubted the validity of such a promotion, but decided to keep his thoughts to himself.

Boone told Frank that his men lived in their homes and periodically met in the jungle for training sessions. For the most part they resisted the Japanese passively, without attacking or unduly antagonizing them, to avoid bringing reprisals onto civilians.[36]

He described how his men kept records of Japanese ships moving into and out of Manila Bay, and Subic Bay near Olongapo. Once a month they passed this information to Lieutenant Ramsey, who had it taken to the southern islands where there was a radio that could reach General MacArthur.[37]

"We also have details that go out to the old battlefields to look for rifles and ammunition. We've built up a pretty good stock." Boone fixed his eyes on Frank. "But sometimes you've got to compete to get anything, what with the Huks and everybody else out there looking for guns too."

At that point there was a sharp noise in the trees behind Boone. He jerked and twisted around to look over his shoulder, his hand reaching for his rifle. A guerrilla at the edge of the clearing looked back at Boone and grinned sheepishly.

Frank asked Boone if they ever actually attacked the Japs. Boone said that occasionally, when they could do so without endangering a village or any Filipino civilians, he would authorize one of his units to assemble in the jungle and ambush a Japanese patrol. The men, especially Ruben Bondoc's men, wanted to strike back at the Japanese and these ambushes were a good way for them to let off steam. Boone admitted, however, that keeping "Captain Magtanggol" under control was one of his more formidable problems.

Some of Boone's men had gotten jobs with the Japanese Army, helping lay land mines around Japanese military installations.

"The men help the Japs lay the mines during the day, and get paid. Then they go back at night and blow up the same mines. The Japs think the guerrillas did it.

"Nobody gets hurt, the men make a little money, and they get to harass the Japs, which is good for morale.

"Everybody wins—except the Japs."[38]

Frank was impressed.

During the torch-lit trek back to the *palay* shed Frank had time to reflect on what he had seen and heard. Boone was obviously an articulate, educated man, about thirty years old, who was able to command the respect of the local Filipinos. He had only been in the Army for two years, and he seemed a little skittish, but he appeared to be honest with Frank, even describing how his original band of thirty followers threw down their weapons and ran away the first time they encountered a few Japanese soldiers.

Frank thought that if he was not able to make contact with Colonel Collier, perhaps he should join John Boone. Here was a ready-made guerrilla organization that appeared to be engaged in sincere efforts to help MacArthur and thus further the war effort. But there were problems. To begin with, Boone moved around constantly, traveling through the jungle on foot and staying a night or two at the headquarters of each of his local organizations. This mode of living offered Boone some protection from the Japanese and helped him maintain control over his men, but Frank knew that in his own weakened physical condition he could not keep up such a pace.[39] He also was concerned that Boone's security was lax—there were simply too many people who knew about him and knew where he was. And, with aggressive hotheads like Captain Magtanggol around, the Japanese would undoubtedly take frequent reprisals on the local villages. That, in turn, would eventually lead to someone turning him in.

On top of everything else, how much good could Boone really do? The information on ship movements and Japanese troop concentrations would, no doubt, be of value to MacArthur sooner or later. But ambushing a few Japanese patrols in the jungle would make little difference to the overall war effort, and it would surely bring grief to the local civilians.

Frank decided to stick with his original plan and join Colonel Collier as soon as possible.

But what if the plan to join Collier fell through? In that case, Frank would move himself and the other three Americans out of the *palay* shed to a new location, deeper in the jungle and higher on the mountain, hopefully high enough to get away from the malaria-infested lowland mosquitoes.[40] They would all be safer hidden deep in the jungle while Frank figured out a way for them to get out of the Philippine Islands and back to the U.S. Army.

Back at camp Payumo finally visited, bringing with him Tivo's daughter Rebecca, a Catholic priest named Father Cabanguis, and a young woman called "Ding" who, like Payumo's bride, was a nurse.[41] They brought some very welcome lettuce, tomatoes, onions, candy, and a towel for Frank. They also brought news that Russia had declared war on Japan and that the war would soon be over.

Frank dismissed the war news as another fanciful rumor, and felt uncomfortable that Payumo had brought more people to the camp. Now two more individuals, Father Cabanguis and nurse Ding, knew about Frank and the other Americans, and knew where they were hiding. Now it was even more important that they not stay at the *palay* shed any longer.

Frank asked Payumo to go to Tala, find Placido, and send him to visit. If Frank could not find Colonel Collier, he intended that the new campsite would be almost halfway back to Tala and he wanted Placido to supply the camp. With both Placido and Tivo providing supplies, they would have some backup if anything happened to either of their benefactors. Payumo promised to contact Placido.

Frank decided not to tell Tivo until everything was ready. No sense in alienating him any further. Eddie Wright, he knew, would disagree. Frank would have a talk with Eddie Wright.

A few days later an unexpected messenger arrived with a typewritten note for Frank:

Dear Sir

Your invitation to the other side has been verified. It came from Col. C thru [name obscured] to Lt. C and so to yourself. I have checked back on it and believe it to be reliable.

My courier to the other side has not yet returned. It seems that [name obscured] is keeping him there to help him thru a serious attack of malaria. I have sent another, to check up on that rumor about them moving but have not received an answer as yet. I will send another message as soon as possible.

I am sending this message because I suppose you are anxious to know what effort I am making.

The route from your place to the other side is a cinch at the present time. No Jap or Constabulary activity anywhere in this district.

My next message will leave you free to make your decision. Till then…

Respectfully,

B [42]

Frank gave the messenger a note to take back, asking for Boone's help getting to Collier's headquarters.

The next morning a worried and agitated Tivo Leonzon appeared with his weekly load of supplies. He stammered out that the Japanese had arrested Delphin Pamintuan for suspected participation in guerrilla activities.[43]

Tivo was visibly shaken. The Japanese had ordered all Filipinos to stay in town, and anyone who went up into the mountains would be considered an outlaw.[44] He urged Eddie Wright to have the Americans get their belongings together and move to a more secluded place, away from his rice paddies, away from his *palay* shed—immediately. It was too dangerous to stay at his shed any longer. Frank readily agreed. Tivo directed two of his sons, Nicholas and Benjamin, to guide the Americans to a small jungle clearing about 300 yards farther upstream and help the Americans construct a *bahay*.[45]

***

In January 1943, Lieutenant General Shegenori Kuroda took over as Japanese commander in the Philippines, and Imperial Headquarters instructed General Kuroda to do something about the guerrillas. Their activities were keeping large numbers of Japanese soldiers tied up on guard duty around various cities and commercial centers in the Philippines. The general devised a comprehensive, two-pronged approach.

First, he ordered a two-month long military crackdown against the guerrillas. [46]

Simultaneously, he had Colonel Akira Nagahama, chief of the *Kempei-tai*, implement a policy called "Attraction." The new policy provided amnesty for any guerrillas or renegade Americans who gave themselves up, good until March 10, 1943. Anyone caught after that date would be shot.[47] General Kuroda also increased the reward for Filipinos turning in Americans or guerrillas to fifty pesos each.

For icing on the cake, General Kuroda announced that once all of the guerrillas gave themselves up, Japan would grant independence to the Philippines.[48] This seemed like an especially brilliant move, because the only reason the Japanese could think of for the widespread pro-American feelings in the Philippines was the fact that the United States had promised the islands their independence, to take effect on July 4, 1946.

The new programs paid off well for Major Nakai and his *Kempei-tai* associates in Balanga, the provincial capital of Bataan. There, two brothers, who were themselves medics for the guerrillas, turned in an American major named Stanley Holmes and six American soldiers for the reward money.[49] Then an American captain named Dallas Vinnette was captured near Orani and with him was a Filipino refugee from a mountain refugee settlement named Tala.[50] Major Nakai had been suspicious of the Tala settlement for some time. He promptly sent a contingent of soldiers up the mountain to Tala to arrest everybody there. All of the men, women and children were brought to the Japanese Army prison in Orani. The captures of Holmes and Vinnette had been a surprise—the only American officer Major Nakai was really looking for in Bataan was a colonel named Frank Loyd.

Reprisals were carried out on several villages known to harbor guerrillas, especially those supporting a man who called himself Captain Magtanggol. Major Nakai's soldiers imprisoned and tortured a number of people in those villages.[51] He was certain the villagers would soon tire of this treatment and turn the guerrilla leaders over to the authorities. In fact, the technique had already worked. A Filipino citizen named Ruben Bondoc revealed that several of Major Nakai's own Filipino agents were actually guerrillas. Although Major Nakai had been certain of their loyalty, the *Kempei-tai* executed all of them.

Recently, Major Nakai had received a more ominous report. An American lieutenant named Henry Clay Conner was rumored to have recently arrived in Bataan or Zambales. The *Kempei-tai* believed that Conner was put ashore by a submarine in advance of a planned American attack.[52] Major Nakai sent a 300-man task force out to look for Lieutenant Conner.

On February 22, 1943 the task force raided two camps on Mount Malasimbo, just north of Dinalupihan. The first raid hit the American refugee camp run by William and Martin Fassoth. It was the third raid on the Fassoths since the conquest of the Philippines, but the camp kept springing up again, each time farther back in the jungle. The task force commander reported to Major Nakai that the raiding party surrounded the camp in the pre-dawn darkness and closed in at first light. They killed a number of Americans and Filipinos in the camp, but unfortunately the two Fassoth brothers escaped once again. A handsome reward was being offered for each of them. [53]

The other raid that day was on a guerrilla headquarters located nearby. Unfortunately again, most of the occupants escaped. But according to the reports Major Nakai received, Lieutenant Conner and two other Americans, named Boone and Ramsey, had been there. [54]

Around the country, the reports said, other Japanese commanders had arrested thousands of people in similar raids. The Philippine guerrilla organization, such as it was, was surely close to collapse.

Major Nakai and most of the Japanese in the Philippines thought it strange that this was the only country in Japan's Greater East Asia Co-Prosperity Sphere where there was a guerrilla problem. In British Malaya, the Dutch East Indies, French Indo-China and the other countries in the Pacific, the natives had, by and large, welcomed the Japanese troops who helped them throw off the shackles of the European colonists. Among the Filipinos, though, it was surprising that so many still supported the old American government.

These Filipinos, he thought to himself, *who can figure them out*?

XI. War News

"Oh, Evelyn. It's Maxie! He's alive!"

Evelyn Loyd had dropped by to visit with Evelyn Noble. For the last several days Evelyn Noble had been unusually happy and upbeat when they talked on the telephone, and Evelyn Loyd wanted to find out what was up.

"How do you know? Where is he?"

In her own restrained way, Evelyn Noble was beside herself with excitement. She said that a man from Army Intelligence had come to her house earlier in the week.

"He said that Maxie is in the mountains. With the guerrillas. He is ALIVE!"

"What about FRANK?"

Evelyn Loyd was joyfully glad for the Noble family, but she was excited too! If they had found Maxie, where was Frank?

"You have to keep this very hush-hush. Very quiet. The man from Intelligence swore me to secrecy. But I *have* to tell you. If Maxie is there, Frank must be with him. Or, at least somewhere nearby." [1]

Evelyn Noble explained that the man would not tell her very much except to say that Maxie was alive, well physically and mentally, he was not a POW, and that he was in touch with Army Intelligence. He praised the work Maxie was doing with the guerrillas. For security reasons, he could not say any more than that, but he was pleased to be able to bring her this news.

"Have you told the girls?"

"Oh, no. They're too young. The war isn't over yet. They'll know everything in due time."

Evelyn Loyd was truly happy for Evelyn Noble. The woman had been extremely depressed ever since the fall of Bataan, ten months ago. Perhaps now she could regain some of her sanity.

As she drove home, Evelyn Loyd felt encouraged. She had always maintained faith that Frank was alive somewhere, and it made sense that Frank and Maxie would be together. They were close friends and they were both adventurous, outdoor types. Maxie and another friend, Martin Moses, had been commanders of Philippine Army regiments in southern Bataan. Frank was stationed nearby, as senior advisor to the Philippine Constabulary troops on the south coast of Bataan. If Maxie had escaped the Japanese there was a good chance Frank had too, and it was likely that they would all be together.

A few days later Evelyn Noble called. She had talked to Dayton Moses, Martin Moses' father. Two intelligence officers visited him also, gave him a similar report on Martin, and asked him not to tell anyone except immediate family.[2] But he had telephoned Evelyn Noble and after a few minutes of cautious, verbal sparring they told each other what they knew. It was obvious that Martin Moses and Maxie Noble were somewhere together in the mountains with the guerrillas. However, Dayton Moses had no news about Frank.

At the weekly meetings of the "Fiddlers' Club," Evelyn Noble soon became something of a celebrity. Word got around that Maxie Noble was a leader of the guerrilla armies in North Luzon, and everyone was excited for her. It was rather romantic to know that her husband was carrying on the war behind the Japs' backs while the rest of the husbands waited it out in prisoner of war camps.[3]

No one talked about Evelyn Loyd's husband, though. Privately, Evelyn Noble assured her that Frank was bound to be safe with Maxie in North Luzon. His name had just not surfaced yet.

As days turned to weeks, Evelyn Loyd waited for her visit from Army Intelligence.

XII. The Dangerous Benefactor

Although Tivo Leonzon continued to supply food as agreed, and even brought newspapers and magazines to Frank Loyd and his companions, there was no sign of the guerrilla, John Boone, or of Frank's friend Jose Payumo. Frank learned that Sam Zozabrado, the Philippine Scout who was supposed to go to Manila, pawn Frank's college ring, buy Atabrine, and bring back money from Colonel Rafael Jalandoni, had never left. Frank was particularly anxious to hear from John Boone. He wanted the guerrilla corporal-turned-captain to take him to Colonel James Collier.

But if Boone could not take him to Colonel Collier, Frank needed to make contact with Placido in order to implement his backup plan—a move farther back in the jungle where the men could be supplied by both Placido and Tivo. Frank's only way to contact Placido was through

Payumo, but it had been a month since the forest ranger last visited the camp.

Something was wrong. Frank began to suspect that Tivo was deliberately keeping Payumo away.

When Tivo's son Nick brought supplies on March 8, 1943, he told Frank that the Japanese had raided John Boone's guerrilla camp on Mount Malasimbo. According to Nick, many of the guerrillas there were killed and all the rest surrendered.[1] Boone had fled north into the Zambales Mountains.

"There is no one left to take you to Colonel Collier."

"You mean Boone, Magtanggol, and *all of* the guerrillas are gone?"

"Yes."

"Where is Jose Payumo? Why hasn't he come up here?"

Nick reported that Payumo was "too busy" to come meet with Frank.[2]

Frank did not believe that either. He wrote a brief letter to Payumo, sealed it, and gave it to Nick to take back. He was certain that the letter would bring Payumo to the camp. If not, it could only be because Tivo was interfering and keeping them cut off from everyone else.

March 9 was Roy Reynolds' daughter's birthday. He had last seen her when she was three months old. Now she was two. The men conducted a brief birthday celebration in her honor.

Frank decided that the time had come to talk to Eddie Wright about his backup plan. He took Eddie aside.

"Look, our situation here is precarious. We need a safer place to hide, and we need to find a source of supplies that is not controlled by Tivo." Frank's low, precise drawl had a way of capturing his listener's attention. "I'll tell you something else, too. We need a stash of food to keep on hand as a reserve. In case Tivo quits us. Or something happens to him."

Eddie looked at Frank. "Tivo is a good, reliable man. I'm not too worried. The Japs haven't ventured south of the highway, and there's no reason for them to. The guerrillas are in the Zambales jungle, on the north side.

"The Japs aren't worried about Tivo, or us—they don't even know we're here.

"Yeah, it would be good to have other contacts," he said to Frank. "But Tivo's done a lot for us. You're being pretty unfair." [3]

Roy Reynolds and Al Romaine joined the conversation, and the four men began to brainstorm ideas about what to do. In spite of Eddie's apparent lack of concern, everyone agreed that it would be good to have an alternate source of supplies. But maybe they could find another benefactor—someone to supplement what Tivo was doing for them rather than move farther back in the jungle. Maybe they could find a way to get out of the jungle altogether. Frank offered to write a letter to an acquaintance in Manila, Lieutenant Colonel Narciso Manzano. Manzano, a Philippine Scout engineer, had been Frank's neighbor at Fort McKinley. Eddie Wright and his wife, Marge, were also friends of the Manzanos.

Frank's letter asked for malaria medicine and money to purchase supplies, and asked if there was any chance of the men being smuggled out of the country to Australia. Sam Zozabrado could deliver the letter, if he ever went to Manila. But the only way Frank could get the letter to Zozabrado was to give it to Tivo. He wrote a note to Zozabrado and asked him to deliver the letter to Manzano. He also reminded Sam to contact Frank's other friend in Manila, Colonel Rafael Jalandoni. The note said to keep these communications secret from Tivo Leonzon.

Eddie Wright disagreed. "Tivo is reliable and honest. He doesn't want anything more than to help."

Frank did not buy it. He placed the letter in a sealed envelope. For good measure, he also wrote a note to Victor

Pamintuan, and asked him to find John Boone and request that Boone take them to Colonel Collier.

On March 12, Tivo came up to the *bahay* with supplies. Frank asked about the letter he had previously given Nick to deliver to Payumo. Had it been delivered?

"No."

Had Tivo or Nick talked to Payumo about coming up to the *bahay*?

"No."

Frank was furious. At this point, the four Americans were at Tivo's mercy. Frank was certain that Tivo was holding them incommunicado on the mountainside for some purpose, although it was not clear why.

Frank maintained his composure and gave the two envelopes to Tivo.[4] There was no other choice. The Americans certainly could not go down to Kulò themselves—with the high level of anti-guerrilla activity going on they would be captured immediately. Tivo Leonzon was truly their only contact with the outside world.

Four days later Nick Leonzon came up to the camp with some extra food, a gift from Victor Pamintuan. Nick could not say whether his father had delivered the letters to Victor or to Sam Zozabrado.

"What about John Boone?" Frank asked.

"When Victor gave this to me to bring here, he said nothing about John Boone."

Frank was more convinced than ever that Tivo and Nick were deliberately keeping them isolated. He wrote a note for Nick to take to his father, telling him to bring Sam Zozabrado up to the *bahay* or Frank was going to come down to the village and get him himself.

Two days later Jose Payumo and Sam Zozabrado showed up, guided by Nick Leonzon.

Payumo took Frank to one side. Out of Nick's earshot, he said that he had gone to Tala to find Placido and arrange for supplies for the new camp. When he got there the settlement was deserted.

"I talked to farmers near the foot of the trail. They say in January, the Japanese arrested everyone in Tala settlement. They herded them all down the mountain to Orani and put them in prison. Men, women, children—everyone. It has been three months now, and they are still there." [5]

Frank was stunned! Placido, his whole family, and everybody else in Tala, were in prison. No wonder he never came back.

Sam Zozabrado's story was less dramatic. According to Zozabrado, his father wanted him to return to their family's home on Cebu Island and he sent him 150 pesos to book passage on a ferry to take him there. It had taken Sam some time to decide what to do, but he had decided to stay in Olongapo for the time being. Now that he had made his decision he would be leaving for Manila soon, to contact Frank's friends. To substantiate his story, Sam showed Frank the 150 pesos.[6]

Frank paid little attention to Sam Zozabrado. That night he prayed for the safety of Placido and his family. He did not want to be responsible for bringing more problems, or even death, to the people who helped him. They had done so much—and their reward was a Japanese prison. Now, more than ever, Frank resolved to find a way to get out of the Philippines and back to the U.S. Army.

***

On his next visit, Tivo Leonzon reported that Major Nakai had issued new orders: all Filipinos were to stay out of the jungle, including the jungle on the south side of the highway, for the next ten days. The amnesty program had expired and the Japanese increased the reward for turning in Americans to 1,000 pesos each.[7] For the first time they were offering Bureau of Constabulary men a reward for each American they caught—a 500 peso bonus in addition to their regular pay.

The newspapers Tivo brought had stories about large numbers of guerrillas, including some Americans, who surrendered under the amnesty plan, and of several guerrilla leaders who were captured or killed in the crackdown. Japanese soldiers stuck the severed head of one of Colonel Claude Thorp's men, red-headed, red-bearded Captain Ralph McGuire, on a pole and paraded it through the villages of Zambales Province as an example of American weakness.[8]

The Japanese were turning up the heat.

Frank asked Tivo to bring additional food supplies to the *bahay* so the men would have a food reserve in case anything happened.

"This is important," Frank said, "in case the Japs come up here looking for us, or if, God forbid, anything should happen to you."

Then Frank handed Tivo his diary pages from January 1 through March 24, 1943 and asked him to give them to Payumo for safekeeping until the end of the war.

Shortly after Tivo left that day, Frank kicked himself mentally when he realized what he had done. His diary contained notes about all of his suspicions and misgivings about Tivo. If Tivo read it, the man would be deeply offended.

Two days later Tivo came back to the *bahay* with the diary. He had read it. He was terribly offended by what Frank Loyd had written about him. He refused to pass the diary on to Payumo.[9]

Frank told Tivo that he had written only his own private thoughts, and that he had not meant to disparage Tivo's character to Payumo or anyone else. Reluctantly, Frank forced himself to apologize to Tivo.

Tivo had wondered about Frank's attitude before. Now, he harbored a deep resentment toward Frank Loyd.

***

On April 8, 1943, Frank and his three companions marked their first anniversary—one full year of hiding in the jungle. Frank Loyd and Eddie Wright hiked farther up the mountain and selected a site for a new camp. They picked a small clearing between two ridges that was well protected. It had only one entrance from the mountainside trail, but there were several possible emergency exits. It was close to the stream and under a heavy canopy of trees that would obscure it from aerial observation. It looked like a good place for a rainy-season *bahay*.

As the two men took turns hacking away brush and undergrowth with their single, dull bolo, they again discussed the possibility of getting off Luzon. They had heard nothing more about Boone or Collier, and with all the anti-guerrilla activity going on both of those men might well be dead. And they might be next. Frank said that if they could get a sailboat large enough to negotiate the ocean winds and currents, they might have a decent chance of making it across the open sea to China. He had been thinking about escaping by boat for some time, and he told Eddie that sailing to China would be more feasible than trying to navigate through the many islands and Japanese naval bases between Luzon and Australia. In crossing the South China Sea they would only have to avoid being stopped by a Japanese warship. That would be largely a matter of luck, but it was a big ocean and luck might be with them. The south coast of China covered the entire area northwest of Luzon, so precise navigation would not be required.[10] To sail the southern route to Australia would be much more difficult.

Eddie listened to Frank's idea with skeptical interest.

Frank went on. “When the rainy season starts, the prevailing winds across the South China Sea shift to the north, toward China. It’s about 800 miles. With the wind behind us I think we can make it in about twelve days.” He said that it would be necessary to complete the trip by the end of June, before typhoons began.

Eddie thought about it. Then he suggested that they go ahead with work on the rainy-season *bahay* since it would be difficult to get an adequate sailboat.

Frank agreed. But the prospect of having two options to choose from, sail to China or wait out the rainy season high up on the mountainside, gave Frank a measure of comfort. At least they were doing something positive about taking control of their destiny.

Back at camp that night, Frank explained his idea to Roy and Al while Eddie listened. Everyone was skeptical, but they all agreed to think about it. Inevitably, the conversation turned to thoughts of home and of their wives and families. Eddie Wright was a man who was passionately in love with his wife, Marge, missed her, and readily said so.[11] She had been pregnant when she left the Philippines on the *Washington* with Evelyn Loyd and the other women. The baby would have been born around the first of January 1942, and would now be more than a year old. Eddie had no idea whether his child was a boy or a girl.

Al Romaine had never been much of an outdoorsman, and was truly miserable here in the woods. As an Army reservist he had done his brief stint of active duty, sent in his correspondence courses regularly, and attended his monthly reserve meetings. But he was intimidated by the jungle and largely unable to fend for himself. Although he was almost forty years old, he had gotten married for the first time shortly before he was called up and sent to the Philippines. Al Romaine longed for his home and his family.[12] But when it came to sailing a boat across the ocean in hopes of getting home, the idea did not appeal to Al.

Roy Reynolds, on the other hand, seemed willing to give it a try. He and Frank had kicked this and several other ideas around in conversations, building "air castles" as they "what-iffed" different possibilities. Roy was a guy who usually kept his spirits up, maintained his health, and occasionally injected a little wry humor. He was fond of assuring the others that when, not if, they all got back home his beautiful wife, Jeannie, and their young daughter would be waiting for him. But the others had better brace themselves, because their wives would no doubt have given them up for dead and found new husbands.[13]

Frank was certain that Evelyn would have faith that he was alive and able to take care of himself. He and Evelyn had hunted and fished together everywhere from the Texas Gulf Coast to the Alaskan wilderness. Frank regretted the agony his family must be going through, not knowing what happened to him or whether he was dead or alive.

Each day, two or three of the men hiked up the trail and continued work on the rainy-season *bahay*. As they worked, the Japanese launched a new drive to finish off the guerrillas on the north side of the highway.[14] The men could hear gunfire coming from across the valley.

Tivo's food deliveries suddenly stopped.

They had never received any of the extra food Frank requested for their reserve, so Frank's concern about their supply situation was now a genuine problem. They carefully rationed what rice they had left, not knowing when, or how, they might get more. They began scrounging the local woods for edible leaves, lizards and snails.

Their supply of Atabrine tablets had long been exhausted and as days passed without sufficient food, the four men grew weaker and more susceptible to malaria. They stripped the bark off a Dita tree, the only one they could find, and boiled it to make tea to stave off the disease. Work on the rainy-season *bahay* came to a halt. The four men had to spend all of their time looking for edible plants and creatures around their camp.

Their food supplies ran out. Days went by when leaves, snails and/or Dita bark tea was their only nourishment.[15] As he grew weaker, Frank's eyesight and hearing began to fade, and his weak arm and leg ached continuously. Al Romaine was having trouble with his vision, too. Areas in front of both of them would fade from light to dark. When Frank tried to read some of the old newspapers Tivo had brought, the letters and words on the page just disappeared. The men attributed their problems to the effects of Dita bark tea, and to vitamin deficiency.[16]

Easter came on April 18 in 1943, and with it came early, monsoon-like rains, and an unexpected visitor, Roque Zozabrado, Sam's brother.[17] Hunger gnawed at Frank and he felt the stirrings of malaria inside as Roque began his story.

Roque said that Sam Zozabrado had gone to Manila two weeks ago, and he managed to meet Colonel Rafael Jalandoni. Jalandoni did not give Sam any money. Instead, he sent a note with a list of questions that only Frank Loyd would be able to answer. Sam had pawned Frank's ring, as instructed, but he only got fifteen pesos for it and was unable to buy any Atabrine. Instead, he brought back sulfanilamide, sodium bicarbonate, and salicylate.[18] Roque handed the medicines to Frank.

Frank was immediately suspicious. He was certain that the gold in his ring should have been worth at least 100 pesos, and Sam's story seemed questionable. Frank thought that Jalandoni would have given Sam a little money based on his previous generosity with Placido, but instead he sent the letter and the list of questions. Jalandoni must be suspicious too.

"Why was Sam gone so long?" Frank asked.

"I apologize for Sam taking so long to come back. When he came back from Manila, he came down sick. Very sick. He was too sick to come and meet you."

Probably caught VD, Frank thought to himself.

"But I am going to Manila myself, now. I will take any messages you want to send."

Frank wrote a brief note to Jalandoni answering his questions. In it, he outlined the plan to sail to China and he asked Jalandoni to give Roque money for supplies. He gave Roque a shopping list of items they needed immediately and told him to use Jalandoni's money to buy the things on the list. The list included shoes, with each man's size. Other problems aside, the wet jungle floor had taken its toll on the men's footgear to the point that none of them had anything on their feet but worn-out soles strapped on by pieces of rags.

As a back-up, Frank gave Roque a note addressed to another contact in Manila, Juan Elizalde. Elizalde, a wealthy businessman and polo player, was a friend of Zero Wilson and he might remember Frank from the days when Frank organized the national shooting matches in Manila.[19] If Jalandoni was unable to help, perhaps Elizalde could.

Roque said that he would leave for Manila that afternoon.

Frank felt a little more confident about Roque. Perhaps he could become their lifeline to Jalandoni or Elizalde and, eventually, their ticket out of the Philippines. As the men watched him head down the trail to Manila, Frank's hopes were piled on Roque's shoulders.

April 20th was Frank Jr.'s fifteenth birthday. But there was no celebration at the small, muddy camp. There was nothing to celebrate with.

On April 27, Tivo Leonzon finally appeared with a load of rice. As the men prepared a fire to cook their first real meal in weeks, Tivo explained that Japanese checkpoints on the roads and trails, and the recent bad weather, had made it impossible to get up the mountainside to make deliveries. The Japanese had backed off, though, and now he could resume his supply runs. However, there was a shortage of vegetables in the villages, so all he could bring was rice.

Frank, hungry and weak, was suspicious of Tivo's excuse for not bringing vegetables. Probably, Tivo just did not want to carry them up the mountain. Without better diets, Frank and the others would soon be too weak to escape if the Japanese located their hideout.

Over the next few weeks Tivo made several small, sporadic deliveries, but the quantities of food he brought would barely last from one delivery to the next. The men began feeling a little better, but what would happen if Tivo stopped coming? Frank again asked Tivo to bring extra supplies so the men would have a reserve on hand for emergencies.

***

As the men slowly regained their strength, they resumed work on the new *bahay*. It measured eleven feet by seventeen feet, much larger than any of the cramped quarters the men lived in previously. It stood nearly six feet off the ground, on stilts made of wooden poles rather than bamboo. It was high enough for the men to build an elevated firebox underneath which could be used for cooking during rainy weather and for warming the *bahay* when the nights grew cool. They made a table and two benches so they would have a place to sit outside. By moving the table under the *bahay*, they could spend time outside even in wet weather.

Instead of a thatched roof and woven-mat sides, the men split bamboo poles and tied them onto the roof and sides of the structure with rattan strips in an overlapping, alternating pattern like a tile roof. As the weather turned windy and rainy, the new *bahay* would be sturdy, comfortable, and dry. They built the entire structure without the use of a single nail.

Frank set up an alarm system consisting of loose vines placed across the approaches to the *bahay*, then strung more vines to the door of the structure where he hung the metal plate from his mess kit. He tied the ends of the vines to a metal fork positioned next to the plate. If anyone disturbed the vines the fork would clank against the plate, hopefully loud enough to wake the men in time to make their escape.

With the help of a Negrito who occasionally visited the camp, Frank cut bamboo poles and rattan straps and made himself a bed. Seeing the new bed, Roy Reynolds, then the others, asked how it was made and began working on their own. Frank wrote in his diary that he had accomplished one of his main objectives—to get the other men interested in working on their own safety, sanitation, and comfort.[20]

As the men moved into their new quarters, the Japanese newspapers reported that more Americans and guerrillas had surrendered, been captured, and been killed. According to the Japanese, guerrilla resistance had been overcome, and therefore the Philippines would be granted independence as promised by General Kuroda.

***

The weather turned sultry and sticky by the time Roque Zozabrado returned on May 8. He reported that on his way to Manila a man stopped him and took him to a meeting of several guerrilla leaders, one of whom was John Boone.

Boone gave Roque an envelope to deliver to a woman at a nightclub in Manila. Remembering Frank and the other Americans, Boone also gave Roque sixty pesos to buy shoes for them. Boone had not fled the area at all, but was in hiding with his Filipina wife's family near Dinalupihan.[21]

When Roque got to Manila, Colonel Jalandoni read Frank's responses to the questions, and he gave Roque some money and assurances of more financial support in the future. Roque had gone shopping, and he turned his purchases over to Frank: 300 Atabrine tablets, one pair of shorts, one pair of pants, one undershirt, some pork sausage, some gauze bandages, and no shoes.

Except for the Atabrine, none of the items Roque delivered matched Frank's list. Frank asked how much money Jalandoni gave him.

"Four hundred pesos."

A considerable sum.

"I could not find any shoes in these large sizes," Roque said, referring to Frank's list. "So I bought you these supplies instead."

Frank estimated the value of all of the items be about 315 pesos—300 pesos for the Atabrine, fifteen for the rest.

Roque confessed to having bought an extra pair of shorts and pants, three more undershirts and four pair of socks, some of which he lost. The rest he kept for himself.

"Where is the rest of the money?"

"I spent it all." [22]

It had been three weeks since Roque left with the shopping list and the letter to Rafael Jalandoni. He had gotten the money, but aside from the Atabrine he had come back with nothing of value. And he even kept part of it for himself.

Frank was angry. He had put a lot of hope in Roque.

As Frank stared at Roque, he began to wonder about the 150 pesos that Sam Zozabrado showed him eight weeks ago. If Sam's father really wanted him to come home, it certainly would not have cost 150 pesos to book passage to Cebu. Sam might have gotten that money from Narciso Manzano in Manila, kept it for himself, and then concocted the story about the trip to Cebu as a cover.[23]

For the moment, Frank decided not to make an issue of it. Roque Zozabrado was still their only real contact with the outside world besides Tivo Leonzon. Roque might still be useful. Tersely, he thanked Roque for his help and sent him on his way.

Once Roque was gone, Eddie Wright spoke directly to Frank.

"We can't trust those guys. We have to rely on Tivo."

After some discussion, the men decided to write a letter to an acquaintance of Roy Reynolds, a Spaniard in Manila named Enrique Brias. Brias was associated with the wealthy Ayala family, he was a friend of Juan Elizalde, and he might be willing to help them financially.[24] They would ask Brias for money, ask his advice about a safer place to hide, and what they could do to assure a safe stream of food supplies.

But how to get the letter to Brias? Nobody trusted the Zozabrado brothers anymore, and Frank and Roy wanted to keep the message to Brias secret from Tivo.

Eddie disagreed. He insisted that they be open with Tivo and tell him what they were planning. If they tried to keep the plans secret and Tivo found out, he would feel betrayed and might quit supplying them altogether.

"Besides," said Eddie, "Tivo has been our benefactor for more than a year. I would be violating my obligations to Tivo if I don't tell him."

Frank decided that he needed to gain control of the situation.

"I'll write the letter to Brias as my own idea, not speaking for the group. We will keep it secret from Tivo. If the plans don't work out for us, and Tivo finds out, you can blame me. I will leave and go somewhere else." [25]

Eddie thought it over briefly.

"Okay."

Frank was a little surprised.

As the conversation continued, he tried to give Eddie several openings, but Eddie did not seem to have any problem with the idea of Frank leaving and going somewhere else. In fact, the prospect of Frank's leaving seemed to add a little enthusiasm to Eddie's voice.

Roy Reynolds changed the subject. "Suppose we have Tivo solicit money from Brias to cover his cost of supporting us. We give him a letter of introduction, and in the letter we ask about food supplies and a safer place to hide. The letter tells Brias not to talk to Tivo about those things. But if Brias sends us any money, we give it to Tivo."

Roy's idea seemed like a good way to get Tivo involved without revealing too much of what they were up to. Everyone agreed to the plan.

Frank began to feel some confidence in their situation. Tivo would be their messenger to Brias, and they could also maintain contact with Colonel Jalandoni through Roque

Zozabrado as a backup. Frank always liked the idea of having a backup.

May 12 was Evelyn's birthday. It had been two years since she left to return to the United States and more than a year since Frank had heard from her. He wrote in his diary:

> Two years tomorrow since I have seen her. If only I could send her my love, and beg forgiveness for not assuring her of it more often when we were together rather than taking it for granted as I always did.[26]

On May 21, Tivo returned from Manila. He had met Brias. Brias sent 100 pesos to the Americans and said that he would try to send a similar amount each month.

Elated, Frank and Roy gave twenty-two pesos to Tivo to reimburse him for his travel expenses. Then they gave him the rest of the money to purchase the emergency supplies Frank had requested.

But there was no letter from Brias about the other matters—food supplies or safer places to hide.

Frank and the others thanked Tivo for his efforts, then gave him another mission. Frank remembered hearing stories of a man named Vincente Bernia who had helped several Americans get to the Fassoth camp in the mountains north of Dinalupihan. Perhaps Tivo could contact Vincente Bernia. Frank explained his plan for sailing a boat out of the Philippines to China. Bernia might have access to a boat of the necessary size, and he was known to be a benefactor to refugee Americans.

Tivo looked at Frank like he was crazy.

"It's very dangerous for me to contact a man like Bernia. I will not take that chance."

Frank sat down and talked to Tivo. After much persuasive conversation, Tivo said that he would think about it.

Frank's sense of confidence was growing. He now had feelers out to four possible sources of help: Enrique Brias had sent them money and promised to send more, Roque Zozabrado had made contact with Rafael Jalandoni and got money and medicine, Sam Zozabrado was supposed to be making contact with Narciso Manzano in Manila, and now Tivo would, hopefully, make contact with Vincente Bernia. Surely one of those people could get them out of Tivo's control, and maybe even get them out of the Philippines. And there was still Colonel Collier.

***

At midnight on May 26, 1943, as Tivo Leonzon and his sons opened concealed compartments in the ends of several special bamboo poles, Tivo was carefully thinking about a serious problem.[27]

Up until January of this year, things had gone reasonably well. His house and farms had been largely spared the destruction that the war brought to many of his neighbors in Bataan. The bombs had missed, the battles were fought to the east and south of his property, and he and his family had survived without anyone being killed or seriously injured. Tivo even made a little profit when the war first got under way by selling produce and rice to the U.S. Army.

Once the Japanese took over, though, Tivo went back to doing business only with his own countrymen. Consorting with the Japanese in any way was against his principles. His neighbors who had done so attracted strong disapproval from the local guerrillas, and they also found their Japanese customers to be more than a little pushy. As the Japanese consolidated their hold on the country, they had turned to high-handed, outright oppression—taking what they wanted and arresting, or even killing, anyone who put up any protest.

Tivo and his family were members of the small Methodist church in Dinalupihan, and they believed in kindness and charity. It seemed natural, therefore, that when he learned of three American officers who had escaped from the Japanese he readily agreed to help them. But that was a year ago. Today, things were different, and he had to be very, very careful.

Tivo's sons finished pouring rice into the open ends of the bamboo poles. After the secret compartments were capped, they tied the poles onto the back of Tivo's carabao, mixed in with a load of regular bamboo.

Things had gone well that first year, Tivo remembered. The three Americans helped protect his crops from bandits and he kept them supplied with food and necessities. They said that once the war was over they would pay him for his services, and Tivo fully expected to collect on that promise. He had faith in General MacArthur, and if the Japanese fought the war the way they ran the Philippines, the Japanese were surely doomed.[28]

In January, this man Loyd happened onto the scene and things had gotten bad, then worse.

Loyd stirred up the other Americans against Tivo and his family—but why? Tivo had yet to figure out the reason.

Loyd brought in other men from the area, Victor Pamintuan and Jose Payumo, for example, and tried to make deals with them to supply the Americans instead of Tivo. Again, why? Surely, Loyd understood that it was both difficult and dangerous for Filipinos to help Americans, much less harbor them. Loyd and the other three were living on Tivo's property, eating Tivo's food, which Tivo brought to them in violation of the Japanese orders. Surely, Loyd understood that Tivo was risking not only his own life but also the lives of all of the male members of his family. If the Japanese found out about Tivo's support of these Americans, they would kill Tivo and all of his sons and burn their family's home to the ground. Ultimately, Tivo had gone to Pamintuan and Payumo and asked them to stay away.

As Tivo tied the last knot on the carabao, he told his sons to remain behind. He would make this delivery himself.

Because of Japanese patrols during the days and roadblocks in the evenings, he had to make the weekly deliveries early in the morning. After midnight, the Leonzon men would load up the carabao, and then proceed up the narrow pathway along the Myete River into the dark, mountainside jungle. As the carabao climbed the path by Tivo's rice paddies, it would step quietly past a few Nipa huts on the left side of the path, just under the trees, where Tivo's sharecroppers and their families lived. In the dim moonlight, or in pitch darkness on some nights, the carabao had to pick its way carefully and silently along.

Before Loyd came along all of this had been unnecessary, since the *palay* shed was just at the south end of the rice fields. When the Japanese launched their drive against the guerrillas in February, however, Tivo had asked the Americans to move farther up the trail. It was then that Tivo had begun the midnight supply runs—such precautions were necessary for the protection of his family.

But when the danger passed, Loyd refused to let the men move back to the *palay* shed. Instead, he had secretly built another *bahay* farther up the mountain, making the supply run even more difficult. The trip up to the clearing where Loyd wanted the supplies dropped took until daybreak. Tivo, or his sons, then had to return in the morning daylight, risking exposure to the Japanese.

As the carabao undulated and swayed beneath Tivo that morning, his patience wore increasingly thin. Inside the bamboo poles strapped to the animal was the third delivery of the food "reserves" Loyd had insisted upon, a full *kavanie* of rice. Nick and his brother-in-law, Tiburcio Paule, had previously delivered seventeen *gántas* of *munggó* beans.[29] Tivo could understand Loyd wanting to have the extra supplies on hand. But Loyd seemed incapable of understanding that such supplies, even the regular weekly supplies, were hard to come by. Tivo was, basically, bringing them produce off his own farm—produce he needed to sell to support his family.

The path up the mountainside crossed the Myete River in two places. As the carabao climbed out onto the bank after the first crossing, Tivo called out his password into the black jungle looming in front of him.

"*Ligtas nà*!" [It is safe!]

Deep within the dark labyrinth of tree trunks, another voice echoed the signal.

"*Ligtas nà*!" [30]

Farther up the river, unseen guerrilla sentries passed the word along. Tivo's carabao could climb the trail in safety along this side of the river, protected by the guerrillas. The Japanese seldom ventured out on night patrols, and they never came to this place after dark. If they did, they would be slaughtered.

Sometimes the Japanese blocked off the trail up the Myete River. At those times it was necessary to take the much longer route around Tama Ridge, to the east. That was the route Nick and Tiburcio had been forced to take when they delivered the *munggó* beans a week ago.

There were food shortages throughout Luzon now. Early in the year, heavy rains and floods had wiped out much of the rice and vegetable crops.[31] Worse than that, the Japanese confiscated many crops without paying the farmers a single peso.[32] In fact, the Japanese had recently made it a practice to pick out a farming village, enter early in the morning and round up all of the males. They would force the men into the fields and make them harvest their neighbors' rice crops, loading the *palay* into Japanese Army trucks. Nobody was paid anything—not the harvesters and not the farmers. In some places, guerrillas had stepped in and tried to protect the crops by shooting at the harvesters. But the attempt backfired horribly. The Japanese soldiers went into the village and shot everyone they thought sympathized with the guerrillas. Hundreds of innocent citizens had been killed.

Confiscation had not happened in Tivo's village so far, but several farmers told him that they were not going to plant crops next year—they planned to live off their seed money until MacArthur returned. To make matters worse, some of the guerrillas also began confiscating crops and other things they wanted, and killing persons they believed did business with the Japanese.[33]

As Tivo neared his destination, the eastern sky began to lighten.

Loyd now wanted Tivo to find a boat for him so he could take the others and sail to China. The man was obviously crazy. He certainly did not look like a sailor. Tivo could not obtain such a boat anyway—the Japanese would immediately want to know what he intended to do with it. And where would they get food to stock it for the trip? Tivo could not purchase those quantities in the marketplace, even if Brias in Manila supplied the money. The Japanese would want to know who was buying such large quantities and why.

Loyd even wanted Tivo to go to Vincente Bernia—a well-known underground leader who was being hunted by the Japs. Every one of Loyd's schemes seemed to end up with Tivo being set up for the Japanese.

At the clearing near the old camp, Wright and Reynolds were already waiting. They unloaded the carabao and poured the rice from the bamboo poles into bags. The men then slung the rice bags on shoulder-poles to carry them up the narrow trail to the new *bahay*.[34] They asked Tivo to come with them for yet another meeting.

When they arrived at the camp, Loyd and Romaine were cooking a pot of rice on the firebox under the *bahay*. Roy Reynolds took Tivo up into the building to show him how it was constructed and the pieces of furniture the men had made. Frank Loyd followed them up the steps.

As soon as they were all inside the room, Loyd asked if Tivo had made contact with Vincente Bernia to secure a boat. Tivo had told Loyd before that it was dangerous for him to even try to contact Bernia. Irritated, he told him so again.

Loyd pressed it. If Tivo was not going to contact Bernia, he should send Victor Pamintuan up to the *bahay* so Loyd could use him as his emissary instead.

Tivo tried to control his temper, but he could not.[35]

"I am not your servant! You *will not* order me to do such things!

"I do not like you. Neither do the others—not Pamintuan, not Payumo, anyone!

"I cannot go running around after Pamintuan or anyone else. I am too busy!"

Tivo was furious. His language would have been much stronger, but in his anger certain English words escaped him.

Frank Loyd bit his tongue and tried to sound conciliatory.

"Tivo, I cannot get these things done if you won't help me. You're just keeping us prisoners here if you won't help us arrange for our own safety or bring someone who will."

Loyd turned and went back outside.

As Reynolds showed Tivo around the *bahay*, they could hear the others outside talking and doing something with the rice.

Cutting Reynolds short, Tivo marched to the front porch of the building and looked down on Loyd and Wright, who were carefully emptying each sack of rice into bamboo joints, then transferring the rice to other containers. To his astonishment, Tivo realized that they were measuring the supplies he brought.

Angered and hurt, sweat beading out on his forehead, Tivo clambered down from the *bahay*, marched over to the bamboo table where the measuring had just been completed, and demanded to know what was going on. He knew now, for certain, that the Americans did not trust him. He also knew that he had not delivered all of the rice that had been ordered, because he was not able to get enough. But no one had even given him the opportunity to say so.

Eddie Wright invited Tivo to sit down on a bench on one side of the table. Al Romaine was seated on the other side, at the opposite end. Roy Reynolds sat down next to Tivo, across from Romaine. Eddie remained standing, slightly behind Tivo.

Frank Loyd walked up to the table and sat down across from Tivo, drawing his pistol as he did so. He set the pistol on the table in front of him, between the two men, pointed at Tivo.

Tivo stared at the gun in astonishment. It was positioned exactly between him and Loyd. It was an obvious threat.

After all he had done for these men, after all the risks and chances he had taken with his own life and the lives of his family, they were now threatening to kill him?

"You are short on rice. There are only ten and one-half *gántas* of beans." It was Loyd speaking, and there was a perverse, angry look in his eye.

"Where is the rest of the rice?"

In Loyd's low, flat drawl the question sounded like nothing short of an accusation.

Tivo could not stand it.

He leaped to his feet and snatched the gun off the table as he went.

As he staggered to get his balance, Tivo grasped the butt of the pistol in both hands with his index fingers looped around the trigger. His arms stiff and straight, he raised the pistol, pointed it directly at Frank Loyd's head and pulled the trigger.

Everyone around the table froze. The hammer snapped, but the weapon did not fire.

Tivo stared down the barrel at Loyd's face. Frank Loyd's small brown eyes were fixed directly on Tivo's eyes. No one moved.

Frank noted with interest that none of the officers around the table made any attempt to grab or to disarm Tivo. Everyone remained in their seats, watching.

The only person who even spoke was Eddie Wright.

“Tivo. TIVO!”

Tivo threw Frank’s gun down on the table and backed off, angry, embarrassed, and emotionally distraught. A black scowl covered his face.

“You are just a coward!” he screamed at Frank.

“If you weren’t with these others here, I would have let you starve a long time ago!”

Realization of what he had done sank slowly into Tivo Leonzon.

If Frank’s gun had been a revolver, like Tivo’s own pistol, Frank would be dead. Tivo did not know he had to chamber a round in the .45 automatic before pulling the trigger.

Tivo walked across the clearing, away from the table and the *bahay*. He sulked for a while with his shoulder against a tree, staring into the jungle. Eddie Wright and Al Romaine both went over to talk with him and tried to pacify him. They asked him to come back to the table and eat with them, but he refused.

Frank Loyd remained seated at the table and picked at his plate of rice while he considered what to do. He knew that it was his own attitude that had provoked Tivo Leonzon. He also knew that without Tivo, the other three Americans probably would not have survived. Their relationship dated back almost a year before Frank arrived on the scene. Frank was the newcomer.

After a while, Frank got up and walked over to Tivo.

"I want you to understand—I was speaking for myself. Not for the other three."

Tivo continued to stare into the dark jungle.

"I will make contact with friends elsewhere. I will find another place to go. I'll do it soon. I promise. But I can't just walk off into the jungle in the middle of the rainy season."

At that point Eddie Wright stepped in front of Frank.

"No." he said. "That's not the way it's gonna be."

Eddie told Tivo that he had to continue providing supplies for all four of the Americans, including Frank, or they would all leave and go elsewhere. Frank, a little surprised, was gratified by Eddie's support. Eddie took Tivo aside and made it clear that Tivo had to take care of them all.

After further discussion with Eddie, Tivo came back to talk to Frank. He apologized for his actions, and pled with Frank to understand his position.

Frank now understood. Life was not simple for Tivo Leonzon—it was dangerous. Very dangerous, thanks to the four Americans. It had been Tivo's choice to help them in spite of the danger, and Frank began to understand that.

As Tivo left the clearing he called back over his shoulder, "I will send my sons with your supplies on Monday."

Only Frank Loyd believed that he would.

XIII. The Shadow Society

Lieutenant Colonel Narciso Manzano was taken prisoner on Bataan with the other USAFFE soldiers when General Edward King surrendered. The Japanese loaded Manzano and other members of General King's staff into a few U.S. Army vehicles and trucked them seventy miles north to Camp O'Donnell. The Japanese commander at O'Donnell ordered them to get the camp ready to receive the thousands of men struggling up the bayside highway on the Death March.

The Philippine Army had local contractors build Camp O'Donnell in 1941 on a patch of flat ground astride a road that runs from Capas, Tarlac, to a barrio named O'Donnell.[1] The camp was built to house the 10,000 men of the 71st Infantry Division, but construction was incomplete when the Japanese attacked. Manzano, a civil engineer by trade, was a diminutive man with bulldog determination.

Looking around the camp, he determined that the approximately one-square-mile area could not possibly accommodate the 70,000 soldiers who were expected to arrive over the next two weeks.[2]

The Death March out of Bataan took each group of Filipino and American prisoners from six to nine days, depending on their starting point. They spent the last day of their journey packed into stinking, hot, railroad boxcars as they were hauled the last thirty miles from the San Fernando railway station to Capas, six miles from the gates of the prison. From there, they walked to the prison camp.

As the famished, dehydrated men stumbled into camp, Manzano began to hear stories of the horrible atrocities that Japanese and Formosan guards had committed each day on the Death March. The men were given little food, and the guards often denied them water even when spigots by the roadside were open and running. Helpless, sick prisoners had been beaten and murdered along the entire length of the road from Bataan to Camp O'Donnell.

In spite of the inadequate facilities at O'Donnell, the Japanese packed 50,000 Filipino soldiers into the south section of the camp and 8,700 Americans into the smaller, north section. Approximately 9,000 men had died, or been killed, on the Death March.[3]

In his "welcoming" speech to the exhausted prisoners Captain Yoshio Tsuneyoshi, the vituperative, portly camp commander, made it clear that any attempt at escape would result in immediate execution. Around the periphery of the camp were wooden guard towers manned by Japanese soldiers with machine guns. Captain Tsuneyoshi explained that he expected the prisoners to establish their own guards inside the camp and to assist their captors in preventing escape. For good measure, he instituted the "ten-man" rule: the guards assigned the prisoners to ten man squads. If any man escaped, all of the rest of the men in his squad would be executed.[4]

The captain made it clear that he considered the men to be "captives," not Prisoners of War. As long as there were guerrillas in the jungle fighting the Japanese, they would remain captives. Once all guerrilla resistance stopped, and only then, they might revert to Prisoner of War status.

Captain Tsuneyoshi concluded his remarks by reminding the men that they were guests of the Emperor. The Japanese government owed them nothing. Anything they got was courtesy of the Imperial Japanese Army.

After this welcoming speech, guards assigned the prisoners to rows of metal and thatched-roof barracks, literally filled to overflowing. There, they slept on two-tiered bamboo slat shelves that served as bunks. There was little running water. Latrines were simply open pits dug along one side of the camp.

Conditions were especially bad on the Filipino side, where the largely untrained and thoroughly demoralized troops had little appreciation for orders, officers or field hygiene. Disease was rampant. As the men ate their meager rations of rice and *munggó* beans, clouds of large, blue flies rose up out of the hot, sticky latrines and covered their food.

Manzano and the other engineering officers did what they could to organize the camp and improve conditions. They assigned mess personnel to the kitchens, although there was little to cook or to eat. Barracks roofs were repaired. The dilapidated water system was repaired and expanded. Hospital barracks, dubbed "wards," were established and staffed by the doctors and medics among the prisoners, although the Japanese provided little medicine to treat the sick or the wounded.

And graves were dug.

The hospital wards, numbered Ward One, Two, Three, etc., included a “Zero” ward. The worst cases were brought to the Zero Ward—men whose dysentery, malaria, gangrene or other infections were so advanced that they had no chance of survival. Men who could not walk, eat, or control their bodies. Men who cast off their rags and few personal possessions, and rolled about on the dirt floor in their own misery, despair and waste until they died. The screaming and the stench from the Zero Ward were overpowering. The smell permeated the camp and could be detected from miles away. The Zero Ward was a place no man approached, save the few medics assigned to check on the unfortunate souls there, and the burial details that came to take them away.

A medical corpsman named Patterson described his first visit to the Zero Ward:

> Upon my arrival I made my first tour through the wards and there I saw things that at that time was for me to force myself to believe. There were American soldiers weighing possibly less than 100 pounds in such condition of starvation it was actually possible to count their vertebra through their stomachs. Many of these men were lying on the floor without blankets and without clothing. Large ulcers two or three inches in diameter were on their backs, abdomen and navels, due to lack of mattresses. These patients, being unable to care for themselves or to move, and the lack of anyone of their buddies capable of looking out for them, were forced to lie on the floor covered entirely with their own feces and urine. Due to these conditions, flies completely covered their bodies.[5]

But the men in the Zero Ward were not the only ones who were dying. The Japanese expected the prisoners to work, not only within the camp but also on projects such as gathering arms and ammunition from the battlefields, repairing roads, and growing vegetables. The hard work combined with the prisoners' meager diet led to more deaths, as did Japanese cruelty. Men on burial details sometimes collapsed from the heat, lack of nutrition and hard labor. They were simply pushed into the mass graves with the other bodies and covered up—sometimes still alive.

In return for their labor, the Japanese paid the prisoners a few centavos to one peso per day. The prisoners were required to use their wages to purchase their own food and medicine.[6] If a man was too sick to work, he was not paid. A small, ruthless black market in food and medicine quickly developed. The ability to pay began to determine who lived and who died.[7]

The Japanese appointed Personnel Officers for each side of the camp: Lieutenant Colonel Narciso Manzano on the Filipino side, and Lieutenant Colonel John E. Olson for the Americans. Every day these two men prepared status reports for the Japanese showing how many men were in the barracks, out on detail, in the hospital, and how many had died and been buried the previous day.

As he prepared his reports, and in meetings with a few other officers, Narciso Manzano vowed that his war with the Japanese was not over yet.[8]

Escape was seldom considered by any of the American prisoners. For the most part, the Americans were too weak, too conspicuous, and too closely watched by the external and internal guards. Most of the Americans were new to the Philippines, could not speak the languages, did not know the countryside or local customs, and had no jungle survival skills other than what they had learned on Bataan. To these men, the Japanese-controlled world outside the wire looked almost as forbidding as the camp itself.

Among the Filipinos, however, escape could mean the difference between survival and death. Some of these men, including the son of William Fassoth, began slipping away. A few would disappear from work details, others would slip through the wire, and others would simply vanish, one way or another. Narciso Manzano and Colonel Nemesio Catalan, the Adjutant on the Filipino side, decided to cover up the defections rather than include them on their daily reports to Captain Tsuneyoshi.[9]

Periodically, the Japanese prison administrators checked the adjutants' reports against their own tallies. Typically, the Japanese counted the men leaving on and returning from work details, the 400 or so bodies committed to graves each day, and prisoners shipped off to and received from other camps. They counted prisoners in their daily formations. But they never went near the Zero Ward, and men who threw away their clothes and identification, or went crazy from cerebral malaria, were sometimes hard to identify. Manzano and Catalan began a regular routine of creative accounting. By juggling the names and numbers of prisoners in the hospital wards, the Zero Ward, out on details, and dying, they were able to cover up for those who escaped, eventually shifting each one into the "dead and buried" column. If the Japanese discovered their deception it would result in their immediate deaths.

On June 6, 1942, the Japanese began moving the American soldiers out of Camp O'Donnell to a new camp, Cabanatuan, on the east side of the Luzon central plain. Conditions there were marginally better than at Camp O'Donnell, and they moved all but the sickest American prisoners out by the first week in July. The Filipino soldiers remained at Camp O'Donnell.

On the 4th of July, Colonels Olson and Manzano reported to the front of Captain Tsuneyoshi's headquarters, a two-story building at the top of a small hill overlooking the camp. There they waited, standing at attention in the hot sun. The two men stood for hours, a few feet apart, but were not allowed to speak. Olson and Manzano had exchanged a glance when they first met that day, but as they stood and waited in the sweltering heat, they never spoke a word. Any infraction by either man would result in a severe beating by the guards. When Tsuneyoshi's squat form finally waddled out onto the porch they delivered their reports, turned, and left.[10]

Colonel Manzano's report that day showed that 19,000 of the 50,000 Filipino soldiers brought to Camp

O'Donnell had already died.[11] Sadly, only a small portion of them were escapees. Colonel Olson's report showed that 1,460 of the 8,700 American soldiers had died.[12] They had all been at Camp O'Donnell less than three months.

The few Filipino civilians who were allowed to visit the camp were horrified at what they saw. Mrs. Josefa Escoda represented a group of young women from Manila's social circles who formed a charitable organization called the "Volunteer Social Aid Committee." [13] These young, Catholic debutantes initially intended to collect food and medicine, and send visitors to cheer up their fighting men who were now prisoners of the Japanese. Once Mrs. Escoda was permitted access to the camp it quickly became obvious that their planned efforts, although desperately needed, were far too small to make any significant difference. They began smuggling letters, news and money to the prisoners through Father Theodore Buttenbruch, a German priest who, as a member of the Chaplains' Aid Association, was permitted regular visits to the prison camps.[14] Within his vast memory Father Buttenbruch shuttled personal messages between family members on the outside and prisoners on the inside of the camps.

Josefa Escoda's husband, Tony, accompanied her to Camp O'Donnell on several visits.[15] For some inexplicable reason (from the Japanese point of view) he was allowed to speak privately with Brigadier General Vincente Lim, former commander of the Philippine Army's 41st Infantry Division. Tony Escoda was a reporter for the *Manila Daily Bulletin*, and he had been the New York *Herald Tribune's* Manila correspondent.

No word of the situation at Camp O'Donnell was ever allowed to appear in the Manila newspapers, of course. But by August 1942, news of the horrible conditions and high death rate at the camp leaked out, causing a major embarrassment to the Japanese government in Tokyo.[16] Captain Tsuneyoshi was relieved of command and replaced by heavy-set, mustachioed Lieutenant Colonel Shiro Ito. He brought a group of U.S. Army doctors and corpsmen in from other prison camps to try to stem the tide of death.[17] But disease and starvation were so bad that Colonel Ito decided to simply parole the surviving Filipino prisoners and thus eliminate the problem.

From September through December 1942, the Japanese gradually paroled the remaining Filipino soldiers to their families and to the mayors of their hometowns, who would be held personally responsible for each man's conduct. Paroles were issued beginning with men from Manila, then men from provinces where there was no guerrilla activity. Men from provinces where guerrillas were still active were to be held in prison until the guerrillas surrendered.

There was another provision. To be paroled, a man had to be well enough to walk. Anyone who was too sick to walk was simply held in camp until he got well or died.[18]

When the authorities were ready to release a group of prisoners, they notified the mayors of their towns and members of their families to come to Camp O'Donnell to get them. On the appointed day, each man was called out by name and he had to walk down a fenced-off passageway to meet his family. If he could not make it, or if there was no one there to claim him, he went back to prison. Some did not even make it back. Consider the experience of Captain Rene Diokno:

> As we gathered near the barbed wire passageway, we were alphabetized and told to wait until our name was called. I had to carry one soldier up to the place. He was starving. I barely managed. I was limping and everything. 'Oh no, don't leave me!' he said. He was desperate. I prayed that there would be someone there to get him. So I talked to him. I saw him afterwards, I saw him later that same day.
>
> Then they made us wait. I was looking for my brother [outside the wire] and when I saw him, I

> called to him. Then my brother tried to jump over the barbed wire. Here comes the Japanese with his bayonet! It's a good thing that at that time he was under instructions not to do that [bayonet the Filipinos]. He was yelling 'Go back! Go back! Back, back, back!' The fellow went back.
>
> Finally, they began to call the names. 'Rene Diokno!' Some of the men could not walk out. When they called the man before me, nobody comes up. The Red Cross man says to me, 'He has died.' I walked out the passage to meet my family. As I walked, I heard them call the man after me. Not again! You know, nobody came. We waited there for a while to see what happened. We learned that that man had died, too.
>
> Think of it. The day they are letting us go home, men are still dying. The man before me and the man after me both died, right there in the line to go home.[19]

By the time Camp O'Donnell closed in January 1943, after eight months of operation, 26,000 of the 50,000 Filipino Prisoners of War there had died.[20]

After the Japanese paroled Narciso Manzano from Camp O'Donnell, he returned to his family home in Manila. But as a civil engineer in the Japanese-occupied Philippines he found little work to do. Nevertheless, he joined the Free Philippines underground, a group organized shortly after the Japanese attack by some young, well-connected professionals in the city.[21] A group financed in part by Juan Elizalde.

Manzano had served in General MacArthur's Military Intelligence Service on Bataan, so he was given that same task in the Free Philippines organization.[22] Each week, he sat in his kitchen late at night and went over scraps of paper that were dropped off by street vendors and various other persons. More papers trickled in from small groups of guerrillas in the mountains around the city. The handwritten reports described the locations of Japanese garrisons; how many men, vehicles, and airplanes were located at each site; where fuel, ammunition dumps, and officers' quarters were located; and docking and sailing of Japanese ships. Manzano consolidated the information and graded the reports as to their importance and probable accuracy. Periodically, he gave his accumulated stack of intelligence reports to a courier to take to Lieutenant Colonel Marcario Peralta, the guerrilla leader on Panay Island, south of Luzon. Colonel Peralta transmitted Manzano's reports to General MacArthur's headquarters by radio.[23]

The most vulnerable links in this chain of communications were the couriers who carried the messages. Couriers were recruited from young men who had specific, legitimate reasons to travel, such as truck drivers, peddlers and fishermen. Government employees who would be familiar to the Japanese and constabulary men along the way, and who would not normally be stopped and questioned, were also good candidates. It was best if they looked not too serious nor wide awake, and it was good for them to carry a couple of extra cigarettes, candy, or loose change in a shirt pocket to distract a constabulary man in case of a personal search. Honest, working-class, traveling men were the best candidates. The papers they carried were, of course, totally incriminating, so the courier had to be willing to face the torture which would surely be applied if caught, and who would be difficult to intimidate. Men with young families at home were not candidates. The couriers' identities were scrupulously guarded, and they had knowledge of as few other members of the underground as possible.[24]

Papers were carried in hollowed out shoe-soles, concealed in hollowed out bananas or other fruit, in food containers, in the false bottoms of bags or packages, or anywhere else their existence could be obscured by legitimate cargo. Road travel was preferable to train travel, due to frequent surprise inspections on the trains.[25] The Free

Philippines couriers would typically take their reports south and leave them at a designated drop point, usually the destination of their cargo, where they would be picked up by Colonel Peralta's courier, coming north to Luzon once per week.[26]

***

On or about the sixth day of March 1943, in Manila, a few well-connected people began to arrive at the door of the elegant home of Señora Joaquin Mencarini on fashionable Taft Avenue.[27] A tall, handsome woman of about forty, the Señora had assembled a select group of Manila citizens who supported various charitable endeavors in the city, including the Remedios Hospital. The Irish Columban Fathers had founded the hospital in a converted school building behind the old Malate Church, ostensibly to care for the poor. In addition to the poor, the priests had asked for and received permission from the Japanese to serve sick and injured Filipino soldiers paroled from the Japanese prison camps. Along with the Filipino soldiers, the hospital also housed a few elderly, sick American and European civilians from the Santo Tomas Internment Camp in Manila.[28]

The hand-picked attendees at this meeting supported another kind of charity, as well.

Among the guests were a wealthy Spaniard named Ramon Amusategui (code name: "Sparkplug") and his pretty wife Lerry ("Screwball"); Father John Lalor ("Morning Glory"), the Irish-Catholic founder of the Remedios Hospital; Doctor and Señora Romeo Atienza who, with nurse "Rosena" Utinsky, had helped care for the sick on Bataan during the terrible malaria epidemic the previous year; and a newcomer to the group: a woman named Claire Phillips ("Highpockets"—so named for her penchant for stuffing intelligence documents into her brassiere, where Japanese sentries, so far, had not looked). Señora Mencarini, herself, went by the code name "Boots." There were several other persons at the meeting, including a well-dressed, young, blue-eyed, blond Spaniard named German, and a prominent Swiss businessman.

Claire Phillips was the American owner and operator of a nightclub in downtown Manila that catered to Japanese military officers. She was a cabaret singer from Portland, Oregon who had been performing at the Manila Hotel ballroom and at the Alcazar Club when the war broke out. When the Japanese invaded the Philippines, she found herself trapped there with her two-year-old daughter, Dian, product of a previous, hasty marriage to a Filipino.

Claire, thirty-three, was a small, dark-haired beauty who used the name "Dorothy Fuentes" on her forged Italian passport. After the Japanese invasion she followed the Fil-American army to Bataan to be with Sergeant John Phillips during the siege—they had met at the Alcazar Club several months before and they married on Bataan.[29] When the American army surrendered, Sergeant Phillips briefly evaded the Japanese but they caught him and he subsequently died of malaria, dysentery and malnutrition in the prison camp at Cabanatuan. Claire, living once again in Manila, learned of John's death from a German priest, Father Buttenbruch, who was a frequent visitor to the prison camps.

Claire explained to the group gathered in Señora Mencarini's parlor that the nightclub she owned, Club Tsubaki, served several purposes. First, it catered exclusively to Japanese officers and therefore was financially successful.[30] A portion of the money made at the club was used to help Father Lalor's Remedios Hospital, where Phillips had worked as a volunteer nurse immediately after the surrender. The rest of the profits were being smuggled to the American prisoners at Cabanatuan in the form of food, medicine and cash. Phillips and her employees at Club Tsubaki also wrote letters to the prisoners to keep their spirits up, and smuggled in bits of war news which they got from the newspapers, radio broadcasts, and their Japanese customers.

There was another, and far more secretive, activity at Club Tsubaki. The girls at the club were skilled at charming information out of tipsy, lonely Japanese. "When do you have to leave?" they would ask a lonely ensign. "No, no. Stay here with me in Manila! Who is your captain—I will talk to him!" Before the night was over, the girl would know the ship's name, destination, sailing schedule, and sometimes the cargoes and names of officers.[31] In addition, intelligence reports were being brought to Club Tsubaki from a guerrilla leader in the hills south of Manila named Colonel Hugh Straughn.[32]

Phillips passed the information collected at the club to General MacArthur's headquarters, although she did not explain to the group gathered in Señora Mencarini's parlor how this was accomplished. In fact, she knew very little about it—she passed her information to Mellie, the Filipina wife of an American guerrilla in the mountains north of Bataan; a man code-named "Compadre." A man whose real name was John Boone.[33]

All of the participants at the meeting were involved in helping Allied prisoners in one way or another. A few were also involved in espionage activities although the others, generally speaking, did not know it. Dr. Atienza, for example, was part of a group headed by General Vincente Lim that included newspaper reporter Tony Escoda. The Swiss businessman, Walter Roeder, was head of the Manila Gas Company and the gas company's laboratories were the source of many of the forged passports used by members of the underground.[34] The gas company also made explosive devices that found their way into the hands of the guerrillas. Roeder maintained contact with a woman named Mona Snyder who, in turn, was a courier between Manuel A. Roxas, a key figure in the Japanese puppet government, and Major Edwin Ramsey's guerrillas in the mountains north of the city. Major Ramsey received intelligence reports from Manuel Roxas, John Boone and a few others, then had them taken by courier to Negros Island in the southern Philippines where they could be transmitted to General MacArthur by radio.[35]

Charitable endeavors on behalf of the Remedios Hospital provided everyone at the meeting with a convenient, legitimate front for the money, goods and intelligence data they collected. A part of the money actually went to the hospital. The rest was smuggled to the prisoners at the Japanese prison camps. The Remedios Hospital was an innocent-looking charity, which was not questioned by the Japanese.[36]

At Cabanatuan, the money and goods were smuggled to the American prisoners through a network devised by an American nurse named Margaret Utinsky. Utinsky lived in Manila under forged Lithuanian papers that identified her as "Rosena" Utinsky, Dr. Atienza's nurse. Like Claire Phillips' sergeant, Margaret Utinsky's husband had starved to death in Cabanatuan.

Each week, Utinsky packed food, clothing, letters and as much currency as she could collect into a truck provided by Juan Elizalde, and sent it to a courageous, short, dark, Igorot girl, a beautician by trade, named Naomi Flores ("Looter").[37] Naomi Flores was a master smuggler who had taken up residence in the village just outside the gates of Cabanatuan prison. Each week, Naomi distributed the money and goods she received from Manila to several vendors who provided supplies to the prison camp. The camp's weekly supplies were carried in by carabao, and the camps' American purchasing officer paid the vendors. But when the prisoners unloaded their purchases, they often found more money than they had just paid buried in the bottoms of the sacks of food they had just purchased, along with letters and bits of news.[38]

Recently, however, the Japanese had become suspicious of Margaret "Rosena" Utinsky and she was being watched. The group of benefactors and amateur spies assembled in Señora Mencarini's living room that day decided to make the Japanese officers' favorite nightspot in

Manila, Club Tsubaki, the new communications center for Manila espionage.

***

Frank Loyd did not know it, but when he asked Tivo Leonzon to contact Vincente Bernia about a sailboat it was already too late. The Japanese caught Vincente Bernia and his brother Arturo in their hideout in the Zambales jungle on April 4, 1943 and killed them both.[39]

When he heard about Bernia's death, William Fassoth called a meeting of the few men remaining at his camp on Mount Malasimbo. On April 6, 1943, William and Martin Fassoth surrendered to the Japanese at San Fernando, Pampanga, near Clark Field. With them were five American soldiers—the last remnants of Fassoth's Camp.[40]

With Thorp, Bernia, and the Fassoth brothers all gone, Frank became increasingly anxious to find a way to get out of the Philippines. It was probably just a matter of time until the Japanese discovered the four Americans on Mount Natib. Frank talked the situation over with Eddie Wright and Roy Reynolds.

"Sam Zozabrado never has made contact with Narciso Manzano, and even if he does it's not likely that Manzano is going to get us on a boat that will get us out of here.

"Furthermore, it's too late to make the crossing to China, even if we can get a big enough sailboat. We're already into the rainy season and by mid-June it's going to get worse. The monsoon winds will do us in before we get halfway there."

Everybody agreed.

Roy had a suggestion. "Maybe we scale back a little. Instead of China, why don't we just get off Luzon to some smaller island farther south—somewhere we can get lost in the islands. Where there's not so many Japs. Then wait it out until MacArthur gets back."

Eddie carried it a step further. "If we can't get passage on a boat, we could go to north Luzon. Up in the mountains with the Igorots. You can bet there's not many Japs there."

Frank had another suggestion, one he had been thinking over for some time.[41] "How about Alaska…or at least the Aleutian Islands."

"What?"

When Frank was stationed in Alaska he had taken an interest in the weather patterns there, particularly the warm winds that blew in from the Pacific during the summer. He explained, "Typhoons have already started in the South China Sea, but they won't hit the Pacific until late summer. The prevailing winds in the Pacific will take us from Luzon straight to Alaska. It's 7,000 miles, so it should take about sixty days to cross. As long as we leave by mid-July, we could get there before it gets too rough or too cold. Then we're home free!" But they would have to leave soon to be able to set sail by July 15.

Roy was skeptical. "That sounds pretty desperate."

To Frank's surprise, Eddie Wright bought into it. As they continued to talk, Eddie really warmed up to the idea. He suggested that they leave Bataan immediately and hike across Luzon to Isabela on the east coast. In the fishing villages along the mountainous coastline they might be able to find, or steal, a big enough sailboat and the necessary provisions.

Frank nixed that idea. Walking across Luzon would be more hazardous than the trip across the Pacific. It would be easier to get a boat in or near Bataan and sail around Luzon.

Frank and Eddie decided to approach Roy's contact in Manila, Enrique Brias, and see if he could help.

Tivo had set up a courier arrangement with the Catholic priest, Father Cabanguis, who made regular trips to Manila on church business. Father Cabanguis visited Brias' home each month, picked up 100 pesos for the Americans, exchanged messages, and brought the money and messages back to Tivo.

Frank had Roy write a letter to Brias. The letter explained their plan to sail east out of the islands, and asked Brias if he could help them secure a large enough sailboat and 1,000 pesos for supplies. Roy gave the letter to Tivo to send to Brias via Father Cabanguis.

The rainy season got steadily worse as the men waited for Brias' reply. Two weeks later Father Cabanguis returned from Manila and gave Tivo 100 pesos and some much-appreciated vitamin and calcium tablets from Brias, but no letter. Brias had told Father Cabanguis that he would talk with some friends about raising 1,000 pesos.

Frank considered it a good sign. Enrique Brias lived at the Elena Apartments in Manila, along with a number of wealthy and influential Filipinos such as Juan Elizalde. If anybody had the means to help the Americans secure a sailboat it would be Enrique Brias and his friends.

When Father Cabanguis returned from his next trip, Frank was anxious for news about the sailboat. Brias sent some malaria medicine and four pair of new shoes, in their correct sizes. Football shoes. With heavy wool socks. Brias was unable to find anything else that would fit them, but at least it was something. By this time, all of their shoes had fallen completely apart and Frank was toughening up his feet in case he had to run from the Japanese, barefoot.

But there was no word from Brias about the sailboat.

Early in July 1943, the four Americans heard bombing and artillery in the distance, somewhere to the east. Tivo reported that there was a big battle going on between the Japanese and the guerrillas at the Layac road junction, in the lowlands just south of Dinalupihan.

Frank was immediately concerned—it was the first time the Japanese had ventured south of the highway in their battles with the guerrillas. He had the men start pulling guard duty each day, sitting in a deer-blind like structure they built over the trail from Kulò. They ran a string of vines from the guard post to their rainy-season *bahay*. A tug on the vine would cause a sheaf of bamboo slats to bang against the side of the hut. One pull was for friends approaching, two a stranger, and three pulls meant Japs. A test run showed that the men at the *bahay* could grab their pistols and emergency packs and get about a 300 yard head start on an approaching Japanese patrol. The guard would have to hide until the Japanese were past, and then sneak off into the jungle on his own.

Pulling his turns at guard duty, Frank fashioned a new pistol holster out of an old shoe, and wove a belt out of rattan. His leather army belt had rotted away in the damp jungle.

Word eventually came back from Enrique Brias about the sailboat. Brias made it clear that he had no means of acquiring such a boat, and it was his advice that if they were in a safe place they should stay put. It was too late anyway. The Pacific Ocean would now be too rough for them to attempt a crossing.

Disappointed, Frank decided to try once more to join Colonel James Collier. He gave Tivo a note to take to Father Cabanguis, asking him to locate Collier. With the note, Frank sent Cabanguis his diary pages from January through July 1943 for safekeeping, with instructions to forward them to Evelyn if he did not survive the war.[42] Included in the diary were instructions to Evelyn to pay Tivo the agreed upon fifty pesos per month for his help. She was also to obtain a good bicycle for each of Tivo's sons, as presents to the boys for helping bring supplies up to the *bahay*.

He wrote letters for Tivo to deliver to Payumo, Boone and their other contacts. But as the weeks went by, the letters drew no response and no one except Tivo and his sons came to the *bahay*. Frank was growing antsy. He hoped at least that Sam Zozabrado had gotten in touch with Narciso Manzano in Manila.

***

As Narciso Manzano perused the scraps of paper arrayed across his kitchen table one night in early August, he was interrupted by a knock at his door. Much to Manzano's surprise, his visitor turned out to be a former Philippine Scout—Sam Zozabrado. Sam had been a private in Manzano's own outfit, the 14th Engineers, at Fort McKinley.

Manzano invited Zozabrado inside and offered him a drink and something to eat, as is the Filipino custom. Sam told Manzano that Colonels Frank Loyd and Eddie Wright were alive and hiding with the guerrillas in the mountains of Bataan. They needed assistance.

Manzano was surprised to hear such good news. The Loyds, Wrights and Manzanos had been social acquaintances at Fort McKinley. Manzano's oldest son was a close friend of Loyd's son, Frank Jr., and the boys often spent the night at each other's home. Evelyn Loyd had taught Manzano's youngest son in the fourth grade at Fort McKinley School.

Narciso Manzano was happy to do what he could. He gave Sam Zozabrado 100 pesos and promised to provide another 100 pesos each month if he could scrape it together.[43] He told Sam to take the money back to Frank and Eddie immediately.

***

On August 9, 1943, Sam Zozabrado walked up the trail into Frank Loyd's camp.

Sam apologized for his inability to come to the camp in April, when his brother Roque had come in his place. He said, however, that he had made every effort to help the Americans as soon as he got well. He immediately returned to Manila and looked up Juan Elizalde. Elizalde had been very generous in his support of the four Americans and had given Sam 100 pesos and two bottles of vitamin pills. Sam had dutifully turned the money and the vitamins over to Mellie, John Boone's wife, to deliver.

"You got it all, didn't you?"

Sam went on to say that he had gone back to Manila a few days ago and contacted Narciso Manzano. Manzano also gave him 100 pesos and a letter, which Sam handed to Frank.

Frank watched Sam carefully as he related this tale. The Americans had not gotten anything from Mellie or John Boone. Frank figured that this was just a cock and bull story, designed to cover up another shakedown. Just as Sam had apparently pocketed the 150 pesos he got back in March, claiming his father had sent it so he could come to Cebu, Sam must have touched Juan Elizalde for another 100 pesos and kept the money for himself. Now Sam was trying to cover it up and lay the blame on Boone. He probably went back to Manila to get more money from Manzano, hoping to confuse the issue or to appease the Americans.

As he had with Roque before, Frank thought carefully about what he would say. Sam had to be straightened out if he was to be of any use in the future. He could also cause major damage by reporting them to the Japanese. If they harmed Sam, or killed him, his brother Roque could get revenge the same way. Revenge was a well-established principle in Filipino society. Frank thought it interesting that Sam and Roque never came up to the camp together.

"You are just protecting Roque with that story."

Frank's statement took Sam by surprise.

Frank chose his words carefully as he told Sam that he knew what was going on. Then he told him what he was going to do.

"As a Philippine Scout, active in the guerrillas, you will have some back pay coming when this war is over. A lot of back pay. About 3,000 pesos, per year."

Frank let that soak in for a minute. In the Philippines, money talks.

"I'm willing to overlook what has happened in the past, up to now. If you help us when we ask you to and do what we say, I'll make sure you get that pay. In fact, I can see to it that you get promoted to sergeant as well."

Frank stared straight into Sam's eyes.

"But if you fuck with me one more time between now and then, it will be a dishonorable discharge and no back pay at all!

"You think it over." [44]

Sam thought it over. His mood became sullen, but he said that he would cooperate.

Frank wrote out a receipt for the money, and a reply to Manzano's note. In it he cautioned Manzano about Zozabrado and asked Manzano about hiring a boat that could take the four Americans to Mindoro, an island just south of the mouth of Manila Bay.[45] He gave the note and the receipt to Sam to deliver to Narciso Manzano.

After Sam left, Frank again read the letter from Manzano. He passed it around for the others to read. Hearing from someone he could trust felt like a breath of fresh air.

Two weeks later, Tivo brought two bottles of vitamin tablets along with his regular supplies. He said that the vitamins were part of a gift from Juan Elizalde, that had been delivered by Sam Zozabrado and Mellie Boone.[46]

XIV. General MacArthur's War

General Douglas MacArthur had a lot on his mind. More than just the war.

Ever since he boarded that PT boat and sped away from Corregidor, Douglas MacArthur had been obsessed about the fate of the thousands of men he left in the Philippines. He named his personal airplane *Bataan*. His staff, at least those officers who had escaped with him, were known as the "Bataan Gang." His statement, "I shall return," had already become one of the most famous quotes in military history.[1] Douglas MacArthur had defined for himself a clear mission—to return to the Philippines and liberate the men he left behind.

On April 4, 1943, ten of those men, led by Captain William E. Dyess, escaped from the Davao prison camp on Mindanao Island. Eventually they made contact with some guerrillas, who took them to Colonel Wendell Fertig's jungle hideout in a remote part of Mindanao. In July, Fertig smuggled Dyess and several of his men onto an American submarine and had them evacuated to Australia.

In Australia, they told their stories to horrified Army intelligence officers. Since before the fall of Bataan, the Japanese had been assuring the rest of the world that they treated prisoners humanely. No one expected that the prison camps would be any better than austere, but the stories the men told about their treatment on the Bataan Death March and at Camp O'Donnell were little short of incredible. The intelligence men passed the word up the chain of command and Secretary of State Cordell Hull immediately protested to the Japanese.[2] But where the public was concerned, for the time being, the men's stories were treated as a military secret.

MacArthur, therefore, was carrying a heavier burden than most generals. Not only did he have a war to fight, but his conscience had long been vexed by thoughts of the men he left behind in the Philippines. Now he learned that the Japanese were murdering, torturing, and starving those men to death. MacArthur, dismayed and angry, sent a letter to President Franklin Roosevelt pleading for aircraft, submarines and aid to the Philippine guerrillas.[3] He was determined to return to the Philippines as he had promised, and liberate his soldiers. But he needed Roosevelt's help.

***

Evelyn Loyd stared blankly at the world map printed in her newspaper. It was August 1943, and the newspapers in San Antonio reported that General MacArthur had conquered New Guinea and the Solomon Islands, and that he and Admiral Chester Nimitz would soon be pushing north through the Pacific.

As usual, the news reports made it sound like everything was going great. The Russians were pushing the Germans back in Europe. General Dwight D. Eisenhower, having conquered North Africa, was attacking the Germans in Italy. MacArthur and Nimitz were attacking the Bismarck and Gilbert Islands—wherever and whatever they were.

But little swastikas still covered the map of Europe. Little rising sun flags still covered Asia and the Pacific.

Evelyn had heard it all before. The fact is the Bismarck Islands and the Gilbert Islands are off the coast of Australia, a long way from the Philippines. The map looked about like it had in 1942. No one knew what was going on in Asia. Radio Tokyo and some newspapers in Argentina were the only sources of news from the other side. It was like a great curtain of silence had descended across the Pacific—from this side were all the optimistic reports of Allied victories, and from the other side there was nothing. And the other side still occupied almost all of the Pacific.

The summer days were hot and it was quiet around the house. Bonnie was off on a vacation trip to Mexico with a girlfriend's family. Frank Jr. was gone a lot, too. He had talked Evelyn into buying him a motor bike and Evelyn worried every time he went out for a ride. That was not often, though. The motor bike was old and Frank Jr. spent most of his time fixing it.

At the Fiddlers' Club luncheons Evelyn Loyd began to recognize a certain feeling in the air. The other women's husbands were prisoners of war, and would be coming home when the war was over. But her husband, Frank Loyd, was missing in action. Presumed dead. What she felt from the other women, was pity.[4]

Second Lieutenant Frank Loyd in a "Jenny" trainer at Kelly Field, San Antonio, Texas, in 1925.

The *USAT Washington* evacuated military families from the Philippines on May 13, 1941. (Courtesy of Joe Wilson.)

Evelyn, Bonnie and Frank Loyd Jr. at Fort Benning, Georgia in 1938.

Major Frank R. Loyd, Manila, The Philippines, 1941.

Roy and Jeannie Reynolds (left foreground) attend a party at the Fort McKinley Officer's Club in 1941. Note the Negrito "village" in the background.

Juan Elizalde, left, after a polo match in 1941. This wealthy Filipino assisted Frank Loyd and other Americans during the war, and financed much of the Philippine resistance out of his own pocket. He was caught, tortured and executed by the Japanese. (Courtesy of Joe Wilson.)

Captain Bartolomeo "Tommy" Cabangbang, leader of the central Luzon penetration party. (Courtesy of Sue Trout.)

Eddie and Marge Wright on May 13, 1941, the day the *Washington* sailed. (Courtesy of James T. Wright.)

Captain Arthur "Maxie" Noble and Major Martin Moses at Fort McKinley in 1941. (Courtesy of Maxine Noble McLean and Bill McLean.)

Eddie Wright helped artist Shelby Dersh develop this painting of combat in the dense jungles of Bataan. It is part of the "Army in Action" series at the U.S. Army's Center of Military History in Washington, D.C. In 1952 it was used to illustrate an article by General Mark Clark in *Esquire* magazine. Eddie suffered a head wound in the action. (Courtesy of Edgar Wright III.)

Japanese invasion currency was brought into the Philippines in huge quantities by the Japanese, resulting in rampant inflation. Millions of counterfeit pesos were smuggled in by the U.S. government to finance the guerrillas.

Fort Santiago, built by the Spanish in the 1500s, became a *Kempei-tai* prison. Political prisoners were held in wooden cages in the fort's courtyard. Hundreds of criminals, guerrillas and persons being investigated by the *Kempei-tai* were kept in the dungeons, without trial. When General MacArthur's liberating army entered Manila, the guards massacred the remaining prisoners in Fort Santiago.

Old Bilibid Prison was used to hold guerrillas, underground suspects and other prisoners before trial. If, after his trial, a prisoner was not told his sentence it meant execution. (Courtesy of the Hudson Barker Collection and Joe Chesnut.)

A "dry-season" *bahay* on Mount Natib. Note the open sides and Nipa-thatched roof.

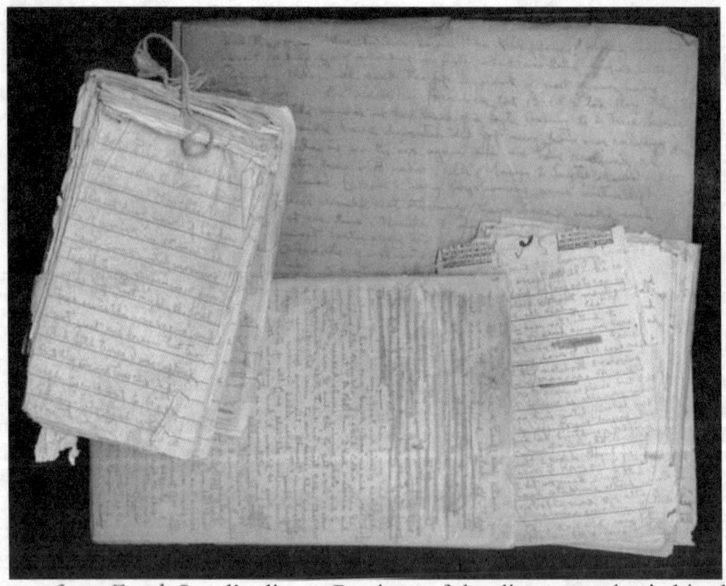

Pages from Frank Loyd's diary. Portions of the diary were buried in the jungle, other portions given to Filipinos to hold until the end of the war. Frank recovered most of it, but parts of the diary were lost.

Evelyn Loyd, right, at one of her many fund-raising activities.

SAN ANTONIO
SUNDAY LIGHT
AN INDEPENDENT TEXAS NEWSPAPER

VOL. LXIII—NO. 257 SAN ANTONIO, TEXAS, SUNDAY, OCTOBER 3, 1943. VOL. LXIII—NO. 257

THEIR FATHERS ARE JAP PRISONERS

The *San Antonio Light* featured a front page picture of (left to right) Gene Pearson, Joe Wilson, Gail Wilson and Frank Loyd Jr. at Central Catholic High School praying for their fathers (photo enhanced).

John and Mellie Boone. (Courtesy of Jeanne Boone.)

Placido Filomeno and two Negritos bring supplies to Frank Loyd and Roy Reynolds on Mount Natib. This photo was actually made after the war by John Boone, who staged the scene and sent it to Frank as a gift. In a letter thanking him, Frank commented that in reality the Negritos would not be wearing pants, and the sacks are too full.

Eddie Wright (far right), two Americans and two Negritos on the day Eddie re-joined U.S. forces near Olongapo, Zambales. (Courtesy of James T. Wright.)

Margaret Utinsky and Claire Phillips aboard ship, returning to the United States in 1945. (Courtesy of Federico Baldassarre.)

Frank Jr. at West Point, about 1947.

Frank Loyd visits with Placido Filomeno (right) and Tiburcio Paule, Tivo Leonzon's son-in-law, in 1954.

Damaso Caballero, Frank's loyal Negrito helper, with his wife Ana, about 1960.

Frank with Rafael Jalandoni, his benefactor and former 4th PC commander, in 1954.

XV. Guerrilla Sunset

In the six months that followed Tivo Leonzon's frustrated attempt to kill Frank, the two men grew to mutually respect each other, and their respect developed into friendship. Tivo was able to pay for most of the supplies he brought to the camp each week out of the money he got from Enrique Brias, and Tivo even solicited contributions from his own friends. The Americans' diet grew to include greens, limes, mangos, guavas and fresh vegetables, as well as the usual rice and *munggó* beans. There was meat or chicken on occasion, and vitamins sent by Brias. The men could feel their hearing and eyesight improving. Their fears of beriberi began to subside. Frank Loyd even began a daily routine of walks and exercises to help him regain strength in his weak arm and leg.

It had become obvious to Frank and his companions that General Douglas MacArthur was not coming back anytime soon. Colonel Claude Thorp was a Japanese prisoner. Colonel James Collier had disappeared. The Japanese were tightening their grip on Luzon, and Major Nakai's men were aggressively hunting for guerrillas and Americans. Frank anxiously awaited a reply to the letter he sent to Narciso Manzano in Manila, hoping that Manzano would be able to find a boat to take them off Luzon to Mindoro, the island just south of Manila Bay.

Frank Loyd's birthday and Roy Reynolds' wedding anniversary were one day apart, September 17 and 18, 1943. Ding, the nurse who had come to the camp with Father Cabanguis, sent them a present of coffee, white sugar, and a quart of home-brewed gin. Frank and Roy looked the bottle over, tasted the liquid gingerly and sniffed the open top.

"What do you think?" asked Roy.

"It has a peculiar smell."

Eddie Wright and Al Romaine observed this conversation from across the table.

"Poor quality gin, if it wasn't distilled and stored properly, is just like moonshine," Frank said, authoritatively. "It can damage the optic nerves. Hurt your eyesight."

"I've heard that. But we could risk a small drink or two." [1]

The suggestion had the desired effect—Eddie and Al consumed little of the stuff, leaving the rest for Frank and Roy. Combined with *kalamansi* [Philippine lime] juice and sugar, it made a pretty good cocktail. Ice would have helped.

A small hen wandered into their clearing that evening. Poor eyesight and too much gin notwithstanding, Frank picked his .45 pistol up off the table, took careful aim, and with one shot knocked the head off the little bird. So the four men celebrated with a good dinner as well.

During the mornings the sounds of axes and bolos chopping into tree trunks echoed through the jungle around the men's camp. *Banka*-makers, including Tivo Leonzon, were on the mountainside hacking thick hardwood trees and shaping them into fishing boats. Once they had the hull properly shaped and hollowed out, the *banka*-makers would carefully push and pull it down the mountain trails and streambeds to a riverside near the bay. There, the hull would get a final smoothing and be fitted with outriggers and other equipment for the buyer. Tivo Leonzon was reputed to be one of the most skilled *banka*-makers on Luzon and he was working on a tree trunk not far from the Americans' *bahay*.

The presence of the *banka*-makers weighed on Frank's nerves. One of them could easily climb up the trail looking for a tree to fell and discover the Americans' hideout. Frank gave orders to the other men that they were to avoid the *banka*-makers at all costs.

The four Americans contended with the damp, rainy weather and looked forward to Tivo's weekly supply run to see what new items he might bring in the way of either food or news. One of the Manila newspapers Tivo brought to the camp carried a story about Colonels Arthur "Maxie" Noble and Martin Moses. [2]

***

After their ill-fated attack on the Itogon Mines, Colonels Noble and Moses withdrew deep into the mountains of northern Luzon. They established their headquarters in Ifugao Province, in the middle of one of the most unusual areas of the world. The steep mountainsides in Ifugao are cloaked with towering, stone-walled rice terraces constructed by indigenous farmers almost 3,000 years ago. The Ifugao natives, descendents of the original builders, maintain and farm the terraces that rise as much as 2,000 feet above the valley floors. The Ifugao are a people who have their own lifestyle and society, and who are notoriously hostile to strangers.

The Japanese, however, had already visited the Ifugao villages and brutally suppressed all resistance to their control. The Ifugao welcomed Moses and Noble as potential protectors and possible saviors. Even these remote, isolated people hated the Japanese and had confidence that one day General MacArthur would be back.

After meeting with Captain Ralph Praeger early in the year and being instructed by General MacArthur to concentrate on gathering intelligence data, Colonels Martin Moses and Maxie Noble ordered their men to hide their weapons, return to their homes, and begin bringing in information about Japanese military installations and activity.[3] In April 1943, they gathered up their collection of intelligence reports and headed farther north to meet again with Ralph Praeger in Kabugao, Kalinga Province. They wanted to get their reports radioed to MacArthur before the coming rainy season made travel across the steep mountainsides nearly impossible.

The two men walked for miles through narrow mountain passes, assisted by native *cargadores* who helped carry their baggage and supplies from mountain to mountain. Unfortunately, Japanese soldiers captured one of the porters when he returned to his home village. The soldiers tortured the *cargador* and several of his neighbors, including their wives and children. They burned their homes to the ground. Eventually they learned that Martin Moses and Maxie Noble were on their way to Kabugao, and that they planned to stop over in a town named Balbalan.[4]

Moses and Noble, unaware of the pursuing Japanese, passed through Balbalan and continued on to Kabugao. There, they met with Ralph Praeger, exchanged radio messages with General MacArthur and met the governor of Kalinga Province, Marcelo Adduru, who was also a guerrilla.

On their return trip south to Ifugao, Moses and Noble stopped overnight in a town named Pinukpuk, headquarters of Major Ali Al-Raschid, a local guerilla leader. That night, the pursuing Japanese raided Kabugao and arrested Governor Adduru. Captain Praeger escaped.[5]

Over the next month Moses and Noble managed to stay just ahead of the pursuing Japanese soldiers and Bureau of Constabulary men, who raided town after town capturing Ali Al-Raschid, five Americans in his guerrilla organization, Lieutenant Charles Arnao, who commanded a small guerrilla unit in the dense Apayao forest, and numerous Filipino guerrillas and sympathizers.[6]

Fully on the run, Moses and Noble made their way south, back toward Ifugao. But at noon on June 3, 1943, after many narrow escapes over more than a month, Colonels Arthur "Maxie" Noble and Martin Moses were captured just south of Balbalan, Kalinga, betrayed again by a tortured Filipino helper.[7]

Their captors beat the two men and took their personal property, including their West Point rings. They were taken to Lubuagan, Bontoc, held briefly, and then transferred to Camp John Hay, Baguio.[8] The Japanese Army held them at Camp John Hay and interrogated them for more than a month. Neither man talked.

On July 11, 1943, Major Godofredo Monsod of the Bureau of Constabulary, with several of his men and a Japanese soldier, walked the two Americans through the streets of Baguio. Major Monsod took the group into the Icoha Restaurant where they sat down for lunch. After they had all eaten, they walked together through the Baguio marketplace. At the market, Major Monsod sent the constables and the Japanese guard away for a few minutes. He allowed Moses and Noble to talk to the gathering crowd.

Maxie Noble was a stooped and worn out man whose swollen lips were still healing from a recent beating. Martin Moses told the crowd to maintain the peace. He said that the American offensive in the Pacific was just gaining momentum and that nobody could stop it. He told the people to be patient and wait.[9]

When the guards returned, the men were transferred from Camp John Hay to the *Kempei-tai* prison in the Whitmarsh Building in downtown Baguio. There, they were crowded into a small, dark, unventilated cell with other captured guerrillas. One bare light bulb lit a room of multiple, crowded cells, where the prisoners were required to sit in rows on the floor of their cell all day, every day, in silence. There was no bathroom or latrine, only an open metal box in the corner of each cell, emptied once per day. In the still, hot air the foul stench of urine and feces was further putrefied by the body odors of the unwashed prisoners. The *Kempei-tai* allowed no one to bathe or even to wash their hands no matter how long they had been confined.[10] Each day the *Kempei-tai* "investigated" a few of their prisoners, consisting of frequent beatings and endless hours of questioning.

Again, no one talked.

***

Frank and his companions continued to wait it out at their mountainside camp, being supplied by Tivo. Early in August Tivo brought a newspaper that contained a brief article about Colonel Hugh Straughn.[11]

***

Hugh Straughn was a short, bulky, sixty-four-year-old veteran of the Spanish-American War who had once been a Lieutenant Colonel in the United States Army. In 1932, he retired in Rizal Province where he had interests in some iron and coal mines.[12] Straughn prospered over the years, and his stocky form became a familiar sight around Manila's social and business circles.

When the USAFFE Army retreated to Bataan, Straughn began raising a small group of Filipinos to fight the Japanese in his home province. He contacted General MacArthur, volunteered his services and asked for instructions. From Corregidor, MacArthur informally inducted Straughn back into the United States Army, authorized him to go ahead with his guerrilla recruiting, but told him to wait for further instructions.

Without waiting for instructions Straughn and his men began blowing up bridges and ambushing Japanese convoys in the provinces south of Manila. Soon volunteers from the towns and countryside joined them, and Straughn's clandestine organization grew. They held out in the mountains south of Manila until the American surrender, which Straughn refused to accept.

For more than a year, Hugh Straughn commanded a growing guerrilla army which covered all of South Luzon and effectively harassed the Japanese. Straughn's command included his own Fil-American Irregular Troops, President Quezon's Own Guerrillas, Terry Hunter's ROTC Guerrillas, and Marking's Guerrillas.[13] As a result, the Japanese hunted and pursued Straughn and he had to live his life on the run in the rugged terrain of south Luzon. The magazine article that crowed about his capture said that he lost more than seventy pounds during his ordeal. The article described Straughn as the chief of all guerrillas in the Philippines.[14] Frank knew that the description was not accurate, but he was saddened by what was sure to be Straughn's fate.

***

In the morning of September 2, 1943, Martin Moses, Maxie Noble, two other Americans, and a small group of Filipino prisoners in Baguio, North Luzon, were bathed, given haircuts, and shaved. The *Kempei-tai* paroled two of the Filipinos and sent them home.[15]

The next morning the rest of the cleaned-up group was put on a truck bound for Manila. The four Americans were in high spirits. They could not have known that they were being transferred to old Bilibid prison in Manila, where prisoners were held for trial.[16]

On September 30, 1943, the Japanese military authorities convened a court martial to try them along with Colonels Claude Thorp, Hugh Straughn, Guillermo Nakar, and twenty-one other men. They kept this group in separate cells, isolated from the other prisoners at Bilibid.

Prison guards brought the men into the courtroom one at a time for the proceedings. The court provided an English-speaking interpreter for each man but there was no defense counsel. An officer read the charges and the defendant was allowed to make a brief statement in his own defense. Then the tribunal sentenced him to death. Each trial took about fifteen minutes.[17]

Late in the morning of Friday, October 8, Bilibid prisoners who happened to be near one of the windows overlooking the prison's dreary, stone-paved courtyard witnessed an ominous sight. Most of them quickly turned away, because to watch would surely attract reprisal from the guards. The few who did watch saw a line of twenty-six nearly naked American and Filipino men, their wrists tied to a central length of chain, stumble across the courtyard toward two trucks waiting at the main gate. The men had been stripped to their undershorts, or Japanese G-strings in some cases, and each man's head was covered with a *bayong*, a native bag made of woven palm leaves.[18]

At noon on that cool, cloudy day at the La Loma Cemetery on the northeast outskirts of the city, one of the trucks unloaded its cargo. Japanese guards led fifteen hooded men, including Colonels Martin Moses and Arthur "Maxie" Noble, inside the walls. They closed the cemetery gates. Passers-by heard a series of shots.[19]

The other truck unloaded its cargo at the nearby Chinese Cemetery. Five Americans, including Colonels Claude A. Thorp and Hugh Straughn, and four Filipinos, including Colonel Guillermo Nakar, were led inside. The guards stood them all in a line and removed the covers from their heads. Colonel Akira Nagahama, chief of the *Kempei-tai*, read their death warrant to them. The guards then re-tied the covers over their heads, except Colonel Straughn's as the old gentleman refused to accept his. The nine men stood at the edge of an open, common grave, about four feet deep. They remained silent, except for Colonel Guillermo Nakar who shouted repeatedly that General MacArthur and the American army would soon be back!

A firing squad composed of Japanese prison guards shot the men. Anyone who was not dead from the first volley received the *coup de grace* from Colonel Nagahama's own pistol. Such was the case of Colonel Hugh Straughn who remained barely alive and kneeling at the edge of the grave. Colonel Nagahama walked up behind him with his pistol and blew his brains out. Guards kicked the bodies into the grave and Straughn's shattered glasses were thrown in on top of him. The bodies were then covered with dirt.[20]

The next evening Colonel Nagahama dropped by Club Tsubaki, the Japanese officers' favorite nightclub in Manila. The proprietress, Dorothy Fuentes, née Claire Phillips, recognized the colonel, approached his table, and sat down to talk.

The morning newspapers had carried stories of the execution of Hugh Straughn, and the American guerrilla commander was the main topic of discussion at Club Tsubaki that night. Claire had helped Hugh Straughn's guerrillas, and felt a certain kinship with him although she had never met the man.[21] Hoping to learn more about him, she asked Nagahama if he had ever met Colonel Straughn. To her horror, Nagahama grinned broadly.

"See dis hand?" he boasted. "Dis is hand dat used gun on him in Chinese Cemetery."[22]

***

By October 1943, the Japanese had captured and executed virtually all of the major guerrilla leaders on Luzon. General Kuroda declared that guerrilla resistance in the islands had ended, so the Japanese granted the Philippines their "independence" on October 14, 1943.[23] Only Japan, Nazi Germany, and Spain recognized the new puppet regime.

Having fulfilled their promise, the Japanese now turned their attention to MacArthur's spies, their underground supporters, and the few Americans who still remained loose in the Philippines.

***

At the end of October, Tivo came to the camp nervous and agitated. He told Frank that a detachment of Japanese soldiers had appeared unexpectedly in Kulò and occupied the schoolhouse. The commander had ordered all Filipinos to stay out of the jungle, and patrols were prowling the woods at the base of the mountain looking for guerrillas. As a result, Tivo and the other *banka*-makers had to stop their work. He could bring no more food supplies until the Japanese went away.

As days passed, then weeks, the Americans' food supplies ran low. They drew rice and *munggó* beans from their reserves, but they had no meat or fruit.

A Negrito wandered by the camp one afternoon, carrying the carcass of a wild pig. The little man was worn out from hiking up the mountain trail with his burden, so Frank gestured for him to sit down, take a rest and have some water. Gratefully, the Negrito took a seat on a log near the *bahay*. Roy Reynolds had learned to speak a little Tagalog, and he began to talk the man into trading some ham for rice and beans. The smell of fresh meat was making everyone's mouth water, but the Americans were reluctant to give up much of their supplies. With protracted haggling, Roy drove a hard bargain. The man finally handed over a good sized ham and took his portion of rice and beans. As Frank watched the Negrito disappear into the jungle he was afraid the man was dissatisfied with the deal and would not come back.

But rice was getting expensive in Bataan, and many Filipinos would no longer trade with the Negritos, so the man did come back. And when he did, he brought more meat, and news from the refugee settlement at Tala Ridge. The Negrito said that Placido Filomeno, Frank's young benefactor at Tala, had been released from the Japanese prison and was back with his family. Frank was relieved to hear it but before he could ask any questions the man also said that he had news about John Boone. The men had not seen or heard from Boone since August, when he sent a note reporting the Allied invasion of Italy.

All was not well with Boone, according to the Negrito. The Japanese had raided Boone's guerrilla headquarters north of Dinalupihan.[24]

"Boom!" said the Negrito, gesturing with his hands. Boone had escaped and was now living nearby.

Frank asked the Negrito if he could find John Boone and bring him to the camp.

On November 9, John Boone came up the trail accompanied by one of his guerrillas.

Boone's story was not good.[25]

A force of seventy Japanese soldiers had raided Boone's headquarters. "All of our supplies and records were lost. The Japs took what they could carry and burned the rest."

"Was anybody hurt? Did the men fight back?" Frank asked.

"No. There were only a few men there, just the headquarters staff. They took off as soon as the Japs appeared. The worst part is, we think they carried off a roster of our new regiment."

Everybody was quiet for a moment.

"How many men is that?" asked Eddie.

"About forty." Boone was obviously depressed.

"How many regiments are there?" Frank asked.

"Three. We're just about to set up a fourth one farther down the bay, near Balanga. During this year we've concentrated on recruiting more people. I think there's about 3,000 all together. Most of them live and work at home. They just come out to the camps for meetings and training, mostly at night. We've been raided before, but this is the first time they've gotten anything of value."

Boone said that he allowed his regimental commanders to run their own organizations pretty much as they saw fit provided they concentrated on recruiting, training and intelligence gathering, and avoided confronting the Japanese.

"I go around to each headquarters every week or two, collect reports and resolve any problems. My wife, Mellie, picks up some stuff for me in Manila from time to time. Every week or so I have a courier take a package of reports to Major Ramsey."

"What does Mellie get from Manila?" Frank was curious.

Boone paused for a moment.

"Nothing too important. Some supplies. Sometimes she gets some money from Claire, a woman at a nightclub who helps us out."

Boone fell silent.

Frank and Eddie counseled Boone. They told him that he needed to get better control of his organization. Frank told Boone that their best policy was to lay low. "Now is not the time to provoke the Japs, especially since they have a roster of your men." Frank wondered what else the Japs might have gotten from Boone.

Everybody agreed that Boone should suspend his training sessions for the time being, until it could be determined what the Japanese might do next.

"Are you still living in Dinalupihan?" Frank asked the question as a test. He wanted to see what Boone would say.

"No. I've got a small *bahay* right across that ridge." Boone waved in the direction of the ridgeline to their west. "Mellie is with me. We're kind of between a little refugee settlement and Kulò. About three clicks* uphill from Kulò."

Frank thought about the Japanese garrison at Kulò.

"You know the Japs are there?"

"Yeah. We'll have to do something about that. Probably we'll go back to Malasimbo."

Boone told the men about the deaths of the Bernia brothers and the surrender of the Fassoth brothers. He said

---

* kilometers.

that Colonel Collier had cleared out of his headquarters camp and moved farther back into the jungle to avoid capture. Boone did not know where Collier was.

"You know, there's a couple of refugee settlements back over that ridgeline." Boone waved in the same direction again.

"If you gents get in trouble and need help, that's a place you could go. There's a guy there named Montano that flat hates the Nips, and has helped me out. If you get over that way, look him up."

They talked a while longer about food, the war, and where in the world MacArthur might be. Eventually Boone stood up, ready to leave.

"I don't know what the Nips are liable to do next, but I'm sorely disturbed, and pissed off about that roster."

Frank was uneasy with what he was hearing. Boone might be mounting a noble effort to recruit and lead guerrillas against the Japanese, but the results his semi-organized villagers could produce would be small, even insignificant, in real military terms. The risk to the villagers and their families, on the other hand, was large. Very large. And that risk could easily lap over onto Frank and his companions.

"Look. I want you to keep quiet about us, okay? Don't say anything to your men about us being here, or where we are. Agreed?"

Boone grinned. "Sure, Colonel. It'll be our little secret. Always has been."

He shook hands all around and headed back down the mountain to lay low at his own *bahay* with Mellie.

The next week Tivo brought a load of supplies up to the camp. He said a guerrilla acquaintance had told him about John Boone's visit. "How is John Boone?" he asked.

Frank and Eddie discussed their situation. It was obvious that Boone had not kept their secret. Besides that, before the Japanese made them stop, some of the *banka*-makers had been working in the woods as close as 400 yards from the *bahay*. Once they came back to work one of those guys might wander up the trail and into camp looking for a likely tree to cut. Frank and Eddie agreed that it was time to move. The rainy season was about over and it was time to construct a dry-season *bahay*. This would be a good time to do it—before the Japanese let the *banka*-makers come back to work.

Frank picked a site even farther up the mountainside, almost inaccessible except through a narrow canyon. There was a trail out the back that provided an escape route. Some friendly Negritos were camped a few hundred yards up the trail, so a surprise visit from the Japanese from that direction was unlikely.

The men worked for several days cutting bamboo and Nipa for the structure and roof thatch, leaving the sides open for ventilation. The day after they moved in, and before they had a chance to dig a run-off ditch around the dirt floor, a final monsoon rain dumped on them, sending an ankle-deep torrent of muddy water gushing through their new home.

As they worked to clean up the mud and mess, Frank Loyd still dreamed of rejoining MacArthur, and he had come up with a new plan.

Having heard nothing from Sam Zozabrado, he wrote a letter for nurse Ding to take to Narciso Manzano. This letter asked Manzano to arrange for Frank and his companions to be smuggled out of the Philippines on a ship. He said he would pay 50,000 pesos to any skipper who could get them to Hawaii, the Solomon Islands or Australia, payable on delivery.[26] Although he knew their chances were slim, Frank was serious. He and Evelyn had some property in Columbus, Georgia they could sell to raise the money. And there was always his wheat farm in Kansas.

Frank knew in his heart there was little chance that the note would get to Manzano or, if it did, that Manzano would be able to act on it. In reality, waiting it out was likely to be their only choice. Still, Frank kept up hope. According to the Japanese newspapers General MacArthur had finally taken New Guinea. If they could survive until MacArthur took nearby Borneo, escape would be much easier. Then the men could participate in the re-invasion and liberation of the Philippines.

***

The intelligence reports coming in from Luzon had impressed General Douglas MacArthur. Guerrilla radio stations in the southern islands sent reports that Clark Field was being used as a training base for Japanese bomber crews, that Manila was the primary supply depot for the Japanese Southern Area Army, and that the old U.S. Navy bases in Manila Bay and Subic Bay were now the Japanese Navy's forward major repair facilities. Spies and guerrillas around Manila reported the locations of Japanese Army warehouses, troop strengths of the Japanese garrisons, and the sailing schedules of some of the 150 freighters and warships that visited Manila Bay each month.[27]

But by the time the reports were couriered from Luzon to the guerrilla radio stations in the southern islands, and transmitted to MacArthur's headquarters, they were as much as a month old—too old to be of much use. If the process could be speeded up, the destinations and cargoes of the ships could be radioed to waiting American submarines while the Japanese ships were still in open waters.

General MacArthur appointed U.S. Navy Lieutenant Commander Charles "Chick" Parsons to solve the problem. Before the war Parsons, a naval reserve officer, lived and worked on Mindanao Island and in Manila. When the Japanese overran the Philippines he posed as a Panamanian diplomat and escaped with his wife and three children to the United States. Parsons' mother-in-law, Mrs. Blanche Jurika, still lived in Manila and close family friends, the Ozamis family, still lived on Mindanao. The patriarch of the Ozamis clan, Senator Jose Ozamis, was a long-time Filipino politician in Manila, and an old friend of General MacArthur.

On March 5, 1943, the submarine *Tambor* deposited Chick Parsons and a small crew of commandos on Mindanao Island.[28] Parsons would remain there for three months. He met with Colonel Wendell Fertig and learned about Fertig's guerrilla organization. He set up several coast-watcher stations on southern islands that overlooked major shipping channels. He visited with the Ozamis family. While he was there, he gave a letter to a courier to deliver to Blanche Jurika, his mother-in-law in Manila.

Senator Ozamis, in Manila, was a close associate of General Vincente Lim, former commander of the 41st Infantry Division on Bataan, and of Manuel Roxas who had been Speaker of the Philippine House of Representatives before the war. Roxas, a thin, popular, and sometimes fiery politician, had served as an aide to General MacArthur on Corregidor but he refused to leave the islands when MacArthur, President Manuel Quezon, and Vice-President Sergio Osmeña departed for points south. President Quezon designated Roxas to take over the government of the Philippines if he and Osmeña were killed before they could return.[29] The Japanese, seeking to lend credibility to their puppet government, made Roxas an assistant to their own Philippine President, Jose Laurel.[30] They had no idea, of course, what Roxas was really up to. Nor did they know of his ties to Narciso Manzano and General Vincente Lim.

After his parole from Camp O'Donnell, General Lim had established a temporary headquarters in his hospital room at the Cancer Institute of the Philippines General Hospital, in Manila. The Cancer Institute was not a place frequented by Japanese, and by having himself admitted as a patient there Lim knew he would be able to avoid being pressed into the service of the puppet government.[31]

Once he settled into his room at the hospital, General Lim began contacting selected men from his old outfit. It was his intention to resurrect the 41st Division, staff it with former soldiers, guerrillas and loyal members of the Bureau of Constabulary, and take over the government of the

Philippines as soon as General MacArthur landed. He would then install Manuel Roxas as provisional president until Quezon returned.[32] In the meantime, Lim devoted himself to intelligence operations.

***

On the night of November 13, 1943, the huge fleet submarine *Narwhal*, rose up out of the South China Sea and deposited nine commandos under the command of Major Lawrence Phillips on the island of Mindoro, just south of the entrance to Manila Bay.[33] The *Narwhal* was one of three submarines General MacArthur had assigned to Chick Parsons to use in making contact with guerrillas and spies in the Philippines. The commandos' mission was to establish a radio station on Mindoro, under the very noses of the Japanese. The spies on Luzon could then bring their intelligence reports to Mindoro by ferry instead of sending them to the southern islands by courier. From Mindoro, the destinations and cargoes of the Japanese ships departing Manila Bay could be quickly radioed to MacArthur's headquarters, and to waiting submarines.

Once the commandos were in place and had their radios in operation, they sent a messenger to Manila to meet with MacArthur's key contact, Senator Jose Ozamis.[34]

Senator Ozamis passed the word around the Manila underground that, henceforth, all intelligence reports were to be taken to General Vincente Lim rather than being couriered to the guerrilla radios in the southern islands.[35] Manuel Roxas contacted Narciso Manzano and told him to submit all of his intelligence data directly to General Lim. Lim would verify the reports and send them by boat to the new commando radio on Mindoro. General Lim, in turn, contacted representatives of guerrilla organizations outside of Manila, including Major Edwin Ramsey, and told them to bring their reports directly to him.

Meanwhile, a Filipino agent named Franco Vera Reyes, a former member of Hugh Straughn's guerrillas, returned to Manila. Reyes was a tall, flashy man—a snappy dresser who often appeared about town in a sharp, yellow suit. He was a published novelist before the war, and a flamboyant businessman who had once been convicted of embezzlement and sentenced to a short stint in prison.[36] He met his old contacts and told them that he had returned to Luzon from Australia aboard the *Narwhal*. While in Australia, the U.S. Navy had assigned him as Chief Liaison Officer for U.S forces in the Philippines, to coordinate the activities of Chick Parsons' submarines from the Luzon end.[37] As might be expected, he carried no U.S. military identification, but as credentials he presented the U.S. War Department's *Philippines Intelligence Guide*, a recently published issue of *Life* magazine, and a letter for Blanche Jurika, Chick Parsons' mother-in-law.

Blanche Jurika's letter was from her daughter, Katsy Parsons, and it contained photographs of Chick and Katsy's children, Blanche's grandchildren, taken recently in Washington, D.C.[38]

Blanche Jurika verified that the letter and the pictures of her grandchildren were genuine. She thanked Reyes for bringing them—she had not seen or heard from her daughter or grandchildren in almost two years—and she agreed to help Reyes while he was in Manila. Franco Vera Reyes' credentials were thus verified, and for several weeks in December he held meetings with various underground and guerrilla leaders in Manila and southern Luzon, including Senator Ozamis, leaders of the Free Philippines underground, and Marking's Guerrillas.

On the evening of January 25, 1944, Narciso Manzano called his wife, Charo, over to the front door of their home and told her that he was leaving on an important mission. Manuel Roxas had ordered Manzano to deliver some secret documents to Colonel Wendell Fertig on Mindanao.[39] From there, if possible, he was to travel to Australia by submarine and deliver Roxas' personal communication to General MacArthur.

Charo said that she understood. Through all of the hardships of the war, she had been a real trooper. She suffered through his absence during the Siege of Bataan, and she kept their family together during his imprisonment at Camp O'Donnell. During the year since he came home, she kept out of the way of his clandestine activities and she sold her own china and silverware to help support the family.[40] She knew that if he was going to Australia it would be months, possibly years, before she would see him again.

He left that night. Traveling by train, sailing *banka*, and on foot, dodging Japanese patrols and making extensive notes on their whereabouts along the way, it took Narciso Manzano more than a month to travel the 1,000 miles to Colonel Fertig's Mindanao headquarters.[41] The documents he carried included five military situation maps showing Japanese defenses on Luzon, with recommended bombing targets.

As Narciso Manzano made his way south, the *Kempei-tai* took Franco Vera Reyes into custody. Then they closed in on the Free Philippines. On the night of Saturday, February 19, they surrounded the Manzano home, rousted everyone out of bed and ransacked the house. They dragged Charo Manzano off to a prison cell at Fort Santiago.[42] Then they went down the street, arrested Blanche Jurika and threw her in the same cell.

More arrests followed. Senator Ozamis. Señora Mencarini. The entire Elizalde family. Virtually everybody in the Free Philippines organization, right down to the couriers—more than ninety persons in all.[43] Japanese troops surrounded and wiped out the commando radio station on Mindoro Island, killing Major Phillips and all but two of his men, whom they captured and later beheaded.[44] Manuel Roxas, General Vincente Lim and newspaper reporter Tony Escoda fled Manila and, for the moment, escaped.[45] For all practical purposes, the Free Philippines organization ceased to exist.[46] With the information they collected in their raids the Japanese launched a major crackdown all over Luzon, extending even to Bataan.

One by one, Filipino operatives brought word of the arrests to Claire Phillips at Club Tsubaki. The Elizalde family, then the Mencarinis, then others... But the Japanese did not seem to suspect Claire. Her regular customers continued to frequent her club. But there were odd clicks and noises on Club Tsubaki's telephone line.[47]

Franco Vera Reyes was a Japanese mole.[48]

XVI. Turning Points

The war had been going on, and Frank had been "missing in action" for two years. Evelyn Loyd was run down, depressed and nervous. She had lost thirty-two pounds. Her hair was turning gray. She was beginning to doubt that Frank was alive. She had pretty much given up on General MacArthur.[1] For her, the last two years had trudged by filled with uncertainty, loneliness and boredom.

Then Radio Tokyo broadcast a report that the Japanese Army had captured Maxie Noble and Martin Moses.[2] Evelyn called her friend Evelyn Noble, and found that she was beside herself with worry. Evelyn Loyd tried to assure her that if the Japanese had captured Maxie, then at least she knew for certain that Maxie was alive and out of danger.

Every six months, all the wives in the Fiddlers' Club received little typewritten cards from their husbands in

Cabanatuan and the other Japanese prison camps. The cards had a pre-printed list of phrases such as "My health is—excellent; good; fair; poor." Each man was allowed to underline the phrase that applied—"excellent" was always underlined—and to write a few comments on the card. The comments were always cheerful and reassuring. Everyone seemed to be doing fine, according to the cards. It made all the women feel happy, even optimistic, to hear that their husbands were in such good shape.

The women wrote letters to their husbands and sent packages of candy, socks, razor blades, underwear and the like whenever the Red Cross said the Japanese would accept them, usually just at Christmas. The prisoners' wives all wished that they could get something more from their husbands than the little cards, or at least more often. But at least they were getting something. Evelyn Noble's husband was a prisoner now. She waited anxiously for her first card.

But there was no word about Frank Loyd, and Evelyn Loyd sometimes felt glad that she had not been notified. She resolved to return to the Philippines someday after the war, and find out what happened to Frank.[3]

Just after New Year's 1944, her telephone rang. On the other end was Evadne McKee, Montgomery McKee's wife, calling from Louisville, Kentucky.

"Evelyn. I've got news for you. You're gonna be thrilled!" The enthusiasm in her voice fairly oozed through the telephone line.

"What is it?"

"I got my card from Montgomery today. Evelyn, across the bottom it says, let me read this to you... 'Am glad to know Mart and Frank are well. Give my regards to Bill and Evelyn'!" [4]

Evelyn's heart leapt into her throat. But then...she was mystified.

"What does that mean? How does he know they are well?"

"I don't know. He knows somehow! I certainly didn't tell him anything about Frank or Mart."

When writing to their prisoner husbands, the wives were only allowed to mention family matters and personal news—nothing about other soldiers or the war. The prisoners, in turn, would often write a comment on the bottom of their cards in response to the letters from home, so their family would know that they got their letters. Evadne assured Evelyn again that she had never mentioned Frank Loyd or Martin Moses in any letter to Montgomery.

What did it mean? Obviously, Montgomery McKee was trying to tell Evadne something—or rather, he was trying to tell the Loyd and Moses families something.

Evadne went on, "You know, some men from the War Department visited Martin Moses' father months ago. He and Bill have known all along that Martin was with the guerrillas in the north...with Maxie Noble. Then we heard that they were captured. But this is the first time we've heard anything about Frank—unless you've been holding out on us!"

To Evelyn, the smile in Evadne's voice was like music.

She was elated! It was the first actual word Evelyn Loyd had heard about Frank in almost two years. If he was not a prisoner—the War Department said that Frank was not on the prisoner of war list—how did Montgomery McKee, locked up in the Cabanatuan prison camp, know he was well? Maybe Evelyn Noble was right all along. Frank really was with Martin Moses and Maxie Noble in North Luzon. When the Japs captured them, they must have all run into Montgomery McKee at the camp. But if so, wouldn't Montgomery have used a different phrase? He would have said something like "I saw Frank and Mart and they are well," not "Am *glad to know* Frank and Mart are well." And what about Maxie?

As soon as she finished talking to Evadne, Evelyn Loyd called Evelyn Noble to share the good news.

Things were finally looking better to Evelyn Loyd. The newspapers were, at last, beginning to focus a little attention on the war in the Pacific. In October, a reporter and photographer showed up at Central Catholic High School inquiring about students whose fathers were in the war. The next day, a photograph of Frank Jr., Gail Wilson, Joe Wilson and another boy was centered on the front page of the *San Antonio Light* newspaper. The picture showed the boys kneeling in front of the chapel altar, praying for the safety of their fathers.[5]

Frank Jr., fifteen years old, was taking flying lessons. Every time he saved up enough money he went to the airport to take one more lesson, and would soon be getting his private pilot's license.[6] He took up marksmanship as a hobby and went deer hunting with a friend from his high school ROTC class.[7] He told Evelyn that he had decided to go to West Point. Inwardly, Evelyn smiled. Frank Jr. applied himself to a lot of things, and did well at them, but studying was not one of those things. If he really wanted to go to West Point, he was going to have to hit the books. Evelyn hoped that the idea of West Point might accomplish what she had been unable to—motivate him to study.

On Friday morning, January 28, 1944, Evelyn was still high on the good news about Frank. She scooped some ground coffee into the little aluminum pot and got breakfast ready for herself and the children. The Fourth War Bond Drive was in town, and she intended to drop by the exhibits after work. The War Bond Drives were the U.S. government's principal method of financing the war, and on Thursday a long caravan of celebrities, military equipment and exhibits had paraded through San Antonio. They set up in Alamo Plaza, just in front of the U.S. Post Office where Evelyn worked in the censorship office. During the weekend there would be more parades, band concerts, patriotic speeches and the like. San Antonio's goal for this particular drive was $8,000,000 and Evelyn intended to drop by and buy some bonds for the children's future education, and to do her part as she always did.

As the smell of fresh coffee drifted through the kitchen, Evelyn sat down and opened the morning newspaper. She expected to find a list of exhibits and a schedule of events for the weekend. Instead, she found a huge headline:

> BATAAN SURVIVORS STARVED, TORTURED, WANTONLY MURDERED BY JAP CAPTORS! [8]

At a joint Army-Navy press conference the government had released the stories of three American soldiers, headed by Lieutenant Colonel William E. Dyess. The men had escaped from a Japanese prison camp and were smuggled out of the Philippines to Australia on a submarine.

Evelyn read about the horrible treatment of American and Filipino soldiers at the hands of the Japanese on the long march from Bataan to Camp O'Donnell. It was a terrible struggle the newspaper referred to as the "March of Death." There were stories of beatings, thirst, starvation, summary executions and outright murder, which were so gruesome the newspapers printed only portions of what they had been told. The paper went on to describe the horrible conditions in the prison camps, including starvation, rampant diseases, and torture of helpless prisoners.

She was horrified. If Frank had been captured, he stepped into *this*.

All over America that day, people were jolted into viewing the war in the Pacific in a new and fearsome light. There had been stories before about Japanese atrocities in China, and tales of Nazi evils in Europe. But never had there been anything like this. Malicious mistreatment and murder of American soldiers—helpless prisoners of war!

The members of the Fiddlers' Club were stunned. Outraged! Horrified…and frightened.

And frustrated—what could they do?

Some of the women decided that the U.S. government had withheld information about conditions in the prison camps to keep from drawing public attention to the Philippines. After all, it had been two years since Pearl Harbor, and President Roosevelt had pursued the war in Europe—not liberation of the Philippines.

Betty Wilson, Zero Wilson's wife, said that she believed the government did not really know about the conditions in the camps until these escapees got to Australia...got back to MacArthur. But they had escaped nine months ago. Why had it taken so long for the story to come out? Betty commented bitterly that the government must have withheld news about the prison camps until the start of the Fourth War Bond Drive.[9]

Evelyn Loyd did not buy those theories. She had personally participated in the war bond drives, the pennies for airplanes drive, and every other fund-raising event she had time to attend. She knew the people who worked in those organizations and refused to believe that any of them could do anything so crass. She believed that until those prisoners escaped and came forward, the U.S. government simply did not know.

Most of the women chose to believe, or tried to believe, the little postcards they received every six months. According to the cards, their husbands were all right. In good health. Happy. It must be some other group of prisoners that were mistreated so badly.

But for some of the women, the cards had stopped coming.

***

In the Pacific, General Douglas MacArthur's difficulties increased. His war with the Japanese, and the fate of the men he had left on Bataan, were intensely personal issues with the General. So were the continuing political battles going on in Washington, thousands of miles away.

There, the inter-service rivalry between the Army and Navy reached ominous, sometimes ridiculous, proportions. Admiral Ernest J. King, the new Chief of Naval Operations, believed that the war in the Pacific should be under the control of the Navy, specifically under Admiral Chester W. Nimitz, Commander in Chief of the Pacific Area. The Pacific, after all, was an ocean and the Navy was, well, the Navy.

General George C. Marshall, Army Chief of Staff, made the argument that General MacArthur was by far the best-qualified commander to fight the Japanese. Of all the United States' senior officers, MacArthur had the most experience in Asia and best knew the "Oriental mind." The Australian government had specifically requested him as Commander in Chief. The Australians, after all, had carried the brunt of the fighting in the Pacific during the early days of the war.

The issue was ultimately resolved by agreeing to a two-pronged attack. Admiral Nimitz took control of the Central Pacific with orders to attack west from Hawaii through the many small islands of Micronesia. His submarines were to cut Japanese shipping lanes and his ships and Marines were to capture island airfields that U.S. bombers could use to attack Japan. General MacArthur, aided by a smaller fleet commanded by Vice Admiral William F. "Bull" Halsey, was given command of the Southwest Pacific and assigned to attack northwest from Australia through the larger islands of Indonesia and the southern Philippines—the "overland" route. His mission was to deny Japanese access to the oil fields and mines of Southeast Asia, and to liberate the Philippines.[10]

Early in 1944, MacArthur began his advance. New Britain, invaded in December, was captured. Halsey's Marines landed on Roi, in the Marshall Islands, and MacArthur's 7th Infantry Division was ready to attack Kwajalein. Admiral Nimitz invaded Eniwetok. The American assault was so effective, in fact, that the Japanese pulled their front line of defense back to Saipan and the Marianas.

Intelligence reports said that the main Japanese fleet had moved from Truk to Palau.

However, another battle was in the works. One which originated with Admiral King in Washington, D.C.

In mid-July, General Marshall ordered Douglas MacArthur to fly to Hawaii for a meeting with "Mr. Big"—President Roosevelt. Marshall did not divulge the purpose of the meeting but obviously something was up. MacArthur had not seen Roosevelt face-to-face in seven years. Although the President traveled to Canada, Africa, and the Middle East for meetings with Churchill and Stalin, he had not set foot in the Pacific since the war began. Moreover, MacArthur had never before been invited to attend any strategy conference on the conduct of the war, whatsoever.

On Wednesday, July 26, the *Bataan* touched down at Hickam Field, Hawaii, after a twenty-six hour trip. That afternoon, MacArthur met President Franklin D. Roosevelt and Admiral Chester W. Nimitz at Pearl Harbor. Their meeting went on for three days.

In front of a large map of the Pacific, the stately Nimitz explained the Navy's, or rather Admiral King's, position: MacArthur's army should proceed overland and capture Mindanao in the southern Philippines. Then they should remain there, with MacArthur's air corps keeping the Japanese air forces on Luzon pinned down, while the U.S. Navy proceeded across the Central Pacific to take Formosa. Nimitz would bypass the rest of the Philippines. Formosa, not the Philippines, would be the jumping-off point for the invasion of Japan, an invasion that would be accomplished by Nimitz' Navy, not MacArthur's Army.[11]

MacArthur, astonished at the prospect of being pulled out of the action once again, remained remarkably composed. He quietly formulated his response to the Navy plan, and when Roosevelt invited his opinion, MacArthur delivered a lengthy and typically eloquent speech.

He reminded President Roosevelt of the political as well as strategic importance of the Philippines—the honor of

America was at stake. Seven thousand American soldiers were being held and mistreated in Japanese prison camps in the Philippines. Seventeen million loyal Filipino Christians were being subjugated by the Japanese. And, MacArthur reminded Roosevelt, he had made them a promise—a promise to return.

To abandon the brave men of Bataan once again, or to turn our backs on the Philippines, America's protégé and protectorate, would be unthinkable.

In a private moment that evening, MacArthur also reminded Roosevelt that, in a few months, a presidential election was coming.[12] The implication was clear.

When MacArthur departed the next day, he had Roosevelt's approval to liberate the Philippines—all of the Philippines.

XVII. Zonification

Before dawn on December 1, 1943, the citizens of Orion, Bataan awoke to noise and commotion in the streets outside their homes. Major Nakai's soldiers were going from house to house, beating their fists on the doors. The soldiers hauled each male occupant outside and sent him stumbling toward the Catholic church at the center of town. They sent the rest of the townspeople, the women and children, to the central market place.

When the men arrived at the church the soldiers made them line up in the aisles. Slowly, the line moved toward the altar. There sat a man who would come to be known as a "scorpion," with a *bayong*, a loose bag, tied over his head. He observed each man through two eye-slits in the bag. If the scorpion raised his hand and pointed at the man standing in front of him, the soldiers pulled that man aside and wired his hands behind his back.

One by one, the soldiers brought each man fingered by the hooded scorpion to the central market. There, a Japanese officer questioned the man in front of his gathered neighbors and family. "How long have you been a guerrilla?" the officer would ask. "Who do you report to?" Whenever the answers were not satisfactory a soldier with a two-by-four wooden club stepped up to the hapless prisoner and beat him to his knees. The questioning then resumed.

As each interrogation was completed, the soldiers blindfolded the prisoner and loaded him into the back of a truck. The officer and his assistant turned their attention to the next prisoner and resumed the process.

The citizens in the market place stood and watched these beatings all day. Late in the afternoon, when the last prisoner was loaded into the truck, the Japanese commander dismissed them. The truck drove away.

The men in the truck could not see where they were being taken, but when it stopped most of them probably sensed that they were near the Japanese military barracks on the outskirts of town. One by one, the soldiers pulled the men out of the back of the truck and led them away.

A Japanese soldier guided each man to a secluded area behind the main barracks. There, the soldier made him kneel in the dirt. With a swift downward stroke, a sword-wielding sergeant chopped off his head.

Thus, by the end of the day the Japanese commander officially declared the village of Orion "Zonafied." As far as the Japanese were concerned, the village was now a guerrilla-free zone. Relatives and village officials who asked were simply told that the men were gone. The Japanese threw the bodies and the severed heads into a common grave and would not let the relatives see or bury their dead.[1]

***

By December 10, word of the zonification of Orion had spread all over Bataan. On that day, one of Roy Reynolds' Negrito friends brought Placido Filomeno to the camp.[2] Frank Loyd had just about given up hope of ever seeing Placido again, so he was surprised and thrilled. Placido appeared to be in reasonably good condition considering that he had spent three months in a *Kempei-tai* prison. Frank introduced Placido to Eddie, Roy and Al. The Negrito hunkered down on his heels nearby while Placido related his story.[3]

"After I bring Colonel Loyd to Kulò, I go back to Tala and the Japanese are waiting. They arrest me and take me to the prison in Orani. My family is there. They are questioned, but not mistreated.

"Then the soldiers beat me with a club! A two-by-four. They put a gun to my head, and they say I have to tell them where Colonel Loyd is.

"I tell them Colonel Loyd has a camp on the mountain, far above Tala, but he is gone. They seemed to already know that much. I thought if I told them something, they maybe let me go.

"But they didn't. They want to know where he went.

"I said, 'I don't know where he went.'

"They didn't believe me. They beat me some more with the club and threaten to kill me. This goes on for weeks.

"Finally, they take me to Balanga, to the *Kempei-tai* headquarters. They let my family go.

"The *Kempeis* question me more about Colonel Loyd and say that I helped him, and that I know where he is. But I tell them nothing.

"They made me kneel on the hard concrete floor for hours and they beat me some more. But still I do not talk. I stay in the jail in Balanga for three months. They question me and beat me every few days.

"Then they want to know about Colonel Loyd. How old is he? What he looks like? How many men does he have? Does he have any guns?

"I tell them, 'Colonel Loyd is an old man. He is sick and he walks with a cane. I never saw anyone come to see him.'

"I tell them only Colonel Loyd is gone and I do not know where. Oh yes—I also tell them Colonel Loyd has a pistol, and he is just about the best shot in the world!

"One day in the interrogation room, the *Kempeis* bring in a man, another prisoner. He is an American—Captain Dallas Vinnette, who was hiding at Francisco Silva's house in Tala. He and I exchange looks when he comes into the room, you know, but we say nothing.

"Vinnette looks sick and badly beaten. They point to me and say I am Colonel Loyd's helper, and they say Vinnette has to tell them what I do for Colonel Loyd.

"Vinnette says nothing. He vouched for me and says only that Colonel Loyd is gone, and that I never helped him.

"A few days later they let me go. They parole me to the mayor of Orani and they say I cannot leave Tala except to come to Orani."

After a few moments, Frank asked, "What happened to Vinnette?"

"I don't know. They took him away. I heard when he got too weak, the *Kempeis* took him to Cabanatuan." [4]

Frank was relieved that Placido and his family were all right, but disturbed that Placido's help to him had cost him three months in the *Kempei-tai* jail, plus the threats and beatings. At least the young man was still alive. In relating his tale, Placido never once complained about what had happened to him.

Placido and Frank talked privately and Frank was impressed by the young man's resilience. He seemed willing, even eager, to help Frank in spite of what had happened to him. His contempt for the Japanese was obvious.

That night Frank thought about their situation. Tivo Leonzon and his family were in extreme danger if the Japanese figured out that he was helping Americans, particularly, it appeared, since he was helping Frank Loyd.

The other three Americans were in danger, also. Too many people knew where they were. It would be just a matter of time before some of John Boone's guerrillas got caught and one of them talked. Besides, any number of Negritos had visited the camp at one time or another and a few Japanese pesos, or bayonets, might easily tempt the Negritos to talk.

Frank was also concerned about Eddie Wright. Eddie had made it clear that he no longer put any stock in Frank's schemes to get out of the islands by boat and return to General MacArthur's forces. Frank's dreams, he said, were hopeless. Before Frank joined the other three men, Eddie had apparently been bitter about the way the USAFFE army was abandoned on Bataan. But more recently Eddie seemed to have resolved that in his own mind. He believed that the army on Bataan was called upon to make a last-ditch stand like the Texans at the Alamo, to stem the Japanese advance in the Pacific. Eddie used to be content to just sit around and wait out the rest of the war in Tivo's care, but recently he had talked about raising a guerrilla battalion of former Philippine Scouts to attack the Japanese. Both plans seemed crazy to Frank. To sit around and do nothing was defeatist, but to try to attack the Japanese with a few salvaged rifles and a rag-tag bunch of Filipinos was plain nuts.

Somewhere, Eddie had obtained a copy of the book *Les Miserables*, and he frequently spoke about the character Jean Valjean. Reading and talking about the hopelessness of Valjean's fictitious situation in the French student's revolt seemed to make Eddie feel that his own real situation was more tolerable. In the story, a police inspector relentlessly hunts down Jean Valjean, just as Major Nakai's soldiers always seemed to be just a step or two away from finding Eddie and his companions. Like Jean Valjean, Eddie Wright idolized and longed to be with the person he loved most, his wife Marge, but he also felt duty and honor-bound to pursue his cause: in this case, defeating the Japanese.[5] Eddie wanted to be with his wife and family, and he wanted to fight the Japs—but he was utterly powerless to do either one.

Al Romaine was even more depressed than Eddie, talking to himself and arguing with every decision. Al refused to obey Frank's orders about keeping quiet in camp during the day when Japanese patrols were active. He refused to dig or use a latrine. Recently, Al had let their cooking fire die out overnight, and then used up all his matches trying to light it again. Frank, enraged, had yelled at Al and told him that from then on Al was to drag a log onto the fire each night and keep the embers burning. Al put up his fists. Pushes turned into blows, and Frank knocked Al over the side of their table. As Al lay on the ground covering his head with his arms, Frank rained jabs on him with his good arm until his anger gave way to pity for Al's helplessness. Nothing had really been hurt but each man's pride. Frank, though, felt guilty about the whole incident.[6]

Al, after all, had a problem. That did not make Frank feel any better.

Everyone was getting on everyone's nerves.

The next morning, Frank took Eddie aside and made a proposal. "Roy and I will set up a separate camp, a 'spike' camp, closer to Tala. We'll develop a second source of supplies with Placido. Each camp will share the supplies they collect with the other. Everybody benefits, and we can reduce the burden on Tivo." [7]

The arrangement would allow Frank and Roy to split off from Eddie and Al but still preserve Tivo's dignity—something Frank knew Eddie would be concerned about. "Tivo's Americans" had made Tivo something of a celebrity in Kulò. Tivo's celebrity made Frank nervous.

On December 12, Frank and Roy followed Placido and his Negrito guide south into the jungle, headed generally toward Tala. They selected a site about two hour's walk from the old camp, 1,800 feet up the mountainside. With their one bolo they constructed a shelter, and Frank and Roy settled in.[8] Placido and the Negrito went back to Tala, about three and a half hours away.

The next week Placido returned with his first load of supplies: a bag of *camotes*, half a dozen huge oranges and fifty Japanese quinine tablets. He also brought the mayor of the Negrito village, Damaso Caballero, who had helped Frank hide in the Orani River gorge during a rainstorm more than a year before, when the Japanese first came to Tala. Damaso was excited to see that Frank was alive and well. He had a rifle that he had salvaged off the battlefields, and he hunted and brought down a wild pig. He gave Placido the hams, kept the head, and Frank and Roy feasted on the liver. They salted and dried the rest of the meat and set part of it aside for Roy to take to Eddie and Al.

The area around the new camp yielded food on its own. There were eels in the mountain streams, Roy bartered a supply of pig meat from a family of Negritos who lived nearby, and Frank shot a monkey that provided stringy but fairly tasty meat. They discovered that the area around the new camp was infested with snakes, "...but," Frank remarked to Roy, "we can eat snakes." [9]

Frank built chicken snares and caught several wild fowl.[10] Then he devised a cage-like trap with a drop-down door that he baited with the monkey skin, and caught a Musong cat. Frank killed the hairy, screaming animal in the cage with his knife, a bloody process that disgusted Roy, then skinned and cooked the Musong, an animal that even the Negritos wouldn't eat.[11]

Each week, one or both of the men made the walk back to Eddie's camp to pick up their share of Tivo's supplies and to leave off portions of whatever food they had been able to acquire. On their second trip they picked up a welcome gift: two sharpened bolo knives. Tivo had brought four of them up to Eddie's camp—a present from a friend.[12]

Frank felt more comfortable with their camp split into two factions. Eddie had always insisted on controlling their relationship with Tivo, and now he was fully in charge of that situation. Placido, Damaso and the local environment seemed more than capable of meeting Frank and Roy's needs. With some distance between them, the men's relationship began to improve.

***

Tivo also seemed happier with the new situation. He began bringing some of his associates up to Eddie Wright's camp once Frank and Roy were gone. Victor Pamintuan and his son Crespin visited Eddie, bringing food and bottle of Scoth (not Scotch) whiskey. Eddie hiked up to Frank and Roy's camp the next morning and brought them some *camotes* and half of a roasted baby pig. Everybody had a tasty lunch, got a good laugh out of the label on the "Scoth" bottle, and a good drink as well.[13]

"Tivo," Eddie said, "brought what sounds like good news. He says some Red Cross ships recently unloaded a bunch of wounded Japs in Manila."

Frank perked up. That meant there was combat in the Pacific, and it must be getting close to the Philippines.

"He also says that MacArthur captured the Admiralty Islands, just north of New Guinea."

Frank was encouraged. If it was true, it was real progress.

"Yeah," Roy glumly pointed out, "but the Admiralty Islands are 2,000 miles from here. They've still got a long way to go."

Some of the news was not so good. In November, the Catholic Church transferred Father Cabanguis out of Dinalupihan, leaving them with no courier to their benefactor in Manila, Enrique Brias. Tivo needed the 100 pesos Brias supplied each month to pay for the food he was bringing to Eddie, so Tivo decided to make the monthly trips to Manila himself.[14] Eddie had agreed, although it was going to be risky if the Japanese questioned Tivo's travels.

Physically, Frank felt better than he had at any time in the past eighteen months. His right arm and left leg were still abnormally small and weak, but only the arm ached, and the pain was tolerable.[15]

On February 5, he climbed by himself to a peak on the north side of Mount Natib called Mount Santa Rosa, 2,000 feet above their campsite. After being stuck in the depths of the Bataan jungle for two years, the blue sky that stretched overhead was inspiring. A gusty breeze wafted across the mountaintop bringing a clean, cool odor to Frank's nostrils.

The dark green treetops covering the mountainside cascaded away from the rocky outcropping where Frank sat and contemplated what to do next. To his north, the green mass of the Zambales Mountains passed across his vision like a jagged wall. Colonel James Collier was over there in Zambales somewhere but, for all practical purposes, nowhere to be found. Vincente Bernia was dead. The sailboat plan had produced nothing, and there had been no word from Narciso Manzano about getting a steamer out of the islands.

Frank looked out over the South China Sea. The American Army was finally moving somewhere in the Pacific. Before long, MacArthur would be back.

It was time to get ready.

Frank again considered Eddie's idea of raising a guerrilla battalion of former Philippine Scouts. Eddie had asked Frank and the other men to help. Frank thought that the idea was admirable, but impractical. How would they recruit them? Where would they put them? Where would they get weapons for them? How could they feed them?

Boone had a more practical setup. His men stayed in their homes, fed themselves, and only came out for training. Once the fighting started they could assemble quickly and they would have built-in logistical support from their nearby families, including medical support for the inevitable casualties.

Frank took a last look at the quiet, smooth surface of the South China Sea. MacArthur was out there, somewhere. The time for escape was over.

Frank decided that he would talk to Roy and Eddie about helping Boone in some way. Considering Boone's lack of military experience, there should be plenty they could do.

Back at camp Frank discussed his ideas with Roy. On "supply day," they both went to Eddie's camp to talk about what to do. While they talked, a nervous and upset Tivo appeared with their supplies. He told the men that the Japanese had caught a retired American sailor named Eddie Hart who lived with his Filipino wife in Dinalupihan.[16] When the Japanese spotted him Hart tried to run away but a Japanese soldier shot him in the leg.

"Mr. Hart gave his watch and ring to some Filipinos who were with the Japs, to take to his wife and children," Tivo said.

"But then the Japs told the Filipinos to bury him. When they started to shovel dirt on him, Mr. Hart cried out to the Japs 'I'm not dead!'

"The Japs fixed that by shooting him in the head!"

For good measure, they publicly hanged the two elderly Filipinos who had been helping Hart.[17]

Then, they arrested another Filipino farmer because someone reported seeing four Americans digging on his farm.

Tivo looked at the four men standing in front of him. He asked Eddie to move his camp to a safer location, farther back in the jungle.[18] The sooner, the better.

Eddie and Al moved the next day.

They set up a new camp in a shallow valley on the side of Mount Natib, above barrio Bamban. Mosquitoes were bad and Eddie soon came down with malaria. In need of medicine, he went down to the barrio and traded his army knife for quinine. But he did not get enough to cure the episode, and his chills and fevers persisted. Finally, racked with fever and nearing delirium, Eddie went back to the barrio. This time he sold his gold pocketwatch and purchased more quinine.[19] Going to the barrio was a desperate act. Fortunately, no one turned him in.

A few days later, Frank and Roy came to Eddie's camp to get their supplies. When he heard about Eddie's visits to Bamban, Frank was mad.

"There's Jap collaborators around. If they turn you in, it's possible...probable, that we'll all pay the price. The big price!"

Eddie, sick with malaria, was not interested in listening to Frank. Al was getting on his nerves, too. They had just had a serious fistfight.[20]

But the quinine had the desired effect, and as he recovered Eddie Wright became increasingly social with the Filipino villagers at the foot of Mount Natib and with the Negritos on the mountain itself.

Eddie had learned enough about the Negritos to avoid going to their villages on feast days. On those occasions they prepared selected delicacies for the village mayor, elders and any honored guests. One such delicacy began by concocting a very rich mixture of meats, spices and vegetables. They fed the raw mixture to a dog. Once the poor animal was practically bursting from overeating, they paused to let the dog digest his food—just enough time for the meal to get to the dog's intestine. At that point the Negritos beat the animal to death, the dog's adrenaline accentuating the flavor of the cuisine, took out the intestine, tied off the ends, and proceeded to roast and eat the "sausage," along with the rest of the dog.[21]

When Eddie did visit, at non-festival times, a celebration was still in order so the Negritos slaughtered a fat pig and roasted it in his honor. At the feast they would give Eddie, as honored guest, the prize delicacy from the pig—a generous portion of its liver extracted while only partially cooked, warm and almost bloody.

With all eyes on him, Eddie made a great show of devouring the entire portion of liver with great gusto and numerous expressions of delight and appreciation, as was his duty. At least it was meat.

Eddie had his reasons. The Negritos and the Filipino villagers were both possible sources of food, medicine and safety. Not only for him, but potentially for the battalion of Philippine Scouts he hoped to raise. Eddie's plan to recruit former Philippine Scouts began to take shape. He went to John Boone's *bahay* to talk about it, and Boone agreed to help, insofar as he could. Boone began sending small quantities of supplies to Eddie's camp, mostly medical items such as bandages and antiseptic that Mellie Boone obtained from Claire Phillips in Manila.[22]

***

Early May brought signs that the rainy season was approaching, so Frank and Roy took their new bolos and built a rainy-season *bahay* with a sturdy bamboo roof, in a small clearing that Damaso found for them.[23]

From their new location Frank and Roy had a narrow view of the sky through the jungle treetops. In the distance they could see patches of overcast grow ominously dark as storms gathered and approached. Breezes, ordinarily welcome, now brought fat raindrops that streaked from the roiling gray overcast and pounded themselves into the hillside. Wherever there was exposed dirt, the ground soon oozed into muddy rivulets. Plants sprang out of the mud and took over everything around them. Vines would appear from nowhere and cover the ground as if to protect the surface from the pounding raindrops. Nipa palm branches grew more than a foot per day.

The rain left the air fresh, void of the heat and dust they had become accustomed to during the dry season. Clothes seemed to stay clean, though limp and damp, except for their pants cuffs and new shoes. The football shoes sent by Brias were constantly wet, and quickly rotted away.

Frank and Roy hiked down the mountainside one day in May to attend an induction ceremony at John Boone's new headquarters near Bamban. Placido Filomeno was going to join Boone's guerrillas, and they wanted to be there and congratulate him.

The ceremony took place on May 10, 1944. Placido was officially sworn in by John Boone and designated a medic. Boone assigned him to the 2nd Regiment at Tala and told him that until combat started Placido was to help treat injuries and illnesses for Filipino families around Tala and Orani.

Boone asked Placido why he wanted to join the guerrillas.

Placido thought about it for a moment, then "...to be a soldier is an honorable profession...and vital in the defense of a sacred cause. I want to serve my country.

"However, I really hate the Nips." [24]

At Boone's headquarters, Frank learned a little more about Boone and his organization. Boone's men were intensely loyal to the American corporal-turned-guerrilla-colonel, to the point that some of them seemed to idolize him. It made sense. Boone's men were basically villagers, not soldiers, and he treated them all with respect. He spoke their language, and he had married a Filipina girl.

Major Ramsey had officially designated Boone's organization the "Bataan Military District." Boone showed Frank a letter he received from Ramsey in March 1944, in which he asked for a list of all Americans known to be alive in Boone's district. In his response, Boone had listed Frank and his companions as alive but "inactive." [25] Frank hoped that Ramsey was in touch with MacArthur's headquarters somehow, and that he had gotten word back to Evelyn.

Frank mentioned that he and Roy were interested in joining Boone's organization.

Boone looked at Frank for a moment. "What are you saying, Colonel? You and the major intend to take command of the Bataan Military District?"

Boone's question caught Frank a little off guard. "No, not at all. You started this command. You've built it up. But we have a lot of training and experience that can be valuable to you.

"Think it over. Figure out how we can best be of help to you, and let me know what you think."

There was a pause. Then, "All right."

Frank had expected a more enthusiastic response, but at least Boone was going to think about it.

Boone took Frank and Roy to meet his wife Mellie and their infant son, Phillip. Mellie turned out to be a slight, attractive woman with high cheekbones and a big smile. She told Frank that she had recently stepped up her trips to Manila, and that she was now going every week to fetch medicine and supplies from Claire Phillips at Club Tsubaki.[26] On one of her recent trips she took little Phillip with her. At the old Malate Church, in the presence of Claire Phillips and an American nurse named Margaret Utinsky, Father John Lalor had christened the child in the Catholic faith.[27] Little Phillip Boone was named after Claire Phillips' husband, who had starved to death in the prison camp at Cabanatuan.

***

At his headquarters in Orani, Major Nakai carefully reviewed his situation map. His troops had kept Bataan pretty well under control since the American surrender. He had two infantry battalions scattered around the larger towns, in platoon-size detachments with supporting artillery. There was a *Kempei-tai* unit of twelve men at the provincial capital in Balanga under Captain Tamura.[28]

The *Kempei-tai* had successfully recruited several pro-Japanese agents, and over the past two and a half years they had captured a number of guerrillas and escaped Americans. The guerrillas were disposed of, and the Americans were shipped off to Cabanatuan.

Recently, however, guerrilla activity had picked up. On May 8, a band of guerrillas ambushed and killed four Bureau of Constabulary men outside of Orion.[29] Major Nakai struck back. One week after the incident his soldiers attacked and killed twenty-five guerrillas in a gunfight north of Dinalupihan.[30]

At seven o'clock in the morning on June 1, 1944, Major Nakai sent his soldiers to surround barrio Saysain, Bagac, on the west coast of Bataan. Soldiers from the Bagac garrison went through the town beating on doors, and ordered all adult men and women to report to the garrison compound. Once everyone was collected, the soldiers sent all of the women and all government employees home. About forty male residents of the town were kept standing under guard in the garrison courtyard.

At that point Japanese officers circulated among the Filipino men, asking about each man's personal status in the community, whether he was a guerrilla, what he knew about the guerrillas, and who he knew who might be a guerrilla. After this "investigation" a few of the men were allowed to leave. The rest were kept at the garrison for three weeks. Every few days Major Nakai's soldiers would select a man out of the group and, in front of the assembled crowd of his neighbors, beat him to death.[31]

Two days after the zonification of Bagac, a new name appeared on Major Nakai's desk—Colonel John Boone. 14th Army headquarters in Manila reported that Colonel John Boone, not Colonel Frank Loyd, was the commander of guerrillas on Bataan. On July 20, they followed up with another report stating that Boone had four regiments of troops at his command.[32]

Where did Boone come from? Major Nakai wondered. Four regiments meant a lot of people. They should not be hard to find. Zonification programs had been successful in wiping out a number of guerrilla hot spots in southern Luzon. Perhaps Bataan needed more zonification.

XVIII. Captain Cabangbang

On the night of August 30, 1944, at Dibut Bay on the east coast of Luzon, the fleet submarine *Narwhal* rose quietly up from beneath the surface in almost total darkness.[1] As soon as she broke through, hatches were thrown open admitting a rush of clean night air into the stale interior of the submarine. Sailors scrambled on deck while small, dark Filipinos leaped aboard from rafts and *bankas* drawn alongside. As the men got to work, Lieutenant Commander Chick Parsons, General MacArthur's guerrilla liaison officer, called eighteen U.S. Army commandos to join him up on deck.

The men blinked in the surrounding darkness and steadied their feet against the gentle roll of the submarine. Dark forms worked hurriedly around them, pulling boxes of cargo up through the open hatches and passing them to the flotilla of rafts that shuttled back and forth to shore along a heavy rope line secured to a distant tree. The *Narwhal* had brought thirty tons of cargo, including carbines, ammunition, K-rations, Spam, and $1 million in counterfeit Japanese currency to the Luzon guerrillas headed by Majors Bernard Anderson and Robert Lapham.[2]

The officer in charge of the commandos reported to Commander Parsons that his men were ready to go ashore. He was a Filipino first lieutenant with an unlikely name: Bartolomeo Cabangbang.[3] He was the leader of a "penetration party" brought to Luzon by Chick Parsons to accomplish a special mission.

Lieutenant Cabangbang was a graduate of the Philippine Military Academy and had been a fledgling pilot in the Philippine Air Corps when the Japanese attacked in 1941. He was wounded on Corregidor, captured by the Japanese, and survived the horrible ordeal of Camp O'Donnell. The Japanese paroled him, assigned him to the Bureau of Constabulary and shipped him off to Cebu Island. On Cebu, Cabangbang deserted the Constabulary and joined a local guerrilla band. Eventually he made his way to Negros Island where he worked for several months as a member of the spy network being formed by another Philippine Air Corps flyer, Major Jesus Villamor.

In October 1943, the U.S. submarine *Cabrilla* picked up Cabangbang and Villamor and took them to Allied headquarters in Australia.[4] There, Lieutenant Cabangbang came to the attention of General MacArthur's staff and they assigned him to the Allied Intelligence Bureau. After special training at the Australian commando school, they put him in charge of a penetration party consisting of five three-man Signal Corps teams. Chick Parsons' submarine brought Cabangbang back to Luzon with his men.

Major Anderson brought hundreds of Filipino *cargadores* to Dibut Bay that night, and Cabangbang and his men fell into line as they lugged their heavy radio equipment up the east face of the Sierra Madre Mountains, then down the long rugged coastline to Major Anderson's headquarters near the Masanga River in Tayabas Province. After discussing the situation and his mission with Anderson, Lieutenant Cabangbang signed on for the time being as Major Anderson's intelligence officer. Anderson's camp was reasonably close to Manila, protected by the high mountains and by Anderson's' guerrillas. Major Anderson told Lieutenant Cabangbang that he could use Anderson's own couriers to contact other guerrilla leaders.

Cabangbang quickly dispatched one of his radio teams to the Hunter's ROTC Guerrillas in southern Luzon, and another to Captain Alejandro Santos' guerrilla organization in Bulacan Province across the mountains, just north of Manila. Since the demise of the Free Philippines organization, Santos' headquarters had become a major collecting point for intelligence reports coming out of the city. Over the next few weeks Lieutenant Cabangbang established observation posts at several towns around Manila and in the Manila railroad station itself. By the end of September 1944, he was in regular radio contact with Lapham's guerrillas and President Quezon's Own Guerrillas, whose radios had been smuggled in by sailing *banka* earlier in the summer.[5] He collected the information he came for, and radioed it back to General MacArthur's headquarters.

***

On Bataan, Tivo Leonzon's activities had attracted the attention of Major Nakai's men, and they put him under surveillance.[6] Tivo was still going to Manila every month to collect 100 pesos from Enrique Brias, but inflation had gotten so bad that 100 pesos would buy only five pints of rice for his four Americans.[7] By the end of August 1944, the Japanese were watching Tivo so closely that he and his sons had to stop bringing food altogether.

Frank Loyd and Roy Reynolds calculated that they had enough rice in their emergency supply to last until the first of October. They could get pig meat from the Negritos, but meat and rice alone lacked vitamins, and vitamin deficiencies such as beriberi could be just as devastating as malaria.[8]

On September 10, Roy Reynolds struck off down a jungle trail toward Kulò. As he neared the village, he found a Filipino who looked friendly and gave the startled man a note to take to Delphin Pamintuan. Pamintuan responded to Roy's plea for help and brought several bags of groceries up to the camp. He promised to bring more when he could, but the Japanese were watching him, too.[9]

The new food source did not hold up for long. A sad and angry Pamintuan came to the camp one afternoon empty-handed. He said that the Japanese had confiscated his rice crop and his carabaos. His two tenant farmers tried to intervene, pleading with the Japanese not to take their rice and farm animals. The Japanese shot them to death for their trouble.[10] Pamintuan could no longer supply food to Frank and Roy.

On September 21, 1944, as Frank and Roy discussed ways to supplement their food supply, the sound of aircraft engines above the trees broke the jungle stillness. With Clark Field nearby, there was nothing unusual about that. But these engines had a different sound—a smoother, heavier, roar. And there were many of them. Lots of them, and they just seemed to keep coming. After a few minutes the distant rumble of explosions from the Pampanga plain, from across Manila Bay, then from nearby Subic Bay, rolled across Bataan. American bombers were blasting the Japanese military bases! The war had at last come back to Luzon.[11]

Shocked and excited by this completely unexpected event, Frank and Roy raced to a lookout point to watch the American airplanes passing overhead. It was an overcast day and the aircraft were in or above the clouds as they crossed Mount Natib. Occasionally the men could glimpse part of a formation through the overcast or as they descended out of the clouds over the Pampanga plain. The bombing went on for hours as American and Japanese fighters engaged in screaming dogfights over Pampanga. Then, stillness. That afternoon the bombers returned for another round.

For the next several days, American fighters and bombers swarmed across central Luzon, bombing Clark Field, Fort Stotsenburg, Manila, and even Corregidor. The Filipinos were excited. The Americans hiding on the mountainsides were electrified. The bemused Negritos, happy for their friends, celebrated.

With the bombing of Luzon, things began to change. Tivo Leonzon came back and brought Jose Payumo with him. They congratulated their American friends on the recent and continuing bombings. The Japanese were still watching Tivo, but the bombing had diverted their attention and Tivo said that he would try to resume food deliveries even though food was scarce all over Luzon. Tivo's spirits were way up and Frank thought to himself that he had never seen Tivo look so happy.

Next, Placido Filomeno showed up at Frank and Roy's camp with at least a week's supply of vegetables and rice, and two bottles of alcohol—one for rubbing and one for drinking, although they were both the same. Congratulations were said all around. After Placido left, Frank and Roy shared their alcohol with the next band of well-wishers to drop by: Damaso Caballero brought most of the Negrito village. The first Negrito to take a sip out of one of the bottles spat it out and exclaimed "Whisky!" in perfect English. He not only knew the American word, but he also knew that this stuff was not fit to drink.[12]

***

Far back in the Zambales Mountains, Colonel Gyles Merrill decided that it was time to get ready for MacArthur's return. He wrote out four principals for guerrilla units to follow in conducting their wartime activities:

1) Protect civilians while defeating the Japs.
2) No fighting until the Allied army arrives.

3) Collect intelligence data to send to General MacArthur.
4) Organize and train guerrilla forces, to be ready when the time comes.

He drew up bookkeeping procedures for use in tracking expenses and designed forms for submitting travel expenses to the U.S. Army after the war. He also created a set of forms for appointing Special Fiscal Agents, and receipts to be given in exchange for donations made to the guerrilla forces by private citizens.[13]

Next, he sent messages to all the American guerrilla leaders he knew of, requiring each of them to report to his headquarters for a conference.[14] The letters to Lieutenants Edwin Ramsey, Clay Conner and Robert Lapham all questioned their use of the rank "major," and ordered the men to bring documentation justifying and authorizing their respective "promotions." They were also to furnish Colonel Merrill with copies of all messages or correspondence they had received from any higher headquarters.[15]

Then he sent a letter to Castro Alejandrino, military commander of the Hukbalahap, proposing that the Huks place themselves under Colonel Merrill's command, thus joining the recognized USAFFE guerrillas.[16] Colonel Merrill assigned Major Roy Tuggle, a pre-war mining engineer who was well known and respected by the Filipinos of central Luzon, to contact the Huk leaders and bring them into the fold.

Finally, he sent a letter through Bernard Anderson to General MacArthur, to let the General know that Colonel Merrill was in charge and awaiting orders:

> TO: Commanding General Southwest Pacific Area:
>
> Request orders and instructions for employment Luzon guerrilla forces be sent to me using my code name Columbus and double transposition code key phrases as follows: 1, the first, middle and last names of the man who lives near my wife and who

is also close friend of Admiral Purnell USN; 2, house number of this friend as for example '1142' total letter both phrases + 2 = twice the sum of the digits of house number. Name and address can be obtained from my wife or Admiral Purnell...

Signed Gyles Merrill,

Col. Cav. GSC Commanding [17]

Before long, the couriers returned with replies to Colonel Merrill's summons.

"Major" Ramsey's message said, "Due to the existing circumstances it will be impossible to attend a conference at this time." [18] In other words, "No."

Seeking to head off an unnecessary and unproductive confrontation, Lieutenant Colonel Peter Calyer talked with Merrill and then sent a well-respected Filipino officer, Captain Jose A. Bernales, to find Ramsey and tell him to report to Colonel Merrill as ordered. Bernales had done intelligence-gathering work with Ramsey during 1943, and Calyer was certain that Ramsey would listen to the advice of his old colleague.

"Major" Lapham replied that he was, "in direct contact with GHQ, SWPA" [MacArthur's headquarters], and that he took his orders from them.[19]

"Major" Conner sent back a rambling letter in which he told how he had developed a Negrito guerrilla force over the past year, and said that the Negrito leaders promoted him to major because they viewed him as the successor to their previous leader and hero, Colonel Thorp, whom they still remembered as "major" from pre-war days.[20]

"Major" Bernard Anderson also wrote back that he took his orders from MacArthur. Anderson said that he could not leave his headquarters for a conference with Merrill, but if Colonel Merrill wanted to come to Major Anderson's for a meeting, he would be willing to see him.[21]

Several other guerrilla leaders, such as "Captains" (Sergeants) Alfred Bruce and Albert Hendrickson in Tarlac

Province, also sent their regrets.[22] In fact, of all the American soldiers Colonel Merrill ordered to attend his conference, not one showed up.

Colonel Merrill was already fuming when he received John Boone's reply to his summons—in fact, two replies.

The first letter was Boone's response to Merrill's request for a list of Americans alive on Bataan Peninsula. Boone listed fourteen Americans, including Lieutenant Colonels Frank Loyd and Eddie Wright.[23] Boone listed himself as a corporal, but signed the letter, "John P. Boone, Brevet Colonel, GFCP, Commanding."

The second letter, dated October 8, was from Frank Loyd, offering Frank's advice with regard to Colonel Merrill's request for the list. It said,

> It will be most difficult, if not actually impossible in many instances--and in all cases I believe inadvisable--to make the necessary changes in commands which would result from assigning the now inactive American officers to guerrilla organizations. The youngsters now with the guerrillas have been with them a long time, have organized them, nursed them along through the dark period, and would now most naturally strongly resent having officers who have heretofore been inactive step in and take over their commands. Furthermore, those Americans who have been with the guerrillas all along are much better qualified because of the fact that they are thoroughly familiar with their areas and are personally acquainted with most of their men...[24]

Merrill was furious! Here was another American officer, a lieutenant colonel in this case, who not only failed to obey Merrill's orders but was also trying to tell him what to do! Seething, he prepared a personal reply to Frank Loyd.

***

By this point in time, Lieutenant Cabangbang could easily have empathized with Colonel Merrill's frustrations had the two men been able to sit down over a cold beer.

As news of MacArthur's victories in New Guinea and the Admiralty Islands spread through Luzon, various guerrilla leaders became increasingly aware of their own potential importance in the coming battle for the Philippines. In the southern islands, Colonels Wendell Fertig and Marcario Peralta had long been at odds over which of them had jurisdiction over what islands. Even though they were both badly damaged by recent Japanese attacks, they maintained remnants of their forces and continued to argue. On Luzon, Majors Bernard Anderson, Edwin Ramsey and Robert Lapham stepped up their recruiting efforts in the mountains around central Luzon and began a frantic contest to expand and organize their relative commands, sometimes at each other's expense.[25] Intelligence messages forwarded to MacArthur's headquarters were cluttered with information about which areas were supposed to be under whose control, requests for arms and supplies, and requests for promotions and unit designations. At times, gunfights broke out between members of rival guerrilla organizations. One message to MacArthur stated, "These happenings seem to suit the Japanese and become a source of their mirth and sneer." [26]

John Boone considered his Bataan guerrillas to be part of Major Ramsey's East Central Luzon Guerrilla Army, although Bernard Anderson also claimed Boone's organization and included Boone's men in the troop counts he sent to MacArthur.[27] Anderson considered Robert Lapham to be under his command as well, and longed to take over Ramsey's organization and to discipline Ramsey.[28] Ramsey, for his part, refused to have anything to do with Anderson.[29] It got so bad at one point that Robert Lapham sent a message to MacArthur's headquarters asking for clarification of everyone's status.[30] Ramsey sent a message asking MacArthur to send a general to take over.[31]

MacArthur, with more important things on his mind, declined to reply.

In October, Lieutenant Cabangbang moved his network control station out of Bernard Anderson's Tayabas headquarters on the east coast, and crossed the mountains to a place in the foothills of the Sierra Madres, twenty miles north of Manila. Here, near Norzagaray municipality in Bulacan Province, he would be centrally located, physically closer to the headquarters of several guerrilla leaders in central Luzon, and protected by the guerrilla organization of Captain Alejo Santos.[32] He dubbed the place, "Victory Hill."

Almost immediately Captain Santos again raised the question "who's in charge here?" Santos had, at various times, been told that he reported to Major Ramsey, to Major Anderson, and to Colonel Merrill.[33]

Lieutenant Cabangbang broke the news—none of them was in charge. General MacArthur had sent specific orders that the various guerrilla commanders were to each operate independently and report directly to the Commanding General.[34] Unified leadership behind Japanese lines, throughout the vastness of the Philippine Islands or even on Luzon itself, was impractical. Santos and everyone else were to lay low, collect and submit intelligence reports, and not try to take over any new areas. It was getting frustrating for Cabangbang. You would think that these people, Americans and Filipinos alike, would focus on the Japanese and cooperate with each other. Santos, for his part, decided that his best bet was to stick with Lieutenant Cabangbang and ignore the other guerrilla "commanders."[35]

In November, Cabangbang brought several more guerrilla organizations into his radio network,[36] and he dispatched a radio team to the guerilla headquarters of Lieutenant Colonel Russell W. Volckmann in northern Luzon.[37] Volckmann operated the best-organized and most ruthless guerrilla organization on Luzon outside of the Huks. As soon as he got his radio up and running, Volckmann radioed back that *he* was the man in charge on Luzon.

Lieutenant Cabangbang's frustration finally hit its limit. He sent General MacArthur a message asking that he send a high-ranking officer to Luzon to take over. He said that the various guerrilla "generals" and "colonels" were not cooperating with him, to the detriment of the war effort.[38] He had tried his best, but MacArthur needed to send an officer who could demand cooperation from the guerrillas.

***

In September 1942, Lieutenant Henry Clay Conner and Sergeant Frank Gyovai had departed the Tala settlement with a band of Huks, intending to become guerrillas. They quickly had a falling out with the Huks, and they wandered about the Luzon central plain for months. Eventually they took refuge in the Zambales Mountains above Fort Stotsenburg with two other Americans, guests of a friendly tribe of Negritos—the same Negritos who had befriended Colonel Thorp several years before. To assure the Negritos' loyalty and protection, and against the advice of Frank Gyovai, Clay Conner married the daughter of the chief of the Negrito tribe.[39]

The Negritos were not much interested in politics, but for their own protection Conner and Gyovai did their best to convince these small forest people that the Japanese were their enemy. They organized them and instructed them in some basic military tactics.

As MacArthur's forces drew near the Philippines, Lieutenant Felipe Maningo, a Philippine Scout, climbed up the mountainside bringing 150 former Scouts with him to join Clay Conner's guerrilla organization, such as it was.[40] Conner set up an observation post in Banaba, a town in the foothills close to Fort Stotsenburg and Clark Field,[41] and Lieutenant Maningo recruited a network of Filipino spies—men who worked at the two Japanese military bases.[42] Doyle Decker, one of the men manning the observation post at Banaba, made contact with Claire Phillips in Manila. They established a courier arrangement to pass information the workers collected on the Japanese bases "through channels" to General MacArthur.[43]

On November 3, 1944, Clay Conner received a courier from Captain Alfred Bruce's headquarters in Tarlac Province, just to his north. The courier brought a message, and with it a small package of supplies recently manufactured in the United States.[44] Al Bruce had just received a two-way radio from a Lieutenant Cabangbang in Bulacan Province. The courier said that Cabangbang had come to Luzon from General MacArthur's headquarters and that someone from MacArthur's headquarters would soon be coming to Conner's site, too.

Conner reasoned that if an officer from General MacArthur's staff was in the Philippines and about to pay him a personal visit, he had better notify Colonel Merrill. Conner wrote a note to Merrill advising him to come to Conner's camp immediately, to meet General MacArthur's representative.[45] As usual, he signed the note "Major H.C. Conner, Jr." He gave the note to one of his Negritos and told him to take it directly to Colonel Merrill.

The Negrito came back with Colonel Merrill's reply, in which Merrill commented, "Congratulations on your promotion. How was it received by you?" [46] The Negrito told Conner that he was to come with him, to a meeting. Concerned about being questioned about his rank once again, Conner followed the Negrito down the mountain to Natividad, Pampanga.

The two men walked down a maze of small paths and animal trails through the jungle that covered the face of the mountain. Occasionally, Conner caught a glimpse of the flat Pampanga plain through the trees, cross-hatched with vegetable and tobacco farms, dark green sugarcane fields, and foot paths. In the distance, along the north shore of Manila Bay, he could make out some of the swamps and fishponds of the Pampanga River delta. Pampanga was not only the home of Fort Stotsenburg and Clark Field, but it also had long been one of the most productive farming areas in the Philippines. Today, many of the fields were fallow—after the Japanese had confiscated so many crops, the Filipino farmers had simply quit planting.

Eventually they came to the elegant wood and stone plantation house of the Jingco family, where Conner met with Lieutenant Colonel Peter D. Calyer, Colonel Gyles Merrill's deputy. Colonel Calyer explained that Colonel Merrill was trying to unite all American guerrillas on Luzon and get them ready for the eventual return of General MacArthur. There would be an important role for Conner and his Negritos, which Colonel Merrill would define once he understood more about Conner's organization. They discussed who was to be in charge of Pampanga Province: "Major" Clay Conner, or "Colonel" Abelardo de Dios—Major Ramsey's man. Calyer said that if Conner was willing to report to Colonel Merrill, as far as he was concerned Conner could be in charge of Pampanga, but he would have to confirm that with Colonel Merrill.[47]

Colonel Calyer also wanted to know why Lieutenant Conner had signed his recent letter "Major" Conner.

Clay Conner explained the necessity of assuming a rank higher than lieutenant in order to command the respect of the Negritos and the Filipinos. He apologized for having done so and suggested that if they thought he had committed a court-martial offense he, Conner, would step aside and Colonel Merrill could appoint a more senior officer to head up his Negrito forces.

Calyer said that would not be necessary. Conner should stay where he was, continue to lead his Negritos and the Philippine Scouts that had joined him in the mountains, and use the rank "major" when dealing with them and other Filipinos. He cautioned him, however, to remember that he was really a lieutenant and that neither Colonel Merrill nor anyone else in the Philippines had authority to promote anybody. As soon as the war was over, Colonel Merrill intended to deal with those who had promoted themselves.

Relieved, Clay Conner agreed.[48]

Back at his headquarters in the mountains, Clay Conner explained the situation to Lieutenant Maningo, Frank Gyovai, and the other three American soldiers hiding with them. Then he and Gyovai explained the situation to the tribal elders. They told them that Major Conner was officially in command of Pampanga Province by order of Colonel Merrill, and that they all needed to begin preparations for the coming war. The Negritos were going to be very important to the war effort, they explained, not only as warriors but also as messengers. The forest people knew the Zambales Mountains far better than anyone else, and Conner had agreed that they would take on the task of carrying messages between Colonel Merrill's headquarters and the other guerrilla organizations on Luzon.[49]

***

Along with his regular load of supplies, Placido brought news to Frank that a team of U.S. Army radiomen came through Tala a few days ago. They were taking a powerful radio to Colonel Merrill, and they told Placido that several teams of radio operators had come to Luzon by submarine under the command of a Lieutenant Cabangbang. Their mission was to gather intelligence information about Japanese installations and activities on Luzon, and radio it back to General MacArthur's headquarters.

Frank was impressed. Clearly, MacArthur must be getting close and clearly Colonel Merrill was somehow included in MacArthur's invasion plans. Boone's men were still hand-carrying their reports of Japanese activity on Bataan to Major Ramsey.[50] Colonel Merrill was much closer. Frank sent Roy down to Eddie Wright's camp with instructions for Eddie to go find Colonels James Collier and Gyles Merrill, and "place our services at their disposal." [51] On November 27, Eddie left for the Jingco Plantation in Natividad, Pampanga, where he expected to find Colonel Collier.

Later that same morning, an American lieutenant named Bob Chapin brought a letter to Frank Loyd from Colonel Merrill. It was Merrill's response to Frank's advice not to put American officers over the existing Filipino guerrilla organizations:

> Your assumption that I contemplated assigning you to a command status in the Guerrilla Forces is entirely in error...
>
> The advice to me contained in your letter is an act of unwarranted impudence and interference that I cannot overlook. You imply that I have no knowledge of what has taken place or is taking place, that I am totally unfamiliar with the condition of the Guerrilla Forces and of the American officers and men who have survived...
>
> Your attitude of defeatism should be kept to yourself. Let me assure you that there are still American officers and men who have not lost the will to fight...
>
> Your letter together with a copy of this reply will be forwarded to higher headquarters for appropriate action.
>
> G. Merrill
> Colonel (Cav) GSC[52]

Frank was astonished. No one had ever chewed him out like that, in person or on paper, since he had been in the United States Army. Higher headquarters? And Merrill had practically called him a coward!

Obviously, there was a misunderstanding. Frank concluded that Merrill must not have discussed his letter with Colonel Collier. James Collier would never have condoned such a reply.[53]

Frank wrote a letter directly to Colonel Collier explaining that he had only intended to express his opinion to Merrill regarding assignment of U.S. officers to command Filipino guerrillas.[54] If Colonel Merrill did not intend to do that, then it was a moot point. In his letter Frank offered his services to Colonels Collier and Merrill, but pointed out that if they did not need him he intended to work in the Bataan Military District as John Boone's advisor.[55]

Frank still had the letter two days later when he got an unexpected visit from an old acquaintance—Sam Zozabrado. After exchanging amenities, Sam held out his hand.

"Colonel, I have something for you."

Frank extended his hand, and Sam Zozabrado dropped five Atabrine tablets and Frank's Iowa State college ring into his palm. It was the ring Sam took with him to Manila as identification when he met Juan Elizalde and Narciso Manzano more than a year ago, back in March 1943. It was the ring Sam had pawned to buy Atabrine tablets for Frank. Frank had long since realized that he misjudged Sam when he accused him of embezzling the 100 pesos sent by Juan Elizalde, but he had not seen Sam since that day.

Frank looked Zozabrado over once again. Sam had redeemed his ring and brought it back. Obviously, the man wanted to set things right.[56]

Frank thanked Sam for his ring and the Atabrine, and the men talked. Sam had become an officer in Boone's guerrillas and was recently promoted to Captain in charge of the Bataan Military District's Military Police detachment.[57] He told Frank that John Boone was still having trouble controlling Captain Magtanggol. Magtanggol, a personal friend of Sam's, had conducted several unauthorized raids on the Japanese, and a few days ago he had killed a Japanese soldier in Hermosa. The Japanese retaliated by raiding Bamban, the site of Eddie Wright's camp, and nearby barrio Bacong, looking for Magtanggol. They killed three men there.[58] Other civilians in the surrounding villages had also been singled out and executed in retaliation for Magtanggol's raids. Civilian support for Boone's guerrillas was being jeopardized.[59]

Sam was on his way to Boone's headquarters to discuss what should be done about Magtanggol. He asked if there was anything that he could do for Colonel Loyd. Frank said that there was. He asked Sam to have Boone's courier deliver the letter to Colonel Collier at the Jingco Plantation.[60]

***

Eddie Wright had unknowingly missed the Japanese raid at Bamban as he walked along the edge of the jungle to the Jingco Plantation. He arrived at mid-day and knocked on the thick wooden doors of the big house. The door opened a crack and a Filipino peered out. Recognizing Eddie as an American, he threw open the door and welcomed Eddie inside.

Silently, the man conducted Eddie down a hallway to a spacious dining room. There, seated around a large mahogany table, were three khaki-uniformed American officers, several well-dressed Filipino women, and one Filipino man. To Eddie's astonishment, they were all eating a sumptuous looking, American-style meal, complete with silverware, real plates, and glasses. The men were clean, clean-shaven, and dressed in clean uniforms. They motioned Eddie to an empty carved-wood chair and invited him to sit down.

The three officers turned out to be Lieutenant Colonel Peter D. Calyer, Major Roy Tuggle, and Captain George E. Crane, who introduced themselves as members of Colonel Gyles Merrill's staff. The women were the sisters who owned the plantation: Arsenia, Maria, Filomena and Remedios Jingco. The Filipino man was Condrado Jingco, their brother, a guerrilla.[61]

Eddie was surprised to learn that the Colonel Collier he had come to see was not full-colonel James "Collier" at all, but rather Lieutenant Colonel Peter D. Calyer, Eddie's West Point classmate, class of '29.[62] Calyer, he learned, reported to Colonel Merrill, not the other way around. Calyer was in Pampanga helping Major Roy Tuggle negotiate a truce with the Hukbalahap on Colonel Merrill's behalf, and they had just signed the agreement.[63] Eddie dutifully offered his services and those of Frank Loyd and Roy Reynolds to Merrill's organization for intelligence gathering duties.

Eddie was astonished by the lifestyle at the Jingco plantation, particularly the food.[64] He stayed on for almost a week, enjoying the clean, hotel-like atmosphere. He and Peter Calyer discussed his idea of raising a battalion of former Philippine Scouts to fight as guerrillas when MacArthur returned.

When Eddie got back to Bataan, he told Frank about Colonel "Calyer," not "Collier." Frank realized what had happened. And he realized that he now had no ally in whatever future dealings he might have with Colonel Merrill.

Peter Calyer had been receptive to Eddie's idea of assembling a battalion of Philippine Scouts, and Eddie began to contact Scouts in the local area to get them organized. General MacArthur had just sent a powerful radio to Colonel Merrill, and Merrill had managed to conclude a treaty with the Hukbalahap. To Eddie, it was obvious that Colonel Merrill was the man in charge on Luzon.

***

As Lieutenant Cabangbang's communications network grew, and as General MacArthur's armies grew closer, Cabangbang found that he was confronted with more unexpected problems.

The Huks were active again and had recently posted leaflets in Pampanga and Bulacan Provinces telling the Filipinos that the USAFFE guerrillas were robbers, that the Huks had been recognized by and were admired by General MacArthur, and that the Huks would soon initiate a communist government in Pampanga Province.[65] They were reported to have killed several USAFFE guerrillas and pro-American government officials.[66] In addition, the rice harvest was approaching and Cabangbang found his net control station at Victory Hill surrounded by bands of armed

Huks who were about to loot the harvest.[67] A battle between the USAFFE guerrillas and the Huks appeared imminent.

Then one of the radio operators Cabangbang had sent to Colonel Merrill's headquarters came back. Merrill's radio was not working properly and the man needed to pick up parts. The radioman told Cabangbang that Colonel Merrill not only claimed to be in charge of all USAFFE guerrillas on Luzon, but that he was also negotiating a treaty with the Hukbalahap.[68]

Cabangbang next received a message from the Huk leadership, citing their "close" association with Colonel Merrill. They insisted that Cabangbang arrange for an aircraft to pick them up and take them to meet General MacArthur. They demanded a face-to-face meeting with the General.[69]

Lieutenant Cabangbang composed a lengthy, tactful reply addressed to "My dear countrymen," in which he said:

> ...it is lamentable that even we, whose fame as real soldiers and heroes has been broadcast throughout the world, are today not united. It is a shame on all of us, that even at this critical day of our national livelihood we cannot agree among ourselves and unite all our war efforts for the furtherance of our common aim--LIBERTY...
>
> General MacArthur calls all of us to unite and cease immediately our petty quarrels and rivalries. Our country demands from all of us our unified war efforts, cooperation and assistance.[70]

Cabangbang's efforts did not go unnoticed at General MacArthur's headquarters. With the Luzon radio net up, running and still expanding, with bickering between the guerrilla commanders more or less under control, and with a great deal of timely intelligence data now flowing smoothly and rapidly into his headquarters, General MacArthur, on December 2, 1944, promoted Lieutenant Cabangbang to Captain.[71]

Emboldened and buoyed by MacArthur's confidence in him, Captain Cabangbang sent messages to all of the Luzon guerrilla commanders, citing MacArthur's authority and telling them that all future communications with MacArthur's headquarters were to go only through him. Unauthorized actions against the Japanese were to cease. All guerrilla units were to sit tight until they received specific instructions from General MacArthur.[72] A few days later, he followed up with another message that clearly told the guerrilla commanders to stop squabbling and follow orders, regardless of their various presumed ranks.[73]

Captain Cabangbang had taken control.

XIX. The Samurai Generals

1944 had gone fairly well for the Japanese Imperial General Staff—up to a point. Premier Hideki Tojo scheduled a major offensive in China to capture Allied air bases, defeat Generalissimo Chiang Kai-shek, and end the long, bloody war there. The China victory was to be accompanied by an invasion of India, designed to secure the western frontier and remove the British from one more country. The Japanese Army and Navy were to hold the Americans and Australians at bay outside of Japan's South Pacific defense perimeter, where they would continue to be little more than an ineffective nuisance. Finally, the Philippine Islands were to be brought fully into Japan's Greater East Asia Co-Prosperity Sphere, ending dissent and guerrilla rebelliousness there.

The June offensive in China resulted in the capture of the Kweilin and Liuchen air bases, which prevented the Americans from launching B-29 strikes from China against

Tokyo.[1] In August the Army successfully completed the China campaign, although Chiang Kai-shek still refused to surrender.[2] So far, so good.

But by September, it was apparent that things elsewhere had taken an ugly turn. Premier Tojo's invasion of India failed miserably. Then General Douglas MacArthur broke through the Japanese defense line in the southern islands and attacked north, reaching Palau. He bypassed several strongholds and left tens of thousands of Japanese troops stranded on now insignificant islands where the fleet could no longer supply or rescue them.

The Japanese Combined Fleet, which had tried for so long to lure the Americans into a decisive battle, had finally gotten its wish at the Battle of the Philippine Sea in June. U.S. Admiral Raymond A. Spruance's Fifth Fleet soundly defeated the Combined Fleet, with horrific losses in Japanese naval aircraft.

Worst of all, in one of the bloodiest battles of the war, the Americans captured Saipan in the Mariana Islands 1300 miles south of Tokyo. Many Japanese considered Saipan to be part of the homeland itself.[3] Virtually every Japanese on the island, soldier and civilian alike, perished in the battle or committed suicide.[4] Mothers leaped off high cliffs with their babies in their arms rather than fall into the hands of the Americans. Because of the fall of Saipan, Premier Tojo was unceremoniously kicked out of the government.[5]

U.S. submarines were sinking Japanese cargo ships at an alarming rate, causing food and fuel shortages in Japan itself.[6] Then the U.S. began to launch B-29 raids on Tokyo from airfields on Saipan.[7] The generals ordered that school children be evacuated from Tokyo to the countryside in anticipation of more bomber attacks.[8]

Clearly, something had to be done.

The Imperial General Staff decided upon a complete change in tactics.

Previously, the Japanese approach to the war had been to take the field aggressively, attack swiftly, and hold the ground they captured. But such aggression had been costly—*banzai* assault tactics resulted in huge numbers of Japanese deaths relative to the number of casualties inflicted on the enemy. The supply of serviceable airplanes was dwindling, and the two-year-long flight-training program could not keep up with the demand for combat pilots.

General Kuniyaki Koiso took over as Premier, replacing Tojo. He had his war planners map out a new strategy, dubbed the "*Sho*" [Victory] Operation. They designed the *Sho* Operation to bring all of Japan's considerable forces to bear against the next enemy offensive and to stop the Americans cold.[9] Wherever the American forces struck next, that place would be designated the decisive battle area. The Army, all of the Japanese naval fleet, and what was left of the air fleet would concentrate there to attack the enemy. Instead of defending the beaches, the Army would pull back, dig in, and wait. They would lure the American troops into inland traps where Japanese soldiers and artillery hidden in underground bunkers could annihilate the Americans in deadly crossfires. The idea was to make it so costly for General MacArthur to gain ground in the Pacific that the American public would be revulsed by the carnage and call off the war before the American Army could reach Japan.[10]

On October 12, the generals and admirals got more bad news. New U.S. carrier-based aircraft, which could out-perform and out-shoot the vaunted Japanese Zero, unexpect-edly attacked Formosa. The 2nd Air Fleet, the best air organization left in the Japanese military, was devastated.[11] As usual, and in direct contrast to reality, the Japanese press depicted the Formosa battle as Japan's biggest victory since Pearl Harbor, claiming that nineteen U.S. aircraft carriers had been damaged or sunk.[12]

But the top generals and admirals knew different. The Japanese had only damaged two American cruisers, while large numbers of their own fighters and bombers were destroyed.

Where would the Americans strike next? Everyone knew that General MacArthur's real objective was the Philippines.[13]

A commission of senior officers went to the Philippines to inspect fortifications there. They reported that General Shegenori Kuroda's defense preparations were unsatisfactory. Kuroda had been ordered to prepare for a possible attack by MacArthur, and he now had more than 400,000 Army soldiers and 20,000 Navy personnel on hand. But as new troops arrived they found that the fortifications they were supposed to occupy were way behind schedule, primarily because construction workers seemed to move so slowly in the Philippines. General Kuroda's food and fuel supplies could only support a few weeks of sustained combat.[14] In spite of recent anti-guerrilla campaigns, guerrilla activity was actually increasing.[15] The puppet Philippine legislature had voted down a conscription bill to draft young Filipino men into the Japanese defense forces.[16] What kind of puppet government was that?

The Imperial General Staff sacked Kuroda. As his replacement they selected two of the most famous and most successful officers in the Japanese military: Lieutenant General Tomoyuki Yamashita—the Tiger of Malaya, and Vice Admiral Takijiro Ohnishi, Chief of General Affairs of Aviation.

Tomoyuki Yamashita was a genuine hero to the Japanese people, and the generals staged plenty of hoopla and public celebration to mark his appointment. On Radio Tokyo, the Tiger of Malaya outlined his expectations: "At last I have MacArthur in my iron trap... The only words I spoke to the British commander during the negotiations for the surrender of Singapore were: 'All I want to hear from you is yes or no!' I expect to put the same question to MacArthur."[17]

Admiral Takijiro Ohnishi, on the other hand, was a thoughtful man who, like many Japanese intellectuals, dabbled in poetry. He had helped Admiral Isoroku Yamamoto plan the attack on Pearl Harbor, and he had been operations officer of the 11th Air Fleet the day it attacked and destroyed General MacArthur's Far East Air Force on the ground at Clark Field—the first day of the war. Pragmatic, heavy-set Admiral Ohnishi knew that it was going to be difficult to stop the American advance.[18] The Americans were shooting down Japanese warplanes as fast as they could be built. Worse, the pilot training schools could not replenish the supply of pilots quickly enough, even if there were enough aircraft. It was a problem that Ohnishi had been contemplating for several months, and he had formulated a potential solution in the back of his mind. His orders from the Admiralty were clear—he was to turn the tide of battle at any cost.[19]

On October 15, a Japanese reconnaissance plane spotted a large U.S. naval force 240 miles east of Manila, apparently headed for Leyte, one of the islands in the middle of the Philippines.[20] The General Staff immediately activated the *Sho* Operation and declared the Philippines the decisive battle area. Imperial Headquarters elected to throw everything they had into the defense of Leyte. They ordered General Yamashita to send the veteran 16th Division from Luzon to Leyte, in spite of his protests that the decisive battle would be better fought on Luzon.[21] They ordered the 2nd Air Fleet, what was left of it after the Formosa debacle, to fly to the Philippines and join the 1st Air Fleet in the defense of the islands.[22] They ordered the Navy's Combined Fleet to sail from the Indies to Leyte Gulf immediately, and stop MacArthur.

***

On October 17, Admiral Ohnishi flew into Manila and immediately convened a meeting of his top naval and air corps officers. With grim determination he advanced his idea for a special attack force. It would be a distinctive force, one that could make a significant difference in the defense of the Philippines and, therefore, the defense of Japan. It would be a force of dedicated young men willing to make the ultimate sacrifice for their country. A force that could extract maximum effect from each aircraft committed to battle.

Admiral Ohnishi's idea was not met with universal enthusiasm.[23]

After the meeting in Manila, Admiral Ohnishi climbed into a waiting limousine and drove to Clark Field to meet with the pilots of the 201st Air Group. He explained to them the dangers facing Japan, the importance of stopping the American advance, and the limited resources they had to work with. He told them that the Japanese battle fleet was on its way to Leyte to sink the American troop transports and thus thwart MacArthur's invasion. But the Japanese battleships had little air cover. It was likely that American carrier-based airplanes would sink the Japanese battleships before they got to Leyte, unless the American carriers could be stopped. The American aircraft carriers were the key—if the 201st Air Group could stop the American carriers, or delay them for only a week, the Japanese battleships would have time to arrive off Leyte and sink the American transports.

The 201st had lost two-thirds of its aircraft in the Battle of the Philippine Sea,[24] and it was down to its last thirty fighter planes. The twenty-three pilots of the 201st understood the gravity of the situation.[25] They agreed to a man to throw themselves against the approaching American aircraft carriers.[26] They elected to call their new attack force "*Kamikaze*" [the Divine Wind], the name given to a typhoon that had destroyed the armada of Kublai Khan in 1281 and thus saved the Empire from the invader.

Gratified by the dedication of his young heroes, Admiral Ohnishi spent that night with the men of the 201st. The next day he returned to Manila to take up his position as commander of the Navy's 1st Air Fleet.[27] He felt certain that the twenty-three Kamikaze pilots of the 201st Air Group would be sufficient to blunt MacArthur's invasion force. If his Kamikazes took the American carriers out of action for just one week, it would provide enough time for the main battle fleet to arrive and sink MacArthur's troopships.[28] The American infantrymen would drown, and the American invasion would thus fail.

***

On October 20, General MacArthur descended on Leyte with a huge landing force—the largest since the Normandy invasion in Europe four months before, the largest ever in the Pacific. More than 500 ships brought four army divisions, over 200,000 troops, to Leyte. As they approached, U.S. carrier-based aircraft swarmed over the cloudy beaches and rainy inland jungles with almost no Japanese opposition.[29] After a heavy naval artillery barrage and extensive bombing, the first wave of men from the U.S. 6th Army went ashore. Resistance at the beaches was surprisingly light.[30] That afternoon, General MacArthur waded ashore from a landing craft, accompanied by his entourage of staff officers and press photographers.

MacArthur had returned.

American airplanes dumped leaflets all over the Philippine Islands announcing the return of General MacArthur and Philippine President Sergio Osmeña.* A radio transmitter was set up and MacArthur and Osmeña made personal appeals over the "Voice of Freedom" for the Filipinos to rise up and strike the Japanese.[31] President Osmeña broadcast from Leyte that the Philippine Army officially confirmed the ranks of all officers and men serving in the USAFFE guerrilla units recognized by General MacArthur.[32]

All over the islands young men volunteered for guerrilla service by the thousands. President Osmeña's

---

* Vice-President Osmeña took over after President Quezon died of tuberculosis in Washington, D.C.

pledge meant that men who served in the guerrillas were going to get paid. In the Philippines, money talks.

***

Admiral Ohnishi, meanwhile, ran into an unexpected problem with his plan to defeat the Americans. For four days his Kamikaze pilots were unable to locate the American aircraft carriers among the late rainy-season fog and clouds.[33]

On October 23, while American transports were still unloading at Leyte, the Japanese Combined Fleet arrived and initiated a three-pronged attack. The Battle of Leyte Gulf, the biggest naval battle of World War II, began. U.S. submarines and superior American radar had no trouble finding the Japanese ships in the rain and fog, including the battleships brought in to sink MacArthur's troop transports. The Imperial Combined Fleet was no longer any match for the Americans. In three days of horrendous fighting, U.S. Admiral Thomas C. Kinkaid's ships and airplanes destroyed a substantial portion of the Japanese Navy.[34]

The naval battle was, for all practical purposes, already lost when, on October 25, Ohnishi's Kamikazes finally located the American carriers and made their first strikes. The results were devastating to the Americans. On that day, the Kamikazes sank one U.S. aircraft carrier, set three others on fire and damaged two more. Eight kamikaze attacks, six carriers out of action.[35] Japanese Navy pilots began volunteering for kamikaze duty all over the Philippines. Admiral Ohnishi was elated by his pilot's success.

When the Emperor's staff informed His Majesty of the feat, it heightened Admiral Ohnishi's elation even further. Until he heard the Emperor's words:

"Was it necessary to go to this extreme? They certainly did a magnificent job."[36]

Ohnishi, upset, interpreted the message to mean that Emperor Hirohito was greatly concerned. He pledged to redouble the efforts of the Kamikaze Corps to relieve His Majesty's concerns.

***

As the Leyte battle waged on, the 2nd Air Fleet flew in from Formosa. Its commander, Admiral Shigeru Fukudome, outranked Admiral Ohnishi and he immediately let it be known that he was opposed to suicide tactics.[37]

Admiral Ohnishi went to Admiral Fukudome's office in Manila and made an almost irrefutable argument: the Japanese fighter pilots were doomed anyway. Every one of them was most likely going to die in combat, so why not give each man the opportunity to do so at maximum cost to the enemy? The kamikaze attack was their best option.[38] After the spectacular success of Ohnishi's pilots on October 25, and with the Japanese Navy virtually knocked out of action, Fukudome had no real choice.

After meeting with Admiral Fukudome, Ohnishi returned to Clark Field. He called his remaining pilots together and made it clear to them that they were heroes and that he would tolerate no criticism of them or of their mission.[39] Since the Americans had successfully landed at Leyte, it was now even more critical that they throw back MacArthur's invasion fleet before it reached Luzon. To that end, more kamikaze volunteers would soon join them.

That night he returned to his quarters. He wrote a poem—about life.[40]

XX. Expectations

On October 19, 1944, Evelyn Loyd listened intently to the news broadcasts about the Leyte invasion. Radio Tokyo announced it first and the U.S. radio networks picked it up immediately.

Evelyn was excited but apprehensive. Soon, she would know. Frank was somewhere in those islands, dead or alive. It was unlikely that Frank would have gone to Leyte, but she was sure that once General MacArthur's troops secured Leyte the General would set his sights on Luzon.

Then the telephone rang. It was Frank's cousin in Kansas, Effie Adee.

Effie said that she had a friend who worked in the War Department in Washington, D.C. In her last letter Effie's friend mentioned that she had seen Frank Loyd's name on a list of American soldiers who were known to be alive and well in the Philippines. Effie was thrilled with the news, but somewhat put out with Evelyn Loyd.

"If the War Department knew Frank was alive, why didn't you tell us? We're family! We've been worried sick!"

Evelyn was stunned. Apparently the War Department knew something about Frank, but they had not notified Evelyn at all.

Evelyn asked Effie who this friend was. Where in the Pentagon did she work? What list had she seen?

Effie became cautious.

"I can't tell you that, Evelyn. I don't want to get her in trouble. This might all be secret. Anyway, I thought you knew. I probably should not have told you about this on the telephone. Who knows who might be listening? I'll write you a letter." [1]

Evelyn was overjoyed, of course. But after Effie hung up and she had time to think about it, she was outraged! After all her phone calls, telegrams and letters to the War Department and to the Red Cross, someone found out that Frank Loyd was alive and nobody told her. She was mad and disgusted. She was mad at the War Department. She was mad at Effie, too.

But was it true?

Evelyn decided to go see an old friend, Lieutenant Colonel Harvey Fisher. The Japanese had captured Harvey Fisher on Bataan in 1942, and interned him in a prison camp on Mindanao. In September 1944, they shipped Fisher and some other prisoners back to Luzon, but a U.S. submarine torpedoed the ship. Fisher swam to shore where he was rescued by some guerrillas. The guerrillas got him onto another U.S. submarine and he was eventually evacuated to the United States. His picture had been in all the newspapers. At first they took him to Washington, but he had just been brought to Brook Army Hospital in San Antonio to recover.

Colonel Fisher told Evelyn that he had heard nothing about Frank Loyd during the entire time he was a prisoner of war. He did know from his contacts in Washington that lists of American guerrillas had been smuggled out of the Philippines, but he doubted that Frank's name was on any of them. The FBI, he assured Evelyn, had already contacted the families of all the men known to be with the guerrillas in the Philippines.[2] Effie must be mistaken. Harvey Fisher discouraged Evelyn from getting her hopes up. Disappointed, Evelyn went home.

Early in November, she got another call. This one was from a man who identified himself as an officer in Naval Intelligence. He wanted to meet with Evelyn—privately. Excited, she invited him over.

He turned out to be a nice-looking young man wearing civilian clothes, a dark trench coat and a hat. Evelyn let him in and they sat down together in her living room. In response to Evelyn's questions the man said that he had no information about Frank and that he really could not comment on anything Effie's friend might have seen. He said, candidly, that he did not want to get Evelyn's hopes up. Frank's status was Missing In Action, and that was all he could confirm.

He did, however, have some questions.

As the conversation progressed, he asked her about the places she had lived and visited in the Philippines. She described Bataan, the jungle, and the time that she and Frank camped there with their children. She described the roads and areas around Manila. And she told him about their last vacation together in the little seacoast village of Legaspi.

"Legaspi? Did you go to the beach there?"

"Yes."

"Tell me about the beaches, and the sand," he said.

Evelyn described what she could remember and mentioned the movies Frank had taken of the children playing on the beach.

"Would you like to see them?"

The man helped Evelyn set up the projector and he watched intently as the children dug in the sand.

When it was over he said, "Mrs. Loyd, I would like to take this film with me. We will keep it for a while and then return it to you. Would you agree to that?"

"Yes. Of course." [3]

The man left with the film.

Now, Evelyn did not know what to think. She told the children what cousin Effie's friend thought she saw, but she also told them what Harvey Fisher and the Naval Intelligence man said. Unlike her friend Evelyn Noble, she wanted her children to know everything. But, like Evelyn Noble, she did not want to raise false hopes.

So she called Evelyn Noble and invited her over for coffee.

Evelyn Noble again tried to convince Evelyn Loyd that Frank was with Maxie Noble and Martin Moses. For some reason, the War Department must be keeping Frank's role in the Philippines a secret, but the fact that Effie's friend had seen his name on a list meant that he was alive. Evelyn Noble assured Evelyn Loyd that she just needed to keep faith.

On December 7, 1944, the third anniversary of the Japanese attacks on the Philippines and Pearl Harbor, the Red Cross called to tell Evelyn Loyd that they were again sending mail to the islands, including mail to men listed as Missing In Action. The clerk said that she was told specifically to call Mrs. Loyd and notify her. Evelyn kept both children home from school the next morning and they all went to the Red Cross office downtown. A volunteer gave each of them one sheet of thin Red Cross stationery and told them that they could write only one page each, but they could write on both sides. They addressed their letters to "Lt. Col. Frank R. Loyd, missing in the Philippine Islands." The volunteer said to write his Army serial number, and place and date of birth in the space labeled "address."

Evelyn wrote that they had all prayed for Frank's safety but that they had heard nothing about him since his letter of March 1942, except for that one mysterious line written on Montgomery McKee's card from prison camp. She told him about her job as a censor at the post office, the new house she had bought at 165 Thorain Boulevard, and that his brother-in-law was somewhere in the Philippines with the 1st Cavalry Division. She inquired about Maxie Noble, and reminded Frank of their planned rendezvous in San Francisco. Bonnie wrote that she was a junior at Incarnate Word High School, tall, with braces, and taking art lessons. Frank Jr. wrote that he was a senior at Central Catholic High School, a six-foot two-inch football player who hoped to get into West Point. He said that he had bought his own 1929 Model "A" Ford, but his proudest accomplishment was earning his pilot's license in just eighteen hours flying time. He told his father that there were questions he wanted to ask about the war but wouldn't because of censorship.[4] Evelyn turned the letters in at the Red Cross desk. The Red Cross volunteer said she would take care of them.

A week later the Red Cross called to say they were sorry, but it was all a mistake. They could not take Evelyn's letters to the Philippines after all. What did she want done with them? Disgusted, Evelyn told them to just throw them away.[5]

About that time, Frank Jr. stuck his head in to tell her that he was going out for the afternoon with some boys from his high school ROTC unit. They had just been issued the new M-1 Garand rifles the Army was using in combat, and their military science professor was taking them to Camp Bullis to practice.[6]

***

On the day General Tomoyuki Yamashita arrived in Manila to take command, he found two large bronze Japanese urns outside the doors of his new quarters—the MacArthur Suite at the Manila Hotel. The urns were inscribed to General Arthur MacArthur from Japanese Emperor Mutsuhito, Emperor Hirohito's grandfather. Jean

MacArthur had left them there when she fled from the hotel in 1941, in hopes that Japanese officers entering the penthouse might treat the furnishings with respect.[7] Castro, the MacArthurs' houseboy, was on hand to serve him.[8]

The next morning Yamashita went to his new headquarters at Fort McKinley. He arrived a little late, but in time to observe the damage done by a guerrilla bomb that exploded beneath his building.[9] Welcome to the Philippines.

General Yamashita's immediate superior, mustachioed Field Marshall Count Hiseichi Terauchi, commanding general of the Southern Army Command, had just returned from Leyte, where he had observed the Japanese defenses.[10] Both men agreed that the defense of the Philippines would have to rely on ground troops, not the air forces or the Navy. Yamashita laid out his defense plan for Field Marshall Terauchi.

If the Americans were not defeated on Leyte, General Yamashita planned to concede the beaches of Luzon and concentrate his troops at three points in the mountains overlooking places where the Americans were most likely to land: Lingayen Gulf, Batangas and Legaspi. Yamashita planned to let the Americans come ashore, where they would initially be concentrated on the beaches. Then his artillery would fire down on them from the mountain strongholds, and Japanese infantry would attack and annihilate them.[11] His troops were already stocking supplies of food, fuel, and ammunition at each site. Electricians were installing communications networks and combat engineers were reinforcing bridges to support tanks and heavy trucks.[12] Field Marshall Terauchi approved.

Terauchi told Yamashita that he was leaving the next day. Although he had maintained his Southern Army Command headquarters in Manila since the early days of the war, Terauchi was moving his headquarters and staff to the safety of Singapore.[13]

It was to be expected. Yamashita had not come to the Philippines to survive. He was there to kill as many

Americans as possible and make it too costly for the U.S. to risk attacking the Japanese homeland. When he said goodbye to his wife in Tokyo he had made it clear that he did not expect to see her again. General Yamashita believed that Admiral Chester Nimitz would attack from Saipan while General Douglas MacArthur attacked simultaneously "overland" from Leyte.[14] He expected to wreak havoc on the Americans. But in the end, he expected to be starved out and die.[15]

XXI. Christmas 1944

"I will do no such thing!" Margaret Utinsky was furious. Lieutenant Colonel Victor Abad, as far as she was concerned, was little short of an idiot.

"I am a nurse! I am here to save lives, not take them!"

Abad grinned at her. She turned and walked out of the little office in the abandoned sugar mill near Tala, Bataan, that Abad used for his 2nd Regiment guerrilla headquarters. She climbed down the steps off the front porch. A light rain soaked through Margaret's clothes as she stumbled down the hillside to the bamboo shelter secluded in a dank, old coffee patch that served as her infirmary. She was glad to get out of Abad's headquarters. It was hot in there and the stench of the guards' unwashed bodies combined with what he had asked her to do had made Margaret nauseous.

As she stood clenching her fists in the one-room infirmary, the image of a young woman and her child burned in Margaret's mind. The woman was sitting in a chair in Abad's back room, just inside the door. Her dark, sweaty clothes loosely coated her thin frame. Strands of black hair stuck to her dark-brown cheeks, shiny with tears. Her child, a boy about five years old, sat in her lap, his large, brown eyes staring uncomprehendingly at Margaret through the open door. Colonel Abad had ordered Margaret to administer a lethal injection of strychnine to both the young woman and her child.[1]

Margaret did not know what to do. Abad claimed that the woman was a traitor, a Japanese spy. He said that the woman and the child too, had been tried and convicted. Margaret had seen no court. None of the guerrillas had gathered in Abad's building to watch a trial as far as she knew. She leaned against the wall of the infirmary, put her face in her hands and tried to think.

After a while, a shadow blotted the cloudy daylight coming through the infirmary door. Margaret looked up.

It was Victor Abad. "Come outside," he said. "I show you something."

Margaret followed him back up the hill and around behind the headquarters building, still trying to think of what she should do, or could do. Margaret could hear the woman crying.

Abad stopped. He leaned his shoulder against the rear corner of the building and nodded toward two men who had dug a hole in the ground near the edge of the jungle. Margaret looked, and she slowly realized that the hole was a grave.

She walked toward it. As she approached she could see dark cloth and a slight movement inside—then the young woman lying on her back in the bottom of the grave, sobbing softly but uncontrollably. Her little boy lay on top of her, his mother's arms wrapped around him, his eyes wide with fear, staring up first at Margaret and then at the guerrilla who stood over the grave, one foot on each side, a .45 caliber pistol in his hand.

"NO!" Margaret staggered back from the grave just as the guerrilla fired. One shot. The bullet passed through both the child and the mother.[2]

As Margaret approached Abad, he was still leaning against the building, grinning slightly, taking in the whole scene. She attacked him. Her small fists pummeled his chest. Her mouth cursed him.

Abad stepped back and grabbed her arms. She fell against his chest, sobbing as he held her. She had to get out of this place. She told him she wanted to go to Colonel Loyd.[3]

Abad shrugged. "You can't make it. Impossible."

Margaret Utinsky had been with the Bataan guerrillas for two months. Things had gotten too hot for her in Manila. In February 1944, the Japanese had arrested most of Margaret's supporters and benefactors. In May, they broke up Naomi Flores' smuggling ring at the Cabanatuan prison camp. Then they arrested Claire Phillips and several of her girls at Club Tsubaki. Other employees brought Claire's little daughter, Dian, to Margaret.[4] For the next several months Margaret cared for the girl while she tried to find out what happened to Claire. But the only word about Claire Phillips was that she was being held in Fort Santiago, had been tortured, and that several American doctors and chaplains at Cabanatuan were thrown into solitary confinement for accepting the medicine and messages sent by Margaret and Claire.[5]

In September, two months ago, Margaret learned that she and Father John Lalor, the priest at the Malate Church who baptized John and Mellie Boone's baby, were both on the Japanese "wanted" list. She packed up a few of Dian's clothes, fled Manila and made her way to Boone's headquarters.[6] Boone welcomed her, commissioned her a second lieutenant in his guerrilla army, and assigned her to work as a nurse in his 2nd Regiment at Tala Ridge, commanded by Lieutenant Colonel Victor Abad.[7] A detail of Boone's men had escorted her and Dian through the jungle to Abad's headquarters in the old sugar mill on Mount Natib, not far from the Tala refugee settlement.

At first, guerrilla life was about what she expected. Abad moved her around every few days, assigned her to various guerrilla details that were about to see action, and the wounded were brought to her for care. There was a serious shortage of bandages and almost no medicine, but the guerrillas had never had *any* professional medical care before, so they were exceptionally grateful for her help. One of the leaders, Captain Ruben Bondoc, who went by the *nom de guerre* "Captain Magtanggol," had even given her new shoes to wear—captured Japanese Army shoes.

Dian, five years old, proved to be an excellent child. She kept to herself and, most importantly, kept quiet. At first the guerrillas were concerned about having a child around, afraid that she might make noises that would give them away to the Japanese. But Dian never cried and they soon accepted her.[8]

Then Abad had begun to act peculiarly. One day he assigned Margaret, as a guerrilla lieutenant, to take charge of a detail of men who were to go get some paint and an American flag to fly over the headquarters—they were to go and get them in Manila.[9] Margaret thought the whole idea was both stupid and crazy, but she did as she was told and wound up once again dodging the Japanese on the streets of Manila.

After Margaret brought the paint and the flag back, things got ugly. The Japanese discovered Abad's headquarters. They attacked and drove the guerrillas out of Tala. They pursued Abad's retreating men and attacked again. And again.[10] Most of the men fled to their homes, leaving Margaret and Dian on the run with Colonel Abad and a few key followers.

In the midst of their running and hiding, Abad and an American officer named Al Romaine brought some food to her and Dian where they were hiding in an old, hollowed out tree. Previously, Margaret had heard rumors about a camp far back on the mountain where a Colonel Loyd lived with his aide, Major Reynolds, and directed the activities of the Bataan guerrillas. In their few moments together, Romaine confirmed the existence of Colonel Loyd's camp and said it was in a very safe place. Margaret resolved then that if things ever got unbearable, that is where she would go.

Today, with the execution of the young Filipina woman, things had gotten unbearable. On top of everything else Dian was sick with pneumonia and Colonel Abad had been unable to obtain any kind of medicine for her.[11]

The next day Colonel Victor Abad gave in. He called for Margaret and presented her to a little man named Damaso Caballero, the mayor of the Negrito village near Tala. He said that Damaso would take her and Dian to Colonel Loyd's camp. Abad gave her a letter of introduction to take to Colonel Loyd.

Damaso's entourage of three young Negritos and eight guerrillas picked up Margaret's clothes and supplies, and little Dian as well. They hiked and climbed all day through the jungle, fording leech-infested streams and swamps until they arrived at their destination at sundown. They were bruised, worn out and bitten. There, standing by a Nipa hut in a small clearing under the jungle canopy, nurse Margaret Utinsky got her first look at the mysterious guerrilla officers, Colonel Frank Loyd and Major Roy Reynolds:

> I came up the hill to see the funniest sight of my life. Outside the hut, standing at the edge of the hill, two men were waiting to greet me. Their shoes were mended with the hides of wild boars, their clothes were patched with pieces of gunny sack. Reynolds had long curly whiskers, his hair hanging down to his shoulders, two front teeth broken off from eating corn. Loyd had dark brown whiskers

clear down to his chest, and he was bent over because he was badly crippled with rheumatism.[12]

Frank and Roy greeted their unexpected visitor, and read her letter of introduction:

> My Dear Col.,
>
> This is to inform the Col. that Lt. Utinsky and the baby will stay temporarily to you secret house for the simple reason that my place is scheduled to be raided for eight consecutive days. She will be there just for safety. Lt. Utinsky is the Chief Headnurse of the Medical Special Unit of the Bay Side of Bataan…
>
> She is a close friend to Col. Boone and she is duly appointed as such and I hope you will do her the best favor possible. Thanks in advance…
>
> Sincerely, Victor L. Abad.[13]

Frank was impressed that the Japanese kept Colonel Abad informed of their raiding schedule.[14]

For months, even years, Frank Loyd had fantasized about various things: about finding a boat that could get him off Luzon, about the delicious dinners served by his old cook Gonzales at the big house in Fort McKinley, of walking up the sidewalk of his home to hug Evelyn and his children, of finding a pretty young nurse deep in the Philippine jungle who would pamper and take care of him.

Margaret Utinsky was an admirable person who at great personal risk had performed wonderful feats of humanity for ill and imprisoned Filipinos and Americans. Frank admired her for that. But she was not young, she was not pretty, and she talked incessantly.[15]

At first Frank and Roy found her stories of supplies smuggled into the Japanese prison camps, of her arrest and torture, of her ingenuity in dodging the authorities, interesting, even inspiring. Then the stories became repetitious, particularly considering that Frank, Roy, and the other men of Bataan had been through some pretty harrowing experiences themselves.

Frank turned his attention to the little girl, Dian. The child was ill, so Frank and Roy made her as comfortable as possible, giving the women their bamboo beds to sleep on, making mango tea, and providing what food they could. The high elevation of Frank and Roy's camp agreed with Dian and over the next few days her condition began to improve.

Christmas was just over a week away. American bombers had flown over dropping Christmas cards to the Filipinos, but little Dian had nothing but the dress on her back. Frank carved a small frame with his knife, stitched a little dress with a piece of gauze and a hand-made wooden needle, stuffed the toy with straw, and gave Dian a doll. It became the most important thing in the child's life.[16]

In response to Frank's request, Boone ordered Colonel Abad to come to Frank's camp to arrange for Mrs. Utinsky's safety while Frank and Roy attended a planning meeting at Boone's headquarters. On December 21, Abad showed up with an entourage of twelve armed guerrillas and his harem of four Filipina girls.[17] Frank told Abad that he and Roy were about to leave for the meeting, and that nurse Utinsky must return to the 2nd Regiment while they were gone. He told Abad to locate her at the Tala settlement where Placido's family could watch over her, and where Abad's guerrillas could still employ her skills as a nurse. He also told Abad that if anything happened to nurse Utinsky, it would be Abad's neck.[18]

That evening, while Abad and his crew made themselves comfortable in the woods around Frank's camp, Frank wrote a letter to Boone answering several issues Boone had raised in his last letter. He made recommendations about areas that Boone's small forces should or should not occupy, how to staff his field hospital, what to do about civilians in combat areas, and other matters related to the start of hostilities. He also recommended that Boone send two American soldiers from his headquarters to Tala to provide security for Mrs. Utinsky. Remembering Boone's previous concern that Frank and Roy intended to take over his command, Frank added, "All of the above is in the nature of suggestion & advice. Use your best judgment and give due consideration to any instructions from higher headquarters which may be in conflict." [19]

The next morning he gave the letter to Abad to take to Boone.

On Saturday, December 23, Frank and Roy got their pistols and other gear together. Abad's men returned to take Margaret Utinsky to Tala.

Margaret refused to go.

A short, strained conversation followed. Finally, Frank showed her how his "metal mess kit and vine" alarm system worked, made certain she had ammunition for her .38 caliber revolver, and pointed out a trail to follow to the Negrito village if anyone came. He had no other choice. He and Roy needed to get to Boone's headquarters. They left Margaret and Dian at the camp.[20]

As they trudged silently down the trail, the men's spirits were low. A few weeks ago Placido brought news of the Leyte invasion, including a copy of the *Manila Tribune*. The Japanese-controlled newspaper claimed that the U.S. Pacific Fleet had been virtually destroyed in the Battle of Leyte Gulf.[21] Since then, Placido had been bringing in bits of news and rumors from Leyte which, for the most part, were not good. After their initial landings, the American forces on Leyte Island pushed inland where they were confronted by a large and powerful Japanese force in the mountains. Currently, the American and Japanese armies were locked in a deadly stalemate in an inland valley. Frank and Roy were going to Boone's headquarters to map out a plan to be sure that the same thing did not happen on Luzon—if MacArthur ever made it to Luzon.

***

In Manila, the *Kempei-tai* divided the city into multiple zones of several blocks each and began zonafying the city.[22] In the past, arrests of suspected guerrillas in Manila had been largely routine. But now some of those arrested were found to have firearms in their possession.[23] To the surprise of the *Kempei-tai,* some even shot back.[24]

The *Kempei-tai* initiated a massive crack-down on suspected spies and underground leaders. They arrested Father Theodore Buttenbruch, the kindly German priest who had smuggled personal messages to the prisoners in Camp O'Donnell and Cabanatuan. They beheaded him.[25] They arrested and executed Colonel Godofredo Monsod, the man who had let Colonels Martin Moses and Maxie Noble talk to the crowd at the marketplace in Baguio.[26] They executed underground suspects who were already in custody, including Tony and Josefa Escoda, Mr. and Mrs. Joaquin Mencarini and General Vincente Lim, organizers of the Manila underground.[27] They took the leaders of the Free Philippines organization to the Chinese Cemetery on the north side of town and beheaded them, including Juan Elizalde and Blanche Jurika, Chick Parsons' mother-in-law.[28] They sentenced Claire Phillips and Ramon Amusategui to death, but Amusategui confessed and took full responsibility for the activities of the Manila underground in an attempt to spare the others. In view of his confession, the Japanese commuted Claire Phillips' death sentence to twelve years in prison.[29] They beat Ramon Amusategui until he was crippled, and then let him die.[30] Intelligence operatives in Manila stopped sending out messages—things had gotten too hot.[31]

At his headquarters at Fort McKinley, General Tomoyuki Yamashita changed his defense plans for Luzon. The Imperial General Staff had insisted that Yamashita defend Leyte and, as a result, 120,000 of his best men were trapped there fighting a losing battle. He needed those men to staff the mountain strongholds overlooking the beaches of Luzon. But with the Japanese fleet in ruins there was no way to bring them back to Luzon, nor was there any way to protect his coastal strongholds from the gunfire of American battleships.[32]

Yamashita decided to abandon the coastal fortifications, divide the 260,000 Japanese Army soldiers he had on Luzon into three groups, and deploy them into the inland mountains surrounding the central plain.[33] The most likely site for the American landing was Lingayen Gulf, and once there, it was a safe bet that General MacArthur would march rapidly south toward Manila.

General Yamashita devised a trap. He deployed his main army, the *Shobu* Group, into the mountains of northern Luzon. He directed the *Shimbu* Group to build fortifications in the Sierra Madres overlooking the east side of the central plain, and the *Kembu* Group to dig into the Zambales Mountains overlooking the west side of the plain. When MacArthur's Army drew abreast of the *Shimbu* and *Kembu* fortifications, Yamashita's troops and artillery would attack from both sides, simultaneously. At the opportune moment, Yamashita's main force would attack from the north, cutting the Americans' supply lines and squeezing them into a trap between the mountain ranges.[34] If it worked, they might actually crush General MacArthur's forces and Yamashita would retain control of the Philippines. In the worst case, if MacArthur's forces proved too strong or landed on some other part of the island, Yamashita would pull back into the mountains and fight a protracted war of attrition when the Americans came after him. Either way, it was a plan designed to inflict maximum casualties on MacArthur's troops, and to give the home forces in Japan as much time as possible to prepare for an American invasion.[35]

***

Major Nakai and two of his infantry companies had been transferred to Leyte, cutting Japanese strength on the Bataan Peninsula by half.[36] 14th Army headquarters assigned the Chief of the *Kempei-tai* detachment at Balanga, Captain

Tamura, to be Commanding Officer of the Dinalupihan garrison. Tamura received secret orders from Manila authorizing him to use drastic measures to eliminate the guerrillas on Bataan.[37]

Tamura appointed Lieutenant Kanesero, a particularly cruel man, to take charge of the *Kempei-tai* detachment in Balanga, the provincial capital halfway down the bay side of the peninsula. Kanesero was ready to execute Tamura's new orders. He did not have to wait long.

Here and there on Bataan, news of the Leyte invasion inspired Boone's men to strike at the Japanese in spite of Boone's orders not to engage in combat. On November 29, Captain Magtanggol and his men marched into Orani wearing Japanese uniforms, shot the Japanese guards and raided City Hall.[38] Then they ambushed a Japanese patrol, killing nineteen.[39] On December 1, a group from the 3rd (Seaside) Regiment on the west coast raided the Japanese-owned Wain logging camp just north of Mariveles. They killed eight Japanese civilians.[40]

Five days later, reprisals began. Lieutenant Kanesero and his men surrounded and zonafied Bagac, the home municipality of Boone's 3rd Regiment. They selected eight Filipinos out of a group of twenty suspects and bayoneted them to death in retaliation for the eight dead Japanese.[41] The soldiers then turned their attention to the 3rd Regiment's headquarters in the hills overlooking the sea, attacked, and wiped it out.

The 3rd Regiment struck back, setting up an ambush on the Pilar-Bagac road. They killed eight Japanese soldiers and captured a truckload of supplies destined for the garrison at Morong, north of Bagac.[42]

Lieutenant Kanesero requested help from Manila. Four hundred Japanese soldiers surrounded Morong, zonafied it and burned the village to the ground. Fearing further reprisals, what was left of the 3rd Regiment evacuated all of the surviving citizens into the mountains.[43]

On December 7, Captain Tamura raided Boone's 1st Regiment guerrilla headquarters on Mount Malasimbo, north of Dinalupihan. The raiders killed two of the men there, and seized a letter and a large quantity of Japanese currency that a courier had just brought from Major Edwin Ramsey.[44]

The next day, Lieutenant Kanesero hit Boone's 4th Regiment headquarters just outside the little village of Tuyo, Balanga, on the bay side.[45] Kanesero zonafied Tuyo and arrested all 150 male residents of the town. The soldiers lined them up and passed them in front of a hooded "scorpion," who fingered twenty men. At midnight the soldiers took the men to the mango trees behind the Balanga Elementary School and beheaded them. Lieutenant Kanesero arrested two sisters of one of the executed men and kept them as prisoners over the next week doing housework for the Japanese soldiers. On the third night of their captivity, the girls were raped and they were raped again every day thereafter. On December 20, a detail of soldiers took them behind the elementary school and killed them—one by bayonet and one by saber.[46]

All month long, Kanesero continued the bloodbath around Balanga. Barrio Montilla on December 9, and Sibacan the next day, where his soldiers killed at least fifty men and they burned the village to the ground.[47] They killed twenty-six more in the zonification of Santa Rosa.[48] Like Boone's 3rd Regiment on the west coast, the 4th Regiment guerrillas began evacuating civilians from the barrios around Balanga.[49]

In Dinalupihan, someone grabbed a drunken Japanese soldier staggering down the street too late at night and strangled him. Immediately afterward, Captain Tamura zonafied Dinalupihan killing twenty guerrilla suspects.[50] Things continued to escalate—the guerrillas shot Captain Tamura's wife, Besing.

The zonifications intensified. Lieutenant Kanesero had barrio Kamachile surrounded and zonafied, arresting all 186 male residents of the village. Behind the Balanga

Elementary School, the soldiers killed eighty of them, including two boys ages five and seven. The barrio was burned.[51]

***

When Frank and Roy arrived at Boone's headquarters near Bamban on December 23, Eddie Wright was there with three other American soldiers who had been hiding in Bataan and Zambales.[52] Eddie had recruited them to help organize his new battalion of Philippine Scouts, and they stopped at Boone's headquarters on their way to confer with Colonel Gyles Merrill.[53] Frank thought to himself that it was the most Americans he had seen in one place in three years.

John Boone was sick with malaria, so Lieutenant Colonel Jose Bernales did the introductions.[54] Bernales, a civil engineer and a capable officer, had been assigned by Major Ramsey to be Boone's Chief of Staff.[55]

Bernales showed everyone around the little thatched-roof headquarters building. The front room was equipped with a few tables and chairs, a typewriter and a Filipino clerk. A message center was in operation, with Negrito runners who provided regular courier service to Boone's four regiments and to other guerrilla headquarters in Pampanga and Bulacan provinces.[56] Boone had appointed a finance officer, and the man was keeping detailed records of donations made to, and expenditures made by, the guerrillas. More than 250,000 pesos in cash and other donations had been sent by citizens in Dinalupihan and by Claire Phillips' contacts in Manila.[57] The finance officer had just received another 175,000 pesos in Japanese invasion currency from Major Ramsey to replace the money lost in the earlier raid.[58]

The next morning, Christmas Eve, the men got down to business. Boone was still out sick but the rest of the officers gathered in the headquarters building where Bernales brought them up to date. Bernales told them about the Japanese raids on Boone's regimental headquarters and the extensive zonifications around Morong, Bagac and Balanga.

He said that Boone had sent Sam Zozabrado to arrest Captain Magtanggol and bring him in. Magtanggol's attacks on the Japanese had caused too much retaliation, jeopardizing civilian support for the guerrillas. Zozabrado, an old friend of Magtanggol's, went unarmed. They got into a fight, and Magtanggol killed him. Then Magtanggol marched on Boone's headquarters. A hasty court-martial had been convened, and Magtanggol was arrested, convicted and executed.[59]

As Bernales talked, a courier from Captain Bartolomeo Cabangbang arrived with messages for Eddie Wright and John Boone.

Bernales opened the letter to John Boone and found instructions from Cabangbang to send a detail of men to pick up a radio and an intelligence team, and bring them back to Bataan.[60]

The men discussed Cabangbang's message. Having direct radio contact with Cabangbang would help, but to do much good against the Japanese the Bataan guerrillas needed better weapons and a supply of ammunition. Bernales described a new type of rifle that Major Ramsey's guerrillas had gotten by submarine—the M1A1 carbine. It packed a .30 caliber punch but was short and lightweight. Ideal for the small Filipinos, and easy to handle in a jungle environment.

Frank decided to appeal directly to General MacArthur. He had served briefly on MacArthur's staff before the war, so he wrote a personal note to the General and requested him to air-drop 500 carbines to the Bataan Military District.[61]

Eddie's message was a letter from Narciso Manzano. Manzano had joined MacArthur's forces on Leyte, and then moved forward as the American Army attacked nearby Mindoro Island.[62] He had transmitted the letter by radio through Captain Cabangbang, inquiring about his friends on Bataan.[63]

Eddie wrote a reply to Manzano and asked him to inform General MacArthur of the need for arms and ammunition in Bataan and Zambales Provinces, and that loyal guerrillas and Philippine Scouts were there to use them. He told Manzano that Colonel Merrill was the senior officer in the area and urged Manzano to contact Merrill about air-dropping arms.[64]

Bernales assigned some men to go back with Cabangbang's courier, deliver Frank and Eddie's notes, and bring back the radio.[65]

Then Bernales passed around a document entitled "General Orders Number 3," from Colonel Merrill. In it, Merrill placed Bataan, South Tarlac and Pampanga Provinces directly under his own control, specifically taking them away from Major Ramsey.[66] Bernales pointed out that Boone now had three people telling him what to do: Colonel Merrill, Major Ramsey, and Captain Cabangbang.

Frank questioned the validity of the order. Merrill cited no higher authority giving him control of Ramsey's units, and there was nothing to indicate that Ramsey had agreed to this change in command.[67]

"I agree," said Bernales. "After all, Major Ramsey helped Boone start the Bataan Military District, and has supported us all through the war. Cabangbang is our contact point with MacArthur, but as far as I'm concerned Major Ramsey is our immediate superior."

"Wait a minute," Eddie Wright broke in. "Colonel Merrill is the senior officer on Luzon. As such, we all owe our allegiance to him. And so does Ramsey. This General Order Number 3 clearly puts Merrill in charge of Bataan. Not Ramsey."

It was mid-day and Eddie had a long hike ahead of him to get to Merrill's headquarters. He and his three assistants left for Colonel Merrill's camp.

The next day, Christmas Day, Boone showed up for the meeting looking weak and pale from malaria. The men turned their attention to what they all had come to do—prepare for MacArthur's invasion. Boone produced a letter from Major Ramsey that said that until MacArthur landed on Luzon his guerrilla units were to gather intelligence data and transmit it to higher headquarters. Once MacArthur landed they were to begin sabotage operations and disrupt Japanese communications and supply lines. But first, each unit was to submit a war plan to Major Ramsey that described exactly what they were going to do and how they were going to do it.

"Well, Colonel," said Boone, "where do we start?"

Frank said that the first order of business was to set their objectives.

Frank believed that U.S. troops might make a landing near Subic Bay followed by a quick thrust into northern Bataan to prevent the Japanese from retreating there as the Americans had done three years before.[68] Boone was skeptical—a landing at Lingayen Gulf or Batangas seemed more likely. In either case, they agreed that the best mission for Boone's guerrillas was to do what they could to prevent the Japanese from entering or crossing Bataan. They stated their objectives in the opening paragraph of the Bataan Military District War Plan:

> In view of the limited men available for combat duty, shortage of arms and ammunitions...and the lack of sufficient food supplies and equipment, it is not intended to take and hold certain important road junctions, places or positions. It is planned to relentlessly attack and harass the enemy by employing HIT-AND-RUN tactics. Unless the situation demands, delaying enemy troop movements, destroying small groups of enemy garrisons... sabotaging enemy military installations such as supply depots and dumps, ammunition dumps,

> gasoline and fuel stores, cutting communications lines, and demolishing small wooden bridges, shall be conducted under cover of darkness. It is not planned to engage the enemy in open combat unless ordered by higher command.[69]

Boone had selected the Japanese airfield at Floridablanca, Pampanga as a sabotage target—large caches of ammunition and fuel were stored there.[70] The two steel bridges over the Calumpit River were another target. There was only one road into Bataan from the Luzon central plain, so destroying those bridges would make it hard for the Japanese to bring in tanks or heavy artillery. He had recently set up a demolition and sabotage unit in Dempe, Pampanga, for the express purpose of blowing the bridges. Frank suggested that Boone's men should blow up the targets and immediately retreat.[71] Boone agreed.

Frank pointed out that on Bataan itself the paved highway ran down the bay side, turned into a dirt road at Mariveles and came back up the west coast. Those roads, with the Olongapo highway and the Pilar-Bagac road running between them, formed boxes around Mount Natib and Mount Mariveles. Due to the steep terrain, this box-shaped road network was the only way the Japanese Army could move around on Bataan. If Boone's guerrillas could inhibit movement on those roads, the Japs would have a tough time getting their troops into position or re-supplying them.

They assigned Boone's 1st Regiment to impede Japanese units using the Dinalupihan-Olongapo highway across the north end of Bataan, and the 2nd and 3rd Regiments were to prevent Japanese troops from moving up or down either of the coasts. They assigned the 4th Regiment to the Pilar-Bagac road across the middle of the peninsula.[72] Southern Bataan was a problem, though, as the 4th Regiment was too small to do much damage in the south. But Boone had intelligence men there. They could monitor Japanese activity and pass reports north. If Boone's guerrilla regiments effectively controlled the north "box," any Japanese in southern Bataan would be isolated there.

With regard to intelligence gathering, Frank suggested that Boone keep a few people in close proximity to each Japanese garrison, and that a weekly intelligence report be sent in from each site, to be consolidated and forwarded to higher headquarters. The reports would include numbers of troops, tanks, artillery, etc., at each place, and the dates and directions of movements into and out of the sites.[73] When analyzed, the reports should give a good picture of where the Japanese were and what they were doing on Bataan. Boone agreed.

The men discussed how each of the American officers could be used most effectively.

Frank, as senior officer, had decided to work with Boone as an advisor.[74] Boone's headquarters near Bamban would serve as the Bataan Military District's main command post and message center, and Boone intended to direct combat operations from there. They decided that Frank would man a forward command post near the bayside highway, coordinate operations along the bay side, and take control of the entire district if the Japanese attacked and wiped out the main command post. They decided to locate the forward command post near Colonel Abad's 2nd Regiment headquarters near Tala, and Frank asked that Placido be assigned to help get the site ready and to serve as his guide. Boone and Frank agreed that once the forward command post was set up, they would exchange messages daily to keep each other apprised of the overall military situation in Bataan. Boone assigned five Negrito runners to the forward command post, to provide communications with Boone's headquarters and the headquarters of the two bayside regiments.

Al Romaine was an electrical engineer and a graduate of the Army Signal School at Fort Benning, so he took a position as technical advisor to Boone's signal section.[75] Al picked a mound-like outcropping on the side of Mount Malasimbo for the radio installation and dubbed it "Signal Hill." [76] Boone assigned two men who had some past radio experience to Al, and told them to get the site ready.[77] Hopefully, they would soon receive their radio from Captain Cabangbang.

Although Roy Reynolds agreed with Frank that it would be wrong for the American officers to usurp Boone's guerrilla command, Roy was not keen on being an "advisor." The men decided that Roy would serve as part of Boone's headquarters staff for the time being, but if a command position became available Roy would take command of troops in the field.[78]

Major Ramsey's letter said to select two sites where supplies could be dropped from airplanes, and gave instructions on how to set them up so pilots could recognize the sites from the air without having to make radio contact. In addition to his signal duties, they put Al Romaine in charge of preparing the reception areas for the air drop.[79]

The men began to get into the details of how to deploy the available men and equipment, and to select specific bridges and telephone lines to be sabotaged. Boone selected sites for civilian evacuation centers in the mountains and assigned men to clear the undergrowth at each place. Fresh water and proper sanitation facilities were going to be a problem. Frank recommended that the Bataan Military District's field hospital be set up at Tala, where Mrs. Utinsky and any other medical personnel who were available could safely treat the wounded.[80]

How long did they have to get ready? American troops had landed on nearby Mindoro Island on December 15. The island would make a good staging area and supply depot for the assault on Luzon, and the flat plateau atop the island was an ideal place to build airstrips. Frank calculated that it would take about a month to build a road to the top, build the airstrips, and move in supplies.[81] Based on that, he calculated that MacArthur would invade Luzon about mid-

January. The men selected January 15, 1945 as the probable date of a U.S. landing on Luzon, the date they would use for planning purposes.

Finally, Boone issued a warning order to the civilian citizens of Bataan telling them to be ready to get out of the towns and go to the evacuation centers in the hills as soon as they were notified about the coming invasion.[82] Until then, they were to stay in their homes so as not to alarm the Japanese.[83]

It took four days to complete the Bataan Military District War Plan, and on December 28, Boone handed the documents to Bernales to be typed and sent to Major Ramsey.[84]

Frank was impressed with John Boone. Even though Boone only had two years Army experience before the war, and not much military training, he was an articulate man who was readily able to think through an idea and turn it into an action plan. He utilized his staff well, and he clearly had a knack for dealing with the Filipinos.[85]

Frank and Roy headed back to their camp on Mount Natib to collect their gear.

When Frank got back to camp, he was physically beat from the arduous climb up the mountainside. The joints in his weak right leg ached, and he feared that he could feel the first signs of malaria in his system.

The two men were pleasantly surprised to find that Margaret Utinsky was not alone at the camp. Placido Filomeno and Pedro Pamintuan had brought groceries for Christmas dinner. The main course was to be chicken rather than turkey, and one of the two live chickens was running around loose in the camp, much to the delight of little Dian. Roy Reynolds took off after it, but after an exhausting, frustrating effort, picked up a gun and fired. The bullet blew the creature apart. Dinner that night consisted of one whole chicken and an appetizer of chicken soup.[86]

***

After a long climb over two rugged Zambales mountains, Eddie Wright and his companions arrived at Colonel Merrill's headquarters in an obscure coastal valley outside the village of Aglao. Eddie found the Colonel in poor health from recent bouts of malaria—Merrill was not immune to mosquitoes after all. Merrill had called Lieutenant Colonel Peter Calyer in from their forward command post at the Jingco sisters' plantation for the meeting, and Calyer had already briefed Merrill on Eddie's plan to form a provisional battalion of Philippine Scouts.

In his presentation the next morning, Eddie said that he intended to recruit former Philippine Scouts by putting the word out over the "bamboo telegraph," asking every former Scout in Bataan and Southern Zambales to come join the war effort. The Scouts were trained soldiers, not guerrillas, and Eddie planned to organize them and use them to disrupt Japanese military operations in the rear areas once General MacArthur's forces landed on Luzon.

To do so, however, would require Colonel Merrill's authorization and support. The men would need weapons, medical supplies, rations, and support troops to help transport the supplies once the battalion took the field. Could Colonel Merrill arrange such support?

Merrill told Eddie that once his radio was working reliably, he would contact MacArthur's headquarters on Leyte and call for weapons, ammunition and medical supplies to be air-dropped at points he had already designated. Major Roy Tuggle, at the Jingco plantation, could arrange to purchase rice and other food for the men. Couriers were available not only for communications within the command, but also to act as *cargadores* for transporting foodstuffs and ammunition. Yes, Colonel Merrill could handle Eddie's support requirements. He duly approved of Eddie's plan and appointed Eddie commander of the new provisional Philippine Scout organization.

"But, Colonel Wright," Merrill said. "I want you to take on bigger responsibilities.

“Lieutenant Clay Conner already has a battalion of Philippine Scouts in Pampanga on the east side of the Zambales Mountains, and Al Bruce has a number of Philippine Scouts in his organization in Tarlac Province. I'm placing Conner's and Bruce's Scout battalions under your command as well.”

Eddie's new organization would be considerably larger than he had envisioned, and would be known not as a battalion, but as the "Provisional *Regiment* of Philippine Scouts." [87]

“In addition, there is the matter of Bataan. ‘Colonel’ Boone and his associate, Lieutenant Colonel Loyd, seem to command a fairly large organization in Bataan that needs leadership and control.”

Colonel Merrill said that he had decided to create a new organization called the "Mountain Group Command." The Mountain Group Command would include Eddie Wright's Provisional Regiment of Philippine Scouts, Boone's Bataan Military District, Conner's Pampanga Military District, and Al Bruce's South Tarlac Military District. Colonel Merrill placed Lieutenant Colonel Eddie Wright in charge of the Mountain Group Command in addition to the Provisional Regiment of Philippine Scouts.[88]

“Your mission will be to prevent the Japanese from crossing the Zambales Mountains to the west coast of Luzon. You can tell Boone all about it when you get back to Bataan.”

Eddie stayed at Colonel Merrill's camp several more days, discussing war plans and conferring with Merrill's officers about the administrative procedures and forms Colonel Merrill had devised.[89] On December 30, Eddie issued his notice to the Philippine Scouts. He gave copies to guerrillas and Negrito runners, who headed for friendly towns in the area.[90]

> SUBJECT: Notice to Assemble
> TO: All Philippine Scouts, Now Free on Luzon, Able to Perform Active Field Duty.

> Under the authority of General Order #4, dated December 30, 1944, issued by the Senior American Officer on Luzon, Commanding Officer Luzon Guerrilla Forces, all Philippine Scouts of all branches are directed to report prior to 20 January 1945 to the place designated by the bearer.

On Wednesday morning, January 3, 1945, Eddie sent detailed instructions to Al Bruce in Tarlac and to Clay Conner in the mountains above Pampanga. Then he headed back to Bataan. In his hand was Merrill's Field Order Number 1, documenting the decisions Merrill had just made, and the organization he had just created.[91] Ahead was a meeting with John Boone.

***

Just after Christmas, Captain Cabangbang received three messages from Colonel Gyles Merrill. Merrill sent the papers by courier, as his radio worked only intermittently and the Japanese were jamming the frequency.

One of the messages was to General MacArthur. In it Colonel Merrill stated that he was in control of Zambales, Bataan, and parts of Tarlac and Pampanga provinces, and he asked MacArthur to confirm his authority in central Luzon.[92] Merrill's strength report stated that he had more than 20,000 men and 1,800 guns under his command, and that the Hukbalahap were under his tactical control. Merrill said that he could take and hold every town in Zambales except Olongapo, but if Captain Cabangbang would send him 1,000 carbines, he could take Olongapo too.[93]

The other messages were for Captain Cabangbang. The first one asked some specific questions:

- What organization tables had General MacArthur authorized for guerrilla units?
- What written authority permitted appointment and promotion of Filipino and American guerrilla officers?

- What geographical areas had been assigned to which guerrilla units?
- What commanders had actually been appointed by General MacArthur on Luzon?

Merrill said he wanted specific orders from General MacArthur on each response, with dates, not just answers to his questions.[94]

The second message requested arms and supplies, to wit:

1,000 Carbines, complete with magazines and ammunition
50 Submachine guns with magazines and ammunition
100 Pistols
200 Hand grenades
50 Time bombs
2,000 Quinine tablets, 5 grain
200 Sulfathiazole tablets
2 Shirts, khaki, size 15½ - 33
2 Trousers, khaki, size 30 - 30[95]

Captain Cabangbang must have felt more frustrated than ever. He had already answered these same questions for almost every guerrilla on Luzon, in some cases more than once. Cabangbang sent a short reply that there were no tables of organization, no written authority for appointing officers, no geographical assignments, and no overall commander had been appointed other than General MacArthur.[96]

***

By January 3, Clay Conner's observation post at Banaba had collected some interesting intelligence information, and his men passed their reports to Conner for review:

Four hundred Japanese airmen and navy men were digging tunnels and constructing concealed concrete bunkers in the east face of the Zambales Mountains, above Fort

Stotsenburg.[97] The work had been going on for weeks and was still in process. Some of the tunnels were huge—large enough to house heavy artillery pieces.[98] The work area was spread across the crotch of a wide gorge called Guligado's Pass overlooking the Luzon central plain. *Peculiar behavior*, Conner thought. The tunnels and bunkers pointed toward Clark Field, Fort Stotsenburg, and the farmlands of the central plain, not north toward Lingayen Gulf.

Convoys of Japanese military trucks loaded with men and equipment were streaming north, moving up the highways from Manila into the mountains of North Luzon. Motorcycles, tanks and staff cars were followed by buses loaded with Japanese civilians. Trains filled with Japanese troops rumbled through the Angeles station, headed north. Foot soldiers tramped northward up both highways pushing wooden carts filled with supplies.[99] Rumor had it that the Japanese commanding general, Yamashita himself, had moved his headquarters to Baguio in the northern mountains and took the Philippines government of President Jose Laurel with him.[100]

Colonel Merrill and Lieutenant Colonel Wright had assigned Conner the task of blocking off the trails across Mount Pinatubo, to prevent the Japanese from moving across the mountains to the Zambales coast. Conner put his Negrito guerrillas to work preparing hundreds of "pig traps" up and down the trails, each consisting of a sharpened bamboo spear triggered by a vine laid across the trail. The pig traps were virtually impossible to detect and were soon tested, with fatal results, by a Japanese scout sent to look for a route across the mountains.[101]

***

Eddie Wright arrived at Boone's headquarters on January 6. Frank Loyd was on his way to the forward command post, so Eddie sat down to talk to Boone, privately. As diplomatically as possible, Eddie told Boone about

Colonel Merrill's decisions and gave him a copy of Field Order Number 1.[102]

Without comment, Boone handed Eddie a message he had just received from Major Ramsey:

> Hereafter, anyone issuing direct orders to you without the consent of this Headquarters should be courteously reminded to adhere to the basic military principles of a chain of command and that all such orders and communications should be routed thru proper military channels.
>
> Your unit is under this command and must obey only orders issued from this Headquarters. [103]

"Look," Eddie said, "in response to your question about conflicting orders, Colonel Merrill has ordered you to ignore any orders from Ramsey.[104]

"Like it or not, Colonel Merrill outranks everybody on Luzon, including Lieutenant Ramsey—and you, Corporal Boone. You have no choice."

Boone was a thin, muscular man with a bony pointed nose and piercing blue eyes that he fixed on Eddie Wright. After considering Eddie's words for a few moments, he pointed out that Ramsey had helped found and build the Bataan Military District, and he had put Boone in charge of it more than two years ago. Merrill's order cited no higher authority requiring that the Bataan Military District be transferred from Ramsey's command to his, and Major Ramsey had never agreed to give up his units to Merrill. Whether Colonel Merrill liked it or not.[105]

A compromise was finally reached: Boone would send the Bataan Military District War Plan to both Colonel Merrill and Major Ramsey, with cover letters asking the two of them to resolve their differences themselves.[106] Along with the war plans went a description of Boone's drop zones which were manned and waiting for arms and supplies. Boone and Eddie Wright agreed to split any arms they received, 50-50.[107]

With those issues temporarily out of the way, Eddie brought up another point, one that would require revision of the just-completed War Plan.

There are three usable passes through the Zambales Mountains along the west coast of Luzon, and Colonel Merrill had ordered the Mountain Group Command to prevent the Japanese Army from using those passes to cross the mountains to the coast.[108] The two passes farther north would be blocked by Al Bruce and Clay Conner. The Dinalupihan-Olongapo highway across northern Bataan was to be blocked by Boone's Bataan Military District and Eddie's 3rd Battalion of Philippine Scouts.

Just east of Olongapo, the highway passes through a winding canyon where the noses of several ridgelines interlock. The area is known locally as the "Zig-zag" road. Eddie Wright, John Boone and Jose Bernales spent that night working out a more detailed plan for Boone's men to occupy the heights above the Zig-zag and ambush any Japanese trying to pass through the canyon on their way to the coast.[109] They allocated one-third of Boone's total ammunition supply to the Zig-zag. The guerrillas would engage the enemy there to the extent their ammunition permitted, and withdraw only when they ran out.

Through the window of Boone's headquarters the next morning, Eddie Wright watched a flight of U.S. planes buzz down the Olongapo highway dropping leaflets that warned Filipino civilians to stay off the roads and to stay away from the Japanese.[110] Within minutes another flight roared in behind them dropping bombs. As if in a dream, one of the planes seemed to fly almost directly overhead and an ear-splitting explosion rocked the little bamboo building. Shrapnel ripped through the *sawali* walls as Boone dove out the door followed by Eddie and everyone else, to get down on the ground. Frightened guerrillas, Scouts, and civilians scattered into the jungle.[111] The American planes careened on up the roadway, dropping bombs on anything that looked suspicious and were gone as quickly as they had come.

Once things calmed down, Eddie and Boone jointly wrote notes to Colonel Merrill telling him that, except for the bombing, their meeting had gone well.[112] Boone sent a runner to Frank Loyd to notify him of the changes ordered by Colonel Merrill.[113]

***

On January 6, at Frank and Roy's camp high up the slopes of Mount Natib, everyone packed up their belongings and utensils. Placido, Damaso Caballero, and the five Negrito runners had arrived to move everybody to the forward command post.[114] Frank told the men to take Mrs. Utinsky and the little girl first. One of the Negritos picked up Dian, and Placido led the group down the mountainside, headed for a spot near Tala.[115]

Meanwhile Roy Reynolds packed his pistol, mess kit, blankets and few personal items, and left to make an inspection tour of Boone's four regimental headquarters.

Frank stayed at the camp with Damaso. When two of the Negrito men came back they gathered up Frank's equipment. One of the men picked up Frank's emergency pack that he had kept with him throughout his time on Bataan. Frank took the pack back and hoisted it onto his own shoulders. The men started, single file, down the mountain. It would take a good two hours to get to the site of the forward command post.[116]

***

While Frank and Damaso were climbing down the steep trail to the new command post, and Eddie Wright and John Boone were discussing Colonel Merrill, Captain Cabangbang received an urgent message from General MacArthur on Leyte.[117] Cabangbang handed a copy of the message to a courier, and told him to take it immediately to Colonel Merrill:

> It is desired that all available means be taken to destroy enemy wire communication…power lines, round houses, rolling stocks, trucks, spurs, tracks

and other means of transportation starting immediately, and exert every effort thru employment of all means available to restrict the movement of enemy forces on the island of Luzon.... In addition, all possible destruction of planes concealed in dispersal areas and oil, ammunition and other supply dumps is desired. ...thus [you have], under local leadership, the opportunity to unleash maximum possible violence against the enemy.

MACARTHUR[118]

XXII. Maximum Violence

According to Evelyn's radio, Leyte had been secured. MacArthur's troops had taken Mindoro just off the coast of Luzon. Luzon was surely next. Evelyn waited with a sense of excitement, but also apprehension and dread.

Then she got a letter from Inez Easley. Inez' husband, "Speck," was one of Frank's best friends dating back to their earliest days in the Army. Speck was a general now, and their son Sandy was a major in his dad's outfit, one of the first units to land on Leyte. Speck had been wounded in the battle.

Inez had a suggestion for Evelyn. Write a letter to Sandy. Ask about Frank. Something important might come of it.[1]

***

A little before dark, Frank Loyd limped into his new command post accompanied by Damaso Caballero and the other two Negritos. Placido Filomeno had selected a small clearing on the west face of Mount Natib above the bayside highway for the forward command post. It was about a mile north of Lieutenant Colonel Victor Abad's 2nd Regiment headquarters at the old sugar mill, and the Tala settlement was a mile and a half on the other side of Abad's camp. Rough trails familiar to the Negritos connected the three sites.

The clearing was well concealed under the thick jungle canopy, with a bare dirt floor held in place by a tangle of rocks and tree roots. It had that musty odor common to places that never dry out.

For the past three hours Frank had climbed across ridgelines and thickly overgrown hillsides, and pulled himself through steep ravines behind his Negrito guides. He was physically exhausted, weak, and feverish with aches in his shoulders and leg.

It was near dusk when they arrived. Margaret Utinsky, little Dian Phillips and the other three Negritos were there to greet them. That night everyone slept wearily on the uneven ground.

The next morning Damaso had his men start work on a shelter. Mrs. Utinsky and Dian busied themselves preparing a cooking fire, Utinsky talking soothingly to the little girl all the while. The child had caught another cold as she climbed through the damp jungle the previous day, and was quietly miserable. Frank, still aching himself, decided that Dian and Utinsky would be better off with Placido's family in Tala. It would be safer there; Dian could be out in the sunshine, and nurse Utinsky could set up her medical aid station.

Placido came from Tala the next day. He, too, had malaria and looked pale and weak. The news he brought was not good.

"There's a new Jap commander in Dinalupihan, Colonel Sanenobu Nagayoshi. He brought more Nips. They camp in the town, in the school, the church, in the theater." [2]

Frank was concerned. A colonel would command a regiment of several thousand troops, much bigger than Major Nakai's thinly spread battalion. Why were they there? Were they an advance guard preparing for a Japanese retreat into Bataan?

Placido said that no Japanese had visited Tala in more than a month. “The Nips in Orani too busy controlling the civilians in town. Besides," Placido said with a certain amount of pride in his voice, "they afraid to come up here."

Frank motioned for Damaso Caballero and Margaret Utinsky to join the conversation. With Placido translating for Damaso, Frank gave them their orders. Damaso was to put his five Negritos on a regular rotation of courier runs to Colonel Victor Abad’s 2nd Regiment headquarters nearby, to the 4th Regiment headquarters farther down the peninsula near Balanga, and to John Boone's headquarters. The men were to convey messages and collect the intelligence reports about Japanese activity along the bayside highway and in southern Bataan. Frank would review and consolidate the reports as they were brought in, and send them on to Colonel Boone. Since Boone’s guerrillas had no radios, the Negrito courier network was going to be very important. One of the five men was to be in Frank's camp at all times, ready to carry emergency messages.

He told Placido to go back to Tala and find someone who would be willing to take care of Mrs. Utinsky and Dian, and to find or build a hut where she could set up her aid station. Placido was also to collect whatever information he could about the Japanese in Orani and bring it to Frank each day.

Placido was immediately enthusiastic. Someone from Tala traveled to Orani almost every day, and information about the Japanese was constantly being passed around on the "bamboo telegraph." He assured Frank that he could bring back plenty of information about the Japs.

Frank told Margaret Utinsky that while she waited for Placido to move her to Tala, she was to write out a list of all of the incidents of Japanese arrests, tortures and executions she could remember during her three years in Manila. He told her to make a second list of all Filipino collaborators she knew about. He told her that she was to give the two lists to American intelligence officers as soon as she was repatriated to U.S. forces.[3]

By nightfall Damaso's men had completed a low, covered bamboo platform for Margaret and Dian to sleep on. The little girl's hacking cough and Frank's malarial chills deprived him of any significant rest that night. He lay on the damp ground and thought about the American forces in Leyte. They were less than 500 miles away.

The next morning, Victor Abad and a few of his bodyguards walked into Frank's camp.

"My men prepare to attack the Japanese," he stated. "I need Placido, your Negritos to carry rice and supplies." [4]

Frank's guard went up. "These men are part of my command post. I need them to maintain communications with Colonel Boone's headquarters. They are assigned to me."

Smiling, Abad reminded Frank that the 2nd Regiment was an important part of Colonel Boone's Bataan Military District, and that while he was sure Frank could put the men to good use in his "advisory" capacity, Abad needed them now or his regiment would be unable to complete its mission. "I return the Negritos when I can." With that he took the five Negritos, more or less at gunpoint, and left.

There was nothing Frank could do about it. He was left alone with Mrs. Utinsky and Dian. Silently, he set to work cutting bamboo poles to make a roof for their shelter. Utinsky and Dian busied themselves with a small fire and began preparing the evening meal.

But the next afternoon, to Frank's surprise, Placido and two of the Negritos returned.

Placido's malaria was worse and he obviously could be of no use, so Frank gave him a few Atabrine tablets and sent him back to Tala. He put the Negritos back to work on the shelter, and building bamboo beds for Mrs. Utinsky and Dian. When the Negritos left for their village that night he tried to tell them to come back early the next day. Frank wanted to get his courier system into operation and test it out. It had been almost a week since he had communicated with John Boone, and that was unacceptable.[5]

***

From a vantage point on the east slope of the Zambales Mountains, Clay Conner watched the men of General Tomoyuki Yamashita's *Kembu* Group feverishly digging into the mountainside at Guligado's Pass, enlarging their network of tunnels and fortifications. General Yamashita's *Shimbu* Group was doing the same thing in the Sierra Madres, far across the Luzon central plain.

Conner studiously observed the workers' routine which, in true Japanese fashion, seldom varied. At about seven o'clock each morning hundreds of soldiers climbed up the steep slope from Clark Field carrying their weapons, papers and work tools. They immediately set to work digging into the mountain, blasting caves, setting wooden forms and pouring concrete. A little before noon they broke for a brief rest, then went back to work. During the day, eight trucks made round-trip hauls up the narrow dirt road from Fort Stotsenburg, bringing building materials, gasoline, heavy weapons and ammunition.[6] Tons of supplies seemed to just disappear into the mountainside.[7] The constant activity reminded Conner of a disturbed anthill.

Each morning before they started work, the Japanese soldiers "stacked" their rifles off to the side of the construction area. Back when they first started they posted guards next to the weapons, but as time went by the guards joined the work crews and now their weapons sat unattended during most of the day.

Colonel Gyles Merrill wanted Conner to keep the Japanese from crossing the Zambales Mountains once General MacArthur attacked. His Negritos' pig-traps could snare hundreds of Japanese, but there would be a lot more than that in a mass movement. Conner needed weapons for his men—and here were the weapons.

Conner had carefully explained his plan to the Negrito chiefs. They had even rehearsed the whole thing in a nearby valley so each man understood exactly what he was to do.

Tomorrow, in the pre-dawn darkness of January 9, 1945, 350 Negrito men would assemble in the jungle alongside the Japanese work site.[8] Once the soldiers arrived and started work, one group of Negritos would run silently out of the jungle toward the waiting rifles, grab the guns and whatever else they could carry, and run back into the jungle. When the Japanese gave chase, their companions waiting in the treeline would rise up with their bows and arrows and shoot the oncoming Japanese. Meanwhile, thirty more Negritos armed with the tribe's only rifles would be positioned on the rocks overhead.[9] As the bow and arrow men withdrew, the riflemen would open fire on the pursuing Japanese. If all went well, the Negritos should acquire rifles, bandoleers of ammunition, and even an automatic weapon or two without taking any casualties of their own.

Today, the Japanese were working on their fortifications, their weapons stacked neatly along the side of the work site. Everything was ready for tomorrow morning. Conner knew that he needed to get on with it. A contingent of Japanese Navy men had recently begun staying overnight at the construction site, continuing the work by lantern light.[10]

But as Conner looked down on Clark Field that day, he saw flights of airplanes taking off. Suddenly, a group of American fighter planes roared overhead and swooped down the mountain slopes to attack the Japanese planes as they lifted off the ground. American bombers flew in behind them and hit the repair shops and fuel supplies the Japanese had hidden in the villages to the north and south of Clark Field—targets that Conner had specified in his recent intelligence reports.[11] The Japanese work crews threw down their shovels, grabbed their guns, and scrambled down the steep hillside. Conner could see Japanese troops and tanks gathering on the highway near Clark Field, then heading north.[12]

The next morning the Japanese work crews did not show up. Conner called off his attack. What was going on?

On Thursday, January 11, one of Colonel Merrill's Negrito couriers came running into Conner's camp with the answer.[13] General MacArthur, he announced, had landed!

***

John Boone got the news on a radio broadcast from the Voice of Freedom—MacArthur's naval armada had sailed into Lingayen Gulf at the north end of the central plain in the early hours of Tuesday, January 9, and began landing troops from his 6th Army.[14] As the fleet of U.S. warships approached Luzon, suicidal Japanese pilots flying airplanes laden with explosives attacked more than thirty ships. Most of the American casualties that day were caused by suicide attacks, not by Japanese troops defending the beaches.

MacArthur was back on Luzon, a little more than eighty miles north of Bataan.

Boone sent a message to Frank Loyd to put the Bataan Military District's War Plan into effect. Frank sent runners to the 2nd and 4th Regiments' headquarters with orders to execute their war plans, start moving civilians out to the evacuation centers and begin attacking targets in their areas.

Margaret Utinsky and Dian were still at Frank's command post. Frank told Placido to go back to Tala, arrange for a place for her, and then come back with some helpers to get Utinsky and the little girl. With the war on in Luzon there would be little reason for the Japanese to visit Tala. But if they discovered Frank's camp, or Colonel Abad's, the women would surely wind up dead.

Frank sent Damaso to Boone's headquarters at Bamban to report that the forward command post was ready.

***

As news of MacArthur's landing at Lingayen spread, former Philippine Scouts began to report to Eddie Wright's camp. In the first week forty Scouts arrived and more than a hundred were expected in the next few days. But a third of the men had malaria. Eddie had no arms to issue, little food to give them, and no quinine or other medicine at all.[15]

Eddie went to John Boone's headquarters nearby, hoping that weapons had been air-dropped to Boone. Many of Boone's men had old weapons and small quantities of ammunition they had salvaged from the Bataan battlefields three years before, but Eddie's Scouts were virtually unarmed. But Boone had received nothing.

Guerrilla intelligence reports estimated that Colonel Nagayoshi now had more than 10,000 infantry troops in and around Dinalupihan.[16] Neither Eddie's Philippine Scouts nor Boone's guerrilla regiments were anywhere near ready to take them on.

As Eddie, Boone and Roy Reynolds discussed their situation, a messenger arrived from Colonel Merrill's headquarters.[17] There was an unconfirmed report that a shipment of arms had been air-dropped to Captain Al Bruce's guerrillas and Scouts in Tarlac, just north of Zambales Province.

Eddie wrote a message back to Merrill saying that if he and Boone were supposed to keep the Japanese from crossing Bataan, as Colonel Merrill had ordered, they had to have arms and ammunition.[18] He also told Boone to send his own messenger to Captain Cabangbang and request an air-drop of arms and medicine directly from him.[19] Eddie knew that he was going around the chain of command, specifically around Colonel Merrill, but maybe Cabangbang could get them some guns.

MacArthur and his troops were still at Lingayen Gulf, having moved only about twenty miles inland since they landed.[20] After General Homma landed at Lingayen in December 1942, he had pushed down the central plain to Manila in less than a week. *What the hell was taking MacArthur so long?*

That afternoon Boone sent a squad of his guerrilla engineers to destroy the ammunition dump at the Palacol Airfield in Floridablanca, Pampanga.[21] It was Boone's second attempt on the ammunition dump, and it was going to be a tough assignment. Most of his dynamite had been used to blow the Calumpit Bridges, and the demolition squad he originally sent to Palacol took what was left. The ammunition dump had not been blown up. And the men had not come back.

The engineers traveled on foot to Floridablanca to case the airfield, which sat temptingly alone on the flat plain outside of town, surrounded by rice and cotton fields. As they watched, the Japanese guards who patrolled the perimeter challenged every Filipino they did not personally recognize. But the men noted that the guards paid little attention to the Filipino farmers who worked in the fields alongside the airfield.

At a bar in Floridablanca that evening, two of the guerrillas approached a somewhat alcoholic farmer whose rice paddies were adjacent to Palacol. Plying him with drinks and appealing to his patriotism, the guerrillas got the farmer to agree to carry a can of gasoline with him to work the next afternoon.

From a hiding place in a patch of trees nearby, the guerrillas encouraged the inebriated farmer to pour gas on the line of huts that separated the airfield from his rice paddies—huts where Japanese bombs and fuel drums were said to be stored. They coaxed the farmer to light a match. The resulting chain reaction set off explosions up and down the airfield that Eddie and Boone could hear all the way back at their headquarters in Bataan. Thirty tons of ammunition and forty tons of bombs were destroyed. Unfortunately, the helpful farmer was too.[22]

***

On Tuesday, January 16, Boone's radio detail finally returned from Captain Cabangbang's headquarters with a radio and two trained operators. They had been gone for almost three weeks. Al Romaine took the men to Signal Hill on the side of Mount Malasimbo, where he had erected an antenna pole and constructed a small shack at the edge of a clearing. After connecting wires and batteries, and laboriously hand-cranking the generator, the men brought the radio to life. Reception was poor, however, and laden with static. The operator worked all afternoon but was barely able to pick up station JWR, Cabangbang's network control station.

The next morning, the radio operators on Signal Hill received a clear message from Colonel Merrill with a request that it be relayed to Captain Cabangbang.[23]

At ten o'clock Al Romaine, John and Mellie Boone and their infant son, and a few others gathered around to see if the operator could send the message. Suddenly, a flight of eight American P-38 fighters burst over the treetops with .50 caliber machine guns chattering. Bullets ricocheted off rocks and tore through the signal panels that had been set up nearby to mark the site of the expected arms drop. Led by Boone, everyone scrambled into ditches and behind rocks as the planes wheeled about for another pass. For fifteen minutes the fast twin-engine fighters swept back and forth, indiscriminately strafing the hilltop. Eventually they left, disappearing as unexpectedly as they had come.

The radio shack was on fire, the signal panels were on fire, several Filipino guerrillas were dead, and part of the radio equipment had been damaged.[24]

The strafing of Signal Hill caused an American casualty, too. Ever since General MacArthur landed at Lingayen, Al Romaine had become deathly afraid that he might perish in the fighting at the last minute. In Al's mind, the P-38s' machine guns that day crystallized the probability of his own death.

Boone decided that he had to get Al off Signal Hill and away from the Filipino guerrillas. The sight of an American officer who was so badly traumatized would kill morale.

Boone assigned Al a Negrito guide, handed him a sheaf of maps and recent intelligence reports, and sent him to meet the American army approaching from the north. The Negritos knew a safe path through the jungle to Pampanga. From there, Filipino guerrillas should be able to smuggle him through the front lines to 6th Army headquarters. Al's mission, Boone said, was to find the man in charge at 6th Army, give him the intelligence reports, and persuade him to air-drop a load of guns, ammunition, and medicine on Signal Hill.[25]

The next day Boone's intelligence men brought in reports that Colonel Nagayoshi's troops were on the move. Columns of Japanese trucks carrying troops and supplies had moved out of Dinalupihan and crossed Bataan to the west. Eight thousand to ten thousand soldiers were moving into positions around Morong on the west coast of Bataan,[26] and entering the Zig-zag pass on the Olongapo highway. It was exactly what Colonel Merrill had ordered Boone and Eddie Wright to keep them from doing.

***

Frank Loyd had reached the point of exasperation with Lieutenant Colonel Victor Abad.

To begin with, Abad had ignored Boone's order to sabotage and attack the Japanese, and instead hung around his own headquarters typing intelligence reports. *Defeating the enemy with typewriters*, Frank thought to himself.[27] He sent a strongly worded note to John Boone and another to Abad, and Boone in turn reprimanded Abad in writing.[28] By the time the bayside guerrillas finally began attacking their assigned targets, a column of Japanese trucks had moved down the bayside highway and across to Morong on the west coast, virtually unmolested.[29]

Placido was laid up in Tala with malaria, so Margaret Utinsky and Dian were still at Frank's forward command post when Abad's men finally attacked the small Japanese garrison at Abucay Hacienda and began to ambush parties of Japanese patrolling the bayside highway.[30] Soon, Abad's wounded were being brought to Frank's command post for Margaret to attend.[31]

The Japanese were nearby, also. Patrols of thirty to fifty men were combing the mountainside looking for guerrillas.[32] Frank's command post was virtually defenseless. Frank ordered Colonel Abad to move Mrs. Utinsky and Dian to Tala.[33] When Abad's men came to get her, Frank told Margaret to stay at Tala until it was safe to join the American troops. Above all, he told her not to go to Abad's headquarters.[34] The Japanese seemed to have no trouble finding Abad, and had raided him several times before.

Frank handed her a letter.

"Show this to the first American soldier you see and he will take you to his commanding officer, who will take you to General MacArthur." [35] He reminded her to give the lists of Japanese atrocities and collaborators to Army Intelligence officers as soon as she contacted U.S. troops.[36] Margaret said that she understood. She and Dian left with Abad's guerrillas.

***

By January 23, John Boone's radio was up and working, at least intermittently, and he was at last able to communicate with Captain Cabangbang's net control station, station JWR. Guerrilla units from as far away as Tarlac were bringing their intelligence reports to Boone to be radioed to Cabangbang. His signal section was overloaded, but one urgent report from Clay Conner was particularly important—it described a large complex of concrete tunnels and bunkers concealed in the mountains above Fort Stotsenburg, at Guligado's Pass. The positions had just been occupied by a large contingent of Japanese troops.[37]

Cabangbang radioed back that he was under pressure from the Japanese and he had to shut down to move to a safer location.[38] He instructed Boone to radio all intelligence reports to General Krueger's 6th Army headquarters in Tarlac, and to radio any other messages directly to MacArthur's headquarters.[39]

Boone still had not received any weapons. Apparently, the arms requests of a mere corporal were not being given any credit at General MacArthur's headquarters.

Eddie Wright came into Boone's headquarters that day to get Roy Reynolds. So Boone talked it over with Eddie Wright. Eddie had 220 Philippine Scouts at his camp now, unarmed. Without weapons there was little they could do to the Japanese, and they were highly vulnerable to attack. Eddie said that desperate times deserved desperate measures. Since Cabangbang had told Boone to make direct contact with MacArthur's headquarters, Eddie told Boone to transmit a request for an arms drop directly to General MacArthur. And to sign Colonel Merrill's name to it.[40]

Boone mulled that one over for a minute. It was rare to see Eddie Wright deviate from proper military procedure, but the suggestion was right up Boone's alley.

Boone sent the message, and signed it "Merrill."

***

Colonel Merrill may have had trouble getting the American guerrilla leaders to obey his orders, but not so Filipinos. To them, Merrill was a full colonel in the United States Army, the senior officer at large in the Philippines, and a Philippine Scout to boot. To Filipino guerrilla leaders like Captain Ramon Magsaysay, Colonel Merrill was clearly their commanding officer. As a result, Colonel Merrill had accumulated a fairly large network of Filipino guerrilla units along the Zambales coast—all headed by Filipino officers.

So when Colonel Merrill ordered Captain Magsaysay to attack the town of Castillejos north of Subic Bay and to clear the Japanese off the Zambales coast, Magsaysay assembled his men and attacked. Magsaysay's guerrillas quickly overcame the Japanese garrison of several hundred men at Castillejos, raised the American flag on the pole in front of the schoolhouse, and turned to the huge San Marcelino airfield on the north side of town.[41] Over the next several days Magsaysay's guerrillas pressured the Japanese throughout southern Zambales, forced them back to Subic Bay and captured the airfield itself. At San Marcelino, they destroyed twenty-five Japanese aircraft and 560 gallons of aviation fuel.[42]

Colonel Merrill radioed General MacArthur and described Eddie Wright's Provisional Regiment of Philippine Scouts. He requested arms drops at three sites in Tarlac and Zambales Provinces.[43]

MacArthur was impressed. He ordered periodic arms drops to Colonel Merrill to begin immediately. The U.S. Army Air Corps dropped Merrill's first arms supply on Mount Pinatubo at ten forty-five the next morning.[44]

As soon as the arms were on the ground, Colonel Merrill summoned Captain Magsaysay to come collect the weapons. He ordered Magsaysay to raise more men who were willing to fight, and to prepare them to fight for a week.[45]

***

Back at Bamban in northern Bataan, Eddie Wright's problems were getting worse. He had managed to obtain some rice and carabao meat to feed his men, but he still had no guns and he desperately needed medicine to avoid an epidemic among his troops. Several of the men who were sick with malaria had become discouraged and left. Several more had tuberculosis. One even had the clap.

If Eddie's men were going to see combat, it needed to be soon. Boone's intelligence reports showed as many as 20,000 Japanese troops in western Bataan, concentrated primarily around the Zig-zag pass.[46]

Boone had specified the Zig-zag as an important target in his intelligence reports, and U.S. bombers plastered the place for four days, but it appeared to have little effect on the well dug-in Japanese.[47] Boone and his men were trying, but their meager supply of ammunition was nearly exhausted.

Then the Japanese fulfilled one of Eddie's worst fears—they struck back. A patrol raided Boone's air-drop site on Signal Hill, the same place that U.S. planes had shot up a few days before, shot the guards, and occupied the area.[48] Another patrol flushed Boone's headquarters out of the clearing near Bamban. John Boone, Jose Bernales and their headquarters personnel fled across the highway to the 1st Regiment headquarters on Mount Malasimbo.[49] The Japanese pursuing Boone passed close by Eddie's camp, and Eddie knew that if his own men were discovered by the Japanese they could do little but run.[50] He either had to get them some weapons, or get them away from Bamban to a more secure place. But where?

***

At ten-thirty in the morning on Saturday, January 27, 1945, Colonel Merrill got his second arms drop. It was five-thirty by the time his *cargadores* were able to haul the thirty-two crates back to Colonel Merrill's camp. There were seven boxes of ammunition, two .50 caliber machine guns, and twenty crates of M-1 carbines. Each crate contained ten of the small, lightweight rifles, a box of waterproof matches, ten pocketknives, a quart jar of sulfa ointment, 1,000 quinine tablets, jars of aspirin and Atabrine, ten donated paper-back books, and ten suits of green underwear in various sizes.[51]

The next day Colonel Merrill wrote a message instructing Eddie Wright to come at once and bring his 3rd Battalion of Philippine Scouts to pick up their weapons.[52] He also reprimanded Eddie Wright in no uncertain terms for using his name on the unauthorized messages that Eddie and Boone had sent to General MacArthur. Merrill and all but one of his staff officers then left for Castillejos, Captain Magsaysay's headquarters on the Zambales coast.

***

In the mountains above Fort Stotsenburg, Lieutenant Clay Conner received a terse message:

> Move all your men away from the area you are now occupying…a distance of six (6) kilometers in a southerly direction is considered sufficient at this time….
>
> Caution: The failure to comply with…these instructions might prove disastrous…[53]

Conner immediately began moving his Negritos and their families south toward Banaba in the foothills. Lieutenant Felipe Maningo's Philippine Scouts fanned out in the lowlands west of Clark Field and encouraged the lowland Filipinos to move to the south as well. They all spent the night in the hills and fields around Banaba, and Conner learned that American forces had captured the nearby town of Angeles, Pampanga, earlier that day. Before dawn the next morning Conner's men fought off a Japanese patrol,[54] then Conner called a meeting of the Filipino and Negrito leaders.

That same morning, Monday, January 29, a column of U.S. tanks and trucks drove out from Angeles, Pampanga, headed toward the foothills south of Fort Stotsenburg. Their mission was to seal off the Japanese' mountainside fortifications while a huge bombing and artillery barrage plastered the caves and bunkers on the mountainside. The bombing would be followed by a tank and infantry assault.

As the tanks drove slowly up the road toward the mountains, one of the commanders spotted a thin cloud of dust rising behind a ridgeline across the flat plain. A small spotter airplane circled overhead. It was hard to tell what the Japanese might be up to, so the tanks stopped. Smells of dust and exhaust fumes hung in the still, hot air. In the distance there was a faint noise—like a mumble of voices intermixed with whoops and shouts.

The three tanks fanned out into the dry rice fields on each side of the road. Infantrymen clamored out of the trucks, brought their rifles to the ready and moved on line with the tanks. Rounds were chambered, safeties off. There was no visible source for the dust cloud—no whirlwind, no vehicles. It just seemed to drift out from the base of the mountain. They proceeded cautiously toward it.

The sound of voices grew stronger as the soldiers approached the ridgeline. It sounded like singing. Behind the ridgeline, a dry riverbed curved to the right and disappeared up into the foothills. Walking down the riverbed toward them was a mass of Filipinos and what appeared to be a few white men with their shirts off. One Filipino was waving an American flag on a pole. As they grew closer the tankers could see that the crowd was actually composed about fifty-fifty of Filipinos and small, black, nearly naked Negritos.

As the crowd approached, the voices became more distinct—they were, in fact, singing. There were almost two thousand people massed together, men and women, some armed, some not, some with bows and arrows or spears, streaming toward the soldiers behind the man who was swinging the American flag in broad circles above his head. They were singing, "California, Here I Come!" [55]

Thus, First Lieutenant Henry Clay Conner and his guerrillas reported for duty that day.

***

Standing on a bare bluff near his forward command post, Frank Loyd listened intently. In the distance he could hear U.S. artillery and bombers pounding the fortifications in the Zambales Mountains above Fort Stotsenburg.[56]

The runner from Boone's headquarters arrived early in the afternoon with a report that part of the U.S. 6th Army had maneuvered around Clark Field and attacked the

Japanese at Fort Stotsenburg.[57] Another column of troops pushed past Stotsenburg and captured Angeles, Pampanga.[58] Frank thought, *Angeles is only about thirty miles away, as the crow flies*. He looked off into the distance, toward Pampanga. *They're getting close.*

Boone's report said that the Japanese were still dug in along the west coast of Bataan and at the Zig-zag pass. Frank wondered why. Why didn't they pull back to Dinalupihan to meet the oncoming American Army? Colonel Merrill had ordered Eddie Wright to keep the Japanese from crossing northern Bataan to the Zambales coast. What did Merrill know about Zambales?

Frank gave the courier a recent intelligence report from south Bataan to take back. The man chatted briefly with Damaso, who was Frank's constant companion these days, and took off. Frank sat down on the edge of his bamboo bunk and swallowed one of his few remaining Atabrine pills. Every day for the past four days he had had chills right at noon. Last night, severe chest pains had kept him awake all night. Malaria was back.[59]

***

When Eddie Wright got Colonel Merrill's message about the arms drop, he immediately set out with an advance party of sixteen Scouts at one o'clock in the morning. The Japanese had taken to hiding in the jungle during the day and coming out at night to move troops and equipment, discipline civilians, and forage for supplies, so Eddie had to take a circuitous route up the east side of Mount Malasimbo and across a high mountain saddle to Aglao. They arrived at Colonel Merrill's camp at ten o'clock in the morning, hungry and worn out.[60] Captain Richard C. Kadel was on hand to meet them and he showed Eddie the cache of 200 weapons that Colonel Merrill had set aside for Eddie's Scouts.[61]

Eddie opened the crates and looked them over. The small, lightweight carbines were excellent weapons for the Filipinos. There were two heavy .50 caliber machine guns, a box of Browning Automatic Rifles, and some mortars. Of particular interest were the quinine and Atabrine pills. Malaria, when treated properly, can be cured relatively easily and Eddie's men would not only be armed, but well, too. Kadel had arranged for supplies of rice and two carabao that could be slaughtered to feed the men. Kadel said that Colonel Merrill was not coming back to this headquarters and Eddie could take all of the supplies left in camp—soap, cigarettes, medicine, toilet articles—anything he could carry.[62]

As Eddie waited for the main body of his Scouts to arrive at Aglao that day, a flotilla of American warships appeared off the Zambales coast. Three of Captain Magsaysay's guerrillas paddled out to the ships in *bankas* to tell the naval officers not to bombard the coastline—southern Zambales was entirely in guerrilla hands. The guerillas were taken to the ship's dining hall while the Navy checked out their story. An officer asked one of the men if Filipino collaborators were likely to be a problem in Zambales. The guerrilla looked up from his plate of bacon and eggs and replied, "No sir. We took care of them three days ago." [63]

In the afternoon of January 29, 1945, the 6th Army's 11th Corps landed unopposed on the Zambales coast. There was not a Japanese in sight. Grinning Filipinos turned out in their Sunday best to welcome the troops at the shoreline. Within hours, Army engineers were preparing the runways at the San Marcelino airfield, and U.S. fighters soon flew in to begin combat operations.[64] Colonel Gyles Merrill reported to Major General Charles Peter Hall, commanding general of 11th Corps, and placed the Zambales and Bataan guerrilla forces under his command.[65]

***

Thus, when Roy Reynolds and the rest of Eddie's troops arrived at Aglao at three o'clock that afternoon, their war had already changed. They just did not know it yet.

Eddie issued weapons and medication, saw to it that the men were properly fed, and put them to work cleaning the Cosmoline off their new carbines. He decided to keep the men at Aglao for two days of weapons training, and to give himself time to lay out a plan before heading down the mountain to engage the Japanese at the Zig-zag.

The next morning, one of Colonel Merrill's Negrito runners came into camp with an urgent message. Lieutenant General Walter A. Krueger, Commanding General of the 6th U.S. Army, was sending an airplane to pick up Eddie at the San Marcelino airfield and fly him across the Zambales Mountains to Krueger's headquarters at the Tarlac Sugar Central.[66] Eddie was to go immediately to San Marcelino.

Leaving Roy Reynolds in charge, Eddie followed the Negrito down the mountain trail to the airfield. While he waited for General Krueger's Piper Cub airplane to arrive, he wrote a letter to his wife Marge.

At 6th Army Headquarters, Eddie was ushered in to meet General Walter Krueger. In his distinct German accent, Krueger congratulated Eddie on the fine job the guerrillas had done, particularly with respect to intelligence reports about Japanese fortifications.

Krueger formally attached Eddie's Provisional Regiment of Philippine Scouts to the 6th U.S. Army. Eddie described the situation at the Zig-zag pass and informed Krueger that no weapons had yet been delivered to John Boone's Bataan Military District. Krueger ordered his men to deliver better radios and a load of ammunition to Boone from 6th Army's own supply, taking it overland by truck.[67] He said that arms were scheduled for air drop to the guerrillas on the west side of Bataan, but not for several more days. He put Eddie Wright in charge of getting those arms to Boone.

***

Late in the afternoon on Thursday, February 1, a Scout at an outpost on the west side of Roy Reynolds' camp spotted movement on the jungle trail below him. A tall green-clad figure appeared wearing a peculiar round helmet. He, in turn, was followed by several more American soldiers. The patrol had been sent up the mountain to find Major Reynolds and the Provisional Regiment of Philippine Scouts.[68]

The U.S. soldiers, who had never heard of the Philippine Scouts, took a long look at the array of partially uniformed Filipinos scattered around Roy's camp cleaning their new weapons. The Scouts were equally impressed by the relatively clean and orderly appearance of the Americans. Both groups were, technically, U.S. Army combat troops. The patrol leader told Roy that General Hall had sent him up the mountain to bring Roy and his men to 11th Corps headquarters on the Zambales coast.

Roy was ready. The Scouts were armed and ready to attack the Japanese at the Zig-zag, or wherever else 11th Corps might want to use them. The next morning they hiked down to the U.S. Army encampment near Olongapo, to the tent of Colonel Potter, Chief of Staff of the 11th Corps. Colonel Potter explained that 11th Corps's mission was to drive across the top of Bataan to Dinalupihan and block any Japanese units that might try to enter Bataan. But the Japanese forces at the Zig-zag had proven to be much tougher than expected. Potter's initial thrust up the road into Bataan was a near disaster, with many casualties. American bodies had been hauled out of the Zig-zag by the truckload.[69]

Colonel Potter's staff was working on plans to bypass the fortifications and trap the Japanese in place. They intended to climb through the mountain foothills instead of going up the road, and once they had the Japanese surrounded they would move across Bataan to Dinalupihan. From there they would head for Manila, joining up with the 6th Army.

"What about us?" asked Roy. "We know this country and can help. We intend to fight our way into Manila with you."

The Colonel looked Roy up and down and peered past him at his group of 200 or so Filipinos and a few Negritos. He said, “Major, if we can’t win this war without you, we’re in a hell of a fix.” [70]

***

Frank and Damaso lay awake and listened to the distant pop-pop-pop of machine-guns and occasional crack of rifle shots coming from the vicinity of the Zig-zag. Neither man could sleep. The noise was not bothersome—it was the fact that American troops were close enough that they could actually hear them.[71]

At dawn an artillery duel started that sounded like it was in their back yard. They awoke to the crash of mortar rounds and the deep boom of bigger guns at Subic Bay, firing on Japanese positions in the Zig-zag. The more distinct sounding Japanese guns along the Olongapo highway opened up on U.S. troops approaching from the west.[72]

Boone's report that day described the American army's capture of Subic Bay and Olongapo. Boone said that he was shifting some of his units south of the Zig-zag to help keep the Japanese bottled up. He had moved more snipers into position along the highway, and he had been forced to move his headquarters to Mount Malasimbo. Boone was pulling together a small force to attack the Japanese headquarters in Dinalupihan.[73] He still had not received any arms or supplies, so it was as much as he could do with the ammunition he had left.

Frank considered Boone's plan. The U.S. Army had attacked the Zig-zag, so they undoubtedly intended to fight their way across the top of Bataan and block it off. Three of Boone's four regiments were located south of the Olongapo highway, so fighting along the highway would cut Boone off from the majority of his command. Frank wrote Boone a note and urged him to move his headquarters to Frank's forward command post immediately.[74]

Frank wrote out a personal request to General MacArthur's headquarters for 3,000 rifles and ammunition to be air-dropped to Boone.[75] In his note, he told Boone to have Bernales smuggle the request through the Japanese lines to the American forces at Subic Bay.[76]

Frank sent runners to the 2nd and 4th Regiments, and directed them to send all future intelligence reports directly to him.[77] He had decided to reroute the Bataan guerrillas' intelligence reports to Eddie Wright's headquarters near Bamban until Boone came back to the south side of the highway. He also issued orders that they should redouble their efforts against the Japanese. Once the American troops started south down the Bataan Peninsula, the fewer Japs the better.

Americans in Olongapo! It would not be long now. Atabrine tablets had suppressed Frank's malaria for the time being, although he still felt weak and run-down. Inside, Frank could feel a bit of enthusiasm stirring for the first time in years.[78]

***

When he got Frank’s note, John Boone sent his operations officer off through the jungle to make contact with the American troops at Subic Bay.[79] He radioed Frank’s request for 3,000 rifles to Captain Cabangbang along with another description of his drop zones.[80] But instead of joining Frank at the forward command post, he took to the jungle himself and went north to Pampanga. He made contact with a U.S. reconnaissance patrol near Fort Stotsenburg, identified himself, and demanded to be taken to 6th Army headquarters in Tarlac.[81] Astonished GIs loaded Boone into the back of a jeep and, escorted by two tanks, took him to General Krueger's headquarters.[82] There, he presented Frank's written request for 3,000 rifles and made a plea for arms, ammunition and medical supplies for his men.[83]

General Krueger abandoned his plan to send the arms by truck and committed to air drop weapons and supplies to Boone's 1st Regiment, instead. Another shipment of weapons would be sent to Boone's 3rd Regiment at Morong by boat, and General Krueger formally attached the regiment to the 11th Corps with the mission of helping block off the south side of the Zig-zag.[84] Eddie Wright's 3rd Battalion of Philippine Scouts was assigned to guard the San Marcelino airfield and to block any Japanese troops that might try to escape north into Zambales.[85]

Boone got back to his headquarters in time to meet the first elements of the 11th Corps as they climbed across the slopes of the Zambales Mountains to Mount Malasimbo, above the Olongapo highway.

At San Marcelino, Eddie Wright waited at the airfield to board the supply plane and guide the pilots to Mount Malasimbo to drop Boone's weapons.[86] He put Roy Reynolds in charge of delivering weapons to the 3rd Regiment guerrillas at Morong by boat, and bringing out their casualties, as well.[87]

But as the supply plane laden with Boone's arms and ammunition touched down at San Marcelino, its landing gear caught in the soft ground and the plane nosed over.[88] It was too badly damaged to take off again. Eddie turned the weapons shipment over to Roy to take to Morong. While he waited for another plane and more weapons, Eddie wrote another letter to Marge.[89]

***

On Sunday, February 4, 1945, guerrillas from Boone's 1st Regiment and soldiers from the 11th Corps attacked Dinalupihan.[90] Colonel Nagayoshi was not there, having moved forward to the Zig-zag to command his doomed troops. The town fell quickly and the 11th Corps linked up with 6th Army forces in the central plain, sealing off Bataan.

The 11th Corps then turned south down the bayside highway, pushing the retreating Japanese in front of them.

The American troops fought their way through Orani at mid-day. As the Japanese withdrew, they slaughtered their prisoners who had been held at the town's municipal building.[91]

Farther south at the provincial capital of Balanga, headquarters of Lieutenant Kanesero's *Kempei-tai* detachment, Japanese soldiers had begun to desert and take off into the mountains, thinking that they might hide safely in the jungle as American soldiers had hidden from them for the past three years. But Balanga was the municipality most frequently decimated by the vicious zonifications the *Kempei-tai* had conducted, and the Filipino guerrillas knew the jungle far better than any Japanese.

One morning, grisly evidence of the Filipino citizens' feelings toward the Japanese appeared in Balanga's town square. There, sitting quietly on a curbstone, the severed head of a Japanese soldier stared blankly at the doors of City Hall.

The next day, that severed head was joined by several more. By the time the Americans arrived on February 5, Balanga was free of Japanese occupation and the town square was almost completely ringed with the heads of the Japanese garrison.[92]

The American soldiers called together officials of the town and local guerrilla leaders. An officer explained that he understood the feelings of the townspeople and of the guerrillas, but that catching and decapitating Japanese soldiers was actually murder, and it had to stop. Everyone agreed.

The number of heads at the town square, however, continued to grow.

***

Tivo Leonzon came up to Frank's command post on Monday, February 5, 1945. He reported that Eddie Wright and his men were gone from Bamban and were attached to the U.S. Army near Subic Bay. Frank had suspended communications with John Boone the previous day—it had gotten too dangerous for the Negrito runners to cross the Olongapo highway. Placido came into camp with a report from Lieutenant Colonel Victor Abad that the 2nd Regiment had completely cleared the Japanese out of their area.

Several Negrito families had gathered near Frank's camp to see what he was going to do. That morning, the women washed his clothes and did their best to make his uniform shirt look presentable.[93] He gave them his food reserves, in thanks: several bushels of corn, rice, *camotes*, some vegetables and a few limes.[94] Frank asked Damaso to lead the way down to the bayside highway. Tivo and Placido both said that they wanted to come along and meet the Americans. The three men talked quietly while Damaso told his family good-bye, a process that consumed a considerable period of time and required copious chatter among the various members of Damaso's clan.[95]

Finally Damaso was ready. He and two of his sons took the lead on the trail down the mountain. If there were Japanese in the bushes on the way down, Damaso must have known how to avoid them as Frank never saw a soul during the two-hour trek down the mountainside.

They arrived at the bayside highway, at a point between Orani and Hermosa. They turned north, walking up the roadway toward Dinalupihan.

Soon Frank spotted a vehicle coming down the road from Hermosa. As it approached, he could see that it was a small, square, truck-like conveyance with two big headlights set at the top of a square, vertical grill, painted dull green. It had no top, the windshield was folded down over the hood, and three Americans were riding inside. The vehicle, which Frank would soon learn was a Jeep, pulled up in front of Frank's little group and stopped. He had never seen anything like it.

The men all stared at each other for a moment in silence. The three American soldiers wore green uniforms with leather boots. Steel helmets that resembled inverted round bowls covered their heads. Instead of leather belts, they wore green webbed belts and harnesses that had ammunition pouches, grenades, knives, pistols and other items attached. Everything was marked "U.S.," but to Frank they looked like apparitions from outer space.

The three soldiers, a lieutenant, a sergeant and a private, were equally stunned. What they saw in front of them looked like a bad jungle dream. There was a stooped, thin, darkly tanned white man with a wide, thick, dark beard, streaked with gray, that hung down to his waist. He wore what appeared to be a clean but tattered khaki-colored uniform shirt with patch pockets and a belt woven out of rattan. One leg was smaller than the other, and his shoes were hide sandals held on by strips of cloth. On his back hung a rattan frame with a tattered, rolled-up piece of canvas tied to it. The only normal-looking thing about him was the .45 caliber military pistol that hung, or rather drooped, from his belt.

Two Filipinos accompanied the man, one toting an ancient bolt-action rifle and the other, an older man, unarmed. With them were three small, black, nearly naked pygmies, two armed with rifles, one with a bow and arrows.

The lieutenant climbed out of the jeep, strode over to the group and confronted Frank.

"Who the hell are you?"

Frank could not suppress a grin. "Lieutenant Colonel Frank R. Loyd, United States Army. I've been waiting for you." [96]

XXIII. 1945

As Frank Loyd climbed into the jeep, Damaso Caballero and his two sons crowded in behind him. Everyone clung to the little vehicle while the driver made a sharp U-turn and sped up the bayside highway to Dinalupihan. There, awe-struck soldiers gathered around to marvel at Frank's sixteen-inch beard and his little black companions. A public relations officer pushed his way through the crowd and Frank asked how to get word of his rescue back to Evelyn.

"Talk to a newspaper reporter. That's the fastest way—she'll hear it on the news." [1]

The officer took Frank to meet Lieutenant Colonel Allen Leonard, commanding officer of the Army battalion at Dinalupihan. Leonard looked Frank up and down, asked where he came from and where he had been, took a couple of pictures, and sent him to the quartermaster tent to draw new uniforms, underwear and shoes. An orderly took Frank to the showers, then to the mess hall. The cooks in the mess tent said that he could have anything he wanted and tried to get him to sit down at a table, but Frank ate standing up and took it slowly.[2] After dinner he autographed a lot of Philippine money for the "GIs," a term he had never heard before, who treated him like a movie star.

At the intelligence officer's tent, he learned from an interpreter that Damaso Caballero expected to go with him to the United States, ever his faithful servant. Frank tactfully convinced Damaso that this would not be necessary, and the officer proceeded to interrogate Damaso and his sons about Japanese positions on Bataan. They refused to say anything, as was typical of the Negritos.

But that night a Japanese patrol threw a hand grenade into the building where Damaso was billeted with some guerrillas, and the next morning Damaso and his sons, only slightly injured, told the Americans everything they knew about the Japanese.[3]

As Frank prepared to enjoy another shower before breakfast, he gazed into a big mirror and marveled at his long, bushy beard. He sadly considered that beard to be his net accomplishment of the past three years.[4] It made him look crazy—like a psychopath. He wondered what Evelyn would think.

Evelyn. Staring at himself in the mirror, Frank was reminded of Enoch Arden, the protagonist in a poem by Alfred Lord Tennyson.[5] In the story, Enoch Arden is shipwrecked on a far shore and comes home years later to find out that his wife is happily married to another man. It reminded Frank of Roy's words about what they all could expect. In the poem, Enoch uses his bushy whiskers as a disguise and he lives out his life loving his former wife and his two children from nearby, but he never reveals himself to them. Frank washed his hair and his beard. He decided not to shave off the whiskers just yet.

At breakfast Frank found John Boone in the mess tent. The two men had not physically seen each other in more than a month—since Frank came to Boone's headquarters for the planning meeting and then left to man the forward command post. Boone described the mad dash he had made to 6th Army headquarters to plead for arms for his men, and he told Frank that Al Romaine was safe in the 6th Army hospital. When Boone asked Frank what had happened to Margaret Utinsky, an incredulous officer seated nearby said that a radio message had come in earlier—a woman named Margaret Utinsky was being brought in from farther down the peninsula. A small airplane was already circling over Dinalupihan, waiting to take Margaret away from the front lines.[6] John Boone shook Frank's hand. He left to return to his guerrilla headquarters on Mount Malasimbo.

A jeep was waiting, and the driver took Frank on a bouncy, high-speed race through the Pampangan farmlands to Guagua at the north end of the fishponds, the headquarters of the 40th Infantry Division. There, he was quickly dubbed "Rip Van Winkle" by the press.[7] He was taken to meet the commanding general of the 40th Division, who turned out to be Major General Rapp Brush, an old acquaintance. Brush had been a Lieutenant Colonel when Frank last saw him. Over lunch Frank told Brush his story, and told him as much as he could remember about the latest Japanese positions on Bataan. He stressed that he was most anxious for assignment to an infantry unit to see the rest of the war through.[8] In response to Frank's request, Brush sent a radio message through Army channels, and he assured Frank that Evelyn would be notified as quickly as possible. He had Frank classified "Project J" (recovered personnel), and sent Frank to 6th Army to be interviewed by Army Intelligence.

The three-hour jeep ride to San Fernando, near Clark Field, was longer and worse than the trip to Guagua. Each bump and jolt aggravated Frank's weak leg and arm, with the pains growing worse as the trip wore on. When the driver finally deposited him at 6th Army, he was given a cigar and the opportunity to talk to more reporters before being interviewed by intelligence officers. He asked for and was given a physical exam at the hospital, which he felt confident he would pass in spite of his lingering malaria. If not, he reasoned, his survival over the past three years would be sufficient proof of his physical condition to obtain a waiver to return to duty.[9] At the hospital, he wrote out a request for an active duty assignment and sent it to General Douglas MacArthur, with copies to General Brush and to Major General Oscar W. Griswold, commander of the 14th Corps. Griswold, he hoped, might remember him from his years as captain of the Army rifle and pistol teams.[10]

He was interrogated again by intelligence officers and, to his surprise, in walked Major Sandy Easley, the young son of one of Frank's old friends, Lieutenant Colonel Speck Easley. Sandy was part of 6th Army's intelligence staff. Frank asked Sandy about his dad.

"It's General Easley, now. Assistant commander of the 96th Infantry Division on Leyte."

The young man was obviously proud of his dad, who had been wounded in the battle for Leyte. Then he handed Frank a letter. "I think you'll want to read this."

From Evelyn Loyd's letter to Sandy, Frank learned that his family was in good health and that Frank Jr. was applying to West Point.

That evening he finally got some time to sit down and write to Evelyn. On the strength of Evelyn's letter to Sandy, Frank shaved off his beard.[11]

***

"Mrs. Loyd, do you want me to answer the door?" Patti Dulligan's voice rang down the hallway of the little house on Thorain Boulevard just as Evelyn was getting out of bed. Patti had spent Friday night, February 9, 1945 with Bonnie, her school chum.[12]

Patti opened the door and took a letter from a mailman waiting on the porch. As Evelyn bustled up the hallway in her bathrobe, Patti turned back into the front room. "Mrs. Loyd, here's a letter for you."

Just as Bonnie stepped into the room, Evelyn took the envelope and ripped it open.

"Ohhhhhh, my God!" Evelyn started to cry.

***

6th Army put Frank Loyd on "casual" status and assigned him to the 92nd Evacuation Hospital at Lingayen to await orders. He hitched a ride to San Fernando to visit Sandy Easley, and talked Sandy into giving him a jeep and a driver to take him back to Bataan. He headed south down the bayside highway to retrieve the footlocker he had buried at the 4th PC Regiment's headquarters near Lamao before the final battle of Bataan. But half way down the peninsula they were stopped by a military police roadblock and told that no traffic was permitted in southern Bataan—guerrillas and 11th Corps troops were still rooting out Japanese in the mountains.

Frank had the driver turn around and go back to Orani, then turn the jeep up the mountain trail toward Tala. Grinding over rocks and tree roots, the jeep made the climb almost two-thirds of the way up to the settlement. At that point they encountered two frightened Filipino men on their way down, who said that they had just seen five Japanese soldiers 400 yards farther up the trail. Frank had his driver back down the trail and return to Orani. There, he waited. It was satisfying, somehow, to sit there in this town recently controlled by the Japanese, and look up at the mountain where the Japs were now hiding instead of Frank.

Word traveled via the "bamboo telegraph" that Frank was looking for Placido Filomeno. About sundown, Placido came into Orani with the metal tin containing a portion of Frank's diary and the jars that Frank had buried in the banana patch more than two years ago. Placido said that a large number of Japs had moved into the mountains above Tala the day Frank went down to meet the Americans on the highway, and they were hiding in the jungle near Frank's old camp. American soldiers had fanned out into the jungle, concealing themselves along trails and streambeds, hiding and waiting. They killed nine Japs just outside Tala two days ago.[13]

***

The War Department's letter to Evelyn had said to keep Frank's discovery confidential, as public knowledge would not be in the best interests of "other Americans who are still in the hands of the enemy." [14] For a week she told no one except Bonnie, Frank Jr., and her sisters.

It was driving her crazy. Evelyn could not sleep at night. She was nearly bursting with the news. But she tried to keep calm and normal in her conversations with the other wives in the Fiddlers' Club, who were calling each other every day to see if anyone had heard anything about their husbands.

All that changed on Saturday morning, February 17, 1945. First, the mailman brought an air mail letter. It began,

> Dearest Evelyn and Mr. & Miss Loyd:
>
> Hope you will excuse for being so late in answering your last letter, of December 1941…

Frank went on to congratulate Frank Jr. on his pilot's license, promise Bonnie that she would go to the finest schools, and describe his beard. He wrote a few pages about where he had been over the past three years. He told Evelyn that he was certain she would understand his desire to stay in the Philippines and see the war to its end, and said that he would try to get permission to fly home for a short leave. He made a brief reference to Enoch Arden and closed with, "Let me know at once whether I shall need whiskers." [15]

Evelyn understood. And she felt like she had just given birth—happy, but weak.[16] Frank really was alive, he was safe, and one day he would be home. She wrote him a long letter, included some snapshots, and had the children each write one. She assured him that he would not need whiskers.

In spite of the "confidentiality" of Frank's status, she called Evelyn Noble and told her the news. Evelyn had heard nothing about Maxie. His name had never been on the prisoner lists.

Then a radio news broadcast announced that American troops found sixteen American soldiers living on Bataan. Roy Reynolds name was mentioned, so Evelyn started calling her other friends. Betty Wilson had no word about Zero, but Jeannie had just gotten a letter from Roy Reynolds.[17]

Before the day was over Evelyn's phone began to ring. Newspaper reporters followed up on wire stories, and Frank's rescue was featured in the next morning's Sunday papers. Beginning that day, Evelyn's life became a string of congratulatory phone calls, mail, and well-wishers knocking on the door. Letters soon jammed her mailbox, including letters from Frank.

***

About the time Frank Loyd joined the U.S. troops at Dinalupihan, elements of the 6th U.S. Army entered Manila. Even though General Tomoyuki Yamashita had taken his army north to the mountains, Japanese naval and air corps personnel still occupied the city. Their commander, Rear Admiral Sanji Iwabachi, ordered them to fight to the death.[18] Over the next four weeks Manila deteriorated into one of the most devastated cities of the war, similar to Warsaw, Poland. The city was virtually leveled by Japanese demolitions, tactical fires and artillery, and by U.S. tank and artillery fire. Fatalistic Japanese soldiers, confronting their own deaths and remembering years of Filipino loyalty to the United

States, decided to take as many Filipinos with them as they could. They went on a rampage of rape and killing, deliberately slaughtering more than 100,000 civilians trapped in the city, the worst Japanese atrocity since the Rape of Nanking.[19] The Catholic priests who had supported the underground and collected food and money for the prisoners of war were singled out for especially gruesome deaths.

Meanwhile, U.S. Marines invaded Iwo Jima to secure airstrips that were being used by the Japanese to attack U.S. bombers. Twenty-two thousand dug-in Japanese defenders would die there, inflicting twenty thousand casualties on their attackers. Once the Marines secured Iwo Jima, the U.S. Army Air Forces began a devastating fire-bombing campaign against Japanese cities.

Because of his physical condition, the Army shipped Frank Loyd to a replacement depot on Leyte, where he got to visit briefly with Speck Easley. General Easley was getting his 96th Division ready to board ship for a new objective—Okinawa.[20]

To his disappointment, Frank Loyd was put on a ship bound for the United States. He arrived at Letterman General Hospital in San Francisco on April 10, 1945 for further medical testing. His requests for a duty assignment had been denied.

***

The knock on the front door caught Evelyn by surprise. She, Bonnie and Frank Jr. had gone to the evening movies at Fort Sam Houston and had just gotten home. It was kind of late for unexpected callers.

Bonnie Loyd pulled the door open, screamed, and threw her arms around Frank's neck. "I just knew it would be you! Anyone else would know to use the doorbell."

Evelyn ran into the room and the scene deteriorated into sobbing and hugs, in spite of Evelyn's earlier promise that there would be no weeping when he came home.[21]

Frank had telephoned from San Francisco four days ago and each day since, except today, April 14. "Today I walked out of the hospital," he explained, grinning, "and availed myself of the free air transportation."

A whirlwind of events began the next morning. Newspaper reporters appeared and photographed Frank in his new uniform eating cake and ice cream. He was granted leave by the Army, and received a promotion to full colonel.

On April 29, Italy fell to the Allies and Hitler committed suicide the next day. A week later Germany surrendered, adding joy and optimism to the rounds of parties held in San Antonio to toast Frank Loyd. Evelyn arranged for the Loyd family to spend a week in a guest cottage on a citrus farm in the Rio Grande Valley, to get re-acquainted.

***

Amid the celebrations of "V-E Day," the bombing of Japan continued and the Joint Chiefs of Staff issued secret orders setting November 1, 1945 as the date for General MacArthur's invasion.[22] Luzon was designated the "jumping off" point. Planning and training for the invasion began. Some of the Philippine guerrillas were to be included in the invasion force.

Even so, the war continued in the Philippines. General Yamashita's plan to destroy MacArthur's army failed, in no small part because the guerrillas had reported the locations and strength of the Japanese fortifications.[23] Even as General MacArthur urged him to get on to Manila, 6th Army commander Lieutenant General Walter Krueger had slowed his advance and sent American divisions into the mountains to attack the Japanese. Thus blocked, Yamashita was unable to spring his trap.

General Yamashita's trap may have failed but in the end his overall strategy prevailed. He made the Americans come after him in the mountains of north Luzon, inflicting 44,000 casualties on American soldiers by mid-August 1944, the longest and bloodiest campaign of the Pacific war. Two hundred thousand Japanese troops died fighting in the Philippines.

General MacArthur's objective of freeing the men he left behind was not achieved. The Japanese had transferred all but the sickest prisoners to Japan, Korea and Manchuria to work in factories and coal mines. Many of them died in unmarked prison ships torpedoed by American submarines and planes, more in the Japanese camps. Two-thirds of the American soldiers captured on Bataan died in Japanese custody.

On August 6, 1945, the first of two atomic bombs descended on Japan. Japanese cities had been so ravaged by carpet bombing and fire bombing that the atomic destruction was actually less than on some previous days when more conventional weapons were used. After the second bomb, Emperor Hirohito told his councilors that he could no longer bear to see his "innocent subjects tormented under the cruelties of war." [24] On August 14, he surrendered.

Epilogue

Colonel Frank R. Loyd was awarded the U.S. Army's Legion of Merit for his actions in the Philippines, and the Philippine Army's Distinguished Conduct Star, the country's second-highest military decoration, for his actions with the Philippine Constabulary during their desperate last-ditch battle on the bayside highway before the surrender of Bataan.

Like many returning veterans he went through a period of depression after the war, and for the rest of his life awoke at night screaming from deep-seated nightmares. After his return home, Evelyn Loyd nursed Frank back to health and stayed by his side as he suffered through months of readjustment and depression. The Army assigned him to be Professor of Military Science and Tactics at the University of Wyoming. He did a stint in the Pentagon and served as Senior Instructor of the Army's Florida Military District. He retired from the service in 1954, classified as physically disabled.[1] He passed away in 1985, a victim of Alzheimer's disease. After Frank's death, Evelyn continued to live alone in their home in San Antonio, well into her nineties. She passed away in May, 2003, two weeks short of her 100th birthday.

In recognition of his work in organizing and commanding the Bataan Military District, John Boone was granted a battlefield commission and served for several years as a U.S. Army major, remaining in the Philippines with his wife and children. Boone corresponded regularly with Frank Loyd and helped Frank retrieve portions of his diary that had been left with various persons on Bataan. He helped Placido Filomeno and other Filipino associates find work in the post-war depression that swept the Philippines. General MacArthur awarded Major John Boone, Lieutenant Colonel Edwin Ramsey and five other guerrilla leaders the Distinguished Service Cross, America's second highest military decoration after the Congressional Medal of Honor.[2]

In 1947, John Boone resigned from the Army, and he and Mellie lived for a time near Subic Bay where he ran a photography shop. When the Korean War broke out he re-enlisted as a master sergeant, was wounded in combat and again decorated for bravery. After the war he and Mellie raised six children until her untimely death of a brain aneurysm in Augusta, Georgia at age forty-two. Sergeant-Major John Boone retired from the U.S. Army in 1964, and passed away in 1980. He and Mellie are buried in Arlington National Cemetery, Washington D.C.

Lieutenant Colonel Eddie Wright returned to California and to his beloved wife Marge. He was awarded the Purple Heart, Silver Star and the Legion of Merit for his actions during the Battle of Bataan. For many years after the war he suffered cyclic depressions. He slept with a loaded carbine hidden under his bed and he kept a .45 caliber pistol in a dresser drawer.[3] In 1959, Eddie retired from the Army and in 1977 he and Marge moved to Paris, Texas, his family home. In February 1997, Marge Wright passed away, and two days after her funeral Eddie Wright followed her, "...his last duty, caring for her, done." [4] Before his death, Eddie Wright took from his safe deposit box the lengthy, detailed diary he had written while on Bataan and burned it. He never allowed anyone to read his diary.

Major Roy Reynolds returned to the United States and found that his wife, Jeannie, had given him up for dead and married another man. He served for a time as an instructor at West Point, and served under General MacArthur again in Korea. He retired from the Army in 1963 as a brigadier general after a distinguished career in Army Intelligence. In 1984, he was one of the founders of the Philippine Scouts Heritage Society (www.philippine-scouts.org). In his later years he suffered from Parkinson's Disease, and he passed away in his sleep in November 2003 at age ninety-three. At the time of his death, he was reviewing a draft of this book.

Major Al Romaine was evacuated from the Philippines to a psychiatric hospital in New Guinea for rest and recuperation, and then to Letterman General Hospital in San Francisco where he suffered a nervous breakdown.[5] He spent most of the next year in hospitals and was discharged from the Army as disabled, suffering from what is today known as "post traumatic stress syndrome." [6] He returned to his home in Louisiana and passed away in 1970.

As former guerrillas and prisoners of war came back from the Philippines, and later from Japan, Evelyn Noble wrote letters and made phone calls searching for Maxie. Some of the men told her what they knew about Maxie but were reluctant to mention rumors of his death.[7] Others told her what they had heard. The Army conducted an extensive investigation into the fate of the guerrilla officers, and on November 9, 1945, three months after the war ended, Evelyn Noble received official notice that Lieutenant Colonel Arthur "Maxie" Noble was presumed dead.[8] Neither his body nor the bodies of the men executed with him were ever identified. The Army set November 1, 1943 as the date of death for all of them, under the assumption that it was the last date that any one of them could still have been alive.[9]

Margaret Utinsky remained in the Philippines for several months and assisted U.S. intelligence officers in hunting down collaborators. Claire Phillips was liberated from the Philippine Women's Correctional Institute, where the Japanese had sentenced her to twelve years at hard labor for espionage.[10] Both women returned to the United States and were awarded the Medal of Freedom, America's highest civilian decoration, for their humanitarian work in smuggling more than one million pesos worth of cash, food and other supplies into the Japanese prisons at Camp O'Donnell and Cabanatuan, at great risk to their own lives.[11] In 1948, Utinsky wrote a book about her exploits entitled "*Miss U*". Claire Phillips wrote a book about her work entitled *Manila Espionage,* with a forward by Major John Boone. The book was made into a movie starring Ann Dvorak.

Placido Filomeno and Tivo Leonzon continued to correspond with Frank Loyd for years after the war. In accordance with their agreements, Frank paid both of them for their services in supplying food to him during the war years. After he retired from the Army, Frank and Evelyn made two trips to the Philippines during the 1950s to visit them and their families.

In 1960, Damaso Caballero and his wife Ana were living in a barrio attached to the U.S. Subic Naval Base, working as domestic servants for an American family. The family heard Damaso's stories about World War II and Colonel Frank Loyd, and contacted the Loyd family. Damaso could neither read nor write, so on January 1, 1961, they made a tape recording of Damaso and his wife speaking to Frank Loyd in their native Negrito dialect. At the end of the tape, Damaso sang Frank a song.[12]

Bonnie Loyd completed her education at Sweetbriar and Bryn Mawr, earning a Masters degree in Art History. She married an architect and opened an art gallery in

Boston, Massachusetts in 1980. She has since moved her gallery to Wellesley where she lives and works as an art historian.

Frank Loyd Jr. graduated from Central Catholic High School in San Antonio the week before Frank Loyd arrived home from the Philippines. After a year of prep school he went to Washington, D.C., lobbied several congressmen, and finally secured an appointment to West Point. He graduated in 1950 and was sent to join General MacArthur's army fighting in Korea. Approximately two weeks after he arrived in Korea, Frank Loyd Jr. was killed in combat.

Frank and Evelyn Loyd are buried in Fort Sam Houston National Cemetery, San Antonio, Texas, next to their son.

Acknowledgements

This book is based primarily on the personal diaries and correspondence of Evelyn and Frank Loyd. Mrs. Evelyn Loyd in San Antonio, Texas, and Leonzon family members in Dinalupihan, Bataan, also provided first-hand accounts. However, to get the complete story of what took place on Bataan during the war, I found it necessary to draw on numerous other sources including original diaries, documents and correspondence, interviews with participants and their descendents, and published accounts of the war. My wife, Coleen, provided invaluable resources in this effort, served as research assistant, made travel arrangements, and poured over piles of documents at the National Archives, MacArthur Memorial, Ernie Pyle Museum and other sites in the United States and in the Philippines.

It would be appropriate to acknowledge the efforts of several other persons who helped compile and review information in this book, particularly Ms. Bonnie Loyd Crane, daughter of Evelyn and Frank Loyd; Ms. Jeanne Boone, daughter of John and Mellie Boone; Mr. Jim Litton, Philippine historian; Mr. Joe Wilson, son of Betty and "Zero" Wilson; Messrs. Jim and Ed Wright, sons of Marge and Eddie Wright; Mr. Jim Zobel, Archivist at the MacArthur Museum; the staff of the Total Army Personnel Command; and particularly the late historian and author Mr. Bernard Norling. I would also like to thank Mr. Cyril Webb for his assistance with on-site research in the Philippines, and Mr. Matt Mims for his cover art and maps. Many others have contributed time, documents and their stories, and although each deserves more credit than space here permits, many of them are listed in the bibliography, more in the end notes.

Compiling the story from all of these different resources has been my responsibility, and while I have made every effort to be as accurate as possible, any errors are my own.

Chris Schaefer

End Notes

I. Separation

[1] The population of the Philippine Islands is among the world's most racially diverse, the larger islands being home to multiple ethnic groups. More than thirty languages are spoken in the Philippines. The Negrito tribes are the most primitive people in the islands, inhabiting the mountains of western Luzon. They are pygmy-sized natives whose ancestors are believed to have migrated from Africa over land bridges that once connected Luzon to Asia.

[2] Attacked by the Japanese in 1937, Chinese Generalissimo Chiang Kai-shek had been able to hold out because of the vast size of his army and of his country, with the aid of American war materials. In the first six months of the war the Japanese captured Shanghai and the five Chinese provinces north of the Yangtze River. For the years after those initial successes the Japanese had been fighting a protracted, bloody, unsuccessful war in an attempt to pin down and defeat Chiang. In the

minds of many Americans, the Japanese' failure to defeat the Chinese after so long substantiated the notion that the Japanese were really not much of a threat to the U.S.

[3] Feis, *The Road to Pearl Harbor*, 268-269.

[4] MacArthur, *Reminiscences*, 210.

[5] Monaghan, *Under The Red Sun*, 9.

[6] MacArthur, *Reminiscences*, 102.

[7] Marquardt, *Before Bataan and After*, 232.

[8] Jose, *The Philippine Army, 1935-1942*, 34-37.

[9] Whitman, *Bataan, Our Last Ditch*, 105.

II. Bataan

[1] Feis, *The Road to Pearl Harbor,* 233-234.

[2] Feis, *The Road to Pearl Harbor,* 215-219, 234. There was no mention of Pearl Harbor. The Japanese' next targets were the Dutch East Indies and Singapore.

[3] Feis, *The Road to Pearl Harbor*, Chapters 29 and 30. The Netherlands had been overrun by the Nazis so the Dutch government was at this time, for all practical purposes, based in Batavia (now Jakarta), Indonesia.

[4] Miller, *War Plan Orange*, 61.

[5] Miller, *War Plan Orange.*

[6] On the west side of the International Dateline, including the Philippines, Hong Kong and Malaya, the date of the attacks was December 8, 1941.

[7] Ancheta, *The Wainwright Papers, Volume 4*, 56.

[8] The exact military population of Bataan at the start of the siege cannot be accurately determined, since most records were lost or destroyed during the battle. However, from an analysis of several sources the author estimates that that there were about 68,500 USAFFE troops on Bataan, 11,500 on Corregidor, and several thousand more in the southern islands. Of the men on Bataan, 55,000 were Filipinos and 13,500 were Americans. On Thursday, January 3, 1941, General Homma's headquarters reported that they had, so far, killed 2,105 Filipino and American soldiers and captured 13,864–Allied Translator and Interceptor Section, Enemy Publications numbers 3 through 5, (MacArthur: Record Group 3, Box 123, folder 5), 7. The vast majority of these men would have been part of the North Luzon Force, and the number does not include the units cut off in the northern mountains that were still fighting. The 13,000 captured probably includes many who deserted. During and after the battle for Luzon there were widespread rumors that large numbers of Filipino soldiers and constabulary men had deserted under fire. While

some men did desert, a comparison of the numbers of troops on hand at the start of the conflict and present on Bataan indicates that desertions were not as wide-spread as rumored, particularly considering the low level of training and preparedness of the Philippine Army, the high percentage of draftees, and anti-colonial sentiments of a significant number of Filipinos.

[9] Loyd, "Speech to Cheyenne, Wyoming, Army Reservists," 10 (Loyd); and "After-battle Report of the Quartermaster Corps, U.S. Army," *The Wainwright Papers, Volume IV*, 63.

[10] Letters, Frank Loyd to Evelyn Loyd, October 14, 1941 and November 12, 1941, (Loyd).

[11] Jones, "An account of the Operations of the South Luzon Force from 24 December'41 to 1 January '42, both Inclusive," (Wilson), 12; and Whitman, *Bataan: Our Last Ditch*, 109.

[12] Letter, Frank Loyd to Evelyn Loyd, March 6, 1942, (Loyd).

[13] Radio message, Marshall to MacArthur, 3 January 1942, cited in James, *The Years of MacArthur, Volume II*, 50-51.

[14] Reynolds would later say that General MacArthur was right about the sky being "black with planes"—Japanese planes. Interview by the author with Brigadier General Royal Reynolds, July 1, 1999.

[15] Young, *The Battle of Bataan*, 29.

[16] The *Banzai* attack, as a military tactic, can only be effective if the enemy's ability to shoot the on-coming Japanese soldiers is limited. With the M-1, a soldier could quickly get off eight shots without taking his finger off the trigger. Charging into a blaze of M-1 and machine gun fire quickly reduced the Japanese ranks. Despite the power of the M-1, however, some Scouts still preferred the more accurate, bolt-action Springfield, and traded their M-1 rifles to Philippine Army soldiers for the older Springfields.

[17] "Anywhere-Anytime," *The Philippine Scouts*, 342-349 (PSHS); Tagarao, *All This Was Bataan*, 37-39; and interview by the author with Brigadier General Royal Reynolds on July 1, 1999.

[18] Smith, "Diary," page 23 (NARA, Philippine Collection, box 143). Lieutenant Commander Douglas E. Smith was commander of the *Oahu*.

[19] Peña, *Bataan's Own*, page 177.

[20] Smith, *Diary*, pages 25-26, (NARA, Philippine Collection, box 143) and letter from Frank Loyd to Evelyn Loyd dated March 6, 1942 (Loyd).

[21] Young, *The Battle of Bataan*, 43, 57 and 73-74; and Tagarao, *All This Was Bataan*, 48-51.

[22] Allied Translator and Interceptor Section, "Enemy Publication No. 151: Combat in Mount Natib Area, Bataan," 1-2 (MacArthur). Also,

Baclagon, *Last 130 Days of the USAFFE*, 29-32; and Peña, *Bataan's Own*, 102-104 and 136.

[23] Gautier, *I Came Back From Bataan*, 44.

[24] MacArthur's behavior during the siege of Bataan was puzzling and uncharacteristic. During World War I he had established a reputation for bravery that was unquestioned, and bordered on foolish. In one example, he and George Patton stood on top of a trench line calmly talking while enemy artillery shells crashed around them, drawing closer with each burst. Finally, as a round exploded only a short distance from the two men, Patton flinched. Having made his point, MacArthur jumped into the trenches with Patton before the next round could kill them both. He designed his own uniforms and dressed flamboyantly, even in battle. Riding crop in hand, his mother's knitted scarf flowing behind him, he would personally lead his infantry troops out of the trenches to attack the Germans. The troops loved him. But during the siege of Bataan, MacArthur remained on Corregidor throughout the battle. The nickname "Dugout Doug" was based on the supposition that he was safely holed up in the Malinta tunnel complex, dug well into the rock. Actually, that was not true as MacArthur lived for most of the battle in a house above ground, and often ventured out in the open during air raids to watch the action and count the enemy bombers, much to the dismay of his staff. Manchester, *American Caesar*, 252-257 and 261-267.

[25] The 9th Cavalry had fought in the Philippines against the *Insurrectos* early in the century. A Philippine Scout corporal named Allen was the son of one of the cavalrymen, who had retired in the Philippines. Since the U.S. Army was still segregated at the time and there were no black units stationed in the Philippines, Allen's appearance attracted attention and he was often asked what outfit he was in. The mischievous Allen would sometimes reply "9th Cavalry" with a straight face, and refuse to give further details on grounds of security, thus starting and perpetuating the rumor. Olson, *O'Donnell: Andersonville of the Pacific*, 69.

[26] Carlos P. Romulo would become the last man to escape from Bataan, sent out on a rickety, overloaded civilian airplane by General Wainwright to prevent him from falling into the hands of the Japanese. Romulo would go on to win a Pulitzer Prize for his book, *I Saw the Fall of the Philippines*, and would become President of the General Assembly of the United Nations.

[27] Wainwright, *General Wainwright's Story*, 53.

[28] Norman, *We Band of Angels*, 60.

[29] The inexperienced 65th Brigade was intended to garrison the Philippines, freeing the crack troops of the 48th Division to join in the

assault on the Japanese' primary objective, the oil-rich Dutch East Indies. Homma's intelligence, faulty at this point, told him there were probably only 25,000 troops on Bataan, based on aerial photographs and on the assumption that most of the Filipino troops had deserted, which they had not. Under the heavy jungle canopy, MacArthur had more than twice that number of men.

[30] Peña, *Bataan's Own*, 148.

[31] Young, *The Battle of Bataan*, 194-195

[32] "The Philippine Campaign—the Japanese Perspective," *Japanese Accounts, Volumes I & II*, (CMH: HRC Geog. S. Philippines, 370.2), 93.

[33] Ancheta, *The Wainwright Papers*, 63; and Whitman, *Bataan: Our Last Ditch*, 314-315.

[34] MacArthur had made at least as many disastrous mistakes as the Pearl Harbor commanders, resulting in the destruction of the Far East Air Force, the last minute retreat to Bataan, and the abandonment of the food and supplies desperately needed by his soldiers. But MacArthur was a well-known general and war hero. Most Americans knew little about MacArthur's errors, and the United States government needed positive things to tell the American people. Therefore, while Kimmel and Short were sacked for their shortcomings, MacArthur was praised. Gailey, *The War in the Pacific*, 117-119.

[35] The rumor about General Yamashita was taken seriously. On March 21, General Wainwright radioed Washington that Yamashita was in command and pressing the attack on Bataan. In actuality, Yamashita had returned to Tokyo where he was hailed as a hero—as big a hero as Admiral Yamamoto, the architect of the Pearl Harbor attack. General Tojo, the aggressive Japanese premier and war minister, saw the conservative Yamashita as a threat to his control of the military government and transferred Yamashita to Manchuria, where he held down the Siberian border for most of the war. Young, *The Battle of Bataan*, 196, and Hoyt, *Japan's War*, 253.

[36] Young, *The Battle of Bataan*, 210.

[37] *Ibid*, 289; and Baclagon, *The Last 130 Days of USAFFE*, 142. Also, James, *The Years of MacArthur, Volume II*, 63.

[38] Manchester, *American Caesar*, 289.

[39] Rogers, *The Good Years: MacArthur and Sutherland*, 186. Also, Manchester, *American Caesar*, 289-290; and Whitney, *MacArthur: His Rendezvous with History*, 46.

[40] MacArthur's departure is described in detail by William Manchester in *American Caesar*, 291-301.

[41] Statement of Doyle Decker to Wayne Sanford, early 1984, page 1, (Indiana: Guerrilla Additions).
[42] Norman, *We Band of Angles*, 78.
[43] Peña, *Bataan's Own*, 171-176; and Gautier, *I Came Back From Bataan*, 50.
[44] Loyd, "Speech to Cheyenne, Wyoming, Army Reservists," 10; Young, *The Battle of Bataan*, 223; Wainwright, *General Wainwright's Story*, 67-68; and Whitman, *Bataan: Our Last Ditch*, 456.
[45] James, *The Years of MacArthur, Vol. II*, 63; and Young, *The Battle of Bataan*, 224.
[46] Wainwright, *General Wainwright's Story*, 74.
[47] Letter, Lieutenant General Masaharu Homma to Major General Jonathon Wainwright, March 19, 1942, (the "Beer Can Message"), (CMH).
[48] Breuer, *The Great Raid on Cabanatuan*, 25.
[49] Young, *The Battle of Bataan*, 239-241
[50] "The Tactical Plan for the Second Offensive on Bataan," *The Philippine Campaign—The Japanese Perspective*, 102-106, (CMH: HRC Geog S. Philippines, 370.2, Japanese Accounts Volumes I and II).
[51] "Thanks to General Wainwright," *The San Antonio Light*, October 31, 1945; and interview by the author with David Topping, May 15, 1999.
[52] Young, *The Battle of Bataan*, 257-258.
[53] Loyd, "Bataan Diary," 97 and 101; and letter, Loyd to Boone, 25 March 1946 (Boone).

III. The Fiddlers' Club

[1] Clark Lee, "Japanese Army in the Philippines Made up of Boys With Small Caliber Rifles; Hundreds Killed," *San Antonio Express*, December 26, 1941, page 1. Nothing could have been further from the truth. In fact, at the beginning of 1942 the Japanese soldiers were possibly the best-trained fighting men in the world, each having completed a rigorous two-year training program which emphasized physical conditioning, bayonet drill, unit tactics, and devotion to the Emperor. Their ability to undertake long marches under harsh conditions was legendary. Lory, *Japan's Military Masters*, Chapters 1 and 3.
[2] The Igorots or "mountain-people" of northern Luzon have a long tradition of headhunting. There were Igorot units in the Philippine Scouts and Igorot soldiers served in the Philippine Army. The Igorots were widely respected by their American officers, and the Japanese, as fierce and fearless warriors.

[3] Ramsdell, Josephine, "Wives of Philippine Defenders Keep Up Spirits in War Jobs," *San Antonio Light*, October 18, 1942.
[4] On December 28, 1941 President Roosevelt and a Navy Department spokesman issued statements to the press that the Allies were following a well-planned campaign to defeat the Japanese and give positive assistance to the Philippines; James, *The Years of MacArthur, Volume II*, 49. On January 3, Army Chief of Staff George C. Marshall sent the message to MacArthur explaining that the navy did not have enough ships to bring the needed reinforcements, but that columns of bombers were on their way from Africa and Hawaii. Whitman, *Bataan: Our Last Ditch*, 9. On January 10, 1942, after President Quezon proposed neutralizing the Philippines to prevent their destruction, Roosevelt replied, "We shall not relax our efforts until the forces which we are now marshalling outside the Philippines Islands return to the Philippines and drive the last remnant of the invaders from your soil." Aluit, *Corregidor*, 32. On February 8, Roosevelt told Quezon, "Although I cannot at this time state the day that help will arrive in the Philippines, I can assure you that every vessel available is bearing to the Southeast Pacific the strength that will eventually crush the enemy and liberate your native land. Vessels in that vicinity have been filled with cargo of necessary supplies and have been dispatched to Manila…A continuous stream of fighters and pursuit planes is traversing the Pacific; already ten squadrons of the foregoing types are ready for combat in the South Pacific area." Aluit, *Corregidor*, 27. On February 10, Roosevelt instructed MacArthur to "keep our flag flying in the Philippines as long as an American soldier or an ounce of food and a round of ammunition remain." Baclagon, *Last 130 Days of the USAFFE*, 227. On February 13, Senator Millard Tidings (Democrat, Maryland) demanded immediate dispatch of fresh troops for the "brave fighters of Bataan," "Big Convoy of Reinforcements to Philippines Held Too Risky," *San Antonio News*, page 1. On March 6, 1942, Walter Farr, a correspondent for the British newspaper *Daily Mail*, filed a report "at sea" in which he described "great convoys of ships carrying American troops, pilots, planes, tanks, and guns," headed across the Southwest Pacific. The report was immediately picked up and carried by U.S. newspapers ("British Writer Describes Shiploads of War Materiel," *San Antonio Express*, March 7, 1942, page 1). The convoy that so impressed Farr was carrying the first, small contingent of U.S. military specialists and aircraft to help with the defense of Australia. Its actual destination was secret, so many readers assumed Farr was aboard the Philippine relief convoy. In fact, no troops, ships or airplanes had been dispatched to the Philippines at all.

[5] "Texas Demos told Victory Must Wait," *San Antonio News*, February 24, 1942, page 8.

[6] "Roosevelt Says Uninterrupted Production Will Bring Victory," *San Antonio News*, February 24, 1942, page 6. It was rumored that when MacArthur heard about the shelling of Santa Barbara he sent a cable from the Philippines to the U.S. Army commander in San Francisco: "If you hold out 30 days we'll send reinforcements." Norman, *We Band of Angels*, 65.

[7] Letter, Evelyn Loyd to Frank Loyd, March 11, 1942, 1 (Loyd).

[8] *Ibid*, 1; and telegram from "Ken" at the War Department to Betty Wilson, March 6, 1942 (both Loyd).

[9] MacArthur kept his wife and infant son with him in Manila when all other military dependents were required to evacuate to the U.S. After the Japanese attack they fled with him to Corregidor. When MacArthur finally agreed to be evacuated, he, his family and several staff officers were taken off Corregidor at night in four PT boats to Mindanao in the southern Philippines. There, they were picked up by a B-17 bomber and flown to Darwin, Australia. Manchester, *American Caesar*, pages 291-309.

[10] Counting the entire Australian Army, most of which was still fighting the Nazis in Egypt and Libya, there were about half as many troops in Australia as MacArthur had left behind on Bataan. Hunt, *The Untold Story of Douglas MacArthur*, 247.

[11] Why Marshall sent the message about airplanes coming across Africa and across the Pacific is not clear, unless one accepts the idea that Roosevelt and Marshall deliberately lied to MacArthur. It is possible that Marshall misunderstood reports from his staff, and was actually referring to a squadron of aircraft in Australia that had been destined to the Philippines but which were dispatched to the Dutch East Indies instead. This possibility seems unlikely, however, given the details that were contained in General Marshall's message.

[12] Even though the U.S. government and U.S. Navy had written off the Philippines, the U.S. Army continued to try to re-supply the troops there by hiring Indonesian and Filipino blockade runners to carry in food and ammunition. $20,000,000 was appropriated by the Army to a small staff of officers under Colonel John A. Robenson in the Dutch East Indies to organize these top secret missions. Out of many attempts, only three blockade-runners made it into the Philippines and only a portion of the cargo of one ship actually got to Corregidor. Underbrink, *Destination Corregidor*, chapters 3 through 8 and chapter 10.

[13] Huff, *My Fifteen Years With General MacArthur*, 96; and Manchester, *American Caesar*, 273. Manchester quotes MacArthur's description of Roosevelt: "...a man who would never tell the truth when a lie would serve him just as well."
[14] There are differing opinions on the reason for this award. William Manchester concluded that it was made to offset Japanese and Nazi propaganda, which was calling MacArthur a coward who had fled from Bataan. Manchester, *American Caesar*, 316. Frazier Hunt indicates that it was initiated by pro-MacArthur, anti-Roosevelt political forces in Congress. Hunt, *The Untold Story of Douglas MacArthur*, 254.

IV. Days of Decision

[1] Whitman, *Bataan: Our Last Ditch*, 543-544.
[2] Loyd, "Bataan Diary," message pad note 2; and Peña, *Bataan's Own*, 185-186.
[3] "Commonwealth of the Philippines General Orders Number 124, Award of the Distinguished Conduct Star," (25 April 1946) to Col. Vincent L. Torres, Col. Gaspar Baylon and Lt. Col. Frank Loyd, page 1 (Loyd).
[4] *Ibid.*
[5] Loyd, "Bataan Diary," message pad notes 7-9; and "National Defense Week Speech," 7 (Loyd). Also, Peña, *Bataan's Own*, 186; and Whitman, *Bataan: Our Last Ditch*, 557-558 and 560-562.
[6] Whitman, *Bataan: Our Last Ditch*, 559-560.
[7] "Commonwealth of the Philippines General Orders Number 124, Award of the Distinguished Conduct Star," (25 April 1946) to Col. Vincent L. Torres, Col. Gaspar Baylon and Lt. Col. Frank Loyd, page 1 (Loyd). Also, Peña, *Bataan's Own*, 186-188; and Young, *The Battle of Bataan*, 281-282. All of these references describe the action which began at noon on April 8, 1942, but do not mention the subsequent action which began about 4:40 pm.
[8] "Commonwealth of the Philippines General Orders Number 124, Award of the Distinguished Conduct Star," (25 April 1946) to Col. Vincent L. Torres, Col. Gaspar Baylon and Lt. Col. Frank Loyd, page 2 (Loyd).
[9] *Ibid.*
[10] *Ibid.* Also, Peña, *Bataan's Own*, 186-188; and Young, *The Battle of Bataan*, 281-282.
[11] "Commonwealth of the Philippines General Orders Number 124, Award of the Distinguished Conduct Star," (25 April 1946) to Col.

Vincent L. Torres, Col. Gaspar Baylon and Lt. Col. Frank Loyd, page 2 (Loyd).
[12] *Ibid.*
[13] *Ibid.*
[14] *Ibid.*
[15] SanGabriel, *The Constabulary Story*, 261; and Peña, *Bataan's Own*, 188. Late in the day, General Francisco did send some units to Jalandoni—the 4th PC units that had been cut off in the previous day's fight at the Mamala River, which had regrouped at PC headquarters. However, the units never made it due to the heavy congestion on the bayside highway and Trail 20 by troops fleeing the other way.
[16] Peña, *Bataan's Own*, 188.
[17] Whitman, *Bataan: Our Last Ditch*, 561.
[18] Loyd, "Bataan Diary," message pad notes 8-10; Note Card 5; and "Speech to Cheyenne Reservists," 10-11 (Loyd).
[19] Loyd, "Bataan Diary," message pad notes 8-10; Note Card 5; and "Speech to Cheyenne Reservists," 10-11 (Loyd). Elements of the 4th PC regrouped after the battle and took up defensive positions farther south on the road at Cabcaben. They held their ground even after the surrender. Returning from the surrender negotiations, Colonel James Collier found a 4th PC major (possibly Baylon) with his .45 caliber pistol drawn and cocked, threatening to shoot a Japanese tank officer who had just demanded his surrender. Behind the Japanese officer was a line of tanks. Behind the PC major was an irrigation ditch filled with constables with rifles at the ready. Col. Collier disarmed the major and told him about the surrender. With tears in his eyes, the PC major asked Collier to inform his men, then walked off into the woods. Whitman, *Bataan: Our Last Ditch*, 593.
[20] Letter, Frank Loyd to Evelyn Loyd, Feb. 7, 1945.
[21] Loyd, "Bataan Diary," message pad note 12; and notes from speeches given by Col. Loyd after the war (Loyd).
[22] Mills and Wools are the correct last names of these two men. Their first names were not recorded in Col. Loyd's notes. For readability, the author has provided fictitious first names. In his notes Col. Loyd referred to Mills as "Capt. Mills," but in a personal conversation with the author he described him as a "Navy lieutenant." The collar insignia for a Navy lieutenant and an Army captain are the same.
[23] This incident was described in a personal communication of Col. Frank R. Loyd to the author in 1963.

[24] Loyd, "Bataan Diary," message pad note 4; and Note Card 6 (Loyd). This is the largest surrender of U.S. troops in any action except the Civil War.
[25] Loyd, Note Card 6; and "Speech to Cheyenne Reservists," 11 (Loyd).
[26] Conner, "We Fought Fear on Luzon," *True*, August 1945, 70.
[27] Sanford, Wayne A., "Col. Claude A. Thorp—The Father of American Guerrilla Warfare," *The World War II Chronicle*, March/April 1989, 7 and 9. Also, Dizon, "Complete Data Covering the Guerrilla Activities of the Late Colonel Claude A. Thorp," (NARA: box 258), 1.
[28] Interview by Doug Clanin with Major Henry Clay Connor, 11 and 15-16. (Indiana) Also, Henry Clay Conner, "We Fought Fear on Luzon," *True*, August 1945, 70.
[29] Interview by the author with Col. John Olson, November 21, 1998. Also, Whitman, *Bataan: Our Last Ditch*, 600.
[30] Horan, "Philippine Guerrillas: Colonel Horan's narrative," (MHI). Also, Norling, *The Intrepid Guerrillas of North Luzon*, Chapter 5.
[31] Personal communication from Col. Frank Loyd to the author, 1963.
[32] Loyd, Note Card 6, and personal communication from Col. Loyd to the author.
[33] "Personal Files of Major General Courtney Whitney," (MacArthur: box 17, folder 1, page 1); and Gautier, *I Came Back from Bataan*, 72.
[34] This story was related by Col. Melvin Rosen, 88th Field Artillery, in an interview with Rhode Island State Senator John A. Patterson on August 2, 1997. Colonel (then Captain) Rosen was one of the prisoners who witnessed this murder. Similar stories are told by virtually all Death March survivors.
[35] Orders came from General Homma to get the thousands of Fil-American prisoners out of Bataan immediately, and thus out of the way of the Japanese Army as it prepared to attack Corregidor. Olson, *O'Donnell: Andersonville of the Pacific*, 18-20.

V. Days of Hope

[1] After laying submerged off Corregidor for two days, the submarine *Permit* sailed on the night of March 16, 1942 evacuating forty army technicians, mostly enlisted men, and numerous bags of mail. General Wainwright had spread the word a few days before that anyone who wanted to write a letter home must do so immediately, so the letters could be taken to Corregidor in time to meet the sub. Sub commander Lieutenant Wreford G. Chapple and his crew withstood two depth charge

attacks by Japanese destroyers before clearing the Philippine Islands and heading for Australia. Underbrink, *Destination Corregidor*, 161-162.

[2] Letter, Evelyn Loyd to Frank Loyd, April 6, 1942, (Loyd).

[3] Letter, Evelyn Loyd to Frank Loyd, February 21, 1945, page 1, (Loyd).

[4] Letter, Major General J. A. Ulio, to Mrs. Frank R. Loyd, June 23, 1942, (Loyd).

[5] Hollister and Strunsky, *From Pearl Harbor Into Tokyo*, 103.

[6] Lieutenant Colonel James H. Doolittle's secret mission had, in fact, been conceived by President Roosevelt shortly after Pearl Harbor as a way to boost American morale. Early in the morning of April 18, 1942, sixteen U.S. Army Air Corps bombers took off from the deck of the newly commissioned aircraft carrier *Hornet*, 800 miles east of Tokyo. After a brief bombing run, the planes attempted to fly past Japan to crash-land in China. All of the aircraft were lost and the Japanese captured some of the crews, but many of the crewmembers survived and Chinese nationalist soldiers rescued them. Hoyt, *Japan's War*, 271-274.

[7] In a propaganda barrage designed to offset the loss of Bataan and Corregidor, the U.S. government began releasing news reports about the naval battle in the Coral Sea and the Doolittle raid on Tokyo. The Coral Sea was described as a great victory although it was actually closer to a draw. The raid on Tokyo left "a swath of destruction 40 miles long and five to twenty miles wide," they said ("Doolittle, 79 Others on Raid Decorated; No U.S. Planes Lost" *San Antonio Express*, May 20, 1942, 1) although the actual damage was negligible. General Doolittle was awarded the Congressional Medal of Honor and all of his crew members were awarded the Distinguished Service Cross, decorations they richly deserved. Doolittle was brought back from China for the award ceremony in President Roosevelt's office. He went along with the excessive damage reports to some degree, making statements like "practically every bomb…hit its mark," and "The performance of the planes [and crews] was magnificent." He confirmed to the gathered newspaper reporters that no American aircraft had been lost, even though they had all been lost.

[8] The author estimates that approximately 67,175 surrendered on Bataan, including 11,796 Americans and 55,379 Filipinos, based on the number who arrived at Camp O'Donnell (Olson, *O'Donnell, Andersonville of the Pacific*, xiii and 235) plus about 8,500 who died on the Death March. The Center of Military History estmates 78,100. "Statistics, Death March, Surrender," CMH 228.01 HRC Geog S. Philippines.

[9] News of the executions was broadcast in the United States and picked up by guerrilla radios in the Philippines. Donald Blackburn, hiding in

northern Luzon, commented, "After some of the things the Japs have done on Luzon those executions could be considered humane treatment." Harkins, *Blackburn's Headhunters*, 151.

VI. Escape and Evade

[1] Letter, Frank Loyd to Evelyn Loyd, February 7, 1945.
[2] This man's name was not recorded in Frank Loyd's diary. The author has supplied a name for readability.
[3] Interview by the author with David Topping, May 19, 1999; and Utinsky, *"Miss U"*, 19-20.
[4] Richard Gordon, interviewed for the PBS American Experience, "MacArthur."
[5] Dialog constructed by the author from descriptions of the aftermath of the Death March. The author estimates that 67,175 American and Filipino troops were captured by the Japanese at the fall of Bataan and marched up the bayside highway. Approximately 8,500 of these men died or were killed by their guards during the five day walk to Camp O'Donnell, the infamous Japanese prison camp at Capas, Tarlac. Exact numbers cannot be determined because no records were kept and it is not clear how many of the 39,000 American soldiers still listed as Missing in Action in the Pacific actually died in the Bataan jungles, on the Death March, or elsewhere. (CMH: 228.01 HRC Geog. S. Philippines, Statistics, Death March, Surrender, 055-056). Also, Olson, *O'Donnell: Andersonville of the Pacific*, 13.
[6] Utinsky, *"Miss U"*, 141.
[7] Military Service Records, Gyles Merrill; and interview by the author with Leon Beck on May 11, 1999. Also, interviews by Wayne Sanford with Leon Beck on March 1 and March 27, 1984, (Indiana: Guerrilla Additions). Also, Sanford, "The Mosquitoes Don't Bite," *The World War II Chronicles*, May/June 1989, pages 8-11.
[8] Fassoth, "Fassoth's Camp," (NARA: box 258), 5-6.
[9] *Ibid*, 11.
[10] Centuries ago the Filipinos began building dikes in the swamplands at the north end of Manila Bay to form pools for raising fish. By 1940 this vast complex of man-made ponds covered almost 100 square miles. Silva, *Geography and Natural Resources of the Philippines*, 150. In 1991 and 1992, nearby Mount Pinatubo blew up in one of the largest volcanic eruptions of the twentieth century. Vast portions of the fishponds, the farmlands at the south end of the central plain, and the U.S. Clark Air Force Base were devastated. Today, much of the area that

comprised the fishponds where Colonel Merrill hid is a moonscape-like wasteland of volcanic ash.

[11] Interview by Doug Clanin with Leon Beck, March 1, 1984, 16-17, (Indiana: Guerrilla Additions).

[12] Interview by Doug Clanin with Leon Beck, March 16, 1984, (Indiana: Guerrilla Additions).

VII. The Sickness at Tala Ridge

[1] Interview by Doug Clanin with Major Henry Clay Connor, (Indiana). Also, Henry Clay Conner, "We Fought Fear on Luzon," *True*, August 1945, 71.

[2] Interview by Wayne Sanford with James Boyd, (Indiana: Guerrilla Additions).

[3] All of these rumors were, of course, completely false.

[4] More than thirty native languages are spoken in the Philippine Islands, broken into as many as eighty dialects. Tagalog is the predominate language in Manila and central Luzon.

[5] This rumor probably referred to the Battle of the Coral Sea, which took place at the same time General Wainwright was surrendering on Corregidor in May 1941. It was considered a draw, although it prevented the Japanese from landing troops at Port Moresby, New Guinea, 350 miles northeast of the coast of Australia. Losses on both sides were heavy. It was the first battle fought entirely by carrier based aircraft—the American and Japanese fleets never came within cannon range of each other. All of the other rumors were, of course, completely untrue.

[6] Loyd, "Bataan Diary," typed transcript, 5. Rice was planted by hand, by a line of Filipino neighbors who would step in unison across a field, bent over and thrusting seedlings into the mud. Often they sang and were accompanied by a musician playing a guitar, banjo or other instrument who would set the pace and entertain the workers.

[7] Loyd, "Bataan Diary," typed transcript, 5.

[8] Certificate of Mariano Vergara Batungbacal Jr., 18 March 1953, *Investigation of Casualty Roster, Bataan Military District*, (NARA: box 245), 1.

[9] As the Fil-American army withdrew into Bataan in December 1941 with the Japanese army hot on their heels, artillery fire and bombing destroyed portions of the irrigation dikes feeding and draining the fishponds at the north end of Manila Bay. Many of the fish farmers fled the fighting, while others joined the USAFFE army and were subsequently sent to Japanese prison camps. The unattended, stagnant

fishponds became huge breeding grounds for anopheles mosquitoes. During May 1942, the prevailing trade winds blew swarms of these mosquitoes southwest across Bataan peninsula and across the rotting, malaria infested bodies lying along the route of the Death March. The resulting epidemic, according to some estimates, killed more than half the population of Bataan peninsula that summer. Henry Clay Conner, "We Fought Fear on Luzon," *True*, August 1945, 72 and 75; Fassoth, "Fassoth's Camp," (NARA: box 258), 8; Utinsky, *Miss "U"*, 20-21; and Phillips and Goldsmith, *Manila Espionage*, 65.

[10] "Rosena" Utinsky was actually Margaret Utinsky, an American nurse traveling under forged Lithuanian papers. Utinsky, *Miss U*, pages 12-22 and 30-31. Also, Hartendorp, *The Japanese Occupation of the Philippines*, Volume II, page 592.

[11] Undated letter, Pierce H. Wade to Wayne Sanford, (Indiana: Guerrilla Additions). Also, Citation for the Silver Star Medal presented to Pierce H. Wade after the war, for his daring action.

[12] Dita bark tea was used by a number of Americans in the jungle as a preventative, or to cure malaria. Although Dita tea did not appear to harm the Negritos, there are reports that in others it can cause blindness and even death. Hunt and Norling, *Behind Japanese Lines*, 43; Lapham and Norling, *Lapham's Raiders*, 43; and interview by Doug Clanin with Major Henry Clay Conner (Indiana).

[13] Loyd, "Bataan Diary," typed transcript, 30-31.

[14] Loyd, "Bataan Diary," typed transcript, 35.

[15] As related by Placido Filomeno after his release from the Japanese prison in Orani. Recorded in Frank Loyd's diary, typed transcript, page 64, and additional comments on Col. Loyd's recorded reading of the diary.

VIII. The Unwelcome Visitors

[1] Conner, "We Fought Fear on Luzon," *True*, August 1945, 72.

[2] Quote paraphrased from Conner, "We Fought Fear on Luzon," *True*, August 1945, 75; and Loyd, "Bataan Diary," typed transcript, 42. More detailed descriptions of neighborhood controls can be found in Steinberg, *Philippine Collaboration in World War II*, 60-61; Mojica, *Terry's Hunters*, 19-21 and 340-341; "Personal Papers of Courtney Whitney," (MacArthur: box 17, folder 1), 10; and in Marquez, *Blood on the Rising Sun*, 236.

[3] Conner, "We Fought Fear on Luzon," *True*, August 1945, 75; and Loyd, "Bataan Diary," typed transcript, 35.

[4] The *Hukbo ng Bayan Laban sa Hapon*, "Hukbalahap" or "Huk" for short, was formed in February 1942 by the leaders of the Philippine Communist and Socialist parties, to oppose the Japanese. The name means, literally, "The Army to Fight Japan." They were probably the best organized guerrillas in the Philippines. For many years after Japan had been defeated the Huks continued to oppose, and attempt to overthrow, the Philippine government. Agoncillo, *History of the Filipino People*, Chapter 24. Also, Taruk, *He Who Rides the Tiger*, 5-6

[5] Conner, "We Fought Fear on Luzon," *True*, August 1945, 75; and Loyd, "Bataan Diary," typed transcript, 35.

[6] Loyd, "Bataan Diary," typed transcript 35. Also, recorded discussion between Vernon Fassoth, Blair Robinett, Winston Jones and Pierce Wade at the 1984 reunion of American Guerrillas in the Philippines, (Indiana: Volume A, Chapter III), 6.

[7] Quinine is a medication derived from the bark of the cinchoa tree and is used to treat malaria. Salicylate is the primary ingredient in aspirin, and is used to treat pain, fever and swelling.

[8] The rumor of sixteen captured was inaccurate. William Fassoth reported that of the sixteen Americans hiding in the camp at the time of the raid on September 25, 1942, six were captured and ten escaped. Three Filipinos were killed by the Japanese during the raid, including a three-year-old child and an old man. Fassoth, "Fassoth's Camp," (NARA: box 258), 20-21. Also, Hunt and Norling, *Behind Japanese Lines*, 44-46 (Ray Hunt was one of the men who escaped during the raid).

[9] Report of Col. Marcelo Adduru, former Governor of Cagayan Province and former Commander of the Cagayan-Apayao Force, 28 July 1947, (NARA: box 258), 7.

[10] Letter, Col. Russell W. Volckmann to General MacArthur's Chief of Staff, 26 November 1945, pages 7-8, (NARA: box 258); and statement of Col. George M. Barnett, 21 November 1945, (IDPF: Arthur Noble).

[11] Letter, Moses to Barnett, 19 September 1944, (NARA: box 249).

[12] Harkins, *Blackburn's Headhunters*, 103. Also, diary of Donald Blackburn (PSHS), and letter, Lt. Col. Martin Moses to Capt. George Barnett, 19 September 1942, (NARA: box 249).

[13] Diary of Donald Blackburn (PSHS); letter, Col. Russell W. Volckmann to General MacArthur's Chief of Staff, 26 November 1945, page 8, (NARA: box 258); and report by Thomas Scoville, "Guerrillas in the Philippines During World War II," (CMH: History Division, 16-19 February, 1969). Also, statements of 1st Lt. Alejo Pacalso, 2nd Lt.

Desiderio Jurado, and others regarding Lt. Col. Arthur Noble and Lt. Col. Martin Moses, February 1946, (IDPF: Arthur Noble).

[14] Norling, *The Intrepid Guerrillas of North Luzon*, 178. Also, diary of Donald Blackburn (PSHS), and letter, Maj. Tom Jones to Evelyn Noble, 22 October 1945, (Noble).

[15] In World War II each soldier was issued one collapsible tent pole and a "shelter-half," a piece of canvas about eight feet long with a row of buttons down one side and a row of buttonholes down the other. For sleeping, two soldiers would button their shelter halves together and pitch a "pup tent" big enough for two persons.

[16] Loyd, "Bataan Diary," 48.

[17] Sanford, "Col. Claude A. Thorp—The Father of American Guerrilla Warfare," *The World War II Chronicle*, March/April 1989, 7-9. The exact composition of Thorp's party varies in different accounts. The referenced article provides the most complete list and is generally in agreement with the numbers mentioned by 1st Lt. Herminia Dizon in her report, "Complete Data Covering the Guerrilla Activities of the Late Colonel Claude A. Thorp," (NARA: box 258), 1.

[18] The raid was successful from the standpoint of killing a Japanese colonel and a number of soldiers, with no American losses. But Japanese reinforcements counter-attacked and the Americans were forced to retreat before they could grab any of the supplies. 1st Lt. Herminia Dizon, "Complete Data Covering the Guerrilla Activities of the Late Colonel Claude A. Thorp," (NARA, box 258), 1-2. Also, Lapham and Norling, *Lapham's Raiders*, 15-17. (Robert Lapham was one of the volunteers in Thorp's party.)

[19] The primary district commanders were: Captain Ralph B. Praeger (26th Cavalry Regiment), Northern Luzon; Captain Joseph R. Barker (26th Cavalry Regiment), East Central Luzon; Captain George J. "Jack" Spies (26th Cavalry Regiment), Southern Luzon; and Captain Ralph McGuire (Philippine Army), Zambales province in West Luzon. Letter, Lt. Col. Claude A. Thorp to Brig. Gen. William E. Brougher, 23 August 1942, (NARA: box 257).

[20] Lt. Col. Claude A. Thorp, "Headquarters Luzon Guerrilla Army, General Orders No. 1," (NARA: box 257).

[21] Letter, Reverend (Colonel) John E. Duffy to Lt. Col. T. H. Metz of the Quartermaster General's Office, May 10, 1949, (IDPF: Claude A. Thorp).

[22] Letter, Merrill to Thorp, August 21, 1942, (NARA: box 257).

[23] Harkins, *Blackburn's Headhunters*, 68-70 (Colonel Thorp is identified as "Colonel Crabtree"). Don Blackburn was one of the officers who brought the letter to Thorp.
[24] Letter, Thorp to Merrill, August 30, 1942, (NARA: box 257).
[25] Letters, Barker to Merrill, 9 Sept. 42; and Merrill to Bell Sept. 17, 1942 (both NARA: box 257). Lapham and Norling, *Lapham's Raiders*, 130. Also, handwritten letter, Thorp to Merrill, 30 August 1942, (NARA: box 257).
[26] Monaghan, *Under the Red Sun*, 143-144.
[27] 1st Lt. Herminia S. Dizon, "Complete Data Covering the Guerrilla Activities of the Late Colonel Claude A. Thorp" (NARA: box 258), 4 and 5. Also, Sanford, "Col. Claude A. Thorp—The Father of American Guerrilla Warfare," *The World War II Chronicle*, March/April 1989, 15.
[28] Frank Loyd told the story of finding the two Japanese soldiers in the stream to his young grandson, Matthew Crane, several times. Each time he told the story he avoided telling the boy exactly what happened to the two soldiers. Later in life, Mr. Crane concluded that Col. Loyd shot and killed them both but that he was reluctant to tell that to a young child, behavior that would be characteristic of Frank Loyd. Interview by the author with Matthew Crane, December 23, 1997. From the point where Frank Loyd and the two soldiers see each other, the author has described a possible scenario based on the experiences of other veterans who found themselves in similar situations.

IX. The Home Front

[1] Interviews by the author with Evelyn Loyd, March 14, 1997 and January 22, 1998; and letters, Evelyn Loyd to Frank Loyd, March 25, 1942 and April 6, 1942, (Loyd).
[2] Letters, Frank Loyd to Evelyn Loyd, March 6, 1942, and Evelyn Loyd to Frank Loyd, February 17, 1945 (Loyd).
[3] "14 San Antonians Listed as Prisoners of War Captured by Japs," *San Antonio Express*, December 16, 1942, 1 and 6; and telegram, Maj. Gen. J. A. Ulio to Mrs. Betty G. Wilson, December 7, 1942, (Wilson). Also, Evelyn Loyd, "Diary," January 21, 1943.
[4] Letter, Lt. Col. Howard F. Bresee to Mrs. Betty G. Wilson, December 19, 1942, (Wilson).
[5] Letter, Maj. Gen. J. A. Ulio to Mrs. Betty G. Wilson, December 29, 1942, with Inclosures, (Wilson).
[6] Evelyn Loyd, "Diary," February 2, 1943.
[7] Evelyn Loyd, "Diary," January and February, 1943.

[8] "Last Automobile Turned Out for Civilian Use," *San Antonio News*, February 11, 1942, B5.
[9] Hoyt, *Japan's War*, 325; and Peña, *Bataan's Own*, 175.
[10] Many top war planners in Washington were of the same opinion as Evelyn Loyd—they thought it might well be impossible to ever force unconditional surrender on Japan. Miller, *War Plan Orange*, 364.
[11] Lory, *Japan's Military Masters*, 172.
[12] Marquardt, *Before Bataan and After*, 263; and Norling, *The Intrepid Guerrillas of North Luzon*, 179.
[13] Evelyn Loyd, "Diary," January 21, 1943.
[14] Whitney, *MacArthur: His Rendezvous with History*, 90.
[15] Hollister and Strunsky, *From Pearl Harbor Into Tokyo*, 132.
[16] MacArthur, *Reminiscences*, 203-204; and Keats, *They Fought Alone*, 171.
[17] Keats, *They Fought Alone*, 182-185 and 194.
[18] MacArthur, *Reminiscences*, 204. Praeger had been in radio contact with the War Department on and off for several months through station KFS, a listening post at Half Moon Bay, California. Norling, *The Intrepid Guerrillas of North Luzon*, 170; and interview by the author with Tom Jones, Praeger's deputy, April 25, 1999.
[19] Norling, *The Intrepid Guerrillas of North Luzon*, 187.
[20] Norling, *The Intrepid Guerrillas of North Luzon*, 190.

X. Joining Collier

[1] Interview by the author with Evelyn Loyd, March 14, 1997. Frank Loyd recovered parts of the diary immediately after Bataan was liberated, other portions were located later and mailed to him by his brother-in-law and by John Boone, and he retrieved some more on a trip to the Philippines in 1954. However, portions of the diary were lost.
[2] Loyd, "Bataan Diary," typed transcript, 49.
[3] Letter, Frank Loyd to Evelyn Loyd, Feb. 7, 1945.
[4] Loyd, "Bataan Diary," typed transcript, 49-50.
[5] Merrill and Calyer were encamped on the lower west slope of the Zambales Mountains above the village of San Marcelino. To get there, Frank Loyd not only had to cross to the north side of the highway but also negotiate rugged mountainsides and deep jungle terrain in order to work his way from the south slope to the west slope of the mountain.
[6] Loyd, "Bataan Diary," typed transcript, 50.
[7] Loyd, "Bataan Diary," typed transcript, 51

[8] Paraphrased from Filomeno, *Defense of Democracy in the Philippines*, 6. Also, Loyd, "Bataan Diary," typed transcript, 51, 64-64a (Loyd).
[9] Loyd, "Bataan Diary," typed transcript, 52.
[10] Certificate of Florentino P. Buenaventura, 27 June 1952, *Bataan Military District Reports of Investigation, GRLA-4*, (NARA: box 245). Terry Adevoso, commander of the Hunters' ROTC Guerrillas, also used the name "Magtanggol."
[11] Loyd, "Bataan Diary," typed transcript, 52.
[12] Loyd, "Bataan Diary," typed transcript, 52, 63.
[13] The guerrillas in the Zambales foothills north of Kulò were organized in May, 1942, by one of Col. Claude Thorp's men, Capt. Ralph McGuire. The Japanese anti-guerrilla campaign early in 1943 resulted in McGuire's betrayal and death, and the death, capture or disbursement of most of his men. The remainder of McGuire's organization was taken over by Antonio Francisco and his executive officer, Cipriano Cid, who built the organization up again and kept it together through the end of the war.
[14] Loyd, "Bataan Diary," typed transcript, 52.
[15] Interview by the author with Jim Wright, December 11, 1998; and Wright family photographs.
[16] Interviews by the author with Brigadier General Royal Reynolds, July 23, 1999, Joe Wilson, October 29, 1998, and Bonnie Loyd Crane, March 20, 2000; and Loyd family photographs.
[17] Frank Loyd's U.S. Army military records and Loyd, "Bataan Diary," typed transcript, 119,123,126-129,131,134.
[18] Interview by the author with Jim Wright, December 11, 1998; and e-mail, Jim Wright to the author, 6 January 1999.
[19] Interview by Rhode Island State Senator John Patterson with Brigadier General Royal Reynolds and Colonel Melvin Rosen , August 2, 1997.
[20] Interview by the author with Brigadier General Royal Reynolds, July 23, 1999.
[21] Interview by the author with Brigadier General Royal Reynolds, July 23, 1999; and Olson, *O'Donnell: Andersonville of the Pacific*, 199. Another group of Filipino soldiers from the 21st Infantry Division was slaughtered in a similar manner, supposedly in retaliation for the heavy casualties they had inflicted on the Japanese at the battle for Mount Samat. Interview by the author with Harry Stempin, May 5, 1999. Mr. Stempin was a company commander in the 57th Infantry Regiment, Philippine Scouts.
[22] Letter, Primitivo Leonzon to undisclosed addressee, 16 Sept. 1947, reprinted in Ashton, *Bataan Diary*, 408-409; and interview by the author with Nicholas Leonzon Jr., May 13, 1998.

[23] Loyd, "Bataan Diary," typed transcript, 98; and Loyd, "Speech to Cheyenne, Wyoming, Army Reserves," 14-15 (Loyd).
[24] Letter, Primitivo Leonzon to undisclosed addressee, 16 Sept. 1947, reprinted in Ashton, *Bataan Diary*, 408-409.
[25] Loyd, "Bataan Diary," typed transcript, 57-58.
[26] Interview by the author with Nicholas Leonzon Jr., Rebecca Leonzon Paule and Tiburcio Paule, May 12, 1998.
[27] Loyd, "Bataan Diary," typed transcript, 55 and 57.
[28] *Ibid*, 60 and 123.
[29] *Ibid*, 55.
[30] Interview by the author with Brigadier General Royal Reynolds, July 23, 1999.
[31] 1st Lt. Herminia Dizon, "Complete Data Covering the Guerrilla Activities of the Late Colonel Claude A. Thorp," (NARA: box 258), 5. Also, Hunt and Norling, *Behind Japanese Lines*, 99.
[32] Loyd, "Bataan Diary," typed transcript, 69, 72 and 101; and letter, "Kuya Sam," [Samuel Zozabrado Jr.] to "Tess" [Tessie Munsgi] January 20, 2004 (Zozabrado).
[33] Depending upon who tells the story, John P. Boone has been described as everything from a villain to a hero. Stories about him vary so wildly that one person who knew him in the Philippines during the war told the author that there must have been two John P. Boones. However, the author has not found any evidence of a second John P. Boone.
[34] Loyd, "Bataan Diary," typed transcript, 56-57 and 122-123
[35] Ramsey and Rivele, *Lieutenant Ramsey's War*, 141-142.
[36] Citation for the award of the Distinguished Service Cross to Major John P. Boone, (MacArthur: individual file on Lieutenant Colonel Bernard Anderson).
[37] Ramsey and Rivele, *Lieutenant Ramsey's War*, 149.
[38] Dialog on Boone's activities paraphrased from Phillips and Goldsmith, *Manila Espionage*, 124.
[39] Loyd, handwritten recap of dispute with Merrill, paragraph 9 (Loyd).
[40] Loyd, "Bataan Diary," typed transcript, 57.
[41] The full name of this nurse was not recorded in Frank Loyd's diary, but she is identified by Francisca Panaflor as Hipolita San Jose, a 2nd Lt. in the Philippine Army nurse corps who treated and cared for the soldiers at the Fassoth camp. "Ding" is a common nickname in the Philippines. Interview by James Litton with 1st Lt. Mariano Pangilinan.
[42] Letter, Boone to Loyd, Feb 15, 1943, (Loyd).

[43] Loyd, "Bataan Diary," typed transcript, 58. This arrest was the first of three times the Japanese arrested Delphin Pamintuan for underground activity during the war.
[44] Letter, Primitivo Leonzon to undisclosed addressee, 16 Sept. 1947, reprinted in Ashton, *Bataan Diary*, 408-409.
[45] Loyd, "Bataan Diary," typed transcript, 58.
[46] "Mojica Study," (CMH), 72. Also, U.S. Army Forces, Pacific, Military Intelligence Section, General Staff, "The Guerrilla Resistance Movement in the Philippines, Vol. I, Intelligence Series," 26 October 1944, (MHI), 10; and Ramsey and Rivele, *Lieutenant Ramsey's War*, 148-149.
[47] The Japanese even offered to redeem surrendering guerrillas' back pay certificates. Mojica, *Terry's Hunters*, 342-343 and 357; and radio message, Lt. Col. Marcario Peralta to General MacArthur, May 26, 1943 (MacArthur: Record Group 16, box 38, folder 10). Also, affidavit of Colonel Irineo Buenconcejo, 27 September 1945, *File 999-23-4, Reference Cases of Fort Santiago Massacre*, (NARA: box 245), 5.
[48] Throughout the country, village mayors and other officials were instructed to make speeches about amnesty and independence to their constituents, and handbills were distributed asking guerrillas to surrender. The handbills purportedly quoted popular, captured guerrilla leaders such as Colonel Guillermo Nakar, praising the Japanese and pleading with the guerrillas to surrender. In fact, Nakar refused to sign any surrender documents at all, and was subsequently executed for it. Harkins, *Blackburn's Headhunters*, 136; and handbill titled "Message to the Guerrillas in the Field," (Indiana: Volume D, Chapter III, Section B, item 14). Also Norling, *The Intrepid Guerrillas of North Luzon*, 98.
[49] *Bataan Military District Reports of Investigation, Annex 2, GRLA-4*, (NARA: box 245), 6.
[50] Loyd, "Bataan Diary," typed transcript, 131 and 136.
[51] Recorded discussion among Vernon Fassoth, Blair Robinette, Winston Jones and Pierce Wade at the 1984 reunion of American Guerrillas in the Philippines, (Indiana: Volume A, Chapter III, 12 and 13); and Loyd, "Bataan Diary," typed transcript, 161.
[52] Interview by Doug Clanin with Henry Clay Conner, (Indiana: binder number eight), 25.
[53] Fassoth, "Fassoth's Camp," (NARA: box 258), 27; Ramsey and Rivele, *Lieutenant Ramsey's War*, 152-154; and Certificate of Santiago K. Sadsad, 15 September 1952, *Bataan Military District Reports of Investigation, GRLA-4*, (NARA: box 245).

[54] Boone's outposts spotted and fired on the approaching Japanese, so the men in the camp were able to withdraw into the jungle without losses. Loyd "Bataan Diary," typed transcript, 60-61; Interview by Doug Clanin with Clay Conner (Indiana); and Edwin Ramsey e-mail to the author, 8 July 2004.

XI. War News

[1] Conversation paraphrased from letter, Evelyn Loyd to Frank Loyd, February 21, 1945, (Loyd); and interviews by the author with Mrs. Loyd.
[2] Letter, Ted Moses to Congressman Fritz Lanham, December 29, 1945, (IDPF: Martin Moses); and Letter, Evelyn Loyd to Frank Loyd, February 21, 1945, 3 (Loyd).
[3] Description of the "Fiddlers' Club": Interviews by the author with Evelyn Loyd and Joe Wilson. Also, Evelyn Loyd's diary entry of May 1, 1943 (Loyd).

XII. The Dangerous Benefactor

[1] Actually, Boone's outpost had detected and fired upon the approaching Japanese, so everyone was able to withdraw into the jungle without losses. Letter, Col. Edwin Ramsey to the author, July 8, 2004. Ramsey was at Boone's headquarters at the time of the raid.
[2] Conversation paraphrased from Loyd "Bataan Diary," typed transcript, 60-61; and interview by Doug Clanin with Clay Conner (Indiana).
[3] Conversation paraphrased from Loyd, "Bataan Diary," typed transcript, 123.
[4] Loyd, "Bataan Diary," typed transcript, 61.
[5] *Ibid*, 62.
[6] *Ibid*, 62 and 101.
[7] *Ibid*, 64.
[8] *Ibid*, 162; and Sanford, "The Organization of Guerrilla Warfare on Luzon, Philippine Islands, April 1942 to January 1943," *The World War II Chronicle*, Jan/Feb 1989, 9.
[9] Loyd, "Bataan Diary," typed transcript, 67.
[10] *Ibid*, 73a.
[11] Interview by the author with Jim Wright, December 11, 1998
[12] Loyd, "Bataan Diary," typed transcript, 126-127.
[13] Interview by the author with Evelyn Loyd, March 14, 1997.
[14] Fassoth, "Fassoth's Camp," (NARA: box 258), 28; and Loyd, "Bataan Diary," typed transcript, 68 and 70.

[15] Various types of vitamin deficiencies can cause all sorts of ailments and diseases, and beriberi was common during the Siege of Bataan and in the Japanese prison camps. Frank Loyd believed that snails were a good source of vitamins. However, freshwater snails can also be a source of worms, which infected many soldiers and POWs.
[16] The author has found no scientific evidence of the effects of Dita bark tea, although Americans in the Philippines often claimed that blindness would result from drinking too much of it.
[17] Loyd, "Bataan Diary," typed transcript, 72, 94 and 102.
[18] Sulfanilamide, the base ingredient of sulpha drugs, is used to treat bacterial infections, especially in wounds. Sodium bicarbonate (baking soda) is an antacid. Originally derived from willow bark, salicylate is the active ingredient in aspirin.
[19] During 1941, Frank Loyd organized gun clubs and shooting competitions among the USAFFE soldiers, working up to national matches where the best marksmen in the Philippines were identified and recognized. Frank spent several years as a member of the U.S. Army rifle and pistol teams before coming to the Philippines. He was designated "Distinguished Marksman" with both weapons, and he was designated "All-American Marksman" in the 1938 U.S. national shooting competitions. The first Philippine national matches were held in May 1941, before the Japanese invasion. Frank and another American officer lost the pistol competition to a Filipino soldier in the final round. After the war, the matches were resumed under the direction of Major Carlos Quirino, who had been a 2nd Lieutenant in the Philippine Constabulary when Frank Loyd was Chief Instructor. Letters, Frank Loyd to Evelyn Loyd, May 22, 1941, 2; and Carlos Quirino to Frank Loyd 1949 and 1955, (Loyd).
[20] Loyd, "Bataan Diary," typed transcript, 73.
[21] John Boone married Filomena Guerrero, daughter of one of his guerrillas, on Feb 19, 1943. Lt. Edwin Ramsey performed the ceremony. "Contract of Marriage" signed by Filomena Guerrero, John Boone and Edwin Ramsey (Boone).
[22] Conversation paraphrased from Loyd, "Bataan Diary," typed transcript, 74.
[23] Loyd, "Bataan Diary," typed transcript, 94 and 101-102. However, Sam Zozabrado's family actually was from Cebu, and they were quite wealthy. Interview by the author with Tessie Musngi, Sam Zozabrado's niece, March 15, 2004.
[24] Loyd, "Bataan Diary," typed transcript, 68 and 103-104.
[25] *Ibid*, 74 and 123-124.

[26] *Ibid*, 75.
[27] Interview by the author with Tiburcio Paule, May 13, 1998. As Tivo Leonzon's son-in-law, Mr. Paule helped load the supplies into the secret compartments in the bamboo, and occasionally made deliveries to the four Americans himself.
[28] The Japanese were notoriously poor administrators, the government of Japan itself being perhaps the best example. During the period leading up to the war many Japanese leaders left office feet first—assassinated by rivals or, in some cases, by subordinates who felt that the government was not moving fast enough in attaining Japan's manifest destiny, domination of the Asiatic world.
[29] A *kavanie* is a little over two bushels. There are 25 *gántas* in a *kavanie*.
[30] Interview by the author with Tiburcio Paule, May 13, 1998.
[31] Pedro Picornell, "Remedios Hospital—Pedro Picornell's Story (1943-45)," *Columban Martyrs of Malate*, 79; and Steinberg, *Philippine Collaboration in World War II*, 91.
[32] Recorded discussion among Vernon Fassoth, Blair Robinette, Winston Jones and Pierce Wade at the 1984 reunion of American Guerrillas in the Philippines, (Indiana: Volume A, Chapter III, 6); and Keats, *They Fought Alone*, 222.
[33] Loyd, "Bataan Diary," typed transcript, 156 and 162.
[34] The Americans had agreed to rendezvous with Tivo each Wednesday morning near the old camp and carry the supplies from there to the new *bahay* themselves. Interview by the author with Nick Leonzon, Jr., May 13, 1998.
[35] Conversations in this section paraphrased from Loyd, "Bataan Diary," typed transcript, 79-81 and 125.

XIII. The Shadow Society

[1] Most American writers refer to the prison as "Camp O'Donnell," as the original Army post appears to have been named after the nearby barrio O'Donnell. Filipino writers generally refer to it as "Capas," after the village and railhead.
[2] Manzano, "Death, Filth in a Jap Concentration Camp," (Manzano), 5 and 6.
[3] Col. John E. Olson, personnel officer for the American side, reported 8,675 American soldiers at Camp O'Donnell on May 2, 1942. Olson, *O'Donnell: Andersonville of the Pacific*, 235. In the prologue to his book, Olson estimates that there were "around 50,000" Filipino soldiers

in the other side of the camp (Olson, xiii), of which over 42,000 were there by the end of April (Olson, 9). The 50,000 figure is consistent with the author's own estimates based on 60,000 Filipino soldiers on Bataan, less 8,000 who died on the Death March, less about 1,000 who evaded the Japanese after the surrender. Estimates of the number of men who died on the Death March vary from 7,000 to 9,000. The higher figure is quoted more often by various sources, but of course no records were kept, whatsoever. These figures do not include the 11,500 men on Corregidor and several thousand men in the southern islands, who held out for one additional month.

[4] Olson, *O'Donnell: Andersonville of the Pacific*, 190, 194 and 208; and interview by the author with David Topping, May 19, 1999.

[5] Quoted in Olson, *O'Donnell: Andersonville of the Pacific*, 102-103.

[6] The practice of paying prisoners for work and charging them for their upkeep began in November 1942, retroactive to August. From the pay, the Japanese even deducted a portion to be placed in a special savings account, a type of War Bond, to help Japan prosecute the war in the Pacific. Phillips and Goldsmith, *Manila Espionage*, 108; and Olson, *O'Donnell: Andersonville of the Pacific*, 109.

[7] Manzano, "Death, Filth in a Jap Concentration Camp," (Manzano), 8-9 and 11, and "Memoirs," (Manzano), Chapter VII—Prison Camp, 6-7; Olson, *O'Donnell: Andersonville of the Pacific*, 143-146 and 160-161; and Tenney *My Hitch in Hell*, 109-110.

[8] Manzano, "History of the Military Intelligence Service Nelson Group," 30 July 1945, (Manzano), 2. Also, letter, Colonel Amado N. Bautista to the Adjutant General, PHILRYCOM, March 17, 1947, paragraph 2, (NARA: box 258).

[9] "General Information on Corregidor, Bataan, Concentration Camps and Guerrillas," (MacArthur: The Papers of Courtney Whitney, Box 17, Subseries 1, Folder 1), 8.

[10] In the author's interview with Col. Olson, he described the day he and Col. Manzano stood in the sun to deliver their reports but were not allowed to speak. On page xiv of *O'Donnell: Andersonville of the Pacific*, Col. Olson mentions that he briefly met Col. Catalan on Capt. Tsuneyoshi's porch the next day, his last day at O'Donnell, where he learned that the Filipinos had been covering up for their escapees.

[11] Interview by the author with Colonel John E. Olson, November 21, 1998.

[12] Olson, *O'Donnell: Andersonville of the Pacific*, Appendix L.

[13] Letter, Lt. Col. E. Carl Engelhart to Board Concerning Services Rendered to American POWs, RFD, PHILRYCON, 18 Jan. 1947, reprinted in Ashton, *Bataan Diary*, 429-434.
[14] Letters, Pilar A. Clemente, Treasurer of the Philippine Women's University, to "To Whom It May Concern," 23 Sept. 1947; and Lt. Col. E. Carl Engelhart to Board Concerning Services Rendered to American POWs, RFD, PHILRYCON, 18 Jan. 1947; both reprinted in Ashton, *Bataan Diary*, 374-376 and 429-434.
[15] Hartendorp, *The Japanese Occupation of the Philippines, Volume II*, 593-596; and Ramsey and Rivele, *Lieutenant Ramsey's War*, 169.
[16] Brackman, *The Other Nuremberg*, 250.
[17] As most of the American prisoners were being transferred to Cabanatuan, the Japanese brought the staff of Hospital #1 on Bataan to Camp O'Donnell, supplemented by some Japanese lab personnel. This team, headed by Colonel James Duckworth, endeavored to clean up the filthy conditions, acquire medicine, and bring some military discipline back into the operation of the camp. Even though they were somewhat successful in their efforts, the problems, sickness and intransigence of the Japanese were overwhelming, and the death rate was only slightly abated. Olson, *O'Donnell: Andersonville of the Pacific*, 99-114.
[18] Interview by the author with Rene Diokno, May 15, 1998. Also, Manzano, "Memoirs," (Manzano), Chapter VII—Prison Camp, 12.
[19] Interview by the author with Rene Diokno, May 15, 1998.
[20] Olson, *O'Donnell: Andersonville of the Pacific*, 163. Also, SanGabriel, *The Constabulary Story*, 267.
[21] Manzano, "Memoirs," Chapter VIII—Luzon, (Manzano), 2.
[22] Manzano, "History of the Military Intelligence Service Nelson Group," 30 July 1945, (Manzano), 2. Also, Central Headquarters, Southwest Pacific Area, Military Intelligence Section, "The Guerrilla Resistance Movement in Central Luzon," (MacArthur: Record Group 16, Box 3, Folder 17), 7.
[23] Manzano, "History of the Military Intelligence Service Nelson Group," 30 July 1945, (Manzano), 3. Also, Lapham and Norling, *Lapham's Raiders*, 74.
[24] Radio message 429, WZE [Peralta] to MacArthur, June 24, 1943 describes the difficulties encountered in traveling through the Japanese occupied Philippines and the techniques and characteristics of the couriers. See also, Lapham and Norling, *Lapham's Raiders*, 74. The communications procedures and the methodology of getting information back to MacArthur were originally worked out by a special commando team headed by Philippine Air Force Captain Jesus Villamor.

MacArthur sent Villamor's Operation Planet team to Negros Island shortly after radio contact was first established with Peralta. The secrecy surrounding identities of the Free Philippines members is mentioned in "Report of Operations, Colonel Manzano, 20 March 1942 to 15 March 1945," to General Jonathon Wainwright, 18 October 1945 (Manzano), 4; in Roces, *Looking for Liling*, 189; and in Taruc, *Born of the People*, 170-171.

[25] Radio message 429, WZE [Peralta] to MacArthur, June 24, 1943; and letter, Harold K. Johnson to Director, Recovered Personnel Division, Headquarters United States Army Forces Western Pacific, 10 Sept. 1946, reprinted in Ashton, *Bataan Diary*, 382-387.

[26] Peralta appears to have had more than ten weekly courier routes in operation between himself and other clandestine groups by this time. Message 291, Peralta to MacArthur, May 31, 1943, (MacArthur: Record Group 16, Box 38, Folder 11).

[27] This meeting is described in Phillips and Goldsmith, *Manila Espionage*, 111-113.

[28] Pedro Picornell, "Remedios Hospital—Pedro Picornell's Story (1943-45)," *Columban Martyrs of Malate*, 78.

[29] In her book, *Manila Espionage*, Claire Phillips claims to have married Sergeant John Phillips near Pilar, Bataan in December 1941. However, other sources indicate that Claire Phillips was still married to her Filipino husband, Manuel Fuentes at the time. Interview (via e-mail) by the author with James Litton, 18 September 2002, and "Investigation of Casualty Roster, Bataan Military District," (NARA box 245), Section V—Conclusions of Investigator.

[30] "Club," in Japan, implies "exclusive." *Tsubaki* is Japanese for camellia, a prized flower. Claire Phillips founded the club specifically to develop a source of intelligence data from Japanese officers. Breuer, *The Great Raid on Cabanatuan*, 104.

[31] Phillips and Goldsmith, *Manila Espionage*, 118-121.

[32] In her book, Claire Phillips claims she was in contact with Boone, Thorp and Straughn. However, Thorp was captured two weeks after Club Tsubaki opened so such contact would have been short lived. Phillips and Goldsmith, *Manila Espionage*, 118-119 and 132.

[33] Filomena "Mellie" Boone would come to Manila and pick up the messages from Claire Phillips, then take them back to Boone's headquarters near Dinalupihan, on Mount Malasimbo. There, they would be combined with reports from Boone's spies around the mouth of Manila Bay and at Subic Bay, and couriered to Edwin Ramsey in Rizal Province, northeast of Manila. Ramsey combined Phillips and Boone's

reports with his own reports and sent them south to Jesus Villamor on Negros Island where they could be transmitted to MacArthur. This circuitous routing could take from several weeks to more than a month. Ramsey also sent copies of his reports to other guerrilla radios in the southern islands, first to Peralta then to Fertig. In October 1944 he obtained a radio from Lt. Cmdr. George Rowe on Mindoro, and from that point forward sent his reports to Rowe. Ramsey "Summary of Organization and Operations of ECLGA," 15 May 1945 (MacArthur). Also, Phillips and Goldsmith, *Manila Espionage*, 106; and Central Headquarters, Southwest Pacific Area, Military Intelligence Section, "The Guerrilla Resistance Movement in Central Luzon," (MacArthur: Record Group 16, Box 3, Folder 17), 3.

[34] In her book, Claire Phillips identifies the Swiss businessman as Charles Ringeness. However, Col. Edwin Ramsey identified the director of the Manila Gas Company who worked as his Chief of Chemical Warfare and who made explosive devices as Walter Roeder. Letter, Col. Edwin Ramsey to the author, July 8, 2004.

[35] Filipino air ace Major Jesus Villamor was brought to Negros by the submarine *Gudgeon* in January, 1943, specifically to establish a spy network in the islands. Villamor and Snyder, *They Never Surrendered*, 3-19.

[36] O'Brien, *Columban Martyrs of Malate*, 79-80.

[37] Utinsky, *Miss "U"*, 52-53.

[38] Letter, Lt. Col. Harold K. Johnson to Director, Recovered Personnel Division, Headquarters United States Army Forces Western Pacific, 10 Sept. 1946, reprinted in Ashton, *Bataan Diary*, 382-387; and Utinsky, *Miss "U"*, 67-72. Father John Lalor set up the collection network in Manila, and Naomi Flores devised and supervised the smuggling procedure at Cabanatuan. Harold K. Johnson was purchasing officer for the camp. Naomi Flores and Father John Lalor are two of the truly unsung heroes of World War II. Harold K. Johnson survived the Japanese prisons and went on to become Chief of Staff of the United States Army.

[39] Handwritten report, "On the Field," by Inman, dated 3/8/43 (actually 4/8/43), (Indiana, brown 3-ring binder labeled "McCoy, Dobesk" on the spine); Loyd, "Bataan Diary," typed transcript, 118; and Hunt and Norling, *Behind Japanese Lines*, 42-43.

[40] Fassoth, "Fassoth's Camp," (NARA: box 258), 26, 29-31; and letters: Doyle Decker to Doug Clanin, June 27, 1985, (Indiana: Guerrilla Additions), 3-4; and Doyle Decker to Wayne Sanford, July 13, 1985, (Indiana: Guerrilla Additions), 2.

[41] Loyd, "Bataan Diary," typed transcript, 77-79 and 89.
[42] Before turning the pages over to Tivo Leonzon, Frank Loyd wrote a watered-down account of Tivo's attempt to shoot Frank, treating the whole thing as a misunderstanding. He kept his original account of the incident, presented in Chapter 13. Both versions appear in the typed transcript, 79-81.
[43] Loyd, "Bataan Diary," typed transcript, 103-104. Also, letter, Eddie Wright to Narciso Manzano, 24 December 1944, (Indiana: Black Binder labeled SWPA I, section regarding John Boone).
[44] Conversation paraphrased from Loyd, "Bataan Diary," typed transcript, 94, 103-104 and 109.
[45] Loyd, "Bataan Diary," typed transcript, 111.
[46] *Ibid*, 109 and 117. Frank's suspicions about Sam Zozabrado were apparently unfounded. Zozabrado's family was, in fact, from Cebu and were quite wealthy.

XIV. General MacArthur's War

[1] Manchester, *American Caesar*, 310-313.
[2] Olson, *O'Donnell: Andersonville of the Pacific*, 210.
[3] Letter, MacArthur to Roosevelt, 20 July 1943, (MacArthur: Record Group 16, Box 63, Folder 4).
[4] Evelyn Loyd, diary entry for September 5, 1943.

XV. Guerrilla Sunset

[1] Conversation paraphrased from Loyd, "Bataan Diary," typed transcript, 109.
[2] Loyd, "Bataan Diary," typed transcript, 84.
[3] Headquarters USFIP, "Supplementary Instructions," March 20, 1943, signed by Colonels Martin Moses and Arthur K. Noble, (NARA: box 259).
[4] Report of 1st Lt. Teofilo Chunan, 26 October 1945, 2; and affidavit of Toribio Dawaton, 4 December 1945, (both IDPF: Colonel Arthur K. Noble).
[5] Report of 1st Lt. Teofilo Chunuan, 26 October 1945, (IDPF: Colonel Arthur K. Noble), 1-2; and report of Colonel Marcelo Adduru, 28 July 1947, Subject: Cagayan-Apayao Force, (NARA: box 258), 5 and 7.
[6] Norling, *The Intrepid Guerrillas of North Luzon*, 205-206.

[7] Report of 1st Lt. Teofilo Chunuan, 26 October 1945, (IDPF: Colonel Arthur K. Noble), 1-2. Also, Hunt and Norling, *Behind Japanese Lines*, 83.
[8] Ramsey and Rivelle, *Lieutenant Ramsey's War*, 240; and Wainwright, *General Wainwright's Story*, 31.
[9] Report of 1st Lt. Teofilo Chunuan, 26 October 1945, (IDPF: Colonel Arthur K. Noble), 1-2.
[10] *Ibid*, 2. Lt. Chunuan was imprisoned with Maxie Noble at the Whitmarsh Building.
[11] Loyd, "Bataan Diary," typed transcript, 104.
[12] Mojica, *Terry's Hunters*, 351-352.
[13] General Headquarters, Southwest Pacific Area, Military Intelligence Section, General Staff, "The Guerrilla Resistance Movement in Central Luzon," 26 October 1944, (MacArthur: Record Group 16, box 3, Folder 17), 8-12. Also, interviews by the Adjutant General's Office, United States Army Forces, Pacific with Mrs. Juanita Pigon, 5 October 1945, Mr. Jose Roxas, 6 October, 1945, and Col. Delgracias Castaneda, 7 October 1945, and others, (IDPF: Col. Hugh Straughn); excerpts from "The History, Activities and Accomplishments of the Fil-American Irregular Troops (FAIT)," (IDPF: Col. Hugh Straughn); and Mojica, *Terry's Hunters*, 295.
[14] Untitled copy of text from *Shin Seiki* weekly tabloid, September 3, 1943, page 11, (IDPF: Colonel Hugh Straughn); and Loyd, "Bataan Diary," typed transcript, 104. Also, Phillips and Goldsmith, *Manila Espionage*, 137. Straughn was the last major guerrilla leader on Luzon to be captured. Guillermo Nakar, who had re-organized the remnants of the Fil-American army in northern Luzon, was captured in September, 1942. His command was taken over by Moses and Noble. Col. Claude Thorp was captured in October 1942, and his central Luzon command was broken up between Captains Ralph McGuire, Joseph R. Barker, and Bernard Anderson. Moses and Noble were captured in June 1943, and their north Luzon command was partially dispersed, and partially divided between Majors Russell Volckmann and Bernard Anderson. After Col. Straughn was captured in September 1943, his FAIT guerrillas largely dispersed and the other groups he led were taken over by their respective commanders. No unified guerrilla command existed after that date, except in the imagination of some of the other guerrilla leaders.
[15] Report of 1st Lt. Teofilo Chunuan, 26 October 1945, (IDPF: Colonel Arthur K. Noble), 2.
[16] *Ibid*, 3; and letter, Maj. Tom Jones to Evelyn Noble, May 14, 1945, (Noble). Maj. Jones was imprisoned with Maxie Noble at Bilibid.

[17] Testimony of 2nd Lt. Richard W. Sakakida, 17 March 1947, *Check Sheet for American Graves Registration* (IDPF: Colonel Martin Moses). Sakakida was a Japanese-American serviceman in Manila who was pressed into the service of the Japanese as an interpreter. He served as the interpreter for Colonel Thorp's trial. See also, Sanford, "Colonel Claude A. Thorp—The Father of American Guerrilla Warfare," *The World War II Chronicle*, March/April 1989, page 15.
[18] Letter, John D. Linehan to the Quartermaster General of the Army, (IDPF: Colonel Martin Moses), 1. Also, Wainwright, *General Wainwright's Story*, 31.
[19] Letter, John D. Linehan to the Quartermaster General of the Army, (IDPF: Colonel Martin Moses), 2.
[20] Affidavits of Ignacio Santos, 28 September 1945 and 5 March 1946, and testimony of 2nd Lt. Richard W. Sakakida, 17 March 1947 (all IDPF: Colonel Hugh Straughn). Santos, a caretaker at the Chinese Cemetery, and Sakakida, an interpreter, both witnessed the executions. Also, Statement of Herminia Dizon, 16 January 1950. (IDPF: Colonel Claude A. Thorp). This description of the execution of the guerrilla commanders on October 8, 1943, is based on the testimony of the two eyewitnesses, Sakakida and Santos, plus Mr. Linehan's description of them being led away from Bilibid Prison. Unfortunately, the recorded testimonies are brief, contradictory, and there is little collaborative evidence other than hearsay. Santos said that men who were not killed by the rifle volley were subsequently beheaded. The author believes it unlikely that a mortally wounded man would or could hold still long enough for beheading, and traditionally the senior officer at a firing squad finishes the job with his pistol. Since Claire Phillips described Col. Nagahama claiming to have killed Straughn with his pistol, the author has described his death accordingly. (Phillips and Goldsmith, *Manila Espionage*, 137.) None of the bodies were recovered after the war, as the graves were unmarked and were largely destroyed by grave-robbers, Filipino relatives trying to dig up and rebury loved ones, and by Allied and Japanese artillery and bombing. Stories about what happened to these men varied widely after the war. One account said that Maxie Noble was skinned alive within sight and sound of the prison compound. Others said that the prisoners were made to dig their own graves, kneel in front of them, and submit to beheading. The U.S. Army conducted extensive investigations into the deaths of each of the men, but the investigators could not even agree on the dates of the deaths, much less what happened to the bodies. All of the men were declared missing in action, presumed dead, with remains unrecoverable. It is possible that all or some of the

executions were conducted on different days in October rather than on October 8 as described here, but based on the above testimonies the author believes they were all executed on the same day, in two different groups. The U.S. Army Graves Registration board selected November 1, 1943 as the official date of death for all of them, under the assumption that it was the latest date that any one of them could possibly still have been alive.

[21] Phillips and Goldsmith, *Manila Espionage*, 118.

[22] Quoted in Phillips and Goldsmith, *Manila Espionage*, 137.

[23] General Hideki Tojo, Japanese War Minister and Prime Minister, came to Manila for the independence ceremony. He slept in the MacArthur Suite at the Manila Hotel. James, *The Years of MacArthur*, 504; and Romulo, *The Manila Hotel*, 121.

[24] Loyd, "Bataan Diary," typed transcript 117.

[25] The following conversation and dialog is paraphrased from Loyd, "Bataan Diary," 116-121 and 150.

[26] Loyd, "Bataan Diary," typed transcript, 111 and 120. In year 2000 dollars, this would be equivalent to an offer of more than $250,000.

[27] Letter, Senator Jose Ozamis to General Douglas MacArthur, January 1,1944, (MacArthur: Record Group 16, Box 38, File 9). Also, Phillips and Goldsmith, *Manila Espionage*, 121.

[28] E-mail, Peter Parsons to the author, 8/4/2002. Also, "Tambor," *Dictionary of American Fighting Ships*.

[29] Manchester, *American Caesar*, 439-442. Also, Hunt and Norling, *Behind Japanese Lines*, 147-149.

[30] Steinberg, *Philippine Collaboration in World War II*, 73-74.

[31] Manzano, "Memoirs," Chapter VIII—Luzon, (Manzano), 4.

[32] Letter, Colonel Amado N. Bautista to the Adjutant General, PHILRYCOM, March 17, 1947, (NARA: box 258), paragraph 7.

[33] This group of American and Filipino commandos was commanded by Major Lawrence Phillips, pre-war manager of the Del Monte Plantation on Mindanao, and no known relation to Claire Phillips. The men were part of the 1st Philippine Regiment, one of two special regiments made up largely of Filipino-Americans, that MacArthur created and began training soon after his arrival in Australia. Mojica, *Terry's Hunters*, 408-409 and 417; and interview by the author with Colonel Tom Jones, April 25, 1999.

[34] Letter, Senator Jose Ozamis to General Douglas MacArthur, January 1, 1944, (MacArthur: Record Group 16, Box 38, File 9). Also, Manzano, "Memoirs," Chapter VIII—Luzon, (Manzano), 10-11.

[35] Major Osmundo Mondoñedo, "Organizational Report," *United States Forces in the Philippines, Military Intelligence Section, Headquarters, Nelson Group*, 1 February 1945, (MacArthur: Record Group 16, Box 3, Folder 11), 1.
[36] Roces, *Looking for Liling*, 226-228; and Manzano, "Memoirs," (Manzano), Chapter VIII—Luzon, 15-16.
[37] Letters, CIO-12 [Reyes] to Bernard Anderson, written December 20 and 23, 1943 (Indiana: Anderson box).
[38] Manzano, "Memoirs," (Manzano), Chapter VIII—Luzon, 16; and interview by the author with Esteban Pirovano, July 22, 2002. Peter Parsons states that he and his family lived in Arlington, Va., for about three months late in 1942, but he does not recall photographs being taken there. E-mails from Peter Parsons, son of Lieutenant Commander "Chick" Parsons, to the author, 14 July 2001 and 14 July 2002.
[39] Major Osmundo Mondoñedo, "Organizational Report," *United States Forces in the Philippines, Military Intelligence Section, Headquarters, Nelson Group*, 1 February 1945, (MacArthur: Record Group 16, Box 3, Folder 11), 1; and Manzano, "Summary of Intelligence Reports Gathered and Submitted by the Military Intelligence Service, Nelson Group," 31 July 1945 (Manzano), 2. Also, coded letter of introduction from Senator Jose Ozamis to Colonel Wendell Fertig, January 21, 1944, (Manzano).
[40] Interview by the author with Allan Manzano, July 28, 2001.
[41] Manzano, "Trip"—notes on places he stopped and Japanese units he observed en route to Fertig's headquarters. (Manzano).
[42] Diary of Marcial P. Lichauco, cited in Manzano, "Memoirs," (Manzano), Chapter VIII, 17. Charo Manzano was held in Fort Santiago as a "hostage," in an attempt to get Narciso Manzano to turn himself in. Eventually she was released.
[43] Manzano, "Memoirs," (Manzano), Chapter VIII-16-17; memorandum, Captain Aurelio L. Lucero to G-1 HPA [Headquarters Philippine Army], 28 September 1945, *Reference Cases of Fort Santiago Massacre*, (NARA: box 245, file 999-23-4), 1 and 4-5; and e-mails, Peter Parsons to the author, 14 and 16 July 2001, and 14 July 2002. Also, Monaghan, *Under the Red Sun*, 236-237.
[44] Interview by the author with Colonel Tom Jones, April 25, 1999; and Mojica, *Terry's Hunters*, 409. In September 1943, (then Captain) Tom Jones, who was Ralph Praeger's deputy, met the two surviving members of the commando team in a dungeon cell in Fort Santiago. Jones survived the war, but the two commandos, Staff Sergeant Arcangel Baniares and T/4 Ramon Vitorio, were subsequently beheaded.

[45] In Manila, Roxas was rumored to have been arrested, but actually fled the city and went to Batangas. Letter, Norbert Schmelkes to Charles "Chick" Parsons, July 22, 1944, (Parsons); and e-mail, Peter Parsons, son of Chick Parsons, to the author, 14 July 2002. General Lim attempted to go to Mindoro, probably to meet or join Major Lawrence Phillips, but failed as the Japanese raided and killed Phillips at this time. In June, 1944, Lim, Tony Escoda, and a few other underground leaders left Manila on a boat again headed for Mindoro, apparently to meet one of Parson's submarines scheduled to put in at Sablayan Point. They were intercepted by a Japanese patrol boat on June 5 and imprisoned in Fort Santiago. Josepha Escoda was arrested in August, 1944. They were all put to death. Letter, Col. Amado N. Bautista to the Adjutant General, Awards and Decorations Section, PHILRYCOM, March 17, 1947, (NARA: box 258).

[46] General Headquarters, Southwest Pacifc Area, Military Intelligence Section, General Staff, "The Guerrilla Resistance Movement in Central Luzon," 26 October 1944, 7-8. Also, Major Osmundo Mondoñedo, "Organizational Report," *United States Forces in the Philippines, Military Intelligence Section, Headquarters, Nelson Group*, 1 February 1945, (MacArthur: Record Group 16, Box 3, Folder 11), 2.

[47] Phillips and Goldsmith, *Manila Espionage*, 162-163.

[48] When researching his book, *Looking for Liling*, Alfredo Roces interviewed Franco Vera Reyes' brother who insisted that Franco Vera Reyes was a guerrilla, not a spy, who paid for his activities with his life. However, other observers disagree: before he left Manila, Narciso Manzano had Franco Vera Reyes tailed, and he was observed visiting Col. Akira Nagahama's *Kempei-tai* office on multiple occasions. Manzano, "Memoirs," Chapter VIII-Luzon, (Manzano), 15-16. Major Edwin Ramsey fed Reyes a false story through an intermediary, and the story quickly turned up in Japanese Army and Bureau of Constabulary circles. Ramsey and Rivele, *Lieutenant Ramsey's War*, 198-200; and letter, Norbert Schmelkes to "Chick" [Parsons], July 22, 1944 (Parsons), 3-4. The Indiana Historical Society has several letters from "CIO-12" to Capt. Bernard Anderson, including one dated Dec 20, 1943 to which Anderson appended a note describing CIO-12 as a Japanese agent, and another dated Dec 23, 1943 with the words "Franco Vera Reyes" written on the back in Bernard Anderson's handwriting. CIO-12 obtained copies of Anderson's guerrilla roster, resulting in a major purge of Anderson's organization. General Headquarters, Southwest Pacific Area, Military Intelligence Section, General Staff, "The Guerrilla Resistance Movement In Central Luzon," 26 October 1944, (MacArthur: Record Group-16,

Box-3, File-17), 6. CIO-12 was Reyes' code name. Shun Force intelligence report, (ADVANTIS Translation No. 33, Jan 7 1945), 415. Samboyd Stagg, whose Methodist missionary mother was associated with Reyes for a short time in Manila, was present when Captain Vincente Gepte, an associate of Gen. Vincente Lim, confronted Reyes about his claims to be connected with Parsons' submarines, after which Reyes ran off and went into hiding for several weeks. Interview by the author with Samboyd Stagg, August 2, 2002. Reyes' ultimate fate is uncertain, but the most prevalent rumor indicates that he was arrested and executed by the Japanese after he exposed the Free Philippines, Phillip's commandos and Anderson's guerrillas, because he had been compromised and therefore had outlived his usefulness. The intelligence guide, magazine and letter that Reyes used for identification were apparently captured from Senator Ozamis' courier and/or other underground operators.

XVI. Turning Points

[1] Evelyn Loyd, diary entries for Jan. 11 and Sept. 5, 1943; and letter, Evelyn Loyd to Frank Loyd, Feb. 17, 1945, (both Loyd).

[2] Bureau of Public Relations, War Department, "Foreign Broadcast Digest No. 473," June 4, 1943, (Noble). Also, letter, Evelyn to Frank Loyd, February 21, 1945, (Loyd), 2.

[3] Evelyn Loyd, diary entry of September 5, 1943.

[4] Prisoner post card, Montgomery McKee to Evadne McKee, cited in letter, Evelyn Loyd to Major General J. A. Ulio, Adjutant General of the U.S. Army, February 25, 1944 (Loyd). Conversation reconstructed from interviews by the author with Evelyn Loyd.

[5] "Their Fathers are Jap Prisoners," *San Antonio Light*, October 3, 1943, page 1.

[6] Letter, Frank Loyd Jr. to his father, Feb. 19, 1945, (Loyd), 2.

[7] Letter, Frank Loyd Jr. to his father, March 3, 1945, (Loyd), 4.

[8] *The San Antonio Express*, January 28, 1944, page 1.

[9] Interview by the author with Joe Wilson, October 29, 1998

[10] Manchester, *American Caesar*, 324-327; and Hollister, From Pearl Harbor Into Tokyo, 157-158.

[11] Hunt, *The Untold Story of Douglas MacArthur*, 300-302. The idea of bypassing the Philippines and capturing Formosa was advanced primarily by Admiral King and by General Hap Arnold, chief of the Army Air Corps, who wanted to establish bomber bases on Formosa. For a general discussion of the issue, see Manchester, *American Caesar*, 420-422.

[12] Manchester, *American Caesar*, 425-430; and Hunt, *The Untold Story of Douglas MacArthur*, 303-305. Roosevelt left Admiral King and General Arnold in Washington when he left for Hawaii. Nimitz, therefore, was at a disadvantage since he was presenting King's concept of the war, not his own. Roosevelt knew that even an unprepared Douglas MacArthur would be a formidable opponent for Nimitz or anyone else to debate. He listened to each man carefully, but one might infer that the result of this meeting was a foregone conclusion.

XVII. Zonification

[1] The first Zonification of Orion occurred on May 8, 1943, and the second on December 1, 1943, according to the Certificate of Peter T. Seeckts, 8 October 1952, *Investigation of Casualty Roster, Bataan Military District*, (NARA: box 245). The description presented here is not based on an eyewitness account of events at Orion that day, but rather on several general descriptions of Zonifications, including Mojica, *Terry's Hunters*, 341-342, 349-351 and 357; Monaghan, *Under the Red Sun*, 147 and 203; and interview by Col. John E. Olson with Master Sergeant Benjamin Austria, October 30, 1988. Sergeant Austria's father, 2nd Lt. Roberto Ben Austria, Philippine Scouts, was killed in a similar Zonification in Guadeloupe, Makati, Rizal in October 1944. The hooded informers were pro-Japanese Filipinos, captured and tortured guerrillas, or other citizens under duress. This process is alleged to have led to abuses by unscrupulous pro-Japanese Filipinos, as it also provided a convenient way to eliminate business rivals and personal enemies.

[2] Loyd, "Bataan Diary," typed transcript, 136.

[3] The following dialog is paraphrased from Loyd, "Bataan Diary," typed transcript, 136-137; and from Filomeno, "Defense of Democracy in the Philippines," 6-7.

[4] Captain Dallas Vinnette was among the prisoners rescued from Cabanatuan prison camp by the U.S. Army 6th Ranger Battalion on January 28, 1945. Sides, *Ghost Soldiers*, prisoner list preceding the Prologue.

[5] E-mail, Jim Wright to the author, 6 March 1999.

[6] Loyd, "Bataan Diary," typed transcript 127-129.

[7] *Ibid,* 121,132,136. Also, letter, Juan [Boone] to Highpockets [Claire Phillips], June 4, 1944, 3.

[8] Loyd, "Bataan Diary," typed transcript 136-137; also interview by the author with Tiburcio Paule, May 13, 1998.

[9] Loyd, "Bataan Diary," typed transcript 148-149.

[10] *Ibid,* 138, 141 and 149.
[11] *Ibid,* 143,147,149-150,151-152
[12] *Ibid,* 137-138, 141-144
[13] *Ibid,* 138
[14] Letter, Primitivo Leonzon to undisclosed addressee, 16 Sept. 1947, reprinted in Ashton, *Bataan Diary*, 408-409.
[15] Loyd, "Bataan Diary," typed transcript 140-141.
[16] *Ibid,* 144-145; and interviews by the author with Vernon Fassoth, April and May 2004.
[17] Certificate of Florentino P. Buenaventura, 27 June 1952, *Investigation of Casualty Roster, Bataan Military District*, (NARA: box 245); and Loyd, "Bataan Diary," typed transcript 144-145.
[18] Loyd, "Bataan Diary," typed transcript, 145.
[19] E-mail, Edgar Wright III to the author, 21 February 1999.
[20] Interview by the author with Jim Wright, December 11, 1998.
[21] E-mail, Edgar Wright III to the author, 21 February 1999.
[22] Interview by the author with Jim Wright, December 11, 1998.
[23] Loyd, "Bataan Diary," typed transcript, 147-148.
[24] Filomeno, "Defense of Democracy in the Philippines," (Loyd), 8-9.
[25] Headquarters, East Central Luzon Guerrilla Area, "Names of American Officers and Soldiers," April 4, 1944, (NARA: box 256, Merrill Correspondence, Rosters, Orders and Miscellaneous Data, 1943-44-45).
[26] Utinsky, *"Miss U"*, 134. Also, Father Gerald Cogan, "Malate Then & Now," *The Far East*, September 1947, 5 and 6.
[27] Phillips and Goldsmith, *Manila Espionage*, 166-167; and Utinsky, *"Miss U"*, 118 and 125.
[28] Certificate of Mariano Vergara Batungbacal, *Investigation of Casualty Roster, Bataan Military District*, (NARA: box 245), 1.
[29] *Ibid*, 2.
[30] 14th Japanese Army Headquarters, "Watari Group Intelligence Report," June 16, 1944, (CMH: Intelligence Reports B, No 152-159), 38.
[31] Certificate of Salvador D. Cruz, 16 January 1952, *Investigation of Casualty Roster, Bataan Military District*, (NARA: box 245), 1-2. Mr. Cruz was one of the men confined at the garrison, and he witnessed the murders.
[32] 14th Japanese Army Headquarters, "Watari Group Intelligence Report," June 2, 1944 and July 20, 1944, (CMH: Intelligence Reports B, No 152-159), 2 and 70. Also, Japanese chart of guerrilla organizations dated 12/13/44, (Indiana: Anderson box); and certificate of Mariano V. Batungbacal, 18 March 1953, *Investigation of Casualty Roster, Bataan Military District*, (NARA: box 245), 3. Mr. Batungbacal worked as an

interpreter for the Japanese authorities and the *Kempei-tai*, in Balanga, Bataan.

XVIII. Captain Cabangbang

[1] "Narwhal," *Dictionary of American Fighting Ships.*
[2] Lapham and Norling, *Lapham's Raiders*, 152-154.
[3] General Headquarters, Southwest Pacific Area, Military Intelligence Section, General Staff, "Guerrilla Resistance Movement in the Philippines," 26 October 1944, (NARA: box 255), 17. Filipino names, those which originate in the languages of the Philippines rather than Spanish, often employ repetitive syllables. Cabangbang is pronounced "ka-bong-bong," and has no actual connotation to gunshots or explosions.
[4] "General Information on Corregidor, Bataan, Concentration Camps and Guerrilla*s*," (MacArthur: Record Group 17, box 1, folder 1). Also, "Cabrilla," *Dictionary of American Fighting Ships*.
[5] General Headquarters, Southwest Pacific Area, Military Intelligence Section, General Staff, "Guerrilla Resistance Movement in the Philippines," 26 October 1944, (NARA: box 255), 6 and 11; and Hunt and Norling, *Behind Japanese Lines*, 157.
[6] Interview by the author with Nick Leonzon and Tiburcio Paule, May 13, 1998.
[7] Loyd, handwritten recap of dispute with Col. Merrill, paragraph 9. (Loyd).
[8] Loyd, "Bataan Diary," typed transcript 153.
[9] *Ibid,* 153.
[10] Letter, Delphin Pamintuan to Frank Loyd, November 11, 1945, 2. (Loyd).
[11] Conner, "The American Air Show," (Indiana: HQ155B, document IIB11). Also, interview by the author with David Topping, May 19, 1999.
[12] Loyd, "Speech to Cheyenne Reservists," (Loyd), 16.
[13] Letter, Merrill to C.O. of the Chinese Overseas Wartime Hsuekkan Militia, 28 August 1944; two pages of instructions beginning "Courier Service: Pedro [Calyer] to Tomas [Merrill], August 29, 1944; and Appointment/Receipt form, 30 August 1944; (all in Indiana: brown 3-ring binder with "McCoy, Dobesk" on the spine).
[14] Letter, Merrill to "Loyal former USAFFE Officers," 4 October 1944, (NARA: box 257, Merrill file); and letter, Calyer to Anderson, October 16, 1944, (MacArthur: Record Group 16, Box 3, File 6). Also, message

number 52, Cabangbang to MacArthur, 20 October 1944, (MacArthur: Record Group 16, Box 17, File 2).

[15] Two pages of instructions beginning "Courier Service: Pedro [Calyer] to Tomas [Merrill], August 29, 1944, (Indiana: brown 3-ring binder with "McCoy, Dobesk" on the spine); letter, Conner to Crane, October 25, 1944, (NARA: box 257, Merrill file); and Lapham and Norling, *Lapham's Raiders*, 114-116.

[16] Letter, Merrill to Alejandrino, 4 October 1944, (Indiana: small, brown 3-ring binder with "McCoy, Dobesk" on spine).

[17] Radiogram, Gyles Merrill to CG, SWPA, 6 October 1944, (NARA: box 257).

[18] Letter, Calyer to Ramsey, 6 September 1944, and 1st Indorsement, 22 September 1944, (NARA: box 256).

[19] Lapham and Norling, *Lapham's Raiders*, 115-116. Lapham was, in fact, in contact with MacArthur. Capt. Robert Ball had traveled by sailboat from Samar Island to the east coast of Luzon to bring a radio to Luzon after Major Lawrence Phillips was killed on Mindoro. Ball made contact with Lapham's men as soon as he landed and set up his radio near Lapham's headquarters. He began transmitting regular intelligence reports from Lapham and Anderson to MacArthur in June 1944. Additional radios were then brought from the southern islands for Anderson and Volckmann. Lapham and Norling, *Lapham's Raiders*, 144-148.

[20] Letter, Conner to Crane, October 25, 1944, (NARA: box 257, Merrill file).

[21] Letter, Anderson to Calyer, 3 November 1944, (MacArthur: Record Group 16, Box 3, File 6).

[22] Lapham and Norling, *Lapham's Raiders*, 116.

[23] Letter, Boone to Merrill, 15 September 1944, (NARA: box 257, Boone file).

[24] Letter, Loyd to Merrill, October 8, 1944, (NARA: box 257, Merrill file).

[25] Santos, "Guerrilla Activities in Luzon", 20 January 1945, (NARA: box 258), 5-9, and Lapham and Norling, *Lapham's Raiders*, 69-71 and 114-121.

[26] Undated message, Western Luzon Guerrilla Forces to General MacArthur, sent through Iloilo, (NARA: box 257, Merrill file).

[27] Santos, "Guerrilla Activities in Luzon", 20 January 1945, (NARA: box 258), 9.

[28] Radio message, Anderson to Manzano, June 19 1944, (Manzano).

[29] Santos, "Guerrilla Activities in Luzon", 20 January 1945, (NARA: box 258), 6 and 9.
[30] Lapham and Norling, *Lapham's Raiders*, 114-115.
[31] Ramsey and Rivele, *Lieutenant Ramsey's War*, 179.
[32] Letter, Caberea to C.O. Kalayaan Area [Anderson], 26 October 1944, (MacArthur Record Group 16, box 3, file 6); and General Headquarters, Southwest Pacific Area, Military Intelligence Section, General Staff, Guerrilla Resistance Movement in the Philippines, 26 October 1944, (MacArthur: Record Group 16, box 3, file 17), page 6 and attached map. Also, Santos, "Guerrilla Activities in Luzon," 20 January 1945, (NARA: box 258), 7.
[33] Santos, "Guerrilla Activities in Luzon", 20 January 1945, (NARA: box 258), 5-9.
[34] Letter, Cabangbang to "All Unit Commanders, USPIF," 8 December 1944, (NARA: box 258, Merrill file); and Lapham and Norling, *Lapham's Raiders*, 117-118.
[35] Santos, "Guerrilla Activities in Luzon", 20 January 1945, (NARA: box 258), 7 and 9; and General Headquarters Southwest Pacific Area, Military Intelligence Section, General Staff, "Guerrilla Resistance Movement in the Philippines," 26 October 1944, (NARA: box 255), 9.
[36] Message, Cabangbang to MacArthur, 20 November 1944, (MacArthur: Record Group 16, Box17, Folder 2); and General Headquarters Southwest Pacific Area, Military Intelligence Section, General Staff, "Guerrilla Resistance Movement in the Philippines," 26 October 1944, (MacArthur: Record Group 16, Box 3, Folder 17), 6 and 10. Also, Mojica, *Terry's Hunters*, 409-410.
[37] Letter, Valera to Volckmann, 27 October 1944, (MacArthur: Record Group 16, box 3, file 6).
[38] Message nr. 99, Cabangbang to MacArthur, 1 November 1944, (MacArthur: Record Group 16, box 17, file 2).
[39] Interview by Doug Clanin with Robert Mailheau, February 21, 1984, (Indiana: Guerrilla Additions, description of Clay Conner). Also, Lapham and Norling, *Lapham's Raiders*, 100-102.
[40] Conner, "We Fought Fear on Luzon," *True*, August 1945, 81.
[41] Monograph by Doyle Decker, page 3; and reminiscences by Doyle Decker , pages 11-13, (both Indiana: Guerrilla Additions).
[42] Report, Lt. H. C. Conner, Jr. to Capt. Crane, October 25, 1944, page 1, (NARA: box257, Merrill file).
[43] The "channels," apparently, were courier to Claire Phillips, courier from Phillips to John Boone, courier to Edwin Ramsey, courier to Jesus

Villamor's radio station on Negros or Wendell Fertig on Mindanao, then radio to MacArthur's intelligence section in Australia.

[44] Handwritten letter, Conner to Crane and Collier, November 3, 1944, (NARA: box 257, Merrill file).

[45] Letters, Conner to "Tomas" [Merrill], November 3, 1944 and November 6, 1944, (NARA: box 257, Merrill file). Conner misunderstood the message from Bruce, which referred to the possibility of one of Cabangbang's men visiting Conner. There was no "representative" of General MacArthur on Luzon.

[46] Letter, Merrill to Conner, 6 November 1944, (NARA: box 257, Merrill file).

[47] Letters, Conner to Merrill, 23 November 1944 and 22 January 1945, (NARA: box 257, Merrill file).

[48] The author's description of this meeting is based on Conner, "We Fought Fear on Luzon," *True*, August 1945, page 86; and letter, Conner to Crane, October 25, 1944, (NARA: box 257, Merrill file).

[49] Report, Conner to Merrill, 23 November 1944, (NARA: box 257, Merrill file).

[50] Loyd, "Bataan Diary," typed transcript, 157.

[51] *Ibid*, 157; and interview by the author with Brig. Gen. Roy Reynolds, July 31, 1999.

[52] Letter, Merrill to Loyd, 26 October 1944, (NARA: box 257, Merrill file).

[53] Loyd, "Bataan Diary," typed transcript, 158.

[54] Notes dated November 26, written on the back of Col. Merrill's letter of 26 October 1944 (Loyd); and Loyd, "Bataan Diary," typed transcript, 154-155 and 166 .

[55] Handwritten copy of letter, Loyd to Collier, November 29, 1944, (Loyd); and Loyd, "Bataan Diary," typed transcript, 157.

[56] Loyd, *Bataan Diary*, typewritten transcript, pages 158 and 160

[57] Affidavits of John P. Boone, 20 Dec 1945, and Lt. Col. Felix Guerrero, 2 July 1946 (both Zozabrado).

[58] Loyd, *Bataan Diary*, typewritten transcript, page 157.

[59] Interview by the author with Vernon Fassoth, April 2004.

[60] Loyd, *Bataan Diary*, typewritten transcript, page 160, and letter, Boone to Tuggle, 6 Dec. 1944, NARA box 257, Boone folder.

[61] Jingco family names from Affidavit of Arsenia J. Jingco, 2 September 1947, (Indiana: Notebook 3).

[62] Loyd, "Bataan Diary," typed transcript, 158. Also letter, Wright to "M" [Narciso Manzano], 24 December 1944, (Indiana: SWPA-I, Boone file).

[63] Loyd, "Bataan Diary," typed transcript, 158. Also, letter, Boone to Tuggle, 6 December 1944, (NARA: box 257, Boone file); and "Agreement For Cooperation," signed by Roy G. Tuggle and Moises Apostle, December 1, 1944, (NARA: box 257).
[64] Loyd, "Bataan Diary," typed transcript, 157-158. Food described in affidavit of Arnsinia J. Jingco, 2 September 1947, (Indiana: Notebook 3).
[65] Hukbalahap leaflet, Nov. 7, 1944, (NARA: box 256); and message number 9, Cabangbang to MacArthur, 4 November 1944, (MacArthur: Record Group 16, box 17, folder 2).
[66] Messages nr. 56 and 142, Cabangbang to MacArthur, 21 October and 14 November 1944, (MacArthur: Record Group 16, box 17, folder 2). Also, letter, Conner to Merrill, 23 November 1944, 6, (NARA: box 257, Merrill file).
[67] Message nr. 296, Cabangbang to MacArthur, 23 November 1944, (MacArthur: Record Group 16, box 17, file 2).
[68] Letter, Conner to Merrill, 23 November 1944, (NARA: box 257, Merrill file), 6.
[69] Handwritten copy of letter to Osmeña, November 23, 1944, (Indiana: brown 3-ring binder with "McCoy, Dobesk" on spine).
[70] Letter, Cabangbang to "Hukbalajaps and other Leaders, in the field," 26 November 1944, (MacArthur: Record Group 16, General files, Philippine project, Hukbalahap, 1943-1945).
[71] Message, MacArthur to Cabangbang, December 2, 1944, (MacArthur: Record Group 16, Box 17, Folder 2).
[72] Memorandum, Cabangbang to "All Unit Commanders, USPIF, In the Field," 2 December 1944, (NARA: Box 257, Merrill file).
[73] Memorandum, Cabangbang to "All Unit Commanders, USPIF, In the Field," 8 December 1944, (MacArthur: Record Group 16, Box 3, Folder 11).

XIX. The Samurai Generals

[1] Hoyt, *Japan's War*, 344-348.
[2] *Ibid*, 364-365.
[3] Although many think of the islands of Hokkaido, Honshu and Kyushu as "mainland" Japan, Japanese thinking included a number of other, more remote, islands. Iwo Jima, for example, was considered to be part of the prefecture of Tokyo. Saipan, in the Mariana chain 1300 miles south of Tokyo, just north of Guam, had been incorporated into the Japanese homeland by settling thousands of Japanese citizens there—its invasion

by and loss to American troops was a huge psychological blow to the Japanese. Hoyt, *Japan's War*, 351.

[4] Hoyt, *Japan's War*, 347-350, 357.

[5] *Ibid*, 350-351.

[6] Blair, *Silent Victory: The U.S. Submarine War Against Japan*, 17.

[7] Hollister, *From Pearl Harbor Into Tokyo*, 185-186.

[8] Hoyt, *Japan's War*, 354 and 372.

[9] Inoguchi, *The Divine Wind*, 6.

[10] In the 1960s and 1970s North Vietnamese General Vo Nguyen Giap employed essentially the same strategy against the United States with a great deal of success. By stringing out the war, publicizing the carnage, and directing lots of propaganda at the American public he eventually won the Vietnam War even though he never won a significant battle. The Japanese, however, had the legacy of Pearl Harbor to overcome, and they never succeeded in discouraging the American public.

[11] Hoyt, *Japan's War*, 372.

[12] Loyd "Bataan Diary," typed transcript, 153; and "U.S. Pacific Fleet Knocked Out," *The Tribune Extra*, Manila, October 27, 1944. Also, Ogawa, *Terraced Hell*, 85.

[13] Colonel Aoshima Ryoichiro and Major Iwano Masataka, "Preparation for Luzon Operations," (CMH: Japanese Monograph no. 7).

[14] Hoyt, *Japan's War*, 366

[15] 14th Japanese Area Army Headquarters, "Shobu Group Headquarters Intelligence Report," September 10, 1944, (CMH: Intelligence Reports B No 1-10), 61; and Colonel Yasuji Okada, "Outline of a Plan for Subjective Operations in the Philippines," (CMH: Japanese monograph no. 3), 12.

[16] Hunt and Norling, *Behind Japanese Lines*, 144; and Steinberg, *Philippine Collaboration in World War II, 97-98.*

[17] Quoted from Rodriguez, *The Bad Guerrillas of Northern Luzon*, 11.

[18] Inoguchi, *The Divine Wind*, 4.

[19] *Ibid*, 184.

[20] *Ibid*, 28.

[21] Colonel Aoshima Ryoichiro and Major Iwano Masataka, "Preparation for Luzon Operations," (CMH: Japanese monograph no. 7), 1.

[22] Inoguchi, *The Divine Wind*, 7.

[23] *Ibid*, 20-21 and 184-187.

[24] Colonel Yasuji Okada, "Shifting Military Strength to Defend the Philippines," (CMH: Japanese monograph no. 3), 40; and Inoguchi, *The Divine Wind*, 9-10.

[25] Inoguchi, *The Divine Wind*, 7-9.

[26] *Ibid*, 10-12
[27] *Ibid*, 21.
[28] *Ibid*, 6-7 and 185.
[29] Gailey, *The War in the Pacific*, 350.
[30] *Ibid*, 350-353.
[31] Hollister, *From Pearl Harbor Into Tokyo*, 183.
[32] "Guerrillas Made Part of PA," *Leyte-Samar Free Philippines*, October 28, 1944.
[33] Nakajima, *The Divine Wind*, Chapter 7.
[34] Manchester, *Goodbye Darkness*, 324-328; and Gailey, *The War in the Pacific*, 347-364. Also, Ogawa, *Terraced Hell*, 33 and 43.
[35] Gailey, *The War in the Pacific*, 361-362.
[36] Nakajima, *The Divine Wind*, 64.
[37] Inoguchi, *The Divine Wind*, 67.
[38] *Ibid*, 8, 186.
[39] *Ibid*, 180.
[40] *In blossom today, then scattered;*
Life is so like a delicate flower.
How can one expect the fragrance to last forever?
Takijiro Ohnishi, as quoted in Inoguchi, *The Divine Wind*, 187.

XX. Expectations

[1] Conversation paraphrased from letters, Effie Adee to Evelyn Loyd, November 8, 1944, and Evelyn Loyd to Frank Loyd, February 17, 1945, (Loyd); and from interviews by the author with Mrs. Loyd.
[2] Letter, Evelyn Loyd to Frank Loyd, February 21, 1945, (Loyd), 3.
[3] Conversation paraphrased from letter, Evelyn to Frank Loyd, February 21, 1945, (Loyd), 2; and from interviews by the author with Mrs. Loyd. If Legaspi was under consideration as a landing point for U.S. troops, the density of the sand, and therefore its ability to support heavy tanks, would be essential information.
[4] Letters, Loyd family members to Frank Loyd, December 8, 1944, (Loyd).
[5] Letter, Evelyn to Frank Loyd, February 21, 1945, (Loyd), 1-2. The Red Cross returned the letters to Mrs. Loyd.
[6] Letter, Frank Loyd Jr. to Frank Loyd, March 3, 1945, (Loyd), 3.
[7] Manchester, *American Caesar*, 250.
[8] Castro, too, had been left behind when the General and his wife departed, with instructions to take care of the suite and its occupants whoever they might be. Romulo, *The Manila Hotel*, 116.

[9] Hoyt, *Japan's War*, 366.
[10] Message nr. 431, Cabangbang to MacArthur, 11 December 1944, (MacArthur: Record Group 16, Box 17, File 2).
[11] Colonel Aoshima Ryoichiro and Major Iwano Masataka, "Preparation for Luzon Operations," (CMH: Japanese monograph no. 7), 1.
[12] Colonel Aoshima Ryoichiro and Major Iwano Masataka, "Events of Japanese Defeat on Luzon," (CMH: Japanese monograph no. 7), 3 and 25.
[13] Message, Cabangbang to MacArthur, 14 December 1944, (MacArthur: Record Group 16, Box 17, File 2). Also, Hoyt, *Japan's War*, 382.
[14] Colonel Aoshima Ryoichiro and Major Iwano Masataka, "Preparation for Luzon Operations," (CMH: Japanese monograph no. 7), 1.
[15] Hoyt, *Japan's War*, 366.

XXI. Christmas 1944

[1] Loyd, "Bataan Diary," typed transcript, 163.
[2] *Ibid*, 163.
[3] Utinsky, *"Miss U"*, 139-140. In her book, Margaret Utinsky says that Dian's illness was her reason for wanting to leave Abad and go to Col. Loyd. In his diary, Col. Loyd describes the execution of the young woman and her child, and what Abad had asked Utinsky to do.
[4] Utinsky, *"Miss U"*, 118.
[5] Phillips and Goldsmith, *Manila Espionage*, 187-191; and Sides, *Ghost Solders*, 200-201.
[6] Utinsky, *"Miss U"*, 119-130; and Loyd, "Bataan Diary," typed transcript, 159 and 163.
[7] Utinsky, *"Miss U"*, 132-133.
[8] *Ibid*, 136 and 139.
[9] Loyd, "Bataan Diary," typed transcript, 163.
[10] Utinsky, *"Miss U"*, 134-136.
[11] *Ibid*, 139-140.
[12] *Ibid*, 141-142.
[13] Letter, Abad to Loyd, December 13 1944, (Loyd).
[14] Loyd, "Bataan Diary," typed transcript, 160.
[15] Letter, Frank Loyd to Evelyn Loyd, March 10, 1942.
[16] Utinsky, *"Miss U"*, 142.
[17] Loyd, "Bataan Diary," typed transcript, 160.
[18] *Ibid*, 160.
[19] Letter, Loyd to Boone, 12/22/44 (Boone).
[20] Utinsky, *"Miss U"*, 142.

[21] "U.S. Pacific Fleet Knocked Out; Troops in Leyte Are Isolated," *The Tribune Extra*, Manila, October 27, 1944.
[22] Monaghan, *Under the Red Sun*, 246-247; O'Brien, *Columban Martyrs of Malate*, vii-viii; and interview by Col. John E. Olson with Master Sergeant Benjamin Austria, October 30, 1988.
[23] 14th Japanese Area Army Headquarters, "Shobu Group Headquarters Intelligence Report," August 27, 1944, (CMH: Intelligence Reports B No 1-10), 41.
[24] Connaughton, Pimlott and Anderson, *The Battle for Manila*, 70. Also, letter, Ramsey to Boone, 6 August 1944, (Boone).
[25] Letters, Pilar A. Clemente, Treasurer of the Philippine Women's University, to "To whom It May Concern," 23 Sept. 1947; and Chaplain (Major) John L Curran to "Board Concerning Services Rendered to American POW'S, Recovered Personnel Division, Philippines-Ryukyus Command," Sept. 9, 1947; both reprinted in Ashton, *Bataan Diary*, 374-381.
[26] Affidavit of Col. Irineo Buenconcejo, 27 September 1945, *Reference Cases of Fort Santiago Massacre*, (NARA: box 245, file 999-23-4), 6. Also, Lapham and Norling, *Lapham's Raiders*, 136-137.
[27] Message nr. 412, Cabangbang to MacArthur, 10 December 1944; and Hartendorp, *The Japanese Occupation of the Philippines, Volume II*, 593. General Lim and Tony Escoda were arrested with several others in a boat on their way to meet a U.S. submarine off Mindoro. The Mencarini's and Josefa Escoda were arrested in Manila by the *Kempei-tai*.
[28] The Elizalde family, except Juan Elizalde, were released when Juan Elizalde claimed full responsibility for their actions and absolved all other family members. There were rumors in Manila after the war that his brother Manolo paid a large bribe to Japanese officials to secure the release of the Elizalde family, but the Japanese refused to include Juan in the deal. Juan Elizalde, Blanche Jurika, Vincente Gepte and twenty-six other leaders were executed in the Chinese Cemetery. Today their remains are buried together there in a large crypt known as the "Heroes Monument."
[29] Phillips, *Manila Espionage*, 207.
[30] *Ibid*, 203.
[31] San Gabriel, *The Constabulary Story*, 294.
[32] Connaughton, Pimlott and Anderson, *The Battle for Manila*, 72.
[33] Gailey, *The War in the Pacific*, 377.
[34] Colonel Aoshima Ryoichiro and Major Iwano Masataka, "Preparation for Luzon Operations," (CMH: Japanese monograph #7), 1. Also, Ogawa, *Terraced Hell*, 33 and 148-149.

[35] Ogawa, *Terraced Hell*, 99.
[36] Certificate of Mariano Vergara Batungbacal, 1, *Investigation of Casualty Roster, Bataan Military District*, (NARA: box 245).
[37] *Ibid*, 3; and "Annex 2, Section V—Conclusions of Investigator," 18 March 1953, *Investigation of Casualty Roster, Bataan Military District*, (NARA: box 245).
[38] Memos Abad to Magtanggol and Abad to Villaruel, Nov 30, 1944 (Boone).
[39] Utinsky, *"Miss U"*, 137; and Loyd, "Bataan Diary," typed transcript, 161.
[40] Certificate of Salvador D. Cruz, 16 January 1952, 2, *Investigation of Casualty Roster, Bataan Military District*, (NARA: Box 245); and Reply, Migano to Boone, 16 Dec 1944 (Boone).
[41] Certificate of Salvador D. Cruz, 16 January 1952, and "Annex 2 Section V—Conclusions of Investigator," 18 March 1953, 2-3, *Investigation of Casualty Roster, Bataan Military District*, (NARA: Box 245).
[42] Certificate of Mariano Vergara Batungbacal, 2, *Investigation of Casualty Roster, Bataan Military District*, (NARA: box 245).
[43] Report from Major Andres Migano to Lt. Col. Gately, 28 Nov. 1944 (Boone), and report from Gately to C.O. ECLGA [Ramsey], 30 November 1944, (NARA: box 246), 2.
[44] Capt. J. Inocencio, "G-3 Periodic Report, Bataan Military District, From 10 December 1944 to 20 December 1944," (NARA: box 257, Boone file); and letter, Boone to Ramsey, 28 December 1944, (NARA: box 246, Bataan Military District folder).
[45] Capt. J. Inocencio, "G-3 Periodic Report, Bataan Military District, From 10 December 1944 to 20 December 1944," (NARA: box 257, Boone file).
[46] Certificate of Mariano V. Batungbacal, 3, *Investigation of Casualty Roster, Bataan Military District*, (NARA: box 245).
[47] *Ibid*; and "Annex 2, Section V—Conclusions of Investigator," 18 March 1953, *Investigation of Casualty Roster, Bataan Military District*, (NARA: box 245).
[48] "Annex 2, Section V—Conclusions of Investigator," 18 March 1953, *Investigation of Casualty Roster, Bataan Military District*, (NARA: box 245).
[49] *Ibid.*
[50] Certificate of Mariano Vergara Batungbacal Jr., *Investigation of Casualty Roster, Bataan Military District*, (NARA: Box 245), 2; and letter, Boone to Tuggle, 6 December 1944, (NARA Box 257).

[51] "Annex 2, Section IV - Findings and Comments," and "Annex 2, Section V—Conclusions of Investigator," 18 March 1953, *Investigation of Casualty Roster, Bataan Military District*, (NARA: box 245).
[52] The men were Captain Lester Chase, Lieutenant Bob Chapin, and Sergeant Frank Bernacki.
[53] Interview by the author with Brig. Gen. Royal Reynolds, July 31, 1999.
[54] Letter, Boone to Ramsey, 28 December 1944, (NARA: box 246, ECLGA/Bataan Military District folder), 2; and letter, Boone to Tuggle, 6 December 1944, (NARA: box 257, Boone file).
[55] Letter, Calyer to Ramsey, 6 September 1944, with three indorsements, (NARA: box 256, Correspondence Regarding Activities of Various Guerrilla & Army Units 3/43 to 1/45); and letter, Boone to Ramsey, 28 December 1944, (NARA: box246: Bataan Military District folder).
[56] Two pages of instructions beginning "Courier Service: Pedro [Calyer] to Tomas [Merrill]," August 29, 1944, (Indiana: brown 3-ring binder with "McCoy, Dobesk" on the spine); and letter, Boone to Merrill 25 December 1944 (NARA: box 257).
[57] Receipts for donations of supplies and money issued to "Highpockets" [Claire Phillips], 15 May 1944; and Financial Report to "C.O. ECLGA," [Ramsey], 15 Sept. 1944 (Boone). Through mid-September Boone had collected more than 250,000 pesos in cash, plus donations of clothing and supplies.
[58] Letter, Gateley to Ramsey, 30 November 1944, (NARA: Box 246, Bataan Military District file), 2.
[59] Loyd, "Bataan Diary," typed transcript, 161; interviews by the author with Tessie Musgni, Zozabrado's niece, on March 15 and March 30 2004; and affidavits of John Boone, Crispin Reyes and Felix Guerrero (Zozabrado). Also, letter, Wright to "M" [Manzano], 24 December 1944, (NARA: box 257, Wright file). Sam Zozabrado's U.S. military records list him as killed in action at the Zig-zag. Vernon Fassoth tells a slightly different version of Magtanggol's death, saying that Boone persuaded Magtanggol's bodyguard to assassinate him in his sleep because no one else was willing to confront Magtanggol. Interview by the author with Vernon Fassoth, April 2004.
[60] Letter, Boone to Ramsey, 28 December 1944, (NARA: box 246, ECLGA/Bataan Military District folder), 3.
[61] Handwritten note, Loyd to C.G., USAFFE, Leyte, 17 December 1944, (Indiana: SWPA-I binder, Boone file), and Loyd, "Bataan Diary," typed transcript, pages 160-161.

[62] Letter, Wright to Merrill, January 12, 1945, (NARA: box 257, Wright file).
[63] Letters, Wright to "M" [Manzano], 24 December 1944; and Boone to Ramsey, 28 December 1944, page 3, (NARA: box 246, ECLGA/Bataan Military District folder).
[64] Letters, Wright to "M" [Manzano], 24 December 1944; and letter, Wright to Merrill, January 12, 1945, (both NARA: box 257, Wright folder).
[65] Memo, Boone to Cabangbang, 24 December 1944, (MacArthur: Record Group 16, box 3, folder 11).
[66] Letter, Calyer to distribution list, December 20, 1944; and General Orders #3, HQ LGF USFIP, December 18, 1944, (both NARA: box 256, Correspondence, Rosters, Orders & Misc. Data file, 1943-44-45).
[67] Loyd, "Bataan Diary," typed transcript, 165.
[68] Letter, Boone to Loyd, 1 February 1945, Loyd family papers.
[69] Headquarters Bataan Military District, "War Plan No. I," 1 January 1945, (NARA: box 257, Boone file).
[70] Letter, Boone to Ramsey, 28 December 1944, (NARA: box 246, ECLGA/Bataan Military District folder).
[71] Letter, Loyd to Boone, 12/22/44 (Boone).
[72] Headquarters, Bataan Military District, "War Plan No. I," 1 January 1945, (NARA: box 257, Boone file).
[73] Letter, Loyd to Boone, 12/22/44 (Boone).
[74] Loyd, "Bataan Diary," typed transcript, 160; and letter, Boone to Tuggle, 6 Dec. 1944, (NARA box 257, Boone folder).
[75] Roster of the Signal Section of the Bataan Military District (Boone).
[76] During the Battle of Bataan in 1942, the area on the side of Mount Mariveles occupied by General King's communications detachment was called "Signal Hill." Boone's Signal Hill, however, was on Mount Malasimbo.
[77] Letter, Boone to Ramsey, 28 December 1944, (NARA: box 246, ECLGA/Bataan Military District folder).
[78] Filomeno, "Defense of Democracy in the Philippines," (Loyd), 8.
[79] Loyd, "Recap of Dispute with Colonel Merrill," November 29, 1944, paragraph 7, (Loyd).
[80] Letter, Loyd to Boone, 12/22/44 (Boone).
[81] Loyd, "Bataan Diary," typed transcript, 159.
[82] Letter, Boone to Ramsey, 28 December 1944, (NARA: box 246, ECLGA/Bataan Military District folder).
[83] Handwritten note, Wright to Merrill, January 7, 1944, (NARA: box 257, Wright file).

[84] Letter, Boone to Ramsey, 28 December 1944, (NARA: box 246, ECLGA/Bataan Military District folder).
[85] Loyd, “Bataan Diary,” typewritten transcript, 162.
[86] *Ibid*; and Utinsky, *"Miss U"*, 143-144.
[87] Letters, Wright to "C.O. Sq. 155 (Lt. O'Conner)" [Conner]; and Wright to "CO South Tarlac Military District" [Sgt. Al Bruce], January 3, 1945, (both NARA: box 257, Wright file); and "Table of Organization, Provisional Regiment of Philippine Scouts," (Indiana: brown, 3-ring binder with "McCoy, Dobesk" on spine). Dialog provided by the author.
[88] Loyd, “Bataan Diary,” 165; and letter, Boone to Merrill, 7 January 1944, (NARA: box 257, Boone file). Dialog provided by the author.
[89] Letters, Wright to "C.O. Sq. 155 (Lt. O’Conner)" [Conner]; and Wright to "CO South Tarlac Military District" [Sgt. Al Bruce], January 3, 1945, (both NARA: box 257, Wright file).
[90] Notice to Assemble, 30 December 1944, (NARA: box 257, Wright file).
[91] Headquarters Luzon Guerrilla Forces, United States Forces in the Philippines, “Field Order # 1,” December 30, 1944, (Indiana: Hq 155 B binder, item II-B-7).
[92] Message number 645, Merrill [through Cabangbang] to MacArthur, 27 December 1944, (MacArthur: Record Group 16, box 17, folder 2).
[93] Message, Merrill to Cabangbang, 19 December 1944. He had sent a similar message on the 15th claiming only 13,000 troops and 800 arms. (both Indiana: SWPA-1 correspondence). Also, message, Cabangbang to MacArthur, December 27, 1944, (MacArthur RG-16,Box-27,Folder-5).
[94] Letter, Merrill to Cabangbang, 15 December 1944, (NARA: box 257, Merrill file).
[95] Memorandum, Merrill to Cabangbang, 16 December 1944, (NARA: box 257, Merrill file).
[96] Letter, Cabangbang to Merrill, 29 December 1944, (NARA: box 257, Merrill file).
[97] Letter, Conner to Merrill, 14 January 1945, (NARA, box 257, Merrill file).
[98] Japanese Navy Captain Sata Naohiro, commander of the 16th Combat Sector, Clark Field, “Recollections and Personal Notes,” (CMH: Japanese monograph #114).
[99] Letter, Conner to Merrill, 14 January 1945, (NARA, box 257, Merrill file).
[100] The rumors were correct. Yamashita transferred his headquarters to Baguio around January 3, 1945. Navy Captain Sata Naohiro (CMH:

Japanese monograph #114). Laurel followed shortly behind, leaving Benigno Ramos in charge in Manila. Mojica, *Terry's Hunters*, 25-26.
[101] Conner, "We Fought Fear on Luzon," *True*, August 1945, 87.
[102] Letter, Wright to Merrill, 7 January 1945, (NARA: box 257, Wright file).
[103] Quoted in letter, Boone to Merrill, 7 January 1944, (NARA: box 257, Boone file).
[104] Dialog paraphrased from letter, Boone to "CO, LGF" [Merrill], 14 January 1945, (Indiana: SWPA-I, Boone file).
[105] Loyd, "Bataan Diary," typed transcript, 165.
[106] Letter, Boone to Merrill, 7 January 1944, (NARA: box 257, Boone file).
[107] *Ibid.*
[108] Headquarters Luzon Guerrilla Forces, United States Forces in the Philippines, "Field Order # 1," December 30, 1944 (Indiana: Hq 155 B binder, item II-B-7). Also, letter, Merrill to Conner, 7 December 1944, (NARA: box 257, Merrill file); and letter, Wright to "CO, LGF" [Merrill], 14 January 1945, (Indiana: brown binder with "McCoy, Dobesk" on spine).
[109] Letter, Boone to Merrill, 7 January 1944, (NARA: box 257, Boone file); handwritten note, Wright to Merrill, January 7, 1944 (NARA: box 257, Wright file); letter, Boone to Ramsey, 8 January 1944, (Boone); and letter, Wright to Merrill, 14 January 1945, (NARA: box 257, Wright file). Also, handwritten notes on Boone's copy of Field Order # 1 (Boone).
[110] Instructions, Guerrero to Unit Commanders, 7 January 1945 (Boone).
[111] Letter, Wright to "Tomas" [Merrill], 7 January 1945, (NARA: box 257, Wright file).
[112] *Ibid.*
[113] Letter, Boone to Loyd, 13 January 1945, (Loyd).
[114] *Ibid*; and Loyd, "Bataan Diary," typed transcript, 161.
[115] Utinsky, *"Miss U"*, 144-146.
[116] Bataan Military District, "War Plan No. I," 1 January 1945, (NARA: box 257, Boone file), 4.
[117] Message, MacArthur to Cabangbang, 10 December 1944, (MacArthur: Record Group 16, box 27, folder 4); memorandum, Cabangbang to Merrill, 12 December 1944, (NARA: box 257, Merrill file); memorandum, Merrill to Cabangbang, 15 December 1944, (Indiana: SWPA-1 correspondence); and message, Cabangbang to Merrill, 15 December 1944, (Indiana: SWPA-1 correspondence).

[118] Message, Cabangbang to Merrill, 6 January 1945, (NARA: box 257, MacArthur file).

XXII. Maximum Violence

[1] Letter, Evelyn Loyd to Sandy Easley, January 11, 1942 (Loyd).
[2] Paraphrased from message number 684, Cabangbang to MacArthur, 31 December 1944, (MacArthur: Record Group 16, box 28, folder 1); and message number 850, Cabangbang to MacArthur, 18 January 1945, (MacArthur: Record Group 16, box 28, folder 2).
[3] Utinsky, *Miss U*, 144-146; and Loyd, "Bataan Diary," typed transcript, 164.
[4] Loyd, "Bataan Diary," typed transcript, 164.
[5] Letter, Wright to Tomas [Merrill], 7 January, 1945, (NARA: box 258, Wright folder).
[6] Radio message, Tuggle to station BZ9 [Boone], 21 January 1945, (Indiana: small, brown binder with "McCoy, Dobesk" on spine).
[7] Letter, Conner to Merrill, 14 January 1945, (NARA, box 257, Merrill file).
[8] Letter, Conner to Merrill, 6 January 1945, (NARA: box 258, Merrill file).
[9] *Ibid.*
[10] Letters, Conner to Merrill, 6 January 1945 and 14 January 1945, (NARA: box 258, Merrill file); and Inoguchi, *The Divine Wind*, 101-103. The Navy men were support personnel of the First Air Fleet which had no planes left so they were now to fight, and die, as infantry. In the next few days they would be joined by the men of the Second Air Fleet. Admiral Ohnishi, his immediate staff, and the surviving pilots of the First and Second Air Fleets had left for Tuguegarao airfield in northern Luzon, to be evacuated to Formosa to establish a Kamikaze training facility. Almost one-third of them were killed by guerrillas as they made their way overland. Navy Captain Sata Naohiro, "Fall of the Philippines," (CMH: Japanese Monograph #114).
[11] Letter, Conner to Merrill, 6 January 1945, (NARA: box 258, Merrill file).
[12] Letter, Conner to Merrill, 14 January 1945, (NARA: box 258, Merrill file).
[13] Conner, "We Fought Fear on Luzon," *True*, August 1945, 87.
[14] Letter, Boone to "C.O. LGF" [Merrill], 14 January 1945, (NARA: box 258, Boone folder).

[15] Letter, Wright to Merrill, January 12, 1945, (NARA: box 257, Wright file).
[16] Bataan Military District, "Letter of Instruction," 17 January 1945, (Indiana: SWPA I, Boone section).
[17] Note, Merrill to Wright, 13 January 1945, (Indiana: small, brown, binder with "McCoy, Dobesk" on spine).
[18] Letter, Wright to "CO, LGF" [Merrill], 14 January 1945; and handwritten note, undated but labeled "Rec'd 18 Jan" (Indiana: small, brown binder with "McCoy, Dobesk" on spine).
[19] Letter, Wright to Merrill, January 12, 1945, (NARA: box 257, Wright file).
[20] D. Holmes Jr., Map III, titled "Sixth Army's Advance, 18-31 January 1945," (Indiana: unlabeled blue box containing miscellaneous papers collected by Wayne Sanford).
[21] Major Jose Inocencio, "Bataan Military District, Operations, From 16 Jan 45 to 19 Jan 45," (NARA: box 257, Boone file).
[22] *Ibid*; and Interview by the author with Jim Wright, December 11, 1998.
[23] Letter, Boone to "C.O. LGF" [Merrill], 18 January 1945, (NARA: box 257, Boone file).
[24] Letter, Boone to "C.O. LGF" [Merrill], 18 January 1945; and Major C. Reyes, "G-2 Report From: 19:00, 16 Jan 45 To: 24:00, 19 Jan 45," 20 January 1945, (both NARA: box 257, Boone file). Also, interviews by Doug Clanin and Wayne Sanford with Leon Beck, December 31, 1983 and January 24, 1984; and by the author with Leon Beck, May 11,1999. Boone's letter, written that same day, says that Signal Hill and his message pick-up panels were strafed by American P-38s, but does not mention casualties or a radio being hit. Leon Beck, who had brought a second radio from Colonel Merrill's headquarters, claims to have a vivid memory of this incident. He states that the planes were Japanese Zeros, several people were killed and wounded, and Merrill's radio set was destroyed. The radio from Cabangbang was soon put into full operation, but there is no mention of the Merrill radio in any of Boone's later correspondence.
[25] Letter, Boone to Loyd, 29 January 1945, (Loyd); and note, Romaine to Conner, 27 January 1945, (Indiana: Guerrilla Additions). Also, intelligence maps of Dinalupihan and Zig-zag prepared by Boone's guerrillas, 16 January 1945, (Boone).
[26] Major C. Reyes, "G-2 Report From: 12:00, 20 Jan 45 To: 12:00, 23 Jan 45," 23 January 1945, (NARA: box 257, Boone file).
[27] Loyd, "Bataan Diary," typed transcript, 167.
[28] Memorandum, Boone to Abad, 21 Jan. 1945 (Boone).

[29] Loyd, "Bataan Diary," typed transcript, 167.
[30] Major Jose Inocencio, "Bataan Military District, Operations, From 16 Jan 45 to 19 Jan 45," (NARA: box 257, Boone file)
[31] Utinsky, *"Miss U"*, 146.
[32] Letter, Wright to "CO LGF" [Merrill], 23 January 1945, (NARA: box 257, Wright file).
[33] Loyd, "Bataan Diary," typed transcript, 167.
[34] *Ibid.*
[35] Utinsky, *"Miss U"*, 146. In her book Margaret Utinsky says that she went from Frank Loyd's camp directly to rejoin U.S. forces. However, Frank Loyd's diary and correspondence with Victor Abad indicate that she went first to Abad's camp, as described here, and then moved to Francisco Silva's house in Tala. From Tala she went to join U.S. forces on February 5, 1945. Loyd, "Bataan Diary," typed transcript, and letter, Abad to Loyd 4 Feb. 1945 (Loyd).
[36] Loyd, "Bataan Diary," typed transcript, 166.
[37] Priority message from Roy C. Tuggle to Radio Station BZ9 [Boone], 21 January 1945 (Indiana: small, brown binder labeled "McCoy, Dobesk" on the spine).
[38] Letter, Boone to Merrill, 23 January 1945, (NARA: box 257, Boone file).
[39] Undated message, Cabangbang to Boone, January 21 1945 (Boone), and radiogram Boone to Merrill, 23 January 1945, (NARA: box 257, Boone file).
[40] Letter, Wright to Merrill, 23 January 1945; and hand-written letter, Merrill to Wright, 28 January 1945, (both NARA: box 257, Wright file).
[41] Letter, "Chow" [Magsaysay] to "Tomas" [Merrill], 19 January 1945, (NARA: box 257, Merrill file). After the war Ramon Magsaysay went into politics and in 1953 became President of the Philippines.
[42] Romulo, *The Magsaysay Story*, 64-66.
[43] Message nr. 1, Merrill to MacArthur, 22 January 1945, (MacArthur: Record Group 16, box 38, folder 5).
[44] Messages Nr 1 through 7, MacArthur to Merrill, 22-25 January 1945, (MacArthur: Record Group 16, box 38, folder 5); and manifest showing 976 lbs. of munitions dropped to Merrill on 23 January 1945 and 4157 lbs. dropped on 27 January 1945, (NARA: box 257, Merrill file).
[45] Letters, "Tomas" [Merrill] to "Chow" [Magsaysay], 23 January 1945 and 25 January 1945, (NARA: box 257, Merrill file).
[46] Report of Capt. Pedro M. Arce, Commander, San Felipe Sector, South Sub-District, District of Zambales, January 25, 1945, Subject: Military

Information (NARA: box 257, Merrill file); and letter, Abad to Loyd, 14 January 1945, (Boone).
[47] Map accompanying "G-2 Report No. 3," 16 January 1945 (Boone); and memorandum, 1st Lt. A. Simsuangco to Wright, 24 January 1944, (NARA: box 257, Wright file).
[48] Letter, Wright to Merrill, 25 January 1945; and memorandum, Wright to "CO, BMD" [Boone], 25 January 1945, (both NARA: box 257, Wright file).
[49] Letter, Boone to Loyd, 29 January 1945, (Loyd).
[50] Letter, Wright to Merrill, 25 January 1945, (NARA: box 257, Wright file).
[51] Interview by Doug Clanin with Leon Beck, (Indiana: Leon Beck's comments, 267-268); and Manifest showing 976 lbs. of munitions dropped to Merrill on 23 January 1945 and 4157 lbs. dropped on 27 January 1945, (NARA: box 257, Merrill file).
[52] Message, Merrill to Wright, 27 January 1945, (NARA: box 257, Wright file); and letter, Boone to Loyd, 29 January 1945, (Loyd).
[53] Instructions, Gardner to Conner, 28 January 1945, (Indiana: Volume B, Chapter II, Section B, document 43).
[54] Conner, "We Fought Fear on Luzon," *True*, August 1945, 87.
[55] Conner, "We Fought Fear on Luzon," *True*, August 1945, 87; and Decker, "Reminiscences," page 13, (Indiana: Guerrilla Additions). Also, Decker, *On A Mountainside*, Chapter 23; and "Duke Student Leads Out Guerrilla Band," *The Charlotte Observer*, February 11, 1945.
[56] Loyd, "National Defense Week Speech," page 14, (Loyd).
[57] "Map 15: Fort Stotsenburg," (Indiana: Volume Hq 155B, Chapter VI, Section A, document 43); and Loyd, "Bataan Diary," 169. This was the 40th Infantry Division under Maj. Gen. Rapp Brush. Connaughton, Pimlott and Anderson, *The Battle for Manila*, 84.
[58] "Map 15: Fort Stotsenburg," (Indiana: Volume Hq 155B, Chapter VI, Section A, document 43); and letter, Boone to Loyd, 29 January 1945, (Loyd). This was the 37th Infantry Division under Maj. Gen. Robert S. Beighter. Connaughton, Pimlott and Anderson, *The Battle for Manila*, page 84.
[59] Loyd, "Bataan Diary," typed transcript, 169; and letter, Loyd to Boone, 1/30/45, (Boone), 3.
[60] Letter, Kadel to Merrill, 30 January 1945, (NARA: box 257, Wright file).
[61] Report, Wright to Merrill, 29 January 1945, (NARA: box 257, Wright file).

[62] Letter, Kadel to Merrill, 30 January 1945, (NARA: box 257, Wright file).
[63] William C. Wilson and Francis McCarthy, "Filipino Guerrillas Rout Japs Week Before Americans Arrive," *The San Antonio Evening News*, Feb. 1, 1945, page 9.
[64] Interview by Doug Clanin with Leon Beck, (Indiana: Leon Beck's comments, page 271).
[65] Message nr. 7, MacArthur to Merrill, February 9, 1945, (MacArthur: Record Group 16, box 38, folder 5).
[66] Message, Krueger to "CG Eleventh Corps" [Lt. Gen. Hall]; and message No. 8, Merrill to Wright, 30 January 1945, (both NARA: box 257, Wright file).
[67] Message, Krueger to "CG Eleventh Corps, Attention Colonel Merrill," (NARA: box 257, Boone file).
[68] Interviews, by Rhode Island State Senator John Patterson with Brig. Gen. Royal Reynolds, August 2, 1997; and by the author, July 31, 1999 .
[69] Astor, *Crisis in the Pacific*, 391.
[70] Interview by Rhode Island State Senator John A. Patterson with Brigadier General Royal Reynolds, August 2, 1997.
[71] Loyd, "Bataan Diary," typed transcript, 170.
[72] *Ibid*, 171; and Astor, *Crisis in the Pacific*, 391.
[73] Letter, Boone to Loyd, 1 February 1945, (Loyd).
[74] Loyd, "Bataan Diary," typed transcript, 171.
[75] *Ibid*, 170; and letter, Loyd to Boone, 30 January 1945, (Boone), 1.
[76] Letter, Loyd to Boone, 30 January 1945, (Boone), 4.
[77] Loyd, "Bataan Diary," typed transcript, 171.
[78] *Ibid*, 172.
[79] Letter, Boone to Commanding General SWPA [MacArthur], 31 Jan 1945 (Boone).
[80] Messages nr, 9 and 14, Boone to Cabangbang (Boone).
[81] Handwritten note, Wright to Merrill, received by Merrill on 5 February 1945, (NARA: box 257, Boone file).
[82] Letter, Abad to Loyd, 4 February 1945, (Loyd).
[83] Letter of Introduction, Boone to Commanding General, 11th Corps, AUS, 3 Feb 45 (Boone).
[84] "The Approach to Manila, 1-4 February 1945" (map), (Indiana: unlabeled blue box containing miscellaneous papers collected by Wayne Sanford relating to guerrillas and POWs in several wars); and Certificate of Macario Linao, Intelligence Officer of the 3rd Regiment, Bataan Military District, 8 March 1952, *Investigation of Casualty Roster, Bataan Military District*, (NARA: box 245).

[85] "The Approach to Manila, 1-4 February 1945" (map), (Indiana: unlabeled blue box containing miscellaneous papers collected by Wayne Sanford relating to guerrillas and POWs in several wars); and interview by the author with Brig. Gen. Royal Reynolds, July 31, 1999.
[86] Col. F. M. Rawolle, "Supply Plan for Bataan Military District," 4 February 1945, (NARA: box 257).
[87] Interview by the author with Brig. Gen. Royal Reynolds, July 31, 1999; Certificate of Macario Linao, Intelligence Officer of the 3rd Regiment, Bataan Military District, 8 March 1952, *Investigation of Casualty Roster, Bataan Military District*, (NARA: box 245); and Col. F. M. Rawolle, "Supply Plan for Bataan Military District," 4 February 1945, (NARA: box 257).
[88] Handwritten note, Wright to Merrill, received by Merrill on 5 February 1945, (NARA: box 257, Boone file).
[89] Letter, Eddie Wright to Marge Wright, February 5, 1945, (Wright).
[90] "The Approach to Manila, 1-4 February 1945" (map), (Indiana: unlabeled blue box containing miscellaneous papers collected by Wayne Sanford relating to guerrillas and POWs in several wars).
[91] Utinsky, *"Miss U"*, 148.
[92] Interview by the author with Maximino de la Peña, Pilar, Bataan, May 13, 1998.
[93] Interview by the author with Evelyn Loyd, March 4, 1997.
[94] Loyd, "Bataan Diary," typed transcript, 172.
[95] Loyd, "National Defense Week Speech," page 14, (Loyd); and personal communication to the author.
[96] Frank Loyd, personal communication to the author.

XXIII. 1945

[1] Letter, Frank Loyd to Evelyn Loyd, February 7, 1945, (Loyd).
[2] Letter, Frank Loyd to Evelyn Loyd, March 12, 1945, (Loyd).
[3] Letter, Frank Loyd "To Whom It May Concern," 27 June 1956, (Loyd); and Frank Loyd personal communication to the author.
[4] Letter, Frank Loyd to Evelyn Loyd, February 7, 1945, (Loyd).
[5] *Ibid.*
[6] Utinsky, *"Miss U"*, 153.
[7] "'Rip Van Winkle' Freed," *The San Antonio Express*, February 20, 1945.
[8] Letter, Frank Loyd to Evelyn Loyd, February 7, 1945, (Loyd).
[9] Loyd, "Recap of Dispute with Merrill," (Loyd) paragraph 10.

[10] Letter, Frank Loyd to Commander in Chief, U.S. Army Forces in the South Pacific; and letter, Frank Loyd to Evelyn Loyd; both February 7, 1945 (Loyd).
[11] Letter, Frank Loyd to Evelyn Loyd, February 7, 1945, (Loyd).
[12] Interview by the author with Patricia Dulligan, April 22, 2004. Also, letter, Frank Loyd Jr. to Frank Loyd, Feb. 19, 1945 (Loyd).
[13] Letter, Frank Loyd to Evelyn Loyd, March 2, 1945 (Loyd).
[14] Letter, Maj. Gen. J. A. Ulio to Mrs. Frank R. Loyd, 8 Feb. 1945 (Loyd).
[15] Letter, Frank Loyd to Evelyn Loyd, February 7, 1945, (Loyd).
[16] Letter, Evelyn Loyd to Frank Loyd, Feb. 17, 1945 (Loyd).
[17] *Ibid.*
[18] Navy Captain Sata Naohiro, "Fall of the Philippines," 15, (CMH: Japanese Monograph #114.)
[19] Connaughton, Pimlott and Anderson, *The Battle for Manila*, Chapters 4 and 5.
[20] General Speck Easly was killed in action on Okinawa.
[21] Letter, Evelyn Loyd to Frank Loyd, April 11, 1945 (Loyd).
[22] Miller, *War Plan Orange*, 366.
[23] Radio message, Tuggle to station BZ9 [Boone], 21 January 1945, (Indiana: Small, brown binder with "McCoy, Dobesk" on spine); and letter, Capt. A. D. Bruce to Col. P. D. Calyer, 26 January 1945, (NARA: box 256).
[24] Hoyt, *Japan's War*, 405.

Epilogue

[1] His service-related disabilities included chronic anxiety and despondency, heart disease, mild hypertension, and neuropathy of the nerves in both legs incurred while "living off the land" as an escapee from the Japanese, July 1942 to April 1945. DD214, Frank Riley Loyd (MilRec).
[2] General Headquarters, United States Army Forces, Pacific, "General Orders…9, Distinguished-Service Cross," 13 June 1945.
[3] Interview by the author with Jim Wright, December 11, 1998.
[4] Edgar Wright III, obituary for Edgar Wright Jr., the West Point *Assembly*, January-February 1998.
[5] Letter, Frank Loyd to Evelyn Loyd, April 13, 1945
[6] Military records, Al Romaine.

[7] Letters, Maj. T.S. Jones to Mrs. Noble, 22 Oct. 1945 (Noble); and Eddie Wright to Marge Wright, undated but written early in 1945 (Wright).

[8] Letter, Maj. Gen. Edward F, Witsell to Mrs. Noble, 9 Nov. 1945 (IDPF).

[9] General Headquarters, United States Army Forces, Pacific, "Review and Determination of the Status of Lt. Col. Arthur K. Noble," 18 Sept. 1945; and "Review and Determination of the Status of Lt. Col. Martin Moses," 17 Sept. 1945, Exhibit A (IDPF).

[10] Phillips, *Manila Espionage*, 207.

[11] Major Harold K. Johnson was camp purchasing officer at Cabanatuan from 8 February 1943 through 20 October 1944, and during that two year period the Japanese authorized total expenditures of about 500,000 pesos for food and other supplies for 6,000 prisoners. The camp's actual expenditures during that period were 1,500,000 pesos, the rest having been smuggled into the camp by the Manila underground. Ramon Amusatigue, Juan Elizalde and Enrique Pirovano were the principal donors, and they were all caught and executed by the Japanese. Letter, Lt. Col. Harold K. Johnson to Director, recovered Personnel Division, Headquarters United States Army Forces Western Pacific, 10 Sept. 1946, reprinted in Ashton, *Bataan Diary*, 382-387. Harold K. Johnson eventually became Chief of Staff of the United States Army.

[12] Tape recording of Damaso and Anna Caballero, and family (Loyd).

Bibliography

Sources of Original Documents

Loyd: Loyd family papers, including the diaries of Colonel Frank R. Loyd and Mrs. Evelyn Loyd, 1941-1945. Provided by Mrs. Loyd and her daughter, Bonnie Loyd Crane.

Boone: Boone family papers, including wartime correspondence between John Boone, Frank Loyd and Edwin Ramsey. Provided by Ms. Jeanne Boone.

CMH: The Center of Military History, Office of the Chief of Military History, Department of the Army, Washington, D.C. Miscellaneous documents relating to Philippine guerrillas, including unpublished diaries, personal accounts and correspondence, and Japanese accounts of the war in the Philippines.

IDPF: Total Army Personnel Command, Department of the Army, Washington, D.C. Individual Deceased Personnel Files.

Indiana: The Indiana State Historical Society, Indianapolis, Indiana. Interviews, correspondence and published articles regarding American guerrillas in the Philippines.

MacArthur: The MacArthur Museum and Archives, Norfolk, Virginia. Personal papers, correspondence and radio transmissions of General Douglas MacArthur, Colonel Courtney Whitney, and others regarding guerrilla activities in the Philippines. Jim Zobel, Archivist.

Manzano: Manzano family papers, including the memoirs of Colonel Narciso L. Manzano. Provided by Mr. Allen Manzano.

MHI: U.S. Army Military History Institute, Carlisle Barracks, Pennsylvania. U.S. Army Forces, Pacific, Intelligence Series, and files titled *Philippine Guerrillas.*

MilRec: National Personnel Records Center, St. Louis, Missouri. Individual military personnel records obtained under the U.S. Freedom of Information Act.

NARA: National Archives and Records Administration, College Park, Maryland. The Philippine Archives Collection—original documents and correspondence pertaining to the pre-war, wartime and post-war activities of the U.S. Army and Navy in the Philippines.

Noble: Noble family papers. Letters from Maxie Noble, and from various persons who had contact with him during the war. Provided by Maxine Noble Mclean, Bill Mclean, and Beverly Noble Hundley.

Parsons: The Chick Parsons archival collection. Correspondence from Norbert Schmelkes, Edwin Ramsey and others regarding the wartime activities of the Philippine underground. Provided by Peter and Michael Parsons.

PSHS: Philippine Scouts Heritage Society, Fort Sam Houston Museum, San Antonio, Texas. Interviews, photographs, news reports and personal narratives of officers and men who served in the Philippine Scouts, compiled by Colonel John E. Olson. Joe Mancuso, Curator.

Wainwright: The Wainwright Papers. Four volumes, including the *Report of Operations of USAFEE and USFIP in the Philippine Islands, 1941-1942*, published by New Day Publishers, Quezon City, Philippine

Islands, in 1980, Celedonio A. Ancheta, Editor. Also available at the National Archives and Records Administration, College Park, Maryland.

Wilson: Wilson family papers, including the diary of Colonel Ovid O. "Zero" Wilson and the correspondence of Colonel Wilson and Mrs. Betty Wilson, 1941-1945. Provided by Mr. Joe Wilson.

Wright: Wright family papers, including the correspondence of Lieutenant Colonel Edgar Wright and Mrs. Marge Wright, 1941-1945. Provided by Mr. James T. Wright of Palo Alto, California and Mr. Edgar Wright III of Washington, D.C.

Interviews

Col. Frank R. Loyd, San Antonio, various dates.
Mrs. Evelyn Loyd, San Antonio, various dates.

MSgt. Ben Austria (by John Olson), Philippine Scout and POW, San Antonio, October 1988
MSgt. Leon Beck, U.S. Army and American guerrilla, San Diego (by telephone), May 11, 1999
Ms. Jeanne Boone, daughter of John and Mellie Boone, Richmond, Virginia (by telephone), October 17, 2003.
Mr. Bill Bowen, son of MSgt William E. Bowen, U.S. Army and American guerrilla, Neenah, Wisconsin (by telephone), April 25, 1999
Mr. Eduardo F. Celestino, Philippine Army and POW, Manila, May 1998
Mr. Henry Clay Conner (by Doug Clanin), U.S. Army and American guerrilla, 1986
Mrs. Bonnie Loyd Crane, daughter of Evelyn and Frank Loyd, San Antonio, April 1997
Mr. Matthew Crane, grandson of Evelyn and Frank Loyd, San Antonio, December 23, 1997
Mr. Rene Diokno, Philippine Army and POW, Manila, May 1998
Mr. James Downey Jr., Philippine Scout and POW, San Antonio, May 1999
Mrs. Ling Hodges, Filipina survivor, Pensacola, Florida, August 11, 1998
Mrs. Beverly Hundley, daughter of Evelyn and Maxie Noble, San Antonio (by telephone), October 17, 2003
Mr. Louis Jurika, son of Tomas Jurika, guerrilla, and grandson of Blanche Jurika of the Manila underground, Miami, Florida (by telephone), August 17, 2002.

Mr. George C. Kintanar, son-in-law of General Mariano Casteneda, Philippine Constabulary and wartime Governor of Cavite Province, Manila, October 2002 (by e-mail)

Mr. Nicholas Leonzon, Jr., grandson of Tivo Leonzon, Dinalupihan, Philippines, May 1998

Mr. Allen Manzano, son of Lt. Col. Narciso Manzano, Philippine Scout, POW and Manila Underground, Carlsbad, California, July 28, 2001

Mr. Homero Martinez, U.S. Army and American POW, Laredo, Texas, March, 2000

Mrs. Maxine Noble McLean, daughter of Evelyn and Maxie Noble, Hilton Head, South Carolina, (by telephone) October 21, 2003

Ms. Tessie Musngi, niece of Sam Zozabrado, Houston, March 15, 2004.

Mr. Tiburcio Paule, benefactor to Frank Loyd and son-in-law of Tivo Leonzon, Dinalupihan, Philippines, May 1998

Mrs. Rebecca Leonzon Paule, daughter of Tivo Leonzon, Dinalupihan, Philippines, May 1998

Mr. Peter Parsons, son of Lt. Cmdr. Charles "Chick" Parsons, MacArthur's guerrilla liaison officer, and grandson of Blanche Jurika of the Manila underground, by e-mail, 2002

Mr. Amado Payumo, brother of Marcell Payumo, Filipino guerrilla, Manila, May, 1998

Mr. Maximinio de la Pena, Filipino guerrilla, Pilar, Philippines, May 1998

Mr. Esteban Pirovano, son of Enrique Pirovano of the Manila underground, Santa Fe, New Mexico, July 2002

Mr. Ralph Praeger, Jr., son of Ralph Praeger, Philippine Scout and American guerrilla, Ogden, Utah (by telephone), March 1999

Col. John E. Olson, Philippine Scout and American POW, San Antonio, November 21, 1998

Brig. Gen. Royal Reynolds, Philippine Scout and American guerrilla, (by John Patterson), Falls Church, Virginia, September 1987

Brig. Gen. Royal Reynolds, Philippine Scout and American guerrilla, Washington, D.C., July 31, 1999

Mr. Harry Stempin, Philippine Scout and POW, San Antonio, May 1999

Mr. Samuel Boyd Stagg, with his mother a member of the Manila underground, Arroyo Grande, Calif. (by telephone), August 2002

Mr. David A. Topping, U.S. Army and POW, San Antonio, May 1999

Mr. Cyril Webb, U.S. Army, New Orleans, Louisiana, various dates

Mr. Joe Wilson, son of Ovid O. "Zero" Wilson, Philippine Scout and POW, San Antonio, October 29, 1998

Mr. Jim Wright, son of Eddie Wright, Philippine Scout and American guerrilla, Palo Alto, Calif. (by telephone), December 11, 1998

Books

Agoncillo, Teodoro A. *History of the Filipino People.* Quezon City, Philippines: Garotech Publishing, Eighth Edition, 1990.

Ancheta, Celedonio A. (Ed.) *Liberation of North Luzon (After-Battle Report).* Navotas, Philippines: Navotas Press, 1983.

—. *The Wainwright Papers, Vols 1-4.* Quezon City, Philippines: New Day Publishers, 1980.

Ashton, Paul. *Bataan Diary*. Self-published, 1984.

Astor, Gerald, *Crises In the Pacific.* New York: Donald I. Fine Books, 1996

Baclagon, Colonel Uldarico S. *Last 130 Days of the USAFFE.* Manila: Astra Ink Corp, 1982

Blair, Clay. *Silent Victory: The U.S. Submarine War Against Japan.* Philadelphia: J.B. Lippincort Company, 1975

Brackman, Arnold *The Other Nuremberg: The Untold Story of the Tokyo War Crimes Trials.*

Breuer, William B. *The Great Raid on Cabanatuan.* New York: John Wiley & Sons, Inc., 1994

Cannon, M. Hamlin. *Leyte: The Return to the Philippines. The U.S. Army in World War II.* Vol. 2, part 5 of *The War in the Pacific.* Washington, D.C.: Department of the Army, 1954

Christman, Calvin L. (Ed.) *America at War; An Anthology of Articles from MHQ: The Quarterly Journal of Military History.* Annapolis: Naval Institute Press, 1995

Connaughton, Richard, John Pimlott and Duncan Anderson, *The Battle for Manila.* London: Bloomsbury Publishing, 1995

Decker, Malcolm *On a Mountainside: The 155th Provisional Guerrilla Battalion Against the Japanese on Luzon.* Las Cruces, New Mexico: Yucca Tree Press 2004.

Department of the Navy, Naval Historical Center, Dictionary of American Naval Fighting Ships, www.history.navy.mil, 2004.

Dyess, William E. *The Dyess Story: The Eye-Witness Account of the Death March from Bataan, and the Narrative of Experiences in Japanese Prison Camps and of Eventual Escape.* New York: G. Putnam's Sons, 1944. Also published as *Bataan Death March.* Lincoln, Nebraska: University of Nebraska Press, 2002.

Feis, Herbert, *The Road to Pearl Harbor.* New York: Atheneum, 1962

Gailey, Harry A. *War in the Pacific.* Novato, California: Presidio Press, 1997

Gautier, James Donovan, with Robert E. Whitmore, *I Came Back from Bataan.* Greenville, SC: Blue
Ridge Publishing, 1997

Gleek, Lewis E., *The Manila Americans.* Manila: Carmelo & Bauermann, Inc., 1977

Harkins, Philip, *Blackburn's Headhunters*, New York: W. W. Norton & Company, 1955.

Hartendorp, A. V. H. *The Japanese Occupation of the Philippines.* Manila: Bookmark Press, 1967

Hollister, Paul, and Robert Strunsky (Ed.), *From Pearl Harbor Into Tokyo.* New York: The Colombia Broadcasting System, 1945.

Hoyt, Edwin P. *Japan's War.* New York: McGraw-Hill Book Company, 1986.

—. *The Lonely Ships: The Life and Death of the U.S. Asiatic Fleet.* New York: David McKay Company, Inc., 1976

Huff, Sidney L., *My Fifteen Years with General MacArthur.* New York: Harper, 1964.

Hunt, Frazier. *The Untold Story of Douglas MacArthur.* New York: Devin-Adair Company, 1954

Hunt, Ray C. and Norling, Bernard. *Behind Japanese Lines.* Lexington, Ky: The University Press of Kentucky, 1986.

Inguchi, Rikihei and Tadashi Nakajima, with Roger Pineau, *The Divine Wind: Japan's Kamikaze Force in World War II.* Annapolis: Naval Institute Press, 1958

James, D. Clayton. *The Years of MacArthur, Volume II: 1941-1945.* Boston: Houghton Mifflin Company, 1975

Jose, Ricardo Trota. *The Philippine Army, 1935-1942.* Manila: Anteneo de Manila University Press, 1992

Kiosaki, Wayne, *A Spy in Their Midst.* New York: Madison Books, 1995.

Knox, Donald, *Death March: The Survivors of Bataan.* New York: Harcourt Brace & Company, 1981

Lapham, Robert and Norling, Bernard. *Lapham's Raiders.* Lexington, Ky: The University Press of Kentucky, 1996

Linn, Brian M., *Guardians of Empire: The U.S. Army and the Pacific, 1902-1940.* Chapel Hill, NC: University of North Carolina Press.

Lory, Hillis. *Japan's Military Masters.* Washington: The Infantry Journal, 1943

MacArthur, General of the Army Douglas. *Reminiscences.* New York: McGraw-Hill, 1964

Manchester, William *American Caesar.* Boston: Little Brown and Company, 1978

Marquardt, Frederick S. *Before Bataan and After.* Indianapolis: The Bobbs-Merrill Company, 1943

Marquez, Adalia. *Blood on the Rising Sun.* New York: DeTanko Publishers, Inc., 1957

Miller, Edward S. *War Plan Orange*. Annaplois: Naval Institute Press, 1991

Mojica, Proculo L. *Terry's Hunters: The True Story of the Hunters ROTC Guerrillas*. Manila: Benipayo Press, 1965.

Monaghan, Forbes J. *Under the Red Sun: A Letter from Manila*. New York: The Declan X. McMullen Company, 1946

Norling, Bernard. *The Intrepid Guerrillas of North Luzon.* Lexington, Ky: The University Press of Kentucky, 1999.

Norman, Elizabeth M. *We Band of Angels.* New York: Random House, 1999

O'Brien, Niall, Editor *Columban Martyrs of Malate.* Manila: Kadena Press, 1995

Olson, Colonel John E. *O'Donnell: Andersonville of the Pacific.* San Antonio: privately printed, 1985

Olson, Colonel John E. (Ed.) *The Philippine Scouts.* San Antonio: privately printed, 1996

Ogawa, Tetsuro *Terraced Hell: A Japanese Memoir of Defeat & Death in Northern Luzon, Philippines.* Rutland, Vermont: Charles E. Tuttle Company, 1972

Paguio, Fr. Wilfredo C., *Bataan: Land of Valor, People of Peace*, Manila: Jardi Press, 1997

Peña, Ambosio. *Bataan's Own.* Manila: Muñoz Press, 1967

Phillips, Claire and Myron B. Goldsmith, *Manila Espionage.* Portland, Oregon: Binfords & Mort, 1947.

Ramsey, Edwin P. and Rivele, Stephen J. *Lieutenant Ramsey's War.* Washington: Brassey's, Inc., 1990

Rodriguez, Ernesto R. *The Bad Guerrillas of North Luzon.* Quezon City, Philippines: J. Burgos Media Services, Inc., 1982

Roces, Alfredo, *Looking for Liling.* Pasig City, Philippines: Anvil Publishing Company, 2000.

Rogers, Paul P., *The Good Years: MacArthur and Sutherland.* New York: Greenwood, 1990.

Romulo, Beth Day, *The Manila Hotel.* Manila: Privately printed, 1987

Romulo, Carlos P., *The Magsaysay Story*. New York: The John Day Company, 1956

Salita, Domingo C., *Geography and Natural Resources of the Philippines.* Quezon City, Philippines: JMC Press, 1997.

SanGabriel, Colonel Reynaldo, *The Constabulary Story.* Quezon City, Philippines: Bustamante Press, 1978

Sides, Hampton, *Ghost Soldiers*. New York: Doubleday, 2001.

Schultz, Duane, *Hero of Bataan: the Story of General Jonathon M. Wainwright*, New York: St. Martin's Press, 1981.

Stahl, Bob, *You're No Good to me Dead: Behind Japanese Lines in the Philippines.* Annapolis: Naval Institute Press, 1995.

Steinberg, David Joel, *Philippine Collaboration in World War II.* Ann Arbor: University of Michigan Press, 1967.

Tagarao, Silvestre L. *All This was Bataan.* Quezon City, Philippines: New Day Publishers, 1991

Taruc, Luis, *Born of the People*, New York, Greenwood Press, 1953.

Tenney, Lester I. *My Hitch in Hell: The Bataan Death March.* Washington: Brassey's, Inc., 1997

Tolischus, Otto D. *Through Japanese Eyes.* Washington: The Infantry Journal, 1946

Underbrink, Robert L. *Destination Corregidor.* Annapolis, Maryland: United States Naval Institute, 1971

Utinsky, Margaret. *"Miss U".* San Antonio: The Naylor Company, 1948

Villamor, Col. Jesus A. and Gerald S. Snyder, *They Never Surrendered.* Quezon City, Philippines: Vera-Reyes, Inc., 1982

Wainwright, General Jonathon. *General Wainwright's Story.* Garden City, NY: Doubleday, 1946

Watson, Mark Skinner. *United States Army in World War II, The War Department, Chief of Staff: Pre-War Plans and Preparations.* Washington: Historical Division, United States Army, 1950

Whitman, John W. *Bataan, Our Last Ditch.* New York: Hippocrene Books, 1990

Whitney, Major General Courtney. *MacArthur: His Rendezvous with History.* Westport, Conn.: Greenwood, 1977

Yap-Diangco, Major Robert T. *The Filipino Guerrilla Tradition.* Manila: R. P. Garcia Publishing Company, 1952.

Young, Donald J. *First 24 Hours of the War in the Pacific.* Shippensburg, PA: Burd Street Press, 1998

—. *The Battle of Bataan.* Jefferson, NC: McFarland & Company, Inc., 1992.

Index